SEXT ED

SEXT ED

Obscenity versus Free Speech in Our Schools

Joseph O. Oluwole and Preston C. Green III, with the assistance of Melissa Stackpole

Foreword by Eunice A. Grippaldi

 PRAEGER

AN IMPRINT OF ABC-CLIO, LLC
Santa Barbara, California • Denver, Colorado • Oxford, England

Library of Congress Cataloging-in-Publication Data

Oluwole, Joseph.
    Sext ed : obscenity versus free speech in our schools / Joseph Oluwole and Preston C. Green III ; with the assistance of Melissa Stackpole ; foreword by Eunice A. Grippaldi
        pages cm
    Includes bibliographical references and index.
    ISBN 978–1–4408–2927–7 (hardback) — ISBN 978–1–4408–2928–4 (ebook) 1. School discipline—Law and legislation—United States. 2. Sexting—Law and legislation—United States. 3. Students—Legal status, laws, etc.—United States. 4. Freedom of expression—United States. 5. Harassment in schools—Law and legislation—United States. 6. Child pornography—Law and legislation—United States. I. Green, Preston C. (Preston Cary) II. Title.
    KF4159.O48   2013
    363.4′702854678—dc23   2012049359

ISBN: 978–1–4408–2927–7
EISBN: 978–1–4408–2928–4

17 16 15 14 13   1 2 3 4 5

This book is also available on the World Wide Web as an eBook.
Visit www.abc-clio.com for details.

Praeger
An Imprint of ABC-CLIO, LLC

ABC-CLIO, LLC
130 Cremona Drive, P.O. Box 1911
Santa Barbara, California 93116-1911

This book is printed on acid-free paper ∞

Manufactured in the United States of America

Contents

Tables and Figures

Tables

Figures

Foreword

In my 40 years in public education as a classroom teacher, district supervisor, building principal, and assistant and deputy superintendent, I have seen many innovations and ideas introduced into the system that have impacted the way we do our work and how learning takes place in schools. In recent years, these innovations have been dwarfed by the impact of technology. Depending on how long you have been in the field, you are nodding your head and thinking about whiteboards, overhead projectors, photocopy machines, computers, and smart boards, to mention just a few. Most of these innovations have impacted the planning and implementation of lessons, helped with ways to best differentiate instruction, and expedited the way we do our jobs. This book addresses a new form of technological innovation that is none of the above, but an amalgamation of the use of technology such as cell phones, not for educational purposes, but for student-to-student communication within the framework of socializing. In response to this, you may say that your district has addressed the use of cell phones by banning them completely at certain times or limiting their use during school hours. Maybe your district was forward-thinking enough to use them as teaching tools. Either way, these decisions deal only with the educational use of technology.

In recent years, the complementary wave to hit the scene that has created the most attention is the use of technology for the socialization of our children; particularly our 12- to 17-year-olds' use of the cell phone to send visual images, better known as digital imaging. Now anyone who has mastered the use of the cell phone to brag about a trip, child, game, or adventure prides himself or herself on being able to take a picture at any moment and send it to a friend or loved one to share what has come to be known as a "Kodak moment." So why is there such a ruckus about our teens' use of this form of communication? The ability to send visual images across cell phones has saved lives and given us opportunities to experience wonders that we never would have on our own. With all that good, the use of digital media as the drug of choice for our tweens and teens to communicate presents visual images that would be considered inappropriate, or even pornographic; hence, the conundrum for many of us. The antiquated laws that guide our decision making can cause us to move far away from our educational role with parents and other caring adults to a law enforcement role, leaving us no choice but a criminal offense for teens who indulge in the practice of sexting.

Once again, you may be nodding your head, but this time probably with a side-to-side motion denoting confusion, frustration, and the need for more information. So the question arises as to how to deal with this form of communication, called sexting, in the context of our daily decision making and guidance of our children at home and in school. One must keep in mind that the operative word is "children." In recent years, when adults have done similar sexting, we waver between indignation at the act and the person to defending their right under the First Amendment's Free Speech Clause. But when it comes to our children, we presently are placed in a void of direction, guided only by child pornography or obscenity laws, or criminal sexting laws.

Who better to help challenge our thinking than Oluwole, Green, and Stackpole? Their skilled backgrounds blended in law, education, and counseling bring to the reader a precise knowledge of all three venues in order to keep our eye on the prize—our children. They take the lid off the law and give us firsthand knowledge and expertise in its imperfection and viability so that we can move forward with a sense of what is right. Their ability to present information in both narrative and graphic formats to help the layperson discern the implications of the present laws and state statutes as well as the bleak outcomes for students who engage in sexting is impeccable. They walk us through case law and present explicit examples to relate to our own experiences in order to shed light on many realities and statistics that can guide our advocacy. They examine the authority of schools to regulate student sexting and present various arguments for decriminalizing it. In our diverse roles as teachers, administrators, parents, and caregivers, we are all child advocates and need to be better equipped to maintain that mission as we navigate the rules, regulations, laws, and influences that are present as we lead and guide our children toward becoming successful adults and knowledgeable decision makers.

Leading our nation's public schools and partnering with parents, care-givers, and the community to create a safe and nurturing environment where children thrive has always been a complex and demanding job. It is becoming ever more so with the advent of various technologies and ways in which we use them to communicate. There is an old Taoist saying: "A thousand-mile journey starts with one step." I believe this book is the first step for educators, parents, caregivers, and lawmakers in doing what's right for our children.

Eunice A. Grippaldi

Retired Assistant Superintendent and Principal,
Livingston Public Schools

Acknowledgments

We would like to thank our families for their support and encouragement throughout the process of researching and writing this book. We would also like to thank Megan Raquet for her tireless assistance with research. Joseph Oluwole would like to express appreciation to his sister-in-law Nike Oluwole and brother Luwi Oluwole for the spirited discussion about our nation's youth and future that inspired the vision for the book.

This book is dedicated to our nation's youth; for the sake of our youth, we hope that we stay true to the caring that is the bedrock of our nation by educating rather than making criminals of our children for student-to-student sexting.

Our deep gratitude goes to Beth Ptalis for her incredible work and distinctive support throughout the process of publishing this book. We would also like to thank Anthony Chiffolo, Rebecca Matheson, and the staff of our publisher, and Bhuvaneswari Rathinam at Premedia Global for their diligence and help. Thank you!

Chapter 1

Introduction

Technology has taken a prominent role in our society today. Indeed, it appears that we can no longer live without some form of technology—this even though we survived as a civilization for generations without technology. The cell phone craze has swept all facets of society, including our children. One need reflect only on the eager anticipation that attends the release of each new iPhone. In fact, many teens in a Pew Research Center focus group indicated that "they would not know how to occupy their time if they did not have their phones."[1] Interestingly, some elementary school students even have cell phones; however, the "real tipping point" for student ownership of cell phones is middle school.[2]

With the ubiquity of cell phones, more and more people, including teenagers, are choosing to use the texting function of cell phones, which allows communication in a similar way to emails. According to the Pew Research Center, "Cell-phone texting has become the preferred channel of basic communication between teens and their friends and cell calling is a close second."[3] In fact, texting has become an "element of teen identity."[4] The Center also found that one out of every three teens sends over 100 texts every day; texting has now exceeded every other mode of communication, including face-to-face interactions, as the primary mode of communication for teens (see Figure 1.1).[5]

Comparative trends for these modes of communication for teens between 2006 and 2009 are shown in Figure 1.2.

Further, the Pew Research Center has found that girls receive and send about 80 text messages daily, while boys receive and send 30 daily.[6] Twelve- and 13-year-olds receive and send about 20 texts daily, while 14- to 17-year-olds receive and send about 60 daily.[7] However, 14- to 17-year-old girls text the most—sending at least 100 texts per day, or a staggering 3,000 texts monthly.[8] Nationally, 20,209 texts are sent out every second by teenagers, and each teenager sends out a text, on average, every 14 minutes.[9]

FIGURE 1.1. Most Teens Text Friends Daily.

The % of teens who contact their friends daily by different methods, by age

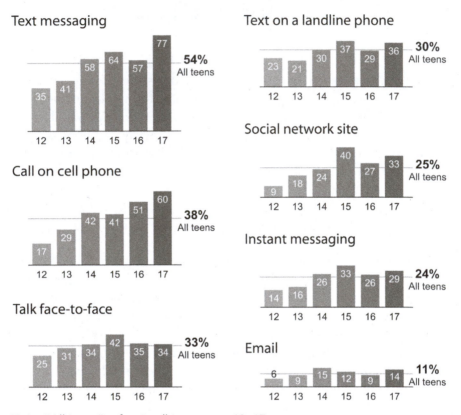

Note: "All teens" refers to all teens ages 12–17.
Source: Amanda Lenhart, Pew Internet and American Life Project, "Teens and Mobile Phones" [2010], available at http://pewinternet.org/Reports/2010/Teens-and-Mobile-Phones/Summary-of-findings.aspx.

Today, cellphones also allow people to send pictures and videos to others. Research shows that 83 percent of teenagers take pictures on their cellphones, and 64 percent use their phones to share pictures.[10] Many students have taken advantage of the cell phone camera function by sending each other sexually explicit messages or partially or wholly nude pictures or videos—a phenomenon called sexting (which stands for *sex* plus

FIGURE 1.2. Texting Takes Off, While Use of Other Communication Channels Remains Stable Over Time.

The % of all teens who have used each communication method to contact their friends daily, since 2006

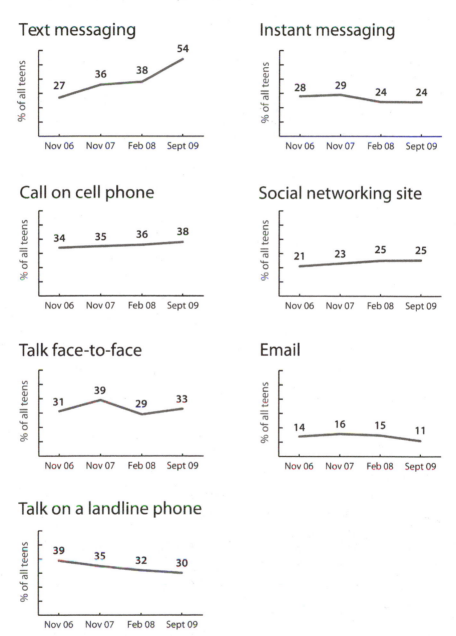

Note: Percentages are for all teens ages 12–17.
Source: Amanda Lenhart, Pew Internet and American Life Project, "Teens and Mobile Phones" [2010], available at http://pewinternet.org/Reports/2010/Teens-and-Mobile-Phones/Summary-of-findings.aspx.

texting). Sexting has also been referred to as LH6 (let's have sex).[11] More broadly, sexting "generally refers to youth writing sexually explicit messages, taking sexually explicit photos of themselves or others in their peer group, and transmitting those photos and/or messages to their peers."[12] Given that a large number of students already use their cell phones for texting to "discuss important *personal* matters,"[13] it is not surprising that they would extend these texts on "personal matters" to sexting. Unfortunately, without realizing it, these students could be setting themselves up for criminal prosecution, even when the sexting is consensual. Students could be prosecuted for producing the sexts, and for possessing and sending the sexts. This is disturbing, particularly because, as legal scholar Terri Day observes, "The overwhelming motive for sexting is as old as the romantic intrigues and motivations of Adam and Eve."[14]

The practice of consensual sexting, which some students might innocuously deem the moral equivalent of erstwhile pictures sent by past generations, before the advent of cell phones, has trapped many students with felony records (under child pornography laws as well as obscenity laws) and sex offender registrations. Detective Eric Hendel of Broward County Sheriff's Office in Florida describes the approach of his office to sexting: "We investigate sexting like any kind of child pornography case, because that's basically what it is."[15] Here, however, is a tragedy: "A child pornography conviction —which could come from sending a racy photo of yourself or receiving said photo from a girlfriend or boyfriend—carries far heavier penalties than most hands-on sexual offenses."[16] This ignores the reality that "sexting is the new form of flirting—an explicit love letter."[17] In fact, psychologists describe sexting as a reflection of "typical teenage hormones."[18]

Given the pervasiveness of teenage sexuality, some of these students might think they are just being teenagers, sexting their partners pictures to memorialize a consensual sexual encounter or to send requested pictures of body parts. However, under current punitive laws, "if you're in possession of a naked picture of a child, you're personally guilty of child pornography."[19] Indeed, even in cases where students can legally have consensual sex, they face the wrath of the law if they memorialize the encounter and sext it; the specter of prosecution for production, possession, or distribution of child pornography hangs over them.

Creative cartoonist Kevin Moore has poignantly conveyed the harsh approach of these statutes in a cartoon (see Figure 1.3).[20]

According to Kevin Clancy, a Texas attorney, it is not necessarily troubled students that sext: "You would be surprised: Eighth-grade, straight-A,

FIGURE 1.3. The Siege Mentality.

Source: Cartoon by Kevin Moore of Moore Toons.

beautiful girls are sending these photos to boys."[21] Terri Day identifies the following as some of the states where sexters have been charged: Alabama, California, Connecticut, Florida, Georgia, Iowa, New Jersey, New York, Pennsylvania, Texas, Utah, Virginia, and Wisconsin.[22]

Further, the sex offender registrations could foreclose students from job opportunities and higher education. Here is a capsule outline of the registry with respect to minors:

In many states, like Florida, if a person is convicted of a crime against children, it automatically triggers registration to the sex offender registry.

Thirty-eight states include juvenile sex offenders in their sex offender registries. Alaska, Florida and Maine will register juveniles only if they are tried as adults. Indiana registers juveniles age 14 and older. South Dakota registers juveniles age 15 and older. Most states allow public access to sex offender registries via the Internet and anyone with a computer can locate registered sex offenders in their neighborhoods.[23]

Moreover, these students find themselves on the same list as rapists and child molesters. This is so despite the fact that sexting has become an integral part of teen culture. Its prosecution surprises even parents. In fact, one parent vividly characterized the prosecution of teen sexting under child pornography laws as "the nuclear weapon of sex charges."[24]

If adults engaged in consensual sexting with other adults, we would likely be outraged and shout from the rooftops for the enforcement of the First Amendment's Free Speech Clause if the government decided to prosecute the adults involved. Should we stand by while students are prosecuted for consensual, noncommercial student-to-student sexting?

Patrick Arthur, a Pennsylvania attorney who has worked on scores of child pornography cases, aptly observes that "the prosecution of minors for photos they took themselves runs counter to the purpose of both state and federal child pornography laws: Preventing the sexual abuse of children by 'dirty old men in raincoats.' It's clearly overkill."[25] As Olympia Meola of the *Richmond Times-Dispatch* rightly notes, "The laws were not written with naughty teenagers in mind."[26]

A fundamental problem is that the law has not caught up with technology. The following thoughtful point about the prosecution of teen sexting, made by legal scholar John A. Humbach, should provide cause for pause in our legal system:

> Whatever else one may make of all this, there is certainly reason to suspect something is profoundly amiss when a system of laws makes serious felony offenders of such a large proportion of its young people. The fact that most of them will probably never be prosecuted is a hardly redeeming point. What kind of justice system turns a blind eye to millions of violators while selectively prosecuting a few? If the laws are sound as written, how can the authorities justify a systematic failure to uncover and prosecute the legions of young felons in our midst? If on the other hand the laws are not sound, how can they be left on the books, a kind of Sword of Damocles for youth, nominally making serious crimes out of conduct that may be deemed, de

facto, too harmless to pursue? Arguably, at least, a self-respecting legal system should either enforce its laws or admit they are wrong and fix them.[27]

Here is the road map for the rest of this book: In Chapter 2, we present statistics on student sexting. We also discuss various instances in which students were charged with crimes for sexting. That chapter concludes with a table laying out the age of consent in various states. In Chapter 3, we set forth various child pornography and obscenity statutes relied on by proponents of prosecuting student sexting. This chapter also includes state statutes specifically enacted for prosecution of student sexting. In Chapter 4, we use case law on obscenity to highlight a First Amendment right for students to consensually sext. Even with agreement that sexts constitute speech, some might wonder if the conduct of sexting itself constitutes free speech. The U.S. Supreme Court has declared that First Amendment "protection does not end at the spoken or written word."[28] Consensual student-to-student sexting constitutes speech because it satisfies the Supreme Court's two-part test for determining if conduct qualifies as symbolic speech under the First Amendment: "In deciding whether particular conduct possesses sufficient communicative elements to bring the First Amendment into play, we have asked [i] whether an intent to convey a particularized message was present, and [ii] [whether] the likelihood was great that the message would be understood by those who viewed it."[29] Consensual student-to-student sexters "intend to convey a particularized message"[30] such as love, affection, romance, or commitment through their sexts; given that a sext is a consensual exchange, "the likelihood is great that the message would be understood by those who view it."[31]

In Chapter 5, we shed light on why it is unconstitutional under the Free Speech Clause to criminalize consensual student-to-student sexting under child pornography statutes; for this, we review obscenity and child pornography precedents. Chapter 6 examines the authority of schools to regulate student sexting. Chapter 7 presents the conclusion to the book, which includes various arguments for decriminalizing student sexting. As First Amendment attorney Lawrence G. Walters pungently declared: "It's time as a society that we step back a little bit and avoid this temptation to lock up our children."[32]

Chapter 2

The Sexting Portrait: The Numbers and the Human Stories

In this chapter, we will examine what the numbers tell us about the practice of sexting and try to put a human face on the sexting numbers and criminalization via examples of students charged with crimes for sexting. We also present data on the age of consent for teenage sex.

The Incidence of Sexting: What Research and Statistics Tell Us

Students tend to engage in consensual sexting with their romantic partners or persons with whom they are seeking to develop relationships. When sexts are shared with romantic partners, they are shared "in lieu of, as a prelude to, or as a part of sexual activity."[1] A ninth/tenth-grade boy told Pew Internet and American Life Project researchers that his sexts were "just between my girlfriend and I. Just my girlfriend sending pictures of herself to me and me sending pictures of myself to her."[2] Similarly, a ninth/tenth-grade girl said, "Yeah, I've sent them to my boyfriend. . . . Everybody does it."[3] Another teenager revealed that sexting is integral to his sexual relationship, noting, "Yes, I do [sext]. I only do it with my girlfriend b/c we have already been sexually active with each other. . . . It's not really a big deal."[4] Sexting also provides an outlet for romantic partners in middle school who are wary of physical sexual contact that early; it is used as an "experimental phase" for teens who are not prepared to be sexually active. In other words, they view sexting as a "safer alternative to real life sexual activity."[5]

For students seeking a romantic relationship with another student, Pew researchers poignantly observe that sexting is now a "form of relationship currency."[6] A high school senior revealed that, as a 14- and 15-year-old, she sent and received sexts. She stated, "Boys usually ask for them or start that type of conversation. My boyfriend, or someone I really liked asked for them."[7] A high school boy, however, noted that "almost all the time it's a single girl sending to a single guy."[8] Still another high school girl reflected, "If a guy wants to hook up with you, he'll send a picture of his private parts or a naked picture of him[self]. It happens about 10 times a month. . . . It's mostly the guys I date or just a guy that . . . really wants to hook up with you."[9] Another high school boy revealed, "Yes I have received some pics that include nudity. Girls will send them sometimes, not often."[10]

The attitude of teenagers toward noncommercial, consensual sexting is evident in other teen revelations to the Pew researchers. For example, a high schooler revealed his thoughts about sexting: "No, [it's not a big deal] we are not having sex, we are sexting. . . . It's not against my religion or anything."[11] Another high schooler echoed this same sentiment, noting, "I know people think [sexting] is dangerous, but to me, it's no big deal because I get them a lot."[12]

The National Campaign to Prevent Teen and Unplanned Pregnancy and CosmoGirl.com commissioned a study of the relationship between sex and technology among teenagers and young adults. The online survey included 1,280 respondents, 653 of whom were teens between the ages of 13 and 19; the other 627 were young adults between the ages of 20 and 26. According to the survey, 20 percent of teens have sexted/posted online nude pictures or videos of themselves. Eighteen percent of teenage girls, 22 percent of teenage boys, and 11 percent of girls between the ages of 13 and 16 reported sexting/posting online nude videos or pictures of themselves. Additionally, 39 percent of teens reported sexting/posting sexually suggestive messages (without pictures or videos). Girls and boys were just about equally likely to have sexted/posted sexually suggestive messages (without pictures or videos): 40 percent of teenage boys and 37 percent of teenage girls. Forty-eight percent of teenagers reported receiving sexually suggestive messages (without pictures or videos).[13]

Teens in the National Campaign study indicated that they mostly sent sexually suggestive content (messages or pictures) to their boyfriends or girlfriends: 67 percent of teen boys sexted/posted sexually suggestive content to their girlfriends, while 71 percent of teen girls sent the same to their boyfriends. Further, 39 percent of teenage boys sent sexually suggestive content to someone they sought to hook up with or date, while 21 percent of teenage girls did the same. Thirty-eight percent of teens indicated that the exchange of sexually suggestive content makes it more likely that they will hook up with someone or date the person. The researchers observed that "many teen boys (29 percent) agree that girls who send such content are expected to date or hook up in real life."[14] When asked the reason for sexting/posting sexually suggestive content, 60 percent of teenage boys and 66 percent of teenage girls revealed that it was "fun or flirtatious."[15] Reinforcing the fact that sexting/posting sexually suggestive content is mostly used by teens for romantic relationships, 52 percent of teenage girls indicated that such sexts/postings were intended for their boyfriends as "a sexy present."[16]

A study of 13- to 17-year-olds conducted by LG Mobile Phones—the cell phone company—found that even though at least 41 percent of teens have sexted, only 11 percent of parents thought their teens had ever sexted.[17] LG Mobile Phones also found that 33 percent of teenagers have received sexts of naked pictures of someone.[18] Further, one in four teenagers believes sexting is not immoral and that many of their peers engage in the practice.[19]

Dr. Sameer Hinduja and Dr. Justin W. Patchin of the Cyberbullying Research Center surveyed about 4,400 students in a large public school district.[20] The students were between the ages of 11 and 18. In their study, 12.9 percent of teenagers admitted to receiving nude or partially nude sexts. In contrast, 7.7 percent revealed that they had sexted such images. Hinduja and Patchin found that boys and girls were equally likely to send naked images in sexts; however, to a significant extent, boys were relatively more likely to report getting sexts of naked images.

In an MTV-Associated Press study of 600 teens and 647 adults, 53 percent of the respondents indicated that they had sent naked pictures of themselves to their boyfriends or girlfriends.[21] Fifteen percent of the respondents admitted to sending out naked pictures to someone they had a crush on, 22 percent of respondents had sent such pictures to someone they hooked up with or dated, and 25 percent had sent them to someone they wanted to date or hook up with. Seventeen percent of the respondents admitted to receiving sexts of naked pictures from someone they had a crush on, 23 percent from someone they had dated or hooked up with, and 16 percent from someone they wanted to hook up with or date. The study also revealed that 44 percent of the respondents had received sexts of naked pictures from their girlfriends or boyfriends.[22] Further, 29 percent of the respondents admitted that they had sexted sexual words to someone they knew.

Like other studies, the Pew research study of teens and sexting, mentioned earlier in this chapter, found that boys and girls are equally likely to sext.[23] In the Pew study, 4 percent of students between 12 and 17 years old reported sending sexually suggestive pictures or videos of themselves to others on their cell phones. While only 4 percent of 12-year-olds reported sending such sexts, 8 percent of 17-year-olds reported sending such texts. On the other hand, 15 percent of students between the ages of 12 and 17 reported receiving sexts from people they knew. Here is the breakdown: 18 percent of students between the ages of 14 and 17 reported receiving sexts, compared to 6 percent of 12- and 13-year-olds; more specifically, 20 percent of 16-year-olds, 30 percent of 17-year-olds, and 4 percent of 12-year-olds reported getting sexts. The researchers found that as students grow older, there is a "steady increase" in the likelihood that they will receive sexts. The relatively low number of students who reported sending sexts could be due to a reluctance of teenagers to admit to researchers that they have sent sexts.

Cox Communications and the National Center for Missing and Exploited Children commissioned a joint study of 655 students between the ages of 13 and 18.[24] The study found that more than 30 percent of students know someone who has sexted and one in five has sexted. The Cox study reported that "most sext senders say these messages are most commonly sent to boyfriends/girlfriends because it's asked of them or to have fun." The study found that 53 percent of girls and 47 percent of boys sext.[25] However, girls are more likely to *send* sexts than boys—65 percent for girls compared to 35 percent for boys.[26] Sixty-one percent of teen sexters are between the ages of 16 to 18, while 39 percent are between the ages of 13 and 15.

Tables 2.1 and 2.2 provide a breakdown of some of the study's findings about to whom and why teens send sexts; the researchers questioned both sext senders (second column) and sext receivers (third column).

The profile of the teen sexter reveals that teen sexters believe to a much more significant extent, relative to all teens, that they are "old enough to

TABLE 2.1 Why Sext Senders *Send* Sexts

	Sext Senders	Sext Receivers
Someone asked me/them to	43%	46%
To have fun	40%	54%
To impress someone	21%	48%
To feel good about myself/themselves	18%	32%
To try to date someone	8%	33%

Source: Cox study 37, available at http://www.cox.com/takecharge/safe_teens_2009/research.html.

TABLE 2.2. Who Sext Senders Send Sexts To

	Sext Senders	Sext Receivers
Boyfriend/girlfriend	60%	75%
Someone I/they had a crush on	21%	49%
Best friend	14%	20%
Friends other than my/their best friend	18%	23%
Classmates	4%	18%

Source: Cox Study 37, http://www.cox.com/takecharge/safe_teens_2009/research.html.

decide for themselves whether sexting is all right";[27] specifically, 76 percent of teen sexters believe this, while only 54 percent of all teens hold this belief. Approximately 50 percent of teenagers believe there is a tendency for adults to "overreact" to sexting.[28] However, sexters are more likely to believe this— 67 percent of sexters—compared to 48 percent of all teens.[29]

Even though the statistics may vary slightly from one study to another, one thing they all reveal is that student sexting is here to stay and a growing part of teenage culture.

Criminalizing Sexting: The Human Account

An online search for news articles about students charged with crimes for sexting yields a multitude of articles. Despite this, the outrage in the media about these prosecutions has been muted. In this section, we attempt to put a face on the tragedy of prosecution of sexting students.

In 2008, ABCNews.com reported that a 15-year-old student at Licking Valley High School in Newark, Ohio, who sexted nude pictures of herself, was arrested, incarcerated, and charged with the felonies "illegal use of a minor in nudity-oriented material" and "possessing criminal tools."[30] ABCNews.com also reported that the girl could be required to register as a sex offender. In Ohio, the possession of criminal tools is a fifth-degree felony,[31] while the illegal use of a minor in nudity-oriented material is a second-degree felony.[32] According to state legislator Jay Hottinger, the law was not intended to apply to minors who send pictures of themselves to friends.[33] That fact did not stop the Licking County prosecutor from seeking to prosecute the 15-year-old and the teens who received the pictures.[34] Fortunately, this ended better than it could have for the girl, as the prosecutor agreed to halt the prosecution if she pled guilty to the lesser charge, something she seemed willing to do to avoid registering as a sex offender.[35] In 2009, in another Ohio case, the *Dayton Daily News* reported that a 14-year-old girl at Kettering Middle School in Dayton faced a charge of "pandering sexual matter involving a minor" after sexts were found on her cell phone showing her in a sexual act with another student.[36]

In Florida, a 17-year-old boy and his 16-year-old girlfriend took pictures of themselves having sex and were charged with directing, producing, or promoting child pornography.[37] In Utah, prosecutors charged a 15-year-old who engaged in consensual sexting with "dealing in material harmful to a minor"—a third-degree felony—and three class-B misdemeanor lewdness counts.[38] The county attorney insisted he was doing this to "send a message to kids."

In Pennsylvania, three girls were charged with "disseminating child pornography" because they sexted their boyfriends.[39] In Alabama, four middle schoolers were arrested for sexting naked pictures of themselves.[40] In Virginia, two students at Spotsylvania High School were charged with "possession of child pornography with intent to distribute and electronic solicitation" for sexting.[41] In Indiana, two middle school students—a 13-year-old girl and a 12-year-old boy—were charged with possession of child pornography and child exploitation.[42] The boy had sexted a picture of his genitals to her and she in turn sexted him a naked picture of herself. The *Chicago Tribune* reported that, if convicted, the students could be required to register as sex offenders.

In New York, Alex, a 16-year-old high school captain of the tennis, basketball, and football teams and leader of his church youth group, engaged in consensual sexting with Laurie, a 15-year-old girl, who had recently enrolled in his school.[43] Alex was at home showering one day after football practice when he received a text from Laurie stating that she wanted to be a cheerleader. Alex responded that he wanted a "cute cheerleader this year." In her reply text, Laurie sent Alex a picture of herself in bra and panties, and another in which she wore only her panties. The text added: "Oh, yeah? Well, is this cute?" Alex followed this with a text to Laurie asking her to send him more pictures. A week later, Alex seemed to have no care in the world as he showered at his family's farmhouse around seven in the morning in preparation for school, when his mother knocked on his door to inform him that a state trooper was downstairs. He was informed that he was facing various felony charges and registration as a sex offender for sexting; he was eventually charged only with a misdemeanor count of "endangering the welfare of a child."[44]

While conceding the sexting was consensual, Tom Splain, Alex's attorney, added, "The thing to bear in mind . . . is she sent him these pictures unsolicited. He's [got] hormones galore—hey, yeah, holy cow! It's Christmas morning!"[45] Alex's parents took him to a sex counselor, who told them what was apparent: "There's no sex problem with your son." As Alex observed, "This is a sixteen-year-old boy and an almost fifteen-year-old girl going through their young adult lives here." Alex's father described the whole episode as the "death of common sense." Alex indicated he would have gladly mowed the lawn of the girl's parents in penance.[46]

In May 2005, Jorge Canal Jr., a student at Perry High School in Iowa, sexted "pictures of his penis and his face" along with the text message "I love you" to C. E., a female classmate. They had been friends for approximately a year.[47] He was subsequently convicted of the serious misdemeanor of "knowingly disseminating obscene material to a minor" for this sexting and ordered to register as a sex offender. The supreme court of Iowa affirmed the conviction.

In Utah, Davis County deputy attorney Ryan Perkins notes that he witnesses "at least one case a week involving teenagers who send or ask for nude photographs via text message."[48] According to *ABC 4 in Utah*, "The majority of his [Perkins's] cases are girls being charged with having or sending pornographic images on their cell phones. He says teenage boys are requesting it and the girls are sending it."[49]

Nationwide Age of Consent

In this section, we present a table from FindTheData showing the minimum age at which persons can consent to sexual relationship in various states.[50] The numbers in the table (Table 2.3) should raise concerns that while students can legally engage in sex in various states, they cannot memorialize it. As you review the table, we want you to ponder this: Does it make sense and comport with notions of fairness for students to be able to legally engage in sexual relations, yet be criminally penalized for sexting?

TABLE 2.3. Age of Consent to Sex in the United States

State	Age of Consent	Minimum Age of Victim	Age Differential between Victim and Defendant	Minimum Age of Defendant to Prosecute
Alabama	16	12	2	16
Alaska	16	N/A*	3	N/A
Arizona	18	15	2 (defendant must be in high school and under 19)	N/A
Arkansas	16	N/A	3 (if victim is under 14)	20 (if victim is 14)
California	18	18	N/A	N/A
Colorado	17	N/A	4 (if victim is under 15), 10 (if victim is under 17)	N/A
Connecticut	16	N/A	2	N/A
Delaware	18	16	N/A	N/A
District of Columbia	16	N/A	4	N/A
Florida	18	16	N/A	24 (if victim is 16)
Georgia	16	16	N/A	N/A
Hawaii	16	14	5	N/A
Idaho	18	18	N/A	N/A
Illinois	17	17	N/A	N/A
Indiana	16	14	N/A	18 (if victim is 14)
Iowa	16	14	4	N/A
Kansas	16	16	N/A	N/A
Louisiana	17	13	3 (if victim is under 15), 2 (if victim is under 17)	N/A
Maine	16	14	5	N/A
Maryland	16	N/A	4	N/A
Massachusetts	16	16	N/A	N/A
Michigan	16	16	N/A	N/A
Minnesota	16	N/A	3 (if victim is under 13), 2 (if victim is under 16)	N/A
Mississippi	16	N/A	2 (if victim is under 14),	N/A

TABLE 2.3. (continued)

State	Age of Consent	Minimum Age of Victim	Age Differential between Victim and Defendant	Minimum Age of Defendant to Prosecute
			3 (if victim is under 16)	
Missouri	17	14	N/A	21 (if victim is 14)
Montana	16	16	N/A	N/A
Nebraska	16	16	N/A	19
Nevada	16	16	N/A	18
New Hampshire	16	16	N/A	N/A
New Jersey	16	13	4	N/A
New Mexico	16	13	4	18 (if victim is 13)
New York	17	17	N/A	N/A
North Carolina	16	N/A	4	12
North Dakota	18	15	N/A	18 (if victim is 15)
Ohio	16	13	N/A	18 (if victim is 13)
Oklahoma	16	14	N/A	18 (if victim is over 14)
Oregon	18	15	3	N/A
Pennsylvania	16	13	4	N/A
Rhode Island	16	14	N/A	18 (if victim is 14)
South Carolina	16	14	Illegal if victim is between 14 and 16 and defendant is older than victim	N/A
South Dakota	16	10	3	N/A
Tennessee	18	13	4	N/A
Texas	17	14	3	N/A
Utah	18	16	10	N/A
Vermont	16	16	N/A	16
Virginia	18	15	N/A	18 (if victim is 15)
Washington	16	N/A	2 (if victim is under 12), 3 (if victim is under 14), 4 (if victim is under 16)	N/A
West Virginia	16	N/A	4 (if victim is under 11)	16, 14 (if victim is under 11)
Wisconsin	18	18	N/A	N/A
Wyoming	16	N/A	4	N/A

Source: FindTheData, Age of Consent & Statutory Rape Laws by State, http://age-of-consent .findthedata.org.

*N/A = not applicable.

Chapter 3

Child Pornography and Obscenity Statutes

In various cases in which students are charged for sexting, the government relies on child pornography and obscenity statutes. In this chapter, we highlight the federal child pornography statutes and various state child pornography, obscenity, and sexting statutes used as the basis for these prosecutions.

Federal Child Pornography Statute

The federal child pornography statute relied on for prosecution of teen sexters is known as the Child Pornography Prevention Act (CPPA).[1] It is important to note that the CPPA covers only sexted images, not written sexts.[2] Subsection 2251(a) of the CPPA provides:

> Any person who employs, uses, persuades, induces, entices, or coerces any minor to engage in, or who has a minor assist any other person to engage in, or who transports any minor in or affecting interstate or foreign commerce, or in any Territory or Possession of the United States, with the intent that such minor engage in, any sexually explicit conduct for the purpose of *producing* any visual depiction of such conduct or for the purpose of *transmitting* a live visual depiction of such conduct, shall be punished as provided under subsection (e), if such person knows or has reason to know that such visual depiction will be transported or transmitted using any means or facility of interstate or foreign commerce or in or affecting interstate or foreign commerce or mailed, if that visual depiction was produced or transmitted using materials that have been mailed, shipped, or transported in or affecting interstate or foreign commerce by any means, including by computer, or if such visual depiction has actually been transported or transmitted using any means or facility of interstate or foreign commerce or in or affecting interstate or foreign commerce or mailed.[3]

Subsection 2251(e) referenced in subsection (a) above sets out the penalty for violating section 2251 of the CPPA. It states in pertinent part: "Any individual who violates, or attempts or conspires to violate, this section shall be fined under this title and imprisoned not less than 15 years nor more than 30 years."[4] This presents a grim future for students convicted of child pornography.

Given that the focus of this book is noncommercial, consensual sexting, it is clear that the word "coerces" in subsection 2251(a) above is inapplicable to our thesis.[5] Nonetheless, proponents of prosecuting even noncommercial, consensual student sexting could seize on the words "uses, persuades, induces, entices" to prosecute both senders and recipients of sexts. An inconvenient truth, however, remains—the title of section 2251 is "Sexual *exploitation* of children" (emphasis added). Noncommercial, consensual student-to-student sexting is clearly not exploitation. In fact, Congress noted that the child pornography laws are designed to ensure children are protected from "those who sexually exploit them, including both child molesters and child pornographers."[6] The very fact that Congress used the words "child molesters" and "child pornographers" in describing the sexual exploitation of children apparently shows that noncommercial, consensual student-to-student sexting is not a target;[7] this should be a cautionary note to proponents of prosecuting noncommercial, consensual sexting.

Moreover, the congressional findings in enacting the federal child pornography laws do not reference noncommercial consensual student-to-student sexting.[8] These findings instead focus on the commercial multibillion-dollar industry of child pornography.[9] In the findings, there is a frequent reference to the "market"[10] for and "traffic" in child pornography.[11] Additionally, the findings focus on "abuse" and "victimization" of children; however, both of these concepts are antithetical to the consent integral to noncommercial consensual sexting.[12] If it is consensual student-to-student sexting, who is the victim and who is the perpetrator? Besides, prosecutions threaten both the student sender of the sext and the student recipient of the sext; so who is the "victim" in such situations?

Another subsection of the CPPA that prosecution proponents could try to use in charging senders of sexts is subsection 2252A(a)(1),[13] which applies to anyone who "knowingly mails, or transports or ships using any means or facility of interstate or foreign commerce or in or affecting interstate or foreign commerce by any means, including by computer, any child pornography."[14] A subsection that could be used to prosecute recipients as well as senders of sexts is subsection 2252A(a)(2), which applies to anyone who "knowingly receives or distributes" the following:

(A) any child pornography that has been mailed, or using any means or facility of interstate or foreign commerce shipped or transported in or affecting interstate or foreign commerce by any means, including by computer; or

(B) any material that contains child pornography that has been mailed, or using any means or facility of interstate or foreign commerce shipped or transported in or affecting interstate or foreign commerce by any means, including by computer.[15]

Under this subsection, convicted student sexters would face a minimum of five years and maximum of 20 years in prison along with a fine.[16]

Student sexters could also be prosecuted for possessing or viewing sexts under subsection 2251A(a)(5) of the CPPA, which applies to anyone who does either of the following:

(A) in the special maritime and territorial jurisdiction of the United States, or on any land or building owned by, leased to, or otherwise used by or under the control of the United States Government ... knowingly possesses, or knowingly accesses with intent to view, any book, magazine, periodical, film, videotape, computer disk, or any other material that contains an image of child pornography; or

(B) knowingly possesses, or knowingly accesses with intent to view, any book, magazine, periodical, film, videotape, computer disk, or any other material that contains an image of child pornography that has been mailed, or shipped or transported using any means or facility of interstate or foreign commerce or in or affecting interstate or foreign commerce by any means, including by computer, or that was produced using materials that have been mailed, or shipped or transported in or affecting interstate or foreign commerce by any means, including by computer.[17]

Under this subsection, convicted student sexters would face a maximum prison term of 10 years or a fine, or they could get both the prison term and a fine.[18]

If the CPPA is deemed applicable to student sexters, then the student sexter who "produces"[19] the "actual sexually explicit conduct"[20] in the sexts is obligated under section 2257 of the CPPA to keep copious records regarding the sexting or face stiff criminal penalties.[21] The word "produces"[22] as used in this section of the CPPA is defined, in pertinent part, as "actually filming, videotaping, photographing, creating a picture, digital image, or digitally- or computer-manipulated image of an actual human being."[23] The term "actual sexually explicit conduct"[24] as used in the section refers to "actual but not simulated conduct."[25] It includes any of the following: "sexual intercourse, including genital-genital, oral-genital, anal-genital, or oral-anal, whether between persons of the same or opposite sex";[26] masturbation;[27] and "lascivious exhibition of the genitals or pubic area of any person."[28] Sexters covered under this section of the CPPA are obligated to "create and maintain *individually identifiable* records pertaining to *every* performer portrayed in such a visual depiction."[29] The term "performer" means "any person portrayed in a visual depiction engaging in, or assisting another person to engage in, sexually explicit conduct."[30]

Courts have relied on the factors the U.S. District Court for the Southern District of California set forth in *United States vs. Dost*[31] to determine "whether a visual depiction of a minor constitutes a lascivious exhibition of the genitals or pubic area"[32] under federal law.[33] These factors, known as the *Dost* factors, are as follows:

1) whether the focal point of the visual depiction is on the child's genitalia or pubic area;
2) whether the setting of the visual depiction is sexually suggestive, i.e., in a place or pose generally associated with sexual activity;
3) whether the child is depicted in an unnatural pose, or in inappropriate attire, considering the age of the child;
4) whether the child is fully or partially clothed, or nude;
5) whether the visual depiction suggests sexual coyness or a willingness to engage in sexual activity;
6) whether the visual depiction is intended or designed to elicit a sexual response in the viewer.[34]

These factors are not exhaustive. As the *Dost* court noted, "a visual depiction need not involve all of these factors to be a lascivious exhibition of the genitals or pubic area. The determination will have to be made based on the overall content of the visual depiction, taking into account the age of the minor."[35] Here is an illustration from the *Dost* court:

Consider a photograph depicting a young girl reclining or sitting on a bed, with a portion of her genitals exposed. Whether this visual depiction contains a "lascivious exhibition of the genitals" will depend on other aspects of the photograph. If, for example, she is dressed in a sexually seductive manner, with her open legs in the foreground, the photograph would most likely constitute a lascivious exhibition of the genitals. The combined effect of the setting, attire, pose, and emphasis on the genitals is designed to elicit a sexual response in the viewer, albeit perhaps not the "average viewer," but perhaps in the pedophile viewer. On the other hand, if the girl is wearing clothing appropriate for her age and is sitting in an ordinary way for her age, the visual depiction may not constitute a "lascivious exhibition" of the genitals, despite the fact that the genitals are visible.[36]

According to the U.S. Third Circuit Court of Appeals, "more than mere nudity is required before an image can qualify as 'lascivious' within the meaning of the statute [CPPA]. A picture is 'lascivious' only if it is sexual in nature. Thus, the statute is violated, for instance, when a picture shows a child nude or partially clothed, when the focus of the image is the child's genitals or pubic area, and when the image is intended to elicit a sexual response in the viewer."[37]

Under the CPPA, each student who "produces" a sext is obligated to determine from an identification document and record the following information about the identity of every performer in each "production": name; date of birth;[38] and any other name the performer has ever used, including aliases, maiden name, nicknames, professional names, or stage names.[39] The law also requires that the student provide the U.S. Attorney General access to inspect the records, possibly at the student's residence, "at *all* reasonable times."[40] The law requires sexters to affix to each copy of every sexted image "a statement describing where the records required by this section with respect to all performers depicted in that copy of the matter [sexted image] may be located."[41] Failure to create and maintain the records is a crime[42] punishable by a maximum prison term of five years and/or a fine.[43]

Despite the fact that these statutory sections (and the state statutes presented later in this chapter) appear to provide grounds for prosecuting student sexters, we will argue later in this book that student sexting, unlike child pornography or obscenity, should be protected under the Free Speech Clause of the U.S. Constitution.

State Child Pornography, Obscenity, and Sexting Statutes

Various states have their own child pornography, obscenity, and sexting laws that could form the basis for prosecuting student sexters. It is critical to set forth the precise language of these laws so that readers can see and read for themselves how easily minors could become criminals, even felons, for consensual sexting.[44] We, as a society, need to see and confront the precise language of these laws that could be used to condemn our youth for consensual sexting. As is evident in the laws discussed in this chapter, it only takes an overzealous prosecution to seize on the language of any of the statutes to charge minors for consensual sexting and, oftentimes, label them as felons, foreclosing life opportunities, including employment and higher education.[45] We must keep in mind that "content-based prohibitions [of speech], enforced by severe criminal penalties, have the constant potential to be a repressive force in the lives and thoughts of a free people."[46] Further, as the U.S. Supreme Court has declared, "the severity of criminal sanctions may well cause speakers to remain silent rather than communicate."[47] Appendix A later in this book sets forth these statutes.[48]

Additionally, Appendix B should bring to focus some of the criminal punishments sexting teens could face, besides those laid out in Appendix A, if convicted of a felony or misdemeanor. This is something to look at, as it highlights what punishments felonies in particular attract and why criminalizing noncommercial consensual student-to-student sexting presents further danger to students.

Chapter 4

Obscenity Precedents and Consensual Sexting

In this chapter, in arguing for a First Amendment right to consensual student sexting, we examine U.S. Supreme Court precedents on obscenity. Legal scholar Amy Adler points out that "in the government's arsenal" against what it deems pornographic, the weapon of obscenity law is the oldest.[1] She observes that obscenity law "began to fall into relative disuse in the 1990s. Yet it has now staged a major comeback and has become a top priority for the FBI and the Department of Justice."[2]

Introduction

Adler provides three reasons for the disuse of obscenity law in the 1990s: (1) there was a pressing need to devote limited enforcement resources to cases arising under child pornography laws (as opposed to obscenity laws);[3] (2) "pornography's increased *cultural presence* posed difficulties for prosecutors";[4] and (3) obscenity law embarrassed the legal system—"Angst is palpable in the cases: Chief Justice Burger referred to the 'tortured history' of the Court obscenity cases. Justice Harlan, terming the obscenity problem 'intractable,' observed that it had 'produced a variety of views among the members of the Court unmatched in any other course of constitutional adjudication.' "[5] Adler explains: the "cases seemed to debase the Court. Obscenity jurisprudence did not emerge from on high; indeed, the Justices literally screened dirty films in the basement. Now the dirty work has fallen to lower court judges and juries who are compelled to view the more extreme, often scatological, hard-core pornography that the government has begun to pursue in obscenity cases."[6]

According to legal counsel Shannon Creasy, until the end of the nineteenth and beginning of the twentieth centuries, the United States hardly regulated sexual expression.[7] Associate Professor of Law David A.

J. Richards recounts the historical development of obscenity law in its incipiency:

> State laws regulating and prohibiting obscenity were adopted only after the passage of the first amendment, as part of the nineteenth century Anglo-American concern over pornography. The earliest law was a Connecticut statute of 1821. The first federal legislation was a customs statute passed in 1842. Even with these laws, prosecutions were relatively few until after the Civil War when the Committee for the Suppression of Vice, led by Anthony Comstock, took up the cudgels for purity in earnest. In short, the evidence for obscenity law contemporaneous with the passage of the first amendment is tenuous at best.[8]

Creasy notes that in seeking to ban obscenity during the period "between the Civil War and the 1930s," courts relied on the English case *Regina vs. Hicklin*,[9] which characterized as obscene "any material that could deprave and corrupt those whose minds are open to such immoral influences." This is the *Hicklin* rule or test. As Creasy aptly points out, the *Hicklin* rule "had the unintended result of assessing materials based on the effect they had on the most susceptible, or sensitive, members of the community. Under *Hicklin*, books and other materials could be judged obscene based on the effect an insignificant, isolated passage had on a child."[10]

Legal author Eric Handelman makes the following observation about the *Hicklin* rule:

> The test fixed a community standard for reading matter based on the feeblest mentality or most suggestible individual in the community. This is quite an anomaly if one considers the material being labeled "obscene" at that time. The *Hicklin* test was not used against magazines that depicted bestiality and sado-masochism, which few dispute are obscene. Instead, this test was used against literature like Theodore Dreiser's *An American Tragedy* and D. H. Lawrence's *Lady Chatterley's Lover*.[11]

Judge Learned Hand's criticism of the *Hicklin* rule finally helped slow its momentum. Particularly, in *United States vs. Kennerley*, Judge Hand noted that the *Hicklin* rule "reduce[d] our treatment of sex to the standard of a child's library in the supposed interest of a salacious few."[12] He questioned if the *Hicklin* rule should be allowed to foster "shame [that] will for long prevent us from adequate portrayal of some of the most serious and beautiful sides of human nature."[13] Further, Justice Hand, who was very critical of the *Hicklin* rule, surmised in *Kennerley* that "to put thought in leash to the average conscience of the time is perhaps tolerable, but to fetter it by the necessities of the lowest and least capable seems a fatal policy."[14]

As Judge Hand declared, we similarly believe with respect to noncommercial consensual student sexting that "truth and beauty are too precious to society at large to be mutilated in the interests of those most likely to pervert them to base uses."[15] The case against prosecuting teens for consensual sexting is evident in Judge Hand's words back in 1913 about the need to match the law to the times: "I hope it is not improper for me to say that the rule as laid down, however consonant it may be with mid-Victorian morals, does not seem to me to answer to the understanding and morality of the present time."[16]

Handelman reveals that the *Hicklin* rule was dealt a "final blow"[17] by the federal circuit and district courts in *United States vs. One Book Entitled Ulysses by James Joyce* and *United States vs. One Book Called "Ulysses."*[18] These courts called for obscenity cases to be decided by "a standard based on the pornographic intent and the effect of the work's dominant theme on the average reader"[19] as opposed to the "lowest and least capable."[20]

Roth vs. United States

In 1957, in *Roth vs. United States*,[21] the U.S. Supreme Court would, for the first time, create a test for deciding obscenity cases[22] and reject the *Hicklin* rule.[23] The Supreme Court *Roth* case was a consolidation of two cases: (1) *Roth vs. United States*, which challenged a federal obscenity law under the First Amendment,[24] and (2) *Alberts vs. California*, which challenged California's obscenity law under the First Amendment.[25] Recall that the Free Speech Clause of the U.S. Constitution provides that "Congress shall make no law . . . abridging the freedom of speech." This amendment is made applicable to the states via the Due Process Clause of the Fourteenth Amendment.[26] In *Roth*, a jury had convicted the appellant for mailing obscene books and circulars; in *Alberts*, the appellant had been convicted for "lewdly keeping for sale obscene and indecent books." The Supreme Court had to decide "whether obscenity is utterance within the area of protected speech."[27]

The Supreme Court ruled that obscenity is excluded from First Amendment protection because "such utterances are no essential part of any exposition of ideas, and are of such slight social value as a step to truth that any benefit that may be derived from them is clearly outweighed by the *social interest in order and morality.*"[28] Under this rationale, consensual sexting should pass constitutional muster since it has more than a "slight social value" to the consenting students; as discussed later herein, it is normal adolescent behavior. Besides, consensual sexting is not a threat to social order. Further, how would social morality be threatened by sexting that is consensual and analogous to love letters? Do love letters threaten social order and social morality?

Indeed, the Supreme Court itself made the following observation in *Roth*:

> The portrayal of sex, e.g., in art, literature and scientific works, is not itself sufficient reason to deny material the constitutional protection of freedom of speech and press. Sex, a great and mysterious motive force in human life, has indisputably been a subject of absorbing interest to mankind through the ages; it is one of the vital problems of human interest and public concern. As to all such problems, this Court said in *Thornhill vs. Alabama*: "The freedom of speech and of the press guaranteed by the Constitution embraces at the least the liberty to discuss publicly and truthfully all matters of public concern without previous restraint or fear of subsequent punishment."[29]

In concluding that obscenity is not protected under the First Amendment, the Court declared that "*implicit* in the history of the First Amendment is the rejection of obscenity as *utterly* without redeeming social importance."[30] The only support the Court cited for this conclusion of implicitness was its reference to a "*universal judgment* that obscenity should be restrained."[31] Yet as David A. J. Richards notes, "the evidence for obscenity law contemporaneous with the passage of the first amendment is tenuous at best."[32] What is the evidence of this "universal judgment"? The Court pointed to the existence of obscenity laws in 48 states, 20 federal obscenity statutes enacted between 1842 and 1856, and an international agreement to suppress circulation of obscenity joined by at least 50 nations.[33] It is difficult to decipher how these independent enactments and agreement support the Court's finding of implicitness.

If the Supreme Court were to rule on sexting today based on its own decision in *Roth*, it would be important for the Court to heed its own words: "All ideas having even the slightest redeeming social importance—unorthodox ideas, controversial ideas, even ideas hateful to the prevailing climate of opinion—have the full protection of the guaranties, unless excludable because they encroach upon the limited area of more important interests."[34] Moreover, the conclusion that obscenity is *"utterly* without redeeming social importance"[35] is fundamentally at odds with the essence of consensual sexting set forth earlier and later herein. If relying on *Roth*, the Court either has to reject its own words in *Roth* or rule that consensual sexting is not obscenity under *Roth*.

The *Roth* court set forth the following test for determining obscenity: "whether to the average person, applying contemporary community standards, the dominant theme of the material taken as a whole appeals to prurient interest."[36] Under this test, if the "contemporary community standards" are those of teenagers as opposed to adults, then consensual sexting might pass muster. If however, "contemporary community standards" are those of adults, the answer is less clear.

Justice Douglas disagreed with the *Roth* test, noting that under this test, "punishment is inflicted for thoughts provoked, not for overt acts nor antisocial conduct. This test cannot be squared with our decisions under the First Amendment."[37] His strong dissenting opinion is apropos to consensual sexting:

> The tests by which these convictions were obtained require only the arousing of sexual thoughts. Yet the arousing of sexual thoughts and desires happens every day in normal life in dozens of ways. Nearly 30 years ago a questionnaire sent to college and normal school women graduates asked what things were most stimulating sexually. Of 409 replies, 9 said "music"; 18 said "pictures"; 29 said "dancing"; 40 said "drama"; 95 said "books"; and 218 said "man." The test of obscenity the Court endorses today gives the censor free range over a vast domain. To allow the State to step in and punish mere speech or publication that the judge or the jury thinks has an undesirable impact on thoughts but that is not shown to be a part of unlawful action is drastically to curtail the First Amendment. As recently stated by two of our outstanding authorities on obscenity, "The danger of influencing a change in the current moral standards of the community, or of shocking or offending readers, or of stimulating sex thoughts or desires apart from objective conduct, can never justify the losses to society that result from interference with literary freedom." If we were certain that impurity of sexual thoughts impelled to action, we would be on less dangerous ground in punishing the distributors of this sex literature. But it is by no means clear that obscene literature, as so defined, is a significant factor in influencing substantial deviations from the community standards.[38]

Echoing Justice Douglas's words in 1957, to criminally punish teens for consensual teen sexting without certainty that the *consensual* sexting "impelled to [criminal] action" puts us on "dangerous ground" under the First Amendment.

Jacobellis vs. Ohio

In 1964, in *Jacobellis vs. Ohio*,[39] the U.S. Supreme Court ruled on an obscenity case involving an appellant who had been convicted of possession and exhibition of an obscene motion picture. The Court ruled that the motion picture was not obscene. Here is Justice Brennan's description of the French film *The Lovers* that was the basis for the case:

> *The Lovers* involves a woman bored with her life and marriage who abandons her husband and family for a young archaeologist with whom she has suddenly fallen in love. There is an explicit love scene in the last reel of the film, and the State's objections are based almost entirely upon that scene. The film was favorably reviewed in a number of national publications, although disparaged in others, and was rated by at least two critics of national stature among the best films of the year in which it was produced.[40]

The key thing that came out of the divided Court in *Jacobellis* was from Justice Stewart's concurring opinion in which he described obscenity as "indefinable."[41] He then provided the most memorial line in the case when he seemed to set forth his test for obscenity as follows: "I know it when I see it."[42] This line is proof that the obscenity jurisprudence is obfuscated and highly subjective; and if that is the case, then consensual sexting should not be merged into this confused jurisprudence.

A Book Named 'John Cleland's Memoirs of a Woman of Pleasure' vs. Attorney General of Commonwealth of Massachusetts

Approximately nine years after *Roth*, a divided Supreme Court would again rule on an obscenity case. In this case—*A Book Named 'John Cleland's Memoirs of a Woman of Pleasure' vs. Attorney General of Commonwealth of Massachusetts*[43]—the book *Memoirs of a Woman of Pleasure* (also known as *Fanny Hill*) was tried and adjudged obscene by the lower courts. In an opinion joined by Justice Fortas and Chief Justice Earl Warren, Justice Brennan elaborated on the *Roth* test, noting that under this test "three elements must coalesce: it must be established that (a) the dominant theme of the material taken as a whole appeals to a prurient interest in sex; (b) the material is patently offensive because it affronts contemporary community standards relating to the description or representation of sexual matters; and (c) the material is utterly without redeeming social value."[44]

Consensual sexting clearly "appeals to a prurient interest in sex." However, is consensual sexting patently offensive? If it is consensual, and particularly where it is sexted solely between teens in relationships who have reached the age at which they are authorized to engage in the ultimate act—sex—how could one say it is patently offensive? In other words, if the teens can legally engage in the sexual act without criminal penalty, how could their mutual memorialization be patently offensive? The answer would hinge on the word "because" and the words "contemporary community standards" in the *Roth* test: "the material is patently offensive *because* it affronts *contemporary community standards* relating to the description or representation of sexual matters." As noted in our discussion of *Roth* earlier in this chapter, it all depends on which community standards are used—those of teens versus those of adults. Some states explicitly include in their statutes that the community standards should be the adult community standards. Are those states not mistaken? After all, teens have their own subculture that is quite distinct from that of adults. As we also noted earlier, it is difficult to argue that consensual sexting is "*utterly* without redeeming social value."[45]

In *A Book Named 'John Cleland's Memoirs of a Woman of Pleasure,'* the Court actually reversed the lower courts' obscenity rulings. Justice Brennan emphasized that, under the *Roth* test, the "*utterly* without redeeming social value" language means that the material must be "unqualifiedly worthless before it can be deemed obscene."[46] Expounding, Justice Brennan revealed that the "social value" of material "can neither be weighed against nor canceled by its prurient appeal or patent offensiveness. Hence, even on the view of the Court below that *Memoirs* possessed only a *modicum* of social value, its judgment must be reversed as being founded on an erroneous interpretation of a federal constitutional standard."[47]

Since consensual sexting would have a "modicum of social value" under the *Roth* test as explained in *A Book Named 'John Cleland's Memoirs of a Woman of Pleasure,'* it should pass constitutional muster. Some would argue that consensual sexting might lead to exploitation of the sexts by others for whom it was not intended. However, just about anything innocent can be abused by someone with wrong motives. An apple is food, in fact delicious fruit, yet in the wrong hands, it can be abused and used as a weapon. Do we then ban apples or criminalize apples due to the potential for abuse? While this is an oversimplification, Justice Brennan's words, in analysis of the book *Memoirs of a Woman of Pleasure*, are not: "All possible uses of the book must therefore be considered, and the mere risk that the book might be exploited by panderers because it so pervasively treats sexual matters cannot alter the fact—given the view of the Massachusetts court attributing to *Memoirs* a modicum of literary and historical value—that the book will have redeeming social importance in the hands of those who publish or distribute it on the basis of that value."[48] Justice Douglas agreed as well:

> The majority [of individuals], needless to say, are somewhere between the over-scrupulous extremes of excitement and frigidity. . . . Everything, every idea, is capable of being obscene if the personality perceiving it so apprehends it. It is for this reason that books, pictures, charades, ritual, the spoken word, can and do lead directly to conduct harmful to the self indulging in it and to others. Heinrich Pommerenke, who was a rapist, abuser, and mass slayer of women in Germany, was prompted to his series of ghastly deeds by Cecil B. DeMille's *The Ten Commandments*. During the scene of the Jewish women dancing about the Golden Calf, all the doubts of his life came clear: Women were the source of the world's trouble and it was his mission to both punish them for this and to execute them. Leaving the theater, he slew his first victim in a park nearby. John George Haigh, the British vampire who sucked his victims' blood through soda straws and dissolved their drained bodies in acid baths, first had his murder-inciting dreams and vampire-longings from watching the "voluptuous" procedure of—an Anglican High Church Service![49]

As the nation considers how to proceed on the criminalization of noncommercial consensual student sexting, we should ponder Justice Douglas's reflective words as a starting point for any action:

> Every time an obscenity case is to be argued here, my office is flooded with letters and postal cards urging me to protect the community or the Nation by striking down the publication. The messages are often identical even down to commas and semicolons. The inference is irresistible that they were all copied from a school or church blackboard. Dozens of postal cards often are mailed from the same precinct. The drives are incessant and the pressures are great. Happily we do not bow to them. I mention them only to emphasize the lack of popular understanding of our constitutional system. Publications and utterances were made immune from majoritarian control by the First Amendment, applicable to the States by reason of the Fourteenth. No exceptions were made,

not even for obscenity. The Court's contrary conclusion in Roth, where obscenity was found to be "outside" the First Amendment, is without justification.[50]

Justice Douglas did not end there. His further poignant words are critical to the debate on consensual sexting and the First Amendment:

The censor is always quick to justify his function in terms that are protective of society. But the First Amendment, written in terms that are absolute, deprives the States of any power to pass on the value, the propriety, or the morality of a particular expression. Perhaps the most frequently assigned justification for censorship is the belief that erotica produce antisocial sexual conduct. But that relationship has yet to be proven. Indeed, if one were to make judgments on the basis of speculation, one might guess that literature of the most pornographic sort would, in many cases, provide a substitute—not a stimulus—for antisocial sexual conduct. As I read the First Amendment, judges cannot gear the literary diet of an entire nation to whatever tepid stuff is incapable of triggering the most demented mind. The First Amendment demands more than a horrible example or two of the perpetrator of a crime of sexual violence, in whose pocket is found a pornographic book, before it allows the Nation to be saddled with a regime of censorship.[51]

Justice Douglas further emphasized that the locus of regulation of students when it comes to "erotic literature" should be the home rather than government censorship.[52] We could extend this to consensual sexting in stating that rather than making felons of and censoring consensual student sexters, whom the laws are often designed to protect, why not keep the locus of regulation for consensual sexting at home? Specifically, Justice Douglas stated that:

Those who are concerned about children and erotic literature would do well to consider the counsel of Judge Bok: "It will be asked whether one would care to have one's young daughter read these books. I suppose that by the time she is old enough to wish to read them she will have learned the biologic facts of life and the words that go with them. There is something seriously wrong at home if those facts have not been met and faced and sorted by then; it is not children so much as parents that should receive our concern about this. I should prefer that my own three daughters meet the facts of life and the literature of the world in my library than behind a neighbor's barn, for I can face the adversary there directly. If the young ladies are appalled by what they read, they can close the book at the bottom of page one; if they read further, they will learn what is in the world and in its people, and no parents who have been discerning with their children need fear the outcome. Nor can they hold it back, for life is a series of little battles and minor issues, and the burden of choice is on us all, every day, young and old."[53]

If you are wondering what the distinction is between *Roth* and *A Book Named 'John Cleland's Memoirs of a Woman of Pleasure,'* here is the Court's expressed distinction:

> While Roth *presumed* "obscenity" to be "utterly without redeeming social importance," *Memoirs* required that to prove obscenity it must be *affirmatively established* that the material is "utterly without redeeming social value." Thus, even as they repeated the words of *Roth*, the *Memoirs* plurality produced a drastically altered test that called on the prosecution to prove a negative, i.e., that the material was "utterly without redeeming social value"—a burden virtually impossible to discharge under our criminal standards of proof. Such considerations caused Mr. Justice Harlan to wonder if the "utterly without redeeming social value" test had any meaning at all.[54]

Ginsberg vs. New York

About two years after the decision in *A Book Named 'John Cleland's Memoirs of a Woman of Pleasure,'* the U.S. Supreme Court would again rule on the intersection of obscenity and the First Amendment. In this case—*Ginsberg vs. New York*[55]—the question before the Court was whether a New York statute that criminalized the sale of obscene material to children below the age of 17 was constitutional. The statute's definition of obscenity was based on whether it appealed to minors below the age of 17, regardless of whether the material would qualify as obscene for adults. The appellant had been convicted for selling "girlie magazines" at two different times to a boy who was only 16 years old.[56] The trial judge determined that the magazines displayed "female . . . buttocks with less than a full opaque covering, or . . . the female breast with less than a fully opaque covering of any portion thereof below the top of the nipple."[57] Additionally, the judge found the magazine pictures "harmful to minors"[58] because they showed nudity in a way that "(i) predominantly appeals to the prurient, shameful, or morbid interest of minors, and (ii) is patently offensive to prevailing standards in the adult community as a whole with respect to what is suitable material for minors, and (iii) is utterly without redeeming social importance for minors."[59]

The appellant argued that "the scope of the constitutional freedom of expression secured to a citizen to read or see material concerned with sex cannot be made to depend upon whether the citizen is an adult or a minor."[60] It is critical to pay attention to the Court's response, as it clearly shows that *Ginsberg* is limited in scope; we would argue that if limited in scope, then clearly it would be a stretch for a court to contextualize consensual sexting in this case since sexting did not exist in 1968 when this decision was made. Here is the Court's response to the appellant's argument: "We have no occasion in this case to consider the impact of the guarantees of freedom of expression upon the totality of the relationship of the minor and the State."[61] Moreover, in the same breath, the Court limited the scope of its decision to the New York statute—a statute that clearly had nothing to do with sexting. Further, the New York statute dealt with commercial distribution, whereas the focus of our book is noncommercial consensual sexting. An additional distinction between our focus and *Ginsberg* lies in the fact that *Ginsberg* dealt with an adult-to-minor exchange, while this book deals with minor-to-minor sexting.

The Court did go on to rule that the New York statute did not violate the free speech rights of minors; in support, the Court pointed to the fact that "suggestions that legislatures might give attention to laws dealing specifically with *safeguarding* children against pornographic material have been made by many judges and commentators"[62] and the need to protect children from "harmful material."[63] The key words in this rationale are *safeguarding* and *harmful*. *Safeguarding* connotes security and safety, while *harmful* connotes injury.

The Court hinged its decision on the need to "safeguard [minors] from *abuses* which might *prevent* their growth into free and independent well-developed men and citizens."[64] The Court also stated that the New York law was passed due to legislative concerns about a "clear and present danger to the people of the state."[65] With sexting that is solely between students mutually consenting to the exchange, what are the security and safety concerns that would justify making felons of these students? What is the abuse that results from noncommercial consensual student-to-student sexting? If there is abuse, are states that permit students under the age of 18 to engage in consensual sex not promoting abuse? How would noncommercial consensual student-to-student sexting *"prevent"* the "growth" of the sexters into "independent well-developed" "citizens," the key word being "prevent"? What is the "clear and present danger" from consensual student-to-student sexting? These are questions that need to be answered thoughtfully. Again, we must keep in mind that in *Ginsberg*, the Court was referring to adult-to-minor commercial distribution, in which case there should definitely be cause for great alarm about abuse, harm, and the need to safeguard minors through legislation.

The New York legislature invoked the "clear and present danger" rationale for enacting the statute in *Ginsberg*. The Supreme Court rejected this rationale, noting that "It is *very doubtful* that this finding [of clear and present danger by the New York legislature] expresses an accepted scientific fact."[66] We must similarly insist on research data in support of criminal legislation against noncommercial consensual student-to-student sexting before enactments, or we risk emotions governing the debate.

In its reasoning to support upholding the New York law and appellant's conviction, the Supreme Court's emphasis on the prime role of parents ironically distinguishes consensual sexting from *Ginsberg's* rationale:

> Constitutional interpretation has consistently recognized that the parents' claim to authority in their own household to direct the rearing of their children is basic in the structure of our society. "It is cardinal with us that the custody, care and nurture of the child reside first in the parents, whose primary function and freedom include preparation for obligations the state can neither supply nor hinder." The legislature could properly conclude that parents and others, teachers for example, who have this primary responsibility for children's well-being are entitled to the support of laws designed to aid discharge of that responsibility. Indeed, subsection 1(f)(ii) of § 484-h expressly recognizes the parental role in assessing sex-related material harmful to minors according "to prevailing standards in the adult community as a whole with respect to what is suitable material for minors." Moreover, the prohibition against sales to minors does not bar parents who so desire from purchasing the magazines for their children.[67]

We agree with the Court's rationale if extended to consensual student sexting: the locus of regulation should be the parents. The Court did go on to declare that because parents are not always available to regulate *sale* of materials to minors, legislatures can step in and "include in a statute designed to regulate the *sale* of pornography to children special standards."[68] It appears evident, however, that the Court limited this declaration to commercial distribution.

In his dissenting opinion in *Ginsberg*, Justice Fortas criticized the Court for not setting forth a standard for distinguishing materials obscene to minors from materials obscene to adults. He opined that the Court had encroached on the traditional realm of parental guidance, an argument that equally applies to criminalization of consensual student-to-student sexting:

This decision does not merely protect children from activities which all sensible parents would condemn. Rather, its undefined and unlimited approval of state censorship in this area denies to children free access to books and works of art to which many parents may wish their children to have uninhibited access. For denial of access to these magazines, without any standard or definition of their allegedly distinguishing characteristics, is also denial of access to great works of art and literature.[69]

Stanley vs. Georgia

Almost a year after *Ginsberg*, in 1969 in *Stanley vs. Georgia*,[70] the U.S. Supreme Court would decide whether an "obscenity statute, insofar as it punishes mere *private possession* of obscene matter, violates the First Amendment, as made applicable to the States by the Fourteenth Amendment."[71] In that case, the appellant had been convicted for possession of obscene films found after a search of his home. The Court acknowledged that this was a case of "first impression"[72] because *Roth* and *Ginsberg* dealt with sale or "public distribution or dissemination" rather than possession.[73] Specifically, the Court noted that "neither *Roth* nor any subsequent decision of this Court dealt with the *precise* problem involved in the present case."[74] Furthermore, the Court noted that "none of the statements cited by the Court in *Roth* for the proposition that 'this Court has always assumed that obscenity is not protected by the freedoms of speech and press' were made *in the context of* a statute punishing mere private possession of obscene material; the cases cited deal for the most part with use of the mails to distribute objectionable material or with some form of public distribution or dissemination."[75]

If the Court was willing to rely on precision of problem presented and context of cases to distinguish *Stanley* from *Roth* and *Ginsberg*, it needs to do the same when presented with its first noncommercial consensual student-to-student sexting case: the Court needs to declare that because there is no precise alignment between its precedents and the issue of noncommercial consensual student-to-student sexting, it is a case of first impression that must be determined anew. After all, this is what the Court did in *Stanley*. In other words, just as the Court was unwilling to extrapolate from *Roth* and *Ginsberg* to *Stanley*, it should be similarly hesitant to extrapolate from its precedents to noncommercial consensual student-to-student sexting. We must keep in mind that sexts did not exist during the years that shaped the Court's obscenity jurisprudence. Context matters, and context should matter. Indeed, the Court itself recognized this in stating, with reference to *Stanley*, that "In this context, we do not believe that this case can be decided simply by citing *Roth*. *Roth* and its progeny certainly do mean that the First and Fourteenth Amendments recognize a valid governmental interest in dealing with the problem of obscenity. But the assertion of that interest cannot, in *every context*, be insulated from all constitutional protections. *Neither* Roth *nor any other decision of this Court reaches that far*."[76]

The phrase "cannot, in every context" should caution the Court against subsuming sexting into its precedents. Besides, the *Stanley* Court declared:

> As the Court said in *Roth* itself, "ceaseless vigilance is the watchword to prevent ... erosion [of First Amendment rights] by Congress or by the States. The door barring federal and state intrusion into this area *cannot be left ajar*; it must be kept tightly closed and opened only the *slightest* crack necessary to prevent encroachment upon more important interests." *Roth* and the cases following it discerned such an "important interest" in the regulation of commercial distribution of obscene material.[77]

The declaration by the Court is clearly a clarion call to avoid eroding First Amendment rights; that call should include a refrain from stifling a First Amendment right to noncommercial consensual student-to-student sexting. The door to censorship of noncommercial consensual student-to-student sexting "cannot be left ajar; it must be kept tightly closed and opened only the slightest crack necessary to prevent encroachment upon more important interests."[78]

Further support for recognizing a First Amendment right to noncommercial consensual student-to-student sexting might be found in the Court's following words: "It is now well established that the Constitution protects the right to receive information and ideas. 'This freedom [of speech and press] ... necessarily protects the right to receive.' This right to receive information and ideas, *regardless of their social worth*, is fundamental to our free society."[79] The Court added that the right to receive information "in the context of ... a prosecution for mere possession of printed or filmed matter in the privacy of a person's own home ... takes on an added dimension."[80]

Consensual sexters are seeking the same right the Court recognized in *Stanley*: "These are the rights that appellant is asserting in the case before us. He is asserting the right to read or observe what he pleases—the right to satisfy his intellectual and *emotional* needs in the privacy of his own home. He is asserting the right to be free from state inquiry into the contents of his library."[81]

We could substitute the word "cell phone" for the word "library" so as to extend this to sexters. Additionally, it is indisputable that one of the needs consensual sexters seek to satisfy through sexting is emotional. Oftentimes, this need is satisfied via sexting at home.

Before we rush to make criminals of our youth, let us consider this Supreme Court declaration: "If the First Amendment means anything, it means that a State has no business telling a man, sitting alone in his own house, what books he may read or what films he may watch. Our whole constitutional heritage rebels at the thought of giving government the power to control men's minds."[82] Again, we could substitute the word "cell phones" for the words "books" and "films" so as to extend this declaration to sexters.

As for the argument often made for criminalizing consensual sexting—that we need to protect the mind of the sexters from the "effects of obscenity"—the Court's response is apt:

> In the face of these traditional notions of individual liberty, Georgia asserts the right to protect the individual's mind from the effects of obscenity. We are not certain that this argument amounts to anything more than the assertion that the State has the right to control the moral content of a person's thoughts. To some, this may be a noble purpose, but it is *wholly inconsistent* with the philosophy of the First Amendment. As the Court said in *Kingsley International Pictures Corp. vs. Regents*, "this argument misconceives what it is that the Constitution protects. Its guarantee is not confined to the expression of ideas that are conventional or shared by a majority. . . . And in the realm of ideas it protects expression which is eloquent no less than that which is unconvincing." Nor is it relevant that obscene materials in general, or the particular films before the Court, are arguably devoid of any ideological content. The line between the transmission of ideas and mere entertainment is much too elusive for this Court to draw, if indeed such a line can be drawn at all. Whatever the power of the state to control public dissemination of ideas inimical to the public morality, it cannot constitutionally premise legislation on the desirability of controlling a person's private thoughts.[83]

Another argument often made for making consensual sexters felons is that "exposure to obscene materials may lead to deviant sexual behavior or crimes of sexual violence"[84] by the sexters. The state of Georgia made the same argument in *Stanley*;[85] the Court's response, then, is apropos here: "There appears to be little empirical basis for that assertion."[86] This was not the end of the Court's response to this assertion. The Court added the following immediately after its response referenced earlier in this paragraph:

But more important, if the State is only concerned about printed or filmed materials inducing antisocial conduct, we believe that in the context of private consumption of ideas and information we should adhere to the view that "among free men, the deterrents ordinarily to be applied to prevent crime are education and punishment for violations of the law." Given the present state of knowledge, the State may no more prohibit mere possession of obscene matter on the ground that it may lead to antisocial conduct than it may prohibit possession of chemistry books on the ground that they may lead to the manufacture of homemade spirits.[87]

In *Stanley*, the Court ruled that private possession of obscene material is constitutionally protected. With that being the rule, why should First Amendment protection not be similarly extended to private possession, by the consenting student sexters, of their own noncommercial consensual student-to-student sexting? Given that the government bears the burden of proof in regulation of free speech, and given the importance of free speech, the Court needs to require "survey-type evidence on the magnitude of the problems" that are often proffered as justifications for regulating sexting when such arguments as above are tendered.[88]

Miller vs. California

About four years after *Stanley*, in 1973 in *Miller vs. California*,[89] the U.S. Supreme Court would set forth a new test for obscenity. In that case, the appellant had been convicted for mailing "unsolicited advertising brochures"[90] of "adult material."[91] The brochures had "some descriptive printed material" but "primarily they consist[ed] of pictures and drawings very explicitly depicting men and women in groups of two or more engaging in a variety of sexual activities, with genitals often prominently displayed."[92] The Court emphasized that the complainants who received the mail "had not requested the brochures."[93] This fact, along with the nature of the mail—advertising—distinguishes *Miller* from noncommercial consensual student-to-student sexting. This is echoed in the Court's characterization of the *Miller* case: "This case involves the application of a State's criminal obscenity statute to a situation in which sexually explicit materials have been *thrust* by *aggressive* sales action upon *un*willing recipients who had in no way indicated any desire to receive such materials."[94] Clearly, noncommercial consensual student-to-student sexting is not "*thrust* by *aggressive sales* action upon *un*willing recipients who had in no way indicated any desire to receive such materials."

Further, given that the *Miller* case dealt with unsolicited advertising of "adult material,"[95] it is not surprising that the Court provided the following rationale for its finding of obscenity in the case: "This Court has recognized that the States have a legitimate interest in prohibiting dissemination or exhibition of obscene material when the mode of dissemination carries with it a significant danger of offending the sensibilities of unwilling recipients or of exposure to juveniles."[96] We are similarly unequivocally against dissemination of "adult material" to any minor and strongly believe that should be a felony. Arguably, given that the Court mentioned juvenile exposure next to "unwilling recipients" and the context of the case itself, it is likely the Court was referring here to adults exposing "adult material" to juveniles; and there is no evidence in the Court's rationale that the Court had in mind noncommercial consensual student-to-student sexting when it made the statement about "unwilling recipients or of exposure to juveniles."

The Court's own cited *Oxford English* and *Webster's* dictionary definitions of obscenity also distinguish *Miller* from noncommercial consensual student-to-student sexting: "Derived from the Latin *obscaenus, ob*, to, plus *caenum*, filth, 'obscene' is defined in the *Webster's Third New International Dictionary* (Unabridged 1969) as '1a: *disgusting* to the senses . . . b: *grossly repugnant* to the generally accepted notions of what is appropriate . . . 2: *offensive or revolting* as countering or violating some ideal or principle.' "[97] Additionally, "*Oxford English Dictionary* (1933 ed.) gives a similar definition, 'offensive to the senses, or to taste or refinement, disgusting, repulsive, filthy, foul, abominable, loathsome.' "[98] Consensual sexters would not describe their noncommercial consensual student-to-student sexting with the words highlighted in the *Oxford English* or *Webster's* definitions. The Court seemed to criticize the *Roth* test for not "reflect[ing] the precise meaning of 'obscene' as traditionally used in the English language" while conceding that the material in *Miller* could more accurately be characterized as pornography.[99]

In establishing the *Miller* test (set forth later herein), the Court emphasized that the test was being created in the context we set forth earlier in this text;[100] in essence, since noncommercial consensual student-to-student sexting was not a context available to the Court in 1973 when the *Miller* test was created, that test should not be used by the Court in noncommercial consensual student-to-student sexting cases. Instead, the Court needs to create another test that would account for the context of noncommercial consensual student-to-student sexting.

Miller would be the first time since *Roth* that a majority of the Court would agree on an obscenity test.[101] Indeed, the Court conceded the elusive nature of the jurisprudence: "We have seen a variety of views among the members of the Court unmatched in any other course of constitutional adjudication."[102] Since that is so—and because of the Court's own declaration that free speech jurisprudence is "an area in which there are few eternal verities"[103]—the Court needs to tread carefully before it subsumes noncommercial consensual student-to-student sexting under its current obscenity jurisprudence.

In 2010, in *Ontario vs. Quon,*[104] which dealt with the Fourth Amendment, the U.S. Supreme Court itself cautioned against eager intervention in technology cases: "The Court must proceed with care when considering the whole concept of privacy expectations in communications made on electronic equipment. . . . The judiciary risks error by elaborating too fully on the Fourth Amendment implications of emerging technology before its role in society has become clear."[105] When it comes to noncommercial consensual student-to-student sexting, should the Court not heed its own words in *Miller*? "We acknowledge, however, the inherent dangers of undertaking to regulate any form of expression. State statutes designed to regulate obscene materials must be *carefully limited*."[106]

The creation of the *Miller* test was a rejection of the plurality test in *A Book Named 'John Cleland's Memoirs of a Woman of Pleasure.'* The *Miller* test is a three-part test: (1) "whether the average person, applying contemporary community standards, would find that the work, taken as a whole, appeals to the prurient interest"; (2) "whether the work depicts or describes, in a patently offensive way, sexual conduct specifically defined by the applicable state law"; and (3) "whether the work, taken as a whole, lacks serious literary, artistic, political, or scientific value."[107] The *Miller* test covers both description and visual representations of sexual conduct.[108]

In the case of noncommercial, consensual student-to-student sexting, it is critical to apply "contemporary community standards" for teens rather than adults, because adults might not fully appreciate the teenage subculture, which is quite different from the adult subculture. After all, the Court itself acknowledged that a national community standard was not appropriate, instead specifying "contemporary community standards" that would vary from community to community.[109] This is even more important given the prominent role of technology in today's teen subculture; a key word to keep in mind under the first prong of the *Miller* test is "contemporary."

The Court's words in *Quon* ring true with the teen subculture: "Cell phone and text message communications are so pervasive that some persons may consider them to be essential means or necessary instruments for self-expression, even self-identification."[110] As the Court admonished in *Quon*, "rapid changes in the dynamics of communication and information transmission are evident not just in the technology itself but in what society accepts as proper behavior."[111]

Moreover, as Justice Douglas observed in his dissenting opinion in *Miller*:

> There are no constitutional guidelines for deciding what is and what is not "obscene." The Court is at large because we deal with tastes and standards. . . . What shocks me may be sustenance for my neighbor. What causes one person to boil up in rage over one pamphlet or movie may reflect only his neurosis, not shared by others. We deal here with a regime of censorship which, if adopted, should be done by constitutional amendment after full debate by the people.[112]

For the "value" element of the third prong of the *Miller* test, Justice Stevens's words in *Smith vs. United States* aptly illustrate the elusive nature of this prong:

> I do not know whether the ugly pictures in this record have any beneficial value. The fact that there is a large demand for comparable materials indicates that they do provide amusement or information, or at least satisfy the curiosity of interested persons. Moreover, there are serious well-intentioned people who are persuaded that they serve a worthwhile purpose. Others believe they arouse passions that lead to the commission of crimes; if that be true, surely there is a mountain of material just within the protected zone that is equally capable of motivating comparable conduct. Moreover, the dire predictions about the baneful effects of these materials are disturbingly reminiscent of arguments formerly made about the availability of what are now valued as works of art. In the end, I believe we must rely on the capacity of the free marketplace of ideas to distinguish that which is useful or beautiful from what which is ugly or worthless.[113]

Justice Harlan echoed these same sentiments in *Cohen vs. California*:[114] "It is nevertheless often true that one man's vulgarity is another's lyric. Indeed, we think it is largely because governmental officials cannot make principled distinctions in this area that the Constitution leaves matters of taste and style so largely to the individual."[115]

If the Court applies the *Miller* test, it is likely that, pursuant to the first prong of the test, sexting "appeals to the prurient interest."[116] However, we need to consider how the Court has defined prurience. According to the Court, "prurience may be constitutionally defined for the purposes of identifying obscenity as that which appeals to a shameful or morbid interest in sex."[117] The teen culture would certainly not describe their noncommercial, consensual student-to-student sexting as a "shameful or morbid interest in sex." If the Court adheres to this definition, then noncommercial, consensual student-to-student sexting might pass muster under *Miller*'s first prong.

While a sext "depicts or describes . . . sexual conduct specifically defined by the applicable state law"[118] such as the laws we set forth earlier, a sext is neither inherently nor necessarily "patently offensive"[119] in the case of noncommercial, consensual student-to-student sexting. If it is consensual, noncommercial, and akin to a love letter, how could it be "patently offensive"? Indeed, elaborating on the "patently offensive" language of its decision, the Court provided a limitation in its focus on commerce that might distinguish *Miller* from noncommercial, consensual student-to-student sexting: "Under the holdings announced today, no one will be subject to prosecution for the sale or exposure of obscene materials unless these materials depict or describe patently offensive 'hard core' sexual conduct specifically defined by the regulating state law, as written or construed. We are satisfied that these specific prerequisites will provide fair notice to a *dealer* in such materials that his *public* and *commercial* activities may bring prosecution."[120]

Justice Douglas's critique of the "offensive" language included in the second prong of the *Miller* test makes a puissant case for First Amendment protection for sexting:

> The idea that the First Amendment permits punishment for ideas that are "offensive" to the particular judge or jury sitting in judgment is astounding. No greater leveler of speech or literature has ever been designed. To give the power to the censor, as we do today, is to make a sharp and radical break with the traditions of a free society. The First Amendment was not fashioned as a vehicle for dispensing tranquilizers to the people. Its prime function was to keep debate open to "offensive" as well as to "staid" people. The tendency throughout history has been to subdue the individual and to exalt the power of government. The use of the standard "offensive" gives authority to government that cuts the very vitals out of the First Amendment. As is

intimated by the Court's opinion, the materials before us may be garbage. But so is much of what is said in political campaigns, in the daily press, on TV, or over the radio. By reason of the First Amendment—and solely because of it—speakers and publishers have not been threatened or subdued because their thoughts and ideas may be "offensive" to some.[121]

In defending its *Miller* decision against the critique of the dissenting justices, the Court further highlighted the commercial and public-exhibition undertones of its decision—undertones absent in noncommercial, consensual student-to-student sexting: "The dissenting Justices sound the alarm of repression. But, in our view, to equate the free and robust exchange of ideas and political debate with *commercial* exploitation of obscene material demeans the grand conception of the First Amendment and its high purposes in the historic struggle for freedom. It is a misuse of the great guarantees of free speech and free press."[122] Besides, it is critical to keep in mind that noncommercial, consensual student-to-student sexting is not "exploitation of obscene material."[123] As the Court itself conceded, "The protection given speech and press was fashioned to assure unfettered interchange of ideas for the bringing about of political and social changes desired by the people ... but the *public* portrayal of hard-core sexual conduct for its own sake, and for the ensuing commercial gain, is a different matter."[124]

Additionally, the argument could be made that in states without sexting laws (in other words, in states that rely solely on obscenity or child pornography laws to prosecute sexters), noncommercial, consensual student-to-student sexting has not been "specifically defined by the applicable state law";[125] this should thus arguably take sexting outside the scope of obscenity pursuant to the *Miller* test's second prong.

As noted earlier, when the *Miller* test was created in 1973, sexting did not exist; and the Court could not have grasped or anticipated today's teen subculture. Thus, it should not be surprising that the third prong of the *Miller* test—"whether the work, taken as a whole, lacks serious literary, artistic, political, or scientific value"—lists only four accepted values for works that would otherwise qualify as obscenity: "literary, artistic, political, or scientific value." While student sexters might argue that sexts have value and more specifically artistic value, pursuant to the third prong of the test, the qualifier—"serious"—fails to take into account fun and the often less "serious" nature of sexting. However, if the Court interprets "serious" as "sincere," then sexting might pass muster under the third prong of the obscenity test.

Under the artistic element, pursuant to distinguished researcher Edward J. Eberle's definition of art, sexts arguably constitute art. Under Eberle's definition, art constitutes a "portal to nonrational, noncognitive, nondiscursive dimensions to human life, offering a fuller conception of the human person."[126] Further, "art functions as a private sphere of freedom not subject or susceptible, on the whole, to the normal rules of society." We contend that a sext constitutes art, because pursuant to Eberle's definition of art, a sext "partakes of the creative process central and unique to human existence."[127] A sext also "provides an avenue to dimensions of human life less accessible by ordinary rational or cognitive processes."[128] As Eberle notes, "art is a crucial part of the process of human definition and self-definition so central to any robust concept of free speech"[129]; so are sexts, as evident in our discussions earlier herein. Eberle's observation that "the artist and his or her viewer share the bond of communicating and sensing life feelings, sharing meanings"[130] clearly applies to noncommercial, consensual student-to-student sexting since the sexter "and his or her viewer share the bond of communicating and sensing life feelings, sharing meanings"[131] through their sexts.

Justice Douglas's dissenting opinion in *Miller* provides a strong foundation for an argument for the Court to extend First Amendment protection to noncommercial, consensual student-to-student sexting, given that it is consensual and noncommercial (we can substitute "noncommercial, consensual student-to-student sexting" for "obscenity" and substitute "use cell phones" for "enter newsstands or bookstalls" in Justice Douglas's opinion that follows to see the opinion's ample application to noncommercial, consensual student-to-student sexting):

> While the right to know is the corollary of the right to speak or publish, no one can be forced by government to listen to disclosure that he finds offensive. That was the basis of my dissent in *Public Utilities Comm'n v. Pollak* where I protested against making streetcar passengers a "captive" audience. There is no "captive audience" problem in these obscenity cases. No one is being compelled to look or to listen. Those who enter newsstands or bookstalls may be offended by what they see. But they are not compelled by the State to frequent those places; and it is only state or governmental action against which the First Amendment, applicable to the States by virtue of the Fourteenth, raises a ban.[132]

First Amendment lawyers H. Franklin Robbins Jr. and Steven G. Mason point out that the Miller test "may be the most vague law that any

American citizen has ever been required to interpret."[133] As they rightly note, "Justice Brennan once explained this problem with chilling reality: The problem is ... that one cannot say with certainty that material is obscene until at least five members of this Court, applying inevitably obscure standards, have pronounced it so."[134]

What the Court observed in 1973 might be similarly applicable to judicial review of sexting today: "One can concede that the 'sexual revolution' of recent years may have had useful byproducts in striking layers of prudery from a subject long irrationally kept from needed ventilation."[135] We need to reflect on Justice Douglas's caution about overregulation that could impair free speech when we deal with sexting, for "we deal with highly emotional, not rational, questions. [After all,] to many the Song of Solomon is obscene."[136]

Paris Adult Theatre I vs. Slaton

On the same day as its *Miller* decision, in *Paris Adult Theatre I vs. Slaton* in 1973,[137] the Court ruled on an obscenity case that involved commercial and public exhibition of material deemed obscene by local officials in Atlanta. The fact that the case involved public exhibition for "paid admission"[138] distinguishes this case from noncommercial, consensual student-to-student sexting. The Court's reasoning did not differ much from *Miller*'s. The critical thing to take out of this case would be from Justice Brennan's dissent critiquing the obscenity jurisprudence: "No other aspect of the First Amendment has, in recent years, demanded so substantial a commitment of our time, generated such disharmony of views, and remained so resistant to the formulation of stable and manageable standards."[139]

Additionally, Justice Brennan cautioned against undermining the First Amendment; and this caution should be heeded in any debates about noncommercial, consensual student-to-student sexting: "We have more than once previously acknowledged that 'constitutionally protected expression ... is often separated from obscenity only by a dim and uncertain line.' Added to the 'perhaps inherent residual vagueness' of each of the current multitude of [obscenity] standards is the further complication that the obscenity of any particular item may depend upon nuances of presentation and the context of its dissemination."[140]

Jenkins vs. Georgia

About a year after the *Miller* decision, in 1974 in *Jenkins vs. Georgia*,[141] the U.S. Supreme Court would seek to clarify the "community standards" element of the first prong of the *Miller* test. Specifically, the Court noted that *Miller* "does not require that juries be instructed in state obscenity cases to apply the standards of a hypothetical *statewide* community."[142] The Court iterated that "*Miller* held that it was constitutionally permissible to permit juries to rely on the understanding of the community from which they came as to contemporary community standards, and the States have considerable latitude in framing statutes under this element of the *Miller* decision." Moreover, "a State may choose to define an obscenity offense in terms of 'contemporary community standards' as defined in *Miller* without further specification, as was done here, or it may choose to define the standards in more precise geographic terms."[143] With this latitude available to states in defining the "contemporary community standards" for noncommercial, consensual student-to-student sexting, states need to exercise responsibility by accounting for the teen subculture, which is different from that of adults.

With respect to the "patently offensive" element of the second prong of the *Miller* test, the Court declared that "it would be wholly at odds with this aspect of *Miller* to uphold an obscenity conviction based upon a defendant's depiction of a woman with a bare midriff, even though a properly charged jury unanimously agreed on a verdict of guilty."[144] This *might* provide some protection under obscenity laws for sexts that only show "a bare midriff." Besides, the Court explicitly ruled that "nudity alone is not enough to make material legally obscene under the *Miller* standards."[145] Overzealous prosecutors of noncommercial, consensual student-to-student sexting might need to be reminded of this; for if the students are merely consensually exchanging nude pictures without more, it is "not enough to make material legally obscene under the *Miller* standards."

Erznoznik vs. City of Jacksonville

In 1975, in *Erznoznik vs. City of Jacksonville*,[146] the U.S. Supreme Court would review a First Amendment challenge to a Jacksonville, Florida, ordinance that prohibited a drive-in theater from showing films with nudity "when its screen is visible from a public street or place."[147] This public exhibition aspect distinguishes this Supreme Court obscenity precedent from the focus of our thesis. The appellant in this case had been charged for "exhibiting a motion picture, visible from public streets, in which female buttocks and bare breasts were shown."[148] The city of Jacksonville argued that the ordinance was part of its "undoubted police power to protect children."[149] The Court, however, noted that while minors' free speech is not coextensive with that of adults, "minors are entitled to a significant measure of First Amendment protection and only in relatively narrow and well-defined circumstances may government bar *public* dissemination of protected materials to them."[150] If the Court made this statement with respect to public dissemination, this should apply even more so to private dissemination, which is what noncommercial, consensual student-to-student sexting entails. The Court criticized the ordinance for prohibiting "scenes from a culture in which nudity is indigenous."[151]

Erznoznik also affirmed the fact that the government cannot wield its power to suppress, as obscene, all exposure of nudity to minors:

> Clearly all nudity cannot be deemed obscene even as to minors. Nor can such a broad restriction be justified by any other governmental interest pertaining to minors. Speech that is neither obscene as to youths nor subject to some other legitimate proscription cannot be suppressed solely to protect the young from ideas or images that a legislative body thinks unsuitable for them. In *most* circumstances, the values protected by the First Amendment are no less applicable when government seeks to control the flow of information to minors.[152]

Concluding Notes

In this chapter, we have provided a review of precedents that support our position that the First Amendment must still be respected with respect to sexting. If noncommercial, consensual student-to-student sexting is not considered art under the *Miller* test, the Court needs to consider updating the *Miller* test or creating an entirely new test to account for the technological component that was clearly not contemplated when the *Miller* test was created. There is a strong case in precedents, as evident in this chapter, for not making students felons for noncommercial, consensual student-to-student sexting. The Court itself acknowledged in *Ashcroft vs. Free Speech Coalition*, in 2002,[153] that "pictures of young children engaged in certain acts might be obscene where similar depictions of adults, *or perhaps even older adolescents*, would not."[154] The Court needs to keep this declaration in mind whenever it considers whether noncommercial, consensual student-to-student sexting is entitled to First Amendment protection; after all, such sexting is essentially conducted by "older adolescents," not "young children."

Chapter 5

Child Pornography Precedents and Consensual Sexting

Introduction

In her article "Inverting the First Amendment," legal scholar Amy Adler provides an excellent analysis of child pornography precedents. As she observes, "child pornography law is the new crucible of the First Amendment. It tests the limits of modern free speech law the way political dissent did in the times of [Justice] Holmes and [Justice] Brandeis."[1] Adler points out that child pornography law "is where popular pressure on courts and legislatures exerts itself most ferociously; it is where the greatest encroachments on free expression are now accepted. Therefore, the law of child pornography is as important for free speech scholars to scrutinize today as was the law of subversive advocacy earlier this century."[2] Yet, as Adler aptly notes, "the law of child pornography has been left to occupy its own peculiar and disagreeable realm" and "has undergone a dramatic growth spurt, unchecked by critical analysis."[3] In this chapter, we provide a dimension of needed critical review of child pornography jurisprudence by scrutinizing it to distinguish it from noncommercial, consensual student sexting.

New York vs. Ferber

In 1982, in *New York vs. Ferber*,[4] the U.S. Supreme Court created the distribution-of-child-pornography jurisprudence as an unprotected category of speech under the First Amendment. Unlike noncommercial, consensual student-to-student sexting, this case involved a commercial transaction in which a bookstore owner, Peter Ferber, sold sexually oriented films to an undercover police officer. What did the films show? They "almost exclusively" showed "young boys masturbating."[5] Ferber was found guilty of violating New York's law prohibiting child pornography dissemination. On appeal, the New York Court of Appeals found the New York law unconstitutional under the First Amendment.[6]

The New York law in question was not unlike any of the other statutes we set forth in Chapter 3. It provided that "a person is guilty of promoting a sexual performance by a child when, knowing the character and content thereof, he produces, directs or promotes any performance which includes sexual conduct by a child less than sixteen years of age."[7] The term "promote" was defined as "to procure, manufacture, issue, sell, give, provide, lend, mail, deliver, transfer, transmute, publish, distribute, circulate, disseminate, present, exhibit or advertise, or to offer or agree to do the same."[8] Sexual performance referred to "any performance or part thereof which includes sexual conduct by a child less than sixteen years of age."[9] "Sexual conduct," in turn, was described as "actual or simulated sexual intercourse, deviate sexual intercourse, . . . masturbation, . . . or lewd exhibition of the genitals,"[10] while "performance" referred to "any play, motion picture, photograph or dance or any other visual representation exhibited before an audience."[11]

According to the Supreme Court, Ferber presented a "single question" to the Court: "To prevent the abuse of children who are made to engage in sexual conduct for commercial purposes, could the New York State Legislature, consistent with the First Amendment, prohibit the dissemination of material which shows children engaged in sexual conduct, regardless of whether such material is obscene?"[12] As the Court itself acknowledged, the sole question before it in Ferber dealt with "the abuse of children" and "commercial purposes." Since both of these—"the abuse of children" and "commercial purposes"—are antithetical to noncommercial, consensual student-to-student sexting, and because the Court acknowledged that it granted certiorari to address the "single question" above, the Court should not extend Ferber to regulation of noncommercial, consensual student-to-student sexting. Moreover, whereas Ferber involved an adult distributing films of children, noncommercial, consensual student-to-student sexting involves consensual student-to-student sexting.

When it comes to noncommercial, consensual student-to-student sexting, the Court needs to heed its own caveat in Ferber: "By focusing on the factual situation before us, and similar cases necessary for development of a constitutional rule, we face flesh-and-blood legal problems with data relevant and adequate to an informed judgment."[13] In Ferber, the Court did not "face flesh-and-blood legal problems with data relevant and adequate to an informed judgment" about noncommercial, consensual student-to-student sexting, especially since the technology for sexting did not even exist then.

Further, as the Court itself conceded in *Ferber*, "Laws directed at the dissemination of child pornography run the risk of suppressing protected expression by allowing the hand of the censor to become *unduly heavy*."[14] In spite of this, the Court identified five reasons for its decision to exclude child pornography distribution from First Amendment protection: (1) the need to protect children from sexual exploitation;[15] (2) the need to close the market for child pornography linked to the "sexual abuse of children";[16] (3) the "economic motive" underlying the production of child pornography;[17] (4) the "exceedingly modest, if not de minimis" value of child pornography;[18] and (5) the consideration that the exclusion was not "incompatible with our earlier decisions."[19] The Court needs to use these very rationales to distinguish noncommercial, consensual student-to-student sexting from *Ferber*.

First, under the rationale of protecting children from sexual exploitation, the Court declared that a "State's interest in *safeguarding* the physical and psychological well-being of a minor is compelling."[20] There is no question that children need to be protected and that the state has a role in protecting them. However, given the context of *Ferber*, which involved adult dissemination of child pornography—an abhorrent act—the Court was justified in arguing for the need to safeguard children from such adults. However, in the case of noncommercial, consensual student-to-student sexting, the safeguarding rationale is greatly diminished; after all, it is a consensual exchange between teenagers. Indeed, since the Court noted that "a democratic society rests, for its continuance, upon the healthy, well-rounded growth of young people into full maturity as citizens"[21] and because self-expression is integral to the full development of adolescents, the Court needs to be hesitant in applying the safeguarding rationale to preclude First Amendment protection for noncommercial, consensual student-to-student sexting.

The Court explained its safeguarding rationale as follows: "The prevention of sexual exploitation and abuse of children constitutes a government objective of surpassing importance."[22] Clearly, in the case of noncommercial, consensual student-to-student sexting, the students are not abusing each other, nor is there exploitation. To support its explanation of the safeguarding rationale, the Court relied on the New York legislature's finding:

> There has been a proliferation of exploitation of children as subjects in sexual performances. The care of children is a sacred trust and should not be abused

by those who seek to *profit* through a *commercial* network based upon the *exploitation of* children. The public policy of the state demands the protection of children from exploitation through sexual performances.[23]

This legislative finding is unequivocally focused on commerce and exploitation—both of which are absent from noncommercial, consensual student-to-student sexting.

The commercial theme of the Court's safeguarding rationale is further evident in the Court's reliance on another New York legislative finding to support the safeguarding rationale, which the Court forcefully stated it would not "second-guess"[24]: In addition, the legislature found "the *sale* of these movies, magazines and photographs depicting the sexual conduct of children to be so abhorrent to the fabric of our society that it urge[d] law enforcement officers to aggressively seek out and prosecute . . . the *peddlers* . . . of this filth by vigorously applying the sanctions contained in this act."[25] Peddling and sale are antithetical to the very concept of noncommercial, consensual student-to-student sexting.

The Court explained the second rationale—the need to close the market for child pornography linked to the "sexual abuse of children"—as follows:

> The distribution of photographs and films depicting sexual activity by juveniles is intrinsically related to the sexual abuse of children in at least two ways. First, the materials produced are a permanent record of the children's participation and the harm to the child is exacerbated by their circulation. Second, the distribution network for child pornography must be closed if the production of material which requires the sexual exploitation of children is to be effectively controlled.[26]

While noncommercial, consensual student-to-student sexting undoubtedly creates a "permanent record of the children's participation," it is non sequitur that noncommercial, consensual student-to-student sexting would cause "harm to the child [that] is exacerbated by their [consensual sexts] circulation." In fact, the essence of noncommercial, consensual student-to-student sexting is connection and relationship-building between the consenting teen sexters. Moreover, given the nature of noncommercial, consensual student-to-student sexting, it is only circulated between the consenting sexters. In other words, unlike the context of *Ferber*, noncommercial, consensual student-to-student sexting does not have a "distribution *network*."

Besides, the reason the Court called for closing "distribution *network*[s]" was to control "the production of material which *requires* the sexual *exploitation* of children." Noncommercial, consensual student-to-student sexting does not *"require"* the exploitation of children, as was the case in *Ferber*. The Court elaborated on the second rationale, stating that "the most expeditious if not the only practical method of law enforcement may be to *dry up the market* for this material by imposing severe criminal penalties on persons selling, advertising, or otherwise promoting the product."[27] Clearly, there is no market to "dry up" with noncommercial, consensual student-to-student sexting.

The commercial theme underlying *Ferber* and distinguishing it from noncommercial, consensual student-to-student sexting is also evident in the Court's elaboration on the second rationale, specifically in the Court's language using the terms "industry," "apparatus," and "market": "While the production of pornographic materials is a low-profile, clandestine industry, the need to market the resulting products requires a visible apparatus of distribution."[28] Justice Brennan's words in his concurring opinion in *Ferber* help amplify our point here: "the Court's assumption of harm to the child resulting from the permanent record and circulation of the child's participation lacks much of its force where the depiction"[29] entails noncommercial, consensual student-to-student sexting. The Court's use of the term "victim" in justifying its second rationale[30] distinguishes *Ferber* from consensual student-to-student sexting, in which there is no victim since it is strictly consensual.

Recall the Court's third rationale for excluding child pornography distribution from First Amendment protection in *Ferber*: "The advertising and selling of child pornography provide an economic motive for and are thus an integral part of the production of such materials, an activity illegal throughout the Nation."[31] Noncommercial, consensual student-to-student sexting is certainly not driven by an "economic motive" of "advertising and selling of child pornography"; instead, it is designed to build bonds between two consenting teen sexters.

The Court expounded on this third rationale, stating that "it rarely has been suggested that the constitutional freedom for speech ... extends its immunity to speech or writing used as an integral part of conduct in violation of a valid criminal statute."[32] This is true. However, in the case of noncommercial, consensual student-to-student sexting, if the conduct referenced in the Court's statement were taken to refer to the sexual acts underlying sexting, as noted earlier, those acts are legal in some states for teenagers; they simply cannot memorialize the acts without violating a criminal law. In other words, our argument for First Amendment protection for noncommercial, consensual student-to-student sexting is not a suggestion "that the constitutional freedom for speech ... extends its immunity to speech or writing used as an integral part of conduct in violation of a valid criminal statute."[33] Why? Because the underlying conduct is not necessarily violative of a criminal statute in every state. As the Supreme Court has noted, "Even where there is an underlying crime, however, the Court has not allowed the suppression of speech in all cases."[34] Before continuing on to the fourth *Ferber* rationale, we want to expound on the third rationale, using three cases to emphasize the absurdity of prosecuting teens for sexting when they can legally engage in the underlying sexual acts.

In *Salter vs. State*,[35] an Indiana appeals court had to decide the fate of a defendant—Salter—who had been convicted of five counts of dissemination of matter harmful to minors and 40 counts of child exploitation. The defendant argued that he should not have been convicted because, under Indiana law, he could legally have consensual relations with the minor— M. B.—with whom he had exchanged several sexually explicit images. The appeals court agreed, finding and reasoning as follows:

> Salter sent the pictures of his genitals to M.B., who, at sixteen, was old enough to consent to sexual relations in Indiana. ... Such sexual activity could involve varying degrees of nudity and necessarily involves some exposure of the genitals. By setting the legal age of consent at sixteen, the Indiana legislature has made an implied policy choice that in-person viewing of another person's genitals is "suitable matter" for a sixteen- or seventeen-year-old child. That being so, how could Salter have known that a picture of his genitals would be "harmful," that is, not "suitable," for M. B.? Asked another way, if such images are harmful to sixteen- and seventeen-year-old children, then why would our legislature allow those children to view the same matter in-person, in the course of sexual activity? These questions reveal the flaw in Indiana Code section 35–49–3–3 as applied to Salter: when read in light of well-established Indiana law setting the age of consent to sexual relations, it did not provide him with fair notice that the State would consider pictures of his genitals harmful to or unsuitable for a sixteen-year-old girl.[36]

The appellate court's finding and reasoning support our discussions earlier in this chapter of noncommercial, consensual student-to-student sexting with respect to *Ferber*'s third rationale. The *Salter* court conceded the controversial nature of its decision: "Because of the nature of Salter's actions and the sheer number of his convictions, we realize that our decision is sure to inspire opposition."[37]

The Vermont Supreme Court appears to support this same reasoning. In *In re G. T.*,[38] a 14-year-old minor—G. T.—appealed his conviction for statutory rape and adjudication as a juvenile delinquent for sexual contact with M. N.—a 12-year-old girl.[39] He argued that, as a minor, the law was supposed to protect—not persecute—him, and that he could not be a victim and perpetrator of a crime under the same law.[40] The Court stated that "under the State's theory in this case, if two persons under sixteen years of age commit consensual, mutual sexual acts with each other, they are both guilty of statutory rape."[41] Additionally, "under the State's theory, both G. T. and M. N. have necessarily committed the crime, and all consensual sexual activity between teenagers is a felony for both participants."[42]

As with noncommercial, consensual student-to-student sexting, which is readily susceptible to selective enforcement under the statutes we covered in Chapter 3, in *In re G. T.*, the Vermont Supreme Court noted that "the selective enforcement of the underlying statute has the hallmarks that other courts have relied upon to find discriminatory prosecution."[43] The Court indicated that it was not "suggesting that we should impose limits on prosecutorial discretion; we are questioning instead a statutory interpretation that necessarily results in this kind of enforcement administration. It is one thing to give discretion in enforcing a legislatively defined crime; it is quite another to give to prosecutors the power to define the crime."[44] In its reasoning reversing G. T.'s adjudication, the Court relied on Professor Sanford H. Kadish's scholarship, which fittingly applies to prosecution of noncommercial, consensual student-to-student sexting:

> One kind of systematic nonenforcement by the police is produced by criminal statutes which seem deliberately to over-criminalize, in the sense of encompassing conduct not the target of legislative concern, in order to assure that suitable suspects will be prevented from escaping through legal loopholes as the result of the inability of the prosecution to prove acts which bring the defendants within the scope of the prohibited conduct. . . .
>
> Insofar as such laws purport to bring within the condemnation of the criminal statute kinds of activities whose moral neutrality, if not innocence, is widely recognized, they raise basic issues of a morally acceptable criminal code. Moreover, these laws are in effect equivalent to enactments of a broad legislative policy against, for example, undesirable gambling, leaving it to the police to further that policy by such arrests as seem to them compatible with it. From one point of view such statutes invite a danger cognate to that of defining a crime by analogy, augmented by the fact that it

is the policeman who is defining criminal conduct rather than a court. That no actual abuse has been demonstrated in police administration of an over-drawn statute ... would not seem to answer the moral and precedential objections to this tactic, any more than the fact that courts in states where the doctrine of common law crimes exists have not in recent years abused it would answer the objections to this doctrine.[45]

To prevent "absurd results," the Vermont Supreme Court took the prudent step that courts considering criminalization of noncommercial, consensual student-to-student sexting should take: construe as inapplicable statutes used to prosecute teens if "the alleged perpetrator is also a victim under the age of consent." The Vermont Supreme Court added, "We agree with the Florida Supreme Court that the statute is intended as a shield for minors and not a sword against them."[46]

The Utah Supreme Court agrees, stating, in *State ex rel. Z. C.*,[47] that "a court should not follow the literal language of a statute if its plain meaning works an absurd result."[48] In that case, Z. C.—a 13-year-old—"engaged in consensual sex with a 12-year-old boy and became pregnant." They both faced delinquency petitions for "sexual abuse of a child."[49] Z. C. was adjudicated a delinquent and, as punishment, compelled to "obey the reasonable requests of her parents, to write an essay regarding her child and the effect of her actions on the child, to have no unsupervised contact with the father of her child, to provide a DNA sample, and to pay a $75 DNA processing fee";[50] the boy received probation. The Utah Supreme Court acknowledged that the plain language of the statute authorized prosecution of Z. C. and the boy; yet in vacating Z. C.'s adjudication, the Court declared that "applying the statute to treat Z. C. as both a victim and a perpetrator of child sex abuse for the same act leads to an absurd result that was not intended by the legislature."[51] In fact, the Court characterized the sexual contact between the minors as "consensual heavy petting."[52] The Court chided the state for using a criminal law designed to protect minors to punish them. After all, with "consensual heavy petting,"[53] "there is no discernible victim that the law seeks to protect, only culpable participants that the State seeks to punish."[54] This same reasoning applies to noncommercial, consensual student-to-student sexting. The Court gave this explanation:

Taking each delinquency adjudication separately, of course, there is only one perpetrator and one victim. In the twelve-year-old boy's adjudication, he stood in the role of perpetrator and Z. C. stood in the role of victim, while in Z. C.'s adjudication, the State simply reversed these roles. In other words, the children were alternatively treated as both victims and perpetrators for the same act. Because it would be unthinkable to file even "civil" juvenile court proceedings against a true victim of such a heinous crime, we conclude that the State's double prosecution of these children is best characterized as charging both as perpetrators for the same act.[55]

Those arguing for full enforcement of the various criminal laws against noncommercial, consensual student-to-student sexting are urged to consider the Utah Supreme Court's response to a similar argument in *State ex rel. Z. C.* In that case, the argument was that the law used to prosecute Z. C. should be given full force because the minors might be adjudicated in juvenile court as opposed to through a full-fledged criminal prosecution. How did the Utah Supreme Court respond? Aptly:

The fact that this is a juvenile court disposition, in which the judge enjoys considerable latitude in crafting punishments and assigning state services designed to help the child, does not change our conclusion. No amount of judicial lenity to compensate for the absurd application of the law changes the fact that the application of the law was absurd to begin with. Moreover, labeling Z. C. with the moniker of "child abuser," even within the juvenile court system, can have serious consequences that were not intended by the legislature. A delinquency adjudication for sexual abuse of a child can lead to sentencing enhancements for any offenses Z. C. might commit while she is a juvenile or even as an adult if her juvenile record is not expunged. Such an adjudication also has the potential to affect any civil proceedings related to the custody of her child or any future attempts to seek child support from the father.[56]

The Utah Supreme Court sharply articulated what we deem as the fallacy of prosecuting sexting minors for child pornography, child abuse, or other crimes for their noncommercial, consensual student-to-student sexting despite its consensual nature: "where there was no evidence of any coercion or force, we conclude that application of the child sex abuse statute produces an absurd result."[57]

Moving to its fourth rationale in *Ferber*, the U.S. Supreme Court declared that "the value of permitting live performances and photographic reproductions of children engaged in lewd sexual conduct is exceedingly modest, if not de minimis."[58] While this is absolutely true for adult production and adult dissemination of child pornography, in the case of noncommercial, consensual student-to-student sexting, sexts have much more than an "exceedingly modest, if not de minimis" value to the sexting teens, as we noted earlier in this book and highlight later as well. In fact, sexts have serious value and meaning to the consensual teen sexters. Additionally, the "production of materials of serious value is not the low-profile, clandestine industry that according to the Court produces purely pornographic materials."[59]

The U.S. Supreme Court pointed out that simulation could serve as a substitute for "live performances and photographic reproductions of children engaged in lewd sexual conduct"[60] where these reproductions are needed for artistic or literary value.[61] However, simulation would be a very poor substitute for noncommercial, consensual student-to-student sexting, which functions as a bond of intimacy between the consenting partners; simulation would amount to encouraging hard-core pornography rather than exchanging pictures of each other.

The *Ferber* court explained its fifth rationale—the exclusion of child pornography distribution is not "incompatible with our earlier decisions"[62]—by stating that its precedents supported the exclusion because "the *evil* to be restricted so overwhelmingly outweighs the expressive interests, if any, at stake, that no process of case-by-case adjudication is required."[63] Following this rationale, the Court should have to identify the "evils" of noncommercial, consensual student-to-student sexting in order not to find its *Ferber* decision incompatible with noncommercial, consensual student-to-student sexting.

The Court placed a limit on the power of states to regulate child pornography, as it had done with its obscenity jurisprudence: "the conduct to be prohibited must be adequately defined by the applicable state law, as written or authoritatively construed."[64] For instance, the Court found this adequate definition in *Ferber*: "the nature of the harm to be combated require[d] that the state offense be limited to works that *visually* depict sexual conduct by children below a specified age."[65]

As an additional restriction on state power, the Court stated that "the category of 'sexual conduct' proscribed must also be suitably limited and described."[66] The Court also noted that "as with obscenity laws, criminal responsibility may not be imposed without some element of scienter on the part of the defendant."[67] The various state statutes that could serve as the basis for prosecuting teen sexters, identified in Chapter 3 (particularly the sexting statutes), appear to satisfy these requirements.

If you are wondering how the Supreme Court distinguished the *Miller* test from *Ferber*, here it is:

> The test for child pornography is separate from the obscenity standard enunciated in *Miller*, but may be compared to it for the purpose of clarity. The *Miller* formulation is adjusted in the following respects: A trier of fact need not find that the material appeals to the prurient interest of the average person; it is not required that sexual conduct portrayed be done so in a patently offensive manner; and the material at issue need not be considered as a whole.[68]

In upholding the New York statute in *Ferber*, the Supreme Court revealed that it "seriously doubt[ed]" and would not "assume" that there would be an expansive use of the statute to encompass protected speech.[69] It seems the majority of the Court failed to comprehend how easily statutes can be stretched to regulate otherwise protected speech. After all, expansion of statutory ambit is essentially what is happening with the efforts to prosecute noncommercial, consensual student-to-student sexting under obscenity and child pornography statutes that were never intended to apply to consensual student sexters. Indeed, in her concurring opinion, Justice O'Connor warned that criminal statutes could be misused to overreach beyond the harms cited by the Court as rationales in *Ferber*.[70]

Some might argue that First Amendment protection need not be explicitly extended to noncommercial, consensual student-to-student sexting because prosecutors will use their discretion to avoid prosecuting such sexting. This is a flawed argument, however, since as noted earlier, even though noncommercial, consensual student-to-student sexting does not present the harms cited in *Ferber*, prosecutors are willing to prosecute consensual teen sexters as child pornographers. In fact, in *United States vs. Stevens*,[71] the Supreme Court confronted a similar argument from the U.S. government as it determined the constitutionality of a federal statute that criminalized the commercial production, possession, or sale of videos of "depictions of animal cruelty."[72] The government argued that the statute should not be ruled violative of the First Amendment because prosecutors would exercise discretion and avoid overreaching in use of the statute: "Not to worry, the Government says: The Executive Branch construes § 48 to reach only 'extreme' cruelty and it neither has brought nor will bring a prosecution for anything less. The Government hits this theme hard, invoking its prosecutorial discretion several times."[73] To this the Supreme Court had an au fait response that should similarly govern with noncommercial, consensual student-to-student sexting: "The First Amendment protects against the Government; it does not leave us at the mercy of noblesse oblige. We would not uphold an unconstitutional statute merely because the Government promised to use it responsibly."[74]

When it comes to noncommercial, consensual student-to-student sexting, the Court needs to heed Justice Stevens's admonition that, to maintain fidelity to the First Amendment, context and content of visual representations must be examined rather than the blanket-prohibition approach of the *Ferber* court:

> A holding that respondent may be punished for selling these two films does not require us to conclude that other users of these very films, or that other motion pictures containing similar scenes, are beyond the pale of constitutional protection. . . . The question whether a specific act of communication is protected by the First Amendment always requires some consideration of both its content and its context.[75]

Osborne vs. Ohio

About eight years after *Ferber* determined the fate of dissemination of child pornography, in 1990 in *Osborne vs. Ohio*,[76] the Supreme Court would decide for the first time whether possession of child pornography is protected under the First Amendment. In that case, the appellant Clyde Osborne was convicted of possession of child pornography after Columbus police found, in his residence, four pictures showing "a nude male adolescent posed in a sexually explicit position."[77] The Ohio statute in question provided that:

> No person shall . . . possess or view any material or performance that shows a minor who is not the person's child or ward in a state of nudity, unless one of the following applies:
>   (a) The material or performance is sold, disseminated, displayed, possessed, controlled, brought or caused to be brought into this state, or presented for a bona fide artistic, medical, scientific, educational, religious, governmental, judicial, or other proper purpose, by or to a physician, psychologist, sociologist, scientist, teacher, person pursuing bona fide studies or research, librarian, clergyman, prosecutor, judge, or other person having a proper interest in the material or performance.

(b) The person knows that the parents, guardian, or custodian has consented in writing to the photographing or use of the minor in a state of nudity and to the manner in which the material or performance is used or transferred.[78]

How did the Court distinguish *Osborne* from its decision on private possession of obscenity in *Stanley*? The Court noted that *Stanley* involved a "paternalistic" government attempt to control "a person's private thoughts."[79] However, in *Osborne*, the state of Ohio was not motivated by "a paternalistic interest in regulating Osborne's mind." Instead, the state was motivated by its desire to "protect the *victims* of child pornography; it hopes to destroy a *market* for the exploitative use of children."[80] The highlighted words should similarly distinguish noncommercial, consensual student-to-student sexting from *Osborne*, as should the context of *Osborne*— the possession of child pornography by an adult.

A look at the Court's language in *Osborne* reveals its concerns about the *market* for child pornography and the need to "dry up" the market. In its rationale, the Court did not merely focus on the commercial context, but also on victimization of children by purveyors and possessors of child pornography. The Court also described the possession of child pornography as a "vice."[81] Adopting *Ferber's* rationale, the Court explained that "as *Ferber* recognized, the materials produced by child pornographers permanently record the *victim's abuse*."[82] In other words, the Court made it clear that *Ferber* was concerned with abuse of children and victimization of children by child pornographers. In fact, in 2010, in a First Amendment case dealing with videos of animal cruelty, Justice Alito would confirm that the *Ferber* decision was founded on the themes of child abuse, commercialization, and victimization:

> The most relevant of our prior decisions is *Ferber*, which concerned child pornography. The Court there held that child pornography is not protected speech, and I believe that *Ferber's* reasoning dictates a similar conclusion here.
>
> In *Ferber*, an important factor—I would say the most important factor—was that child pornography involves the commission of a crime that inflicts severe personal injury to the children who are made to engage in sexual conduct for commercial purposes. The *Ferber* Court repeatedly described the production of child pornography as child "abuse," "molestation," or "exploitation." ("In recent years, the exploitive use of children in the production of pornography has become a serious national problem"); ("Sexual molestation by adults is often involved in the production of child sexual performances"). As later noted

in *Ashcroft v. Free Speech Coalition*, in *Ferber* "the production of the work, not its content, was the target of the statute." (*Ferber* involved "speech that itself is the record of sexual abuse.")

Second, *Ferber* emphasized the fact that these underlying crimes could not be effectively combated without targeting the distribution of child pornography. As the Court put it, "the distribution network for child pornography must be closed if the production of material which requires the sexual exploitation of children is to be effectively controlled." The Court added: "There is no serious contention that the legislature was unjustified in believing that it is difficult, if not impossible, to halt the exploitation of children by pursuing only those who produce the photographs and movies. . . . The most expeditious if not the only practical method of law enforcement may be to dry up the market for this material by imposing severe criminal penalties on persons selling, advertising, or otherwise promoting the product." ("The advertising and selling of child pornography provide an economic motive for and are thus an integral part of the production of such materials.")

Third, the Ferber Court noted that the value of child pornography "is exceedingly modest, if not de minimis," and that any such value was "overwhelmingly outweigh[ed]" by "the evil to be restricted."[83]

The *Osborne* court explained that the exclusion of possession of child pornography from First Amendment protection was needed because "pedophiles use child pornography to seduce other children into sexual activity."[84] In support, the Court cited the finding of the Attorney General's Commission on Pornography that "child pornography is often used as part of a method of seducing child victims. A child who is reluctant to engage in sexual activity with an adult or to pose for sexually explicit photos can sometimes be convinced by viewing other children having 'fun' participating in the activity."[85]

In all the preceding rationales given by the Court and through its opinion, it is evident that at the core of the Court's decision in *Osborne*, as in *Ferber*, was the criminalization of adult victimization and abuse of children—pedophilia. There is not a hint of concern about noncommercial, consensual student-to-student sexting in the Court's opinion. While some would argue that the memorialization that sexting produces could end up in the hands of pedophiles, the Supreme Court has a pertinent terse response: "Congress may pass valid laws to protect children from abuse, and it has. The prospect of crime, however, by itself does not justify laws suppressing protected speech."[86] As the Court has clearly stated, "among free men, the deterrents ordinarily to be applied to prevent crime are education and punishment for violations of the law, not abridgment of the rights of free speech."[87] In other words, the law should not be used to abridge free speech, as we believe would occur with criminalization of noncommercial, consensual student-to-student sexting.

Moreover, by its very nature, noncommercial, consensual student-to-student sexting is not produced through victimization or abuse of children. Possibly, noncommercial, consensual student-to-student sexting would instead fall within the category of "viewing or possessing innocuous photographs of naked children" that the *Osborne* court implied constituted protected speech.[88]

Even if all the rationales the Court identified in *Ferber* and *Osborne* were to justify limiting First Amendment protection for noncommercial, consensual student-to-student sexting, do those rationales justify making criminals of consensual teen sexters? Do they justify statutes making felons of the very people the Court's rationales seek to protect?

The Court pointed out that in child pornography and obscenity cases, in determining which depictions may be prohibited, courts must examine the lewdness of the depiction. Specifically, the Court declared, "We do not agree that this distinction between body areas and specific body parts is constitutionally significant: The crucial question is whether the depiction is lewd, not whether the depiction happens to focus on the genitals or the buttocks."[89]

Ashcroft vs. Free Speech Coalition

In 2002, in *Ashcroft vs. Free Speech Coalition*,[90] the U.S. Supreme Court ruled that virtual child pornography—pornographic materials that "appear to depict minors but were produced by means other than using real children, such as through the use of youthful-looking adults or computer-imaging technology"[91]—is protected speech under the First Amendment. In its rationale for this decision, the Court pointed out that the federal statute at issue was flawed because it prohibited "visual depiction of an idea—that of teenagers engaging in sexual activity—that is a fact of modern society and has been a theme in art and literature throughout the ages."[92] What a powerful statement that is! It clearly supports noncommercial, consensual student-to-student sexting. The Court noted that under the federal statute it invalidated, "images are prohibited so long as the persons appear to be under 18 years of age."[93] Critical of this statutory provision, the Court observed, as we alluded to earlier in this book, that "this is higher than the legal age for marriage in many States, as well as the age at which persons may consent to sexual relations."[94]

The Court pointed out that "48 States permit 16-year-olds to marry with parental consent" and "in 39 States and the District of Columbia, the age of consent is 16 or younger."[95] Besides, as the Court emphasized, "It is, of course, undeniable that some youths engage in sexual activity before the legal age . . . on their own inclination."[96] The Court also noted that teenage sexual activity has been around since the days of William Shakespeare:

> William Shakespeare created the most famous pair of teenage lovers, one of whom is just 13 years of age. See Romeo and Juliet, act I, sc. 2, l. 9 ("She hath not seen the change of fourteen years"). In the drama, Shakespeare portrays the relationship as something splendid and innocent, but not juvenile. The work has inspired no less than 40 motion pictures, some of which suggest that the teenagers consummated their relationship. Shakespeare may not have written sexually explicit scenes for the Elizabethan audience, but were modern directors to adopt a less conventional approach, that fact alone would not compel the conclusion that the work was obscene.[97]

The Court observed that teenage sexual activity is evident in modern culture, as can be seen in various movies:

> Contemporary movies pursue similar themes. Last year's Academy Awards featured the movie, Traffic, which was nominated for Best Picture. The film portrays a teenager, identified as a 16-year-old, who becomes addicted to drugs. The viewer sees the degradation of her addiction, which in the end leads her to a filthy room to trade sex for drugs. The year before, American Beauty won the Academy Award for Best Picture. In the course of the movie, a teenage girl engages in sexual relations with her teenage boyfriend. . . .
>
> Our society, like other cultures, has empathy and enduring fascination with the lives and destinies of the young. Art and literature express the vital interest we all have in the formative years we ourselves once knew, when wounds can be so grievous, disappointment so profound, and mistaken choices so tragic, but when moral acts and self-fulfillment are still in reach. Whether or not the films we mention violate the CPPA, they explore themes within the wide sweep of the statute's prohibitions. If these films, or hundreds of others of lesser note that explore those subjects, contain a single graphic depiction of sexual activity within the statutory definition, the possessor of the film would be subject to severe punishment without inquiry into the work's redeeming value. This is inconsistent with an essential First

Amendment rule: The artistic merit of a work does not depend on the presence of a single explicit scene.[98]

Free Speech Coalition confirmed that both the *Ferber* and *Osborne* decisions were focused on child abuse, victimization, and commercialization of visual depictions of children. For example, the Court observed that *Osborne* "*anchored its holding* in the concern for the participants, those whom it called the 'victims of child pornography.' It [*Osborne*] did not suggest that, absent this concern, other governmental interests would suffice."[99] This statement by the Court would seem to provide a safe harbor for noncommercial, consensual student-to-student sexting. Additionally, the Court clarified that *Ferber* involved "speech that itself is the record of sexual abuse."[100] Clearly, noncommercial, consensual student-to-student sexting is not "speech that itself is the record of sexual abuse."

In *Free Speech Coalition*, the Court was critical of the federal statute criminalizing virtual child pornography because the statute "prohibits speech that records no crime and creates no victims by its production";[101] is this not the same situation with noncommercial, consensual student-to-student sexting? The following reasoning by the Court with respect to virtual child pornography similarly applies to noncommercial, consensual student-to-student sexting; we could as well just substitute the words "noncommercial, consensual student-to-student sexting" for the words "virtual child pornography": "Virtual child pornography is not 'intrinsically related' to the sexual abuse of children, as were the materials in *Ferber*. While the Government asserts that the images can lead to actual instances of child abuse, the causal link is contingent and indirect. The harm does not necessarily follow from the speech, but depends upon some unquantified potential for subsequent criminal acts."[102]

Prosecutors eager to prosecute noncommercial, consensual student-to-student sexting and courts willing to uphold such prosecutions might want to consider the Court's following clarification of *Ferber*:

The Government says these indirect harms are sufficient because, as *Ferber* acknowledged, child pornography rarely can be valuable speech. ("The value of permitting live performances and photographic reproductions of children engaged in lewd sexual conduct is exceedingly modest, if not de minimis"). This argument, however, suffers from two flaws. First, *Ferber*'s judgment about child pornography was based upon how it was made, not on what it communicated. The case reaffirmed that where the speech is *neither obscene nor the product of sexual abuse*, it does *not* fall outside the protection of the First Amendment. ... The second flaw in the Government's position is that *Ferber* did not hold that child pornography is by definition without value. On the contrary, the Court recognized some works in this category might have significant value.[103]

In response to the government's arguments that virtual child pornography should be unprotected speech because it could lead pedophiles to abuse children, the Court made a profound statement that equally should apply when such arguments are raised against First Amendment protection for noncommercial, consensual student-to-student sexting:

> The Government seeks to justify its prohibitions in other ways. It argues that the CPPA is necessary because pedophiles may use virtual child pornography to seduce children. There are many things innocent in themselves, however, such as cartoons, video games, and candy, that might be used for immoral purposes, yet we would not expect those to be prohibited because they can be misused. The Government, of course, may punish *adults* who provide unsuitable materials to children and it may enforce criminal penalties for unlawful solicitation.[104]

The Court likewise dismissed the government's argument that "virtual child pornography whets the appetites of pedophiles and encourages them to engage in illegal conduct"[105] with reasoning that should similarly cover noncommercial, consensual student-to-student sexting: "This rationale cannot sustain the provision in question. The mere tendency of speech to encourage unlawful acts is not a sufficient reason for banning it. ... The government may not prohibit speech because it increases the chance an unlawful act will be committed at some indefinite future time."[106] Additionally, the Court stated that in *Ferber*, "the Government has shown no more than a remote connection between speech that might encourage thoughts or impulses and any resulting child abuse. Without a significantly stronger, more direct connection, the Government may not prohibit speech on the ground that it may encourage pedophiles to engage in illegal conduct."[107] As we have indicated, we strongly believe that the government should severely punish adults who possess child pornography or provide it to children; however, we do not believe noncommercial, consensual student-to-student sexters should be made criminals.

The Supreme Court's statement in *Free Speech Coalition* was clear:

The Government may not suppress lawful speech as the means to suppress unlawful speech. Protected speech does not become unprotected merely because it resembles the latter. The Constitution requires the reverse. The possible harm to society in permitting some unprotected speech to go unpunished is outweighed by the possibility that protected speech of others may be muted.[108]

Chapter 6

The Authority of Schools to Regulate Student Speech

Introduction

According to the Pew Research Center, "most schools treat the phone as a disruptive force that must be managed and often excluded from the school and the classroom."[1] Here are the statistics:

- 12 percent of all students say they can have their phone at school at *any* time.
- 62 percent of all students say they can have their phone in school, just not in class.
- 24 percent of teens attend schools that ban all cell phones from school grounds.
- Still, 65 percent of cell-owning teens at schools that completely ban phones bring their phones to school every day.
- 58 percent of cell-owning teens at schools that ban phones have sent a text message during class.
- 43 percent of all teens who take their phones to school say they text in class at least once a day.
- 64 percent of teens with cell phones have texted in class; 25 percent have made or received a call during class time.[2]

It is not unexpected that with such stringent approaches to cell phone use, many students resort to hiding the phones because of the "if they can see it, they can take it philosophy"[3] of schools. The Pew study notes that teens believe schools arbitrarily enforce cell phone policies. A high schooler explains, "Our [cell phone] rules are just like whatever the teachers feels [sic] like."[4]

In certain schools, parents are required to pick up seized phones, while others return the phones to students at the end of the school day or class. Some teens believe teachers play favorites with enforcement. A middle schooler reveals that "it's kind of messed up, but if you're one of the favorites, and I'm one of the favorites with some of my teachers, they just let you use your phone."[5]

While there might be justifiable grounds for excluding the cell phone from the classroom, its total exclusion from the school, in a bid to prevent or curtail sexting, seems a little too drastic; particularly because as the U.S. Supreme Court has clearly stated, the free speech rights of students do not end at the schoolhouse gate.[6] Indeed, some schools even prohibit students from using cell phones in their cars. However, students will be students; and, given that there is an innate need in each human to express himself or herself, it is no surprise that the Pew study found that "even though most schools treat the phone as something to be contained and regulated, teens are nevertheless still texting frequently in class."[7] Pew points out that "despite these restrictions, teens are still *overwhelmingly* taking their phones to school—77% take their phones with them to school every school day and another 7% take their phone to school at least several times a week. Less than 10% of teens take their phone to school less often and just 8% say they never take their phone to school."[8] Nonetheless, the protection of constitutional rights should not be dependent on whether students are able to find a way to circumvent restrictions on free speech rights.

As Figure 6.1 indicates, roughly 65 percent of students at schools that completely exclude cell phones still take their cell phones to school daily.

Additionally, students text during class; this, we agree, is disruptive and needs to be regulated so as not to take away from focus on the lessons. The numbers of students texting during classes are surprising: "Nearly one-third (31%) of teens who take their phones to school text in class several times a day and another 12% of those teens say they text in class at least once a day."[9] This is further evident in Figure 6.2 (though the numbers are still low enough at 31% to undermine the need for a blanket prohibition of cell phone use or texting at school, which very well could be a First Amendment right).

Even with school regulations, students find surreptitious ways to text—"behind stacks of books, under desktops, inside of bags, and one even described having an older phone that he kept in his bag to surrender to teachers when he got caught texting in class." Further, Pew reports that "in-class texting varies little with regard to the aggressiveness of a school's

FIGURE 6.1. Teens Who Take Their Phones to School.

How often do you take your phone to school?

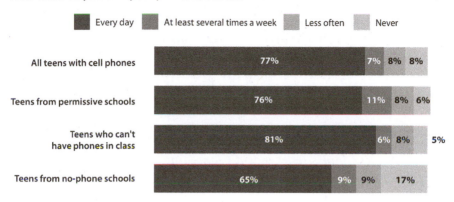

Note: Survey conducted from June 26-September 24, 2009. N = 625 teen cell phone owners ages 12–17 and the margin of error is +/– 5%. For smaller subgroups, the margin of error may be larger.
Source: Amanda Lenhart, Pew Internet and American Life Project, "Teens and Mobile Phones" [2010], available at http://pewinternet.org/~/media//Files/Reports/2010/PIP-Teens-and-Mobile-2010-with-topline.pdf.

FIGURE 6.2. 31% of Teens Who Take Their Phones to School Send Text Messages Every Day during Class Time.

Of teens who take their phones to school, the % who do each activity (frequency)

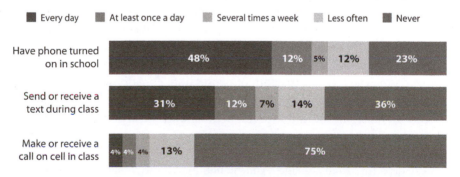

Note: Survey conducted June 26-September 24, 2009. N = 625 teen cell phone owners ages 12–17 and the margin of error is +/– 5%. For smaller subgroups the margin of error may be larger.
Source: Amanda Lenhart, Pew Internet and American Life Project, "Teens and Mobile Phones" [2010], available at http://pewinternet.org/~/media//Files/Reports/2010/PIP-Teens-and-Mobile-2010-with-topline.pdf.

regulation of its students' mobile phones."[10] This information should educate schools that more regulation is not the answer. However, we believe texting during noninstructional time should be protected under the First Amendment even if texting during instructional time is regulated.

The Supreme Court has provided us four cases to use as the basis for analyzing the free speech rights of students vis-à-vis the school district. We examine these cases next in order to determine the extent of schools' authority to regulate student sexting.

Tinker vs. Des Moines Independent Community School District

Tinker vs. Des Moines Independent Community School District[11] was the very first case in which the U.S. Supreme Court recognized student free speech as a protected First Amendment right.

During the Vietnam War, various students wore armbands to school in protest of the war and in advocacy of peace. Elementary, junior high, and high school students were represented in the armband protest. Five such students were suspended from school for wearing the armbands, even though they caused no disruption at the school. Some of the students subsequently sued the school district and school officials, seeking nominal damages and an injunction against the disciplinary action.

Throughout its opinion, the U.S. Supreme Court empowered students with the right to free expression. If you were a student who had felt depowered or unempowered by the absence of free speech protection for students, you would have come out of *Tinker* feeling jubilant. Right away, the Court emphasized that schools cannot rely on the mere "fear of a disturbance" to regulate student speech. Specifically, the Court declared that "in our system, undifferentiated fear or apprehension of disturbance is not enough to overcome the right to freedom of expression."[12] Additionally, the Court accentuated the fact that our Constitution does not allow our educational system to foster monolithic speech or to silence dissent or views that are in the minority:

> Any departure from absolute regimentation may cause trouble. Any variation from the majority's opinion may inspire fear. Any word spoken, *in class, in the lunchroom, or on the campus,* that deviates from the views of another person may start an argument or cause a disturbance. But our Constitution says we must take this risk and our history says that it is this sort of hazardous freedom—this kind of openness—that is the basis of our national strength and of

the independence and vigor of Americans who grow up and live in this *relatively permissive*, often disputatious, society.[13]

In any discussions about regulating student speech, we must not lose sight of an important principle—the fact that schools "are educating the young for citizenship is reason for scrupulous protection of Constitutional freedoms of the individual, if we are not to strangle the free mind at its source and teach youth to discount important principles of our government as mere platitudes."[14] The *Tinker* court warned schools that "*more than* a mere desire to avoid the discomfort and unpleasantness that always accompany an unpopular viewpoint" is required in order to prohibit student speech.[15] What is the "more than" that the Constitution requires? According to the Court, the Constitution requires that to regulate speech, schools must show a reasonable forecast of or actual material and substantial disruption of the school's work or infringement of other students' rights; this is the *Tinker* test. The Court found no evidence of a reasonable forecast of or actual "material and substantial"[16] disruption of the school's work or infringement in the *Tinker* case.[17] The students were merely engaged in "silent, passive expression of opinion, unaccompanied by any disorder or disturbance on the part of petitioners."[18]

A school's "urgent wish to avoid the controversy which might result from the expression" is an insufficient ground under the Constitution for regulating student speech.[19] The Court observed that the school officials in *Tinker* had decided to regulate the student speech because the Vietnam War was a "subject of a major controversy." At the time of the school's regulation of the speech, "debate over the Viet Nam war had become vehement in many localities." Additionally, "a protest march against the war had been recently held in Washington, D.C. A wave of draft card burning incidents protesting the war had swept the country. At that time two highly publicized draft card burning cases were pending in this Court. Both individuals supporting the war and those opposing it were quite vocal in expressing their views."[20]

Despite the hot-button nature of the war at the time, the Court ruled that controversialism without material and substantial disruption or infringement of the rights of other students is insufficient grounds to regulate student speech.

Today, sexting, while not akin to war, is the "subject of a major controversy." If we follow *Tinker*'s rationale, we know that the controversial nature of sexting alone is not a basis for school regulation of student speech. In essence, based on *Tinker*'s rationale, in order to regulate noncommercial, consensual student-to-student sexting, schools should have to show that such sexting presents a reasonable forecast of or actual material and substantial disruption of the school's work or infringement of other students' rights.

Schools must be wary of selective regulation of student speech. In *Tinker*, the Court chided school officials for selectively regulating the armbands while allowing other "symbols of political or controversial significance": "The record shows that students in some of the schools wore buttons relating to national political campaigns, and some even wore the Iron Cross, traditionally a symbol of Nazism. The order prohibiting the wearing of armbands did not extend to these. Instead, a particular symbol—black armbands worn to exhibit opposition to this Nation's involvement in Vietnam—was singled out for prohibition."[21] This would suggest that if schools selectively regulate noncommercial, consensual student-to-student sexting while allowing other forms of texting, they could lose a court challenge if they fail to satisfy the *Tinker* test. As the Supreme Court indicated in *Tinker*, "Clearly, the prohibition of expression of one particular opinion, at least without evidence that it is necessary to avoid material and substantial interference with schoolwork or discipline, is not constitutionally permissible."[22]

Given the prevailing highly paternalistic attitudes toward students up until *Tinker* was decided, it should not be surprising that the Court went out of its way to explicitly acknowledge that the U.S. Constitution actually regards students as persons: "Students *in* school as well as *out of* school are 'persons' under our Constitution."[23] They are not only persons in and out of school; they actually have "fundamental rights which the State must respect."[24] What a shock that must have been to those who considered students as property and consequently subject to the absolute control of the school. In essence, the Court acknowledged that students have recognized minds of their own. When we dehumanize students by failing to acknowledge their individuality and instead seek conformity, we undermine the very premise of the right to free expression.

The Court emphasized that students are not robots to be programmed with the government's choice of message. The Court pointed out that "in our system, state-operated schools may not be enclaves of totalitarianism. School officials do not possess absolute authority over their students. . . . In our system, students may not be regarded as closed-circuit recipients of only that which the State chooses to communicate. They may not be confined to the expression of those *sentiments* that are officially approved."[25]

Sexts express sentiments and feelings; and as the Court stated, "school officials cannot suppress expressions of *feelings* with which they do not wish to contend."[26] Furthermore, it does "violence to both letter and spirit of the Constitution,"[27] and we as a people reject "the principle that a State might so conduct its schools as to foster a homogeneous people."[28]

Students should not have to seek official approval to engage in noncommercial, consensual student-to-student sexting—a medium for expressing sentiments and feelings. It is true that not all students sext. Nevertheless, we must protect those who do; after all, we are not a "homogeneous people."[29] Given that schools have a role in helping students define their identities and the fact that speech, including sexting, is part of the process of self-expression and self-identity, schools should not deprive students of this right; nor should punishment attend noncommercial, consensual student-to-student sexting unless there is material and substantial disruption to the school's work or infringement of rights of others. Since it is of the consensual sort, the sexting we refer to herein would not infringe on the rights of others.

Besides, "the vigilant protection of constitutional freedoms is nowhere more vital than in the community of American schools."[30] Before clamping down on noncommercial, consensual student-to-student sexting, let us ask ourselves: should the school not be "peculiarly the marketplace of ideas"?[31] After all, our future as well as the full development of "We the People" (individually and corporately) is dependent on whether we can train our children that effective and democratic learning comes "through wide exposure to that robust exchange of ideas which discovers truth out of a multitude of tongues, [rather] than through any kind of authoritative selection."[32]

The *Tinker* court poignantly declared that "it can hardly be argued that either students or teachers shed their constitutional rights to freedom of speech or expression at the schoolhouse gate."[33] The Court underscored the fact that the principles we highlighted earlier in the chapter are not limited to "supervised and ordained discussion which takes place in the classroom."[34] After all, as the Court eloquently pointed out, "The principal use to which the schools are dedicated is to accommodate students during prescribed hours for the purpose of certain types of activities. Among those activities is *personal intercommunication* among the students."[35] It is undeniable that noncommercial, consensual student-to-student sexting *is* "personal intercommunication among the students" involved. As the Court observed, "personal intercommunication among the students" constitutes "not only an inevitable part of the process of attending school; it is also an important part of the educational process."[36] If we are to uphold the integrity of *Tinker*, we need to be cognizant of the fact that "a student's rights, therefore, do not embrace merely the classroom hours. When he is in the *cafeteria, or on the playing field, or on the campus during the author-ized hours*, he may express his opinions, even on *controversial subjects*, ... if he does so without materially and substantially interfer [ing] with the requirements of appropriate discipline in the operation of the school and without colliding with the rights of others."[37]

Is there any other reason in *Tinker* to extend First Amendment protec-tion to noncommercial, consensual student-to-student sexting? Certainly! First Amendment protection should be extended because "under our Constitution, free speech is not a right that is given only to be so circum-scribed that it exists in principle but not in fact. Freedom of expression would not truly exist if the right could be exercised only in an area that a benevolent government has provided as a safe haven for crackpots." More-over, as the Court stated, "The Constitution says that Congress (and the States) may not abridge the right to free speech. This provision means what it says. ... We do not confine the permissible exercise of First Amendment rights to a telephone booth or the four corners of a pamphlet, or to super-vised and ordained discussion in a school classroom."[38]

Bethel School District No. 403 vs. Fraser

In 1986, the U.S. Supreme Court would rule on its second student free speech case—*Bethel School District No. 403 vs. Fraser*.[39] In that case, the issue before the Court was "whether the First Amendment prevents a school district from disciplining a high school student for giving a lewd speech at a school assembly."[40] This very statement, by the Court, of the issue before it distinguishes *Fraser* from noncommercial, consensual student-to-student sexting—noncommercial, consensual student-to-student sexting is not before a school assembly nor is it publicly disseminated. Instead, it is private interpersonal communication on private, rather than school, cell phones. Noncommercial, consensual student-to-student sexting could also be distin-guished from *Fraser* because the school assembly was "part of a school-sponsored educational program in self-government,"[41] while noncommercial, consensual student-to-student sexting is not. Further, students were required to either attend the assembly or go to study hall; there is no obligation or mandate but rather consent with noncommercial, consensual student-to-student sexting.

In *Fraser*, during his nominating speech in support of his colleague, a high school student gave what the Court characterized as an "elaborate, graphic, and explicit sexual metaphor."[42] The student gave the speech at a school assembly attended by about 600 high schoolers, many of them 14-year-olds. Here is the content of the speech:

> I know a man who is firm—he's firm in his pants, he's firm in his shirt, his character is firm—but most . . . of all, his belief in you, the students of Bethel, is firm. Jeff Kuhlman is a man who takes his point and pounds it in. If necessary, he'll take an issue and nail it to the wall. He doesn't attack things in spurts—he drives hard, pushing and pushing until finally—he succeeds. Jeff is a man who will go to the very end—even the climax, for each and every one of you. So vote for Jeff for A. S. B. vice-president—he'll never come between you and the best our high school can be.[43]

There were various student reactions to the speech, including yelling and hooting, embarrassment, bewilderment, and gesturing simulating the sexual activities referenced in the speech. While noncommercial, consensual student-to-student sexting could elicit any of these reactions from the mutual sexters, the fact that the sexting is consensual effectively ensures that the reactions would not be negative in the sense of the *Fraser* reactions.

School officials in *Fraser* disciplined the student for his speech, pursuant to school policy regulating obscene speech that materially and substantially (this language is from the *Tinker* test) disrupted education. He was suspended and disqualified from candidacy for graduation speaker. The student sued, alleging a First Amendment violation and seeking monetary damages as well as an injunction.

Given the public nature of the dissemination of the speech in *Fraser*, it is not astonishing that the Court called for the teaching of civility as a value in public schools. In contrast, noncommercial, consensual student-to-student sexting is not a threat to civility; and it is private speech. Further, in its call for teaching civility, the Court's expressed underlying concern was for the sustenance of our "democratic political system." In this respect, the Court called for the balancing of the "sensibilities of others" against the "tolerance of divergent political and religious views, even when the views expressed may be unpopular."[44] This balancing simply should not apply to noncommercial, consensual student-to-student sexting, since the sexting is consensual. After all, the sensibilities of the parties are willingly exposed to the sexts in the case of noncommercial, consensual student-to-student sexting. Consequently, there is not a divergence or unpopularity of the expression in the sexts.

In its call for civility, the Court reasoned that in the U.S. Congress, "there are rules prohibiting the use of expressions *offensive* to other participants in the debate."[45] This reasoning further highlights the distinctions between noncommercial, consensual student-to-student sexting and *Fraser*: the public nature of the *Fraser* communication versus the highly-private nature of *Fraser*, and the fact that *Fraser* targeted offensive or offending speech, which is not the nature of noncommercial, consensual student-to-student sexting between the sexters as "participants."

In *Fraser*, the Court appeared to focus its concerns on the nature of the student's speech as "offensive," "vulgar," "highly offensive," "plainly offensive," "acutely insulting,"[46] or "seriously damaging" or "highly threatening to others" with respect to "public discourse."[47]

Justice Brennan wrote a concurring opinion to "express my understanding of the breadth of the Court's holding."[48] In his concurrence, he pointed out that, in spite of the above characterizations of speech by the *Fraser* Court, the student's speech was "far removed from the very narrow class of 'obscene' speech which the Court has held is not protected by the First Amendment."[49] He opined that the student's speech was "no more obscene, lewd, or sexually explicit than the bulk of programs currently appearing on prime time television or in the local cinema. Thus, I disagree with the Court's suggestion that school officials could punish respondent's speech out of a need to protect younger students." Justice Brennan warned that "the authority school officials have to regulate such speech by high school students is not limitless."[50]

Climactically, the Court articulated the *Fraser* test: schools can regulate student speech that is "lewd, indecent, or offensive speech and conduct such as that indulged in by this confused boy."[51] When iterated in public discourse and courtrooms, though, the *Fraser* test itself is never articulated with the "confused boy" phrase. However, it is important to include the language "conduct such as that indulged in by this confused boy" to distinguish the fact that students engaged in noncommercial, consensual student-to-student sexting are not "confused" and are not engaged in "conduct such as that indulged in by this confused boy." Just after articulating the *Fraser* test, the Court made this declaration: "This Court's First Amendment jurisprudence has acknowledged limitations on the otherwise absolute interest of the speaker in reaching an unlimited audience where the speech is sexually explicit and the audience may include children."[52] This concern with an "unlimited audience" where students could incidentally or accidentally be exposed to sexual speech differs from the intentionally consensual nature of the communication that occurs with noncommercial, consensual student-to-student sexting.

The Court followed the preceding declaration with expressed concern for the "captive audience" nature of the student's speech in *Fraser*.[53] Given that noncommercial, consensual student-to-student sexting is a consensual exchange, however, no "captive audience" is subjected to the sexts. In upholding the school's discipline of the student, the Court expressed further concern for the "*unsuspecting* audience of teenage students";[54] by its very nature, noncommercial, consensual student-to-student sexting is not communication with an "unsuspecting audience."

Justice Stevens cautioned judges against assuming the role of arbiters of student speech, noting that the student in *Fraser* was "probably in a better position to determine whether an audience composed of 600 of his contemporaries would be offended by the use of a four-letter word—or a sexual metaphor—than is a group of judges who are at least two generations and 3,000 miles away from the scene of the crime."[55] Similarly, the students consensually sexting are in a better position to judge the offensiveness of their sexts; the sexters should be afforded the First Amendment right to make this judgment themselves. Justice Stevens also chided the Court for its discordant opinion, noting that "when a more orthodox message is being conveyed to a similar audience, four Members of today's majority would treat high school students like college students rather than like children"[56] and, consequently, uphold the right of the student to deliver the speech.[57]

We believe that noncommercial, consensual student-to-student sexting should be disciplined only if it materially and substantially disrupts the school or infringes the rights of others. This is similar to Justice Stevens's reasoning with respect to the *Fraser* speech. Justice Stevens poignantly stated:

> Justice Sutherland taught us that a nuisance may be merely a right thing in the wrong place,—like a pig in the parlor instead of the barnyard. Vulgar language, like vulgar animals, may be acceptable in some contexts and intolerable in others. Indeed, even ordinary, inoffensive speech may be wholly unacceptable in some settings. It seems fairly obvious that respondent's speech would be inappropriate in certain classroom and formal social settings. On the other hand, in a locker room or perhaps in a school corridor the metaphor in the speech might be regarded as rather routine comment. If this be true, and if respondent's audience consisted almost entirely of young people with whom he conversed on a daily basis, can we—at this distance—confidently assert that he must have known that the school administration would punish him for delivering it?[58]

Reasoning from Justice Stevens's wise words, in the case of noncommercial, consensual student-to-student sexting, a nuisance should be found only when there is material and substantial disruption.

Hazelwood School District vs. Kuhlmeier

In 1988, in *Hazelwood School District vs. Kuhlmeier*,[59] the U.S. Supreme Court would make its third ruling on student free speech. In that case, the Court was presented with school-sponsored speech, which is clearly not the same as noncommercial, consensual student-to-student sexting—private interpersonal communication. Specifically, in *Kuhlmeier*, the Court had to decide "the extent to which educators may exercise editorial control over the contents of a high school newspaper produced as part of the school's journalism curriculum."[60]

The high school principal had precluded the newspaper from publishing an article on the "impact of divorce on students at the school" and another on teenage pregnancy.[61] The high school principal had a practice of reviewing news articles for approval prior to publication, a practice that is clearly not existent with noncommercial, consensual student-to-student sexting. The principal censored the pregnancy article due to concerns that the privacy of students covered in the article was not adequately protected. Since noncommercial, consensual student-to-student sexting is consensual, the principal should not sit as arbiter of the privacy of consensual communication where it does not cause material and substantial disruption per *Tinker*.

The principal also censored the pregnancy article because of his concerns that the subjects of birth control and sexual activity, covered in the article, were "inappropriate for some of the younger students at the school."[62] While this might be a valid concern for a school newspaper, with sexting, if the sexting is private, consensual and causes no material and substantial disruption to the school, the principal should not be the moral arbiter of free speech.

The principal censored the divorce article due to his concerns that those parents covered in a negative light in the publication had neither given their consent nor been forewarned of the article; these are similarly not concerns for noncommercial, consensual student-to-student sexting. For both articles, the principal also believed there was insufficient time to address his concerns before the publication deadline; this as well is not a concern for noncommercial, consensual student-to-student sexting. The newspaper was funded in part by the school board as well as by newspaper sale proceeds, further distinguishing *Kuhlmeier* from noncommercial, consensual student-to-student sexting, which is not school-funded.

In finding no First Amendment violation, the Supreme Court pointed out that public schools are not traditional public forums like parks and streets—places where people traditionally communicate—unless it is shown from the school's practice or policy that it has opened up its facilities to "indiscriminate use by the general public or by some segment of the public, such as student organizations."[63] If the school is not so shown, "school officials may impose reasonable restrictions on the speech of students, teachers, and other members of the school community."[64] Given that the newspaper was a school facility that had not been opened up in practice or policy to indiscriminate public or student use, but was rather reserved as a part of the journalism class laboratory, the Court ruled that the newspaper was not a public forum. The Court pointed out that the school "exercised a great deal of control over Spectrum [the newspaper]." Indeed, the school had "final authority with respect to almost every aspect of the production and publication of Spectrum, including its content."[65] Clearly, schools could not have such degree of control over noncommercial, consensual student-to-student sexting without committing a constitutional foul. Further, student cell phones used for noncommercial, consensual student-to-student sexting are not school properties or school facilities. As private property, the concept of public forum should not apply to them. Additionally, unlike the newspaper in *Kuhlmeier*, student cell phones and sexting are not part of the school curriculum.

The Court distinguished *Tinker* from *Kuhlmeier* as follows: *Tinker* involved personal student speech, while *Kuhlmeier* involved school-sponsored speech. In other words, in *Kuhlmeier*, the school was the "publisher" of the speech, whereas in *Tinker*—as with noncommercial, consensual student-to-student sexting—the student was the publisher. The Court characterized the *Kuhlmeier* type of speech as involving activities that "may fairly be characterized as part of the school curriculum, whether or not they occur in a traditional classroom setting, so long as they are supervised by faculty members and designed to impart particular knowledge or skills to student participants and audiences."[66]

Noncommercial, consensual student-to-student sexting is more akin to the student speech in *Tinker* in that the sexting is a "student's personal expression that happens to occur on the school premises."[67] If students sought to publish sexts in a school newspaper, then sexting would be subject to the *Kuhlmeier* test—"educators do not offend the First Amendment by exercising editorial control over the style and content of student speech in school-sponsored expressive activities so long as their actions are reasonably related to legitimate pedagogical concerns."[68] Publication of sexts, however, is not of the nature of noncommercial, consensual student-to-student sexting discussed herein.

Justice Brennan's piercing criticism of the *Kuhlmeier* test should provide cause for pause to those eager to jump on the ideas embraced in the *Kuhlmeier* test to regulate student speech:

> Free student expression undoubtedly sometimes interferes with the effectiveness of the school's pedagogical functions. Some brands of student expression do so by directly preventing the school from pursuing its pedagogical mission: The young polemic who stands on a soapbox during calculus class to deliver an eloquent political diatribe interferes with the legitimate teaching of calculus. And the student who delivers a lewd endorsement of a student-government candidate might so extremely distract an impressionable high school audience as to interfere with the orderly operation of the school. Other student speech, however, frustrates the school's legitimate pedagogical purposes merely by expressing a message that conflicts with the school's, without directly interfering with the school's expression of its message: A student who responds to a political science teacher's question with the retort, socialism is good, subverts the school's inculcation of the message that capitalism is better. Even the maverick who sits in class passively sporting a symbol of protest against a government policy or the gossip who sits in the student commons swapping stories of sexual escapade could readily muddle a clear official message condoning the government policy or condemning teenage sex. Likewise, the student newspaper that, like Spectrum, conveys a moral position at odds with the school's official stance might subvert the administration's legitimate inculcation of its own perception of community values.[69]

Justice Brennan opined further:

> If mere incompatibility with the school's pedagogical message were a constitutionally sufficient justification for the suppression of student speech, school officials could censor each of the students or student organizations in the foregoing hypotheticals, converting our public schools into enclaves of totalitarianism that strangle the free mind at its source. The First Amendment permits no such blanket censorship authority. While the constitutional rights of students in public school are not automatically coextensive with the rights of adults in other settings, students in the public schools do not shed their constitutional rights to freedom of speech or expression at the schoolhouse gate. Just as the public on the street corner must, in the interest of fostering enlightened opinion, tolerate speech that tempt[s] [the listener] to throw [the speaker] off the street, public educators must accommodate some student expression even if it offends them or offers views or values that contradict those the school wishes to inculcate.[70]

As Justice Brennan opined in his dissent, "The mere fact of school sponsorship does not, as the Court suggests, license ... thought control in the high school, whether through school suppression of disfavored viewpoints or through official assessment of topic sensitivity. The former would constitute unabashed and unconstitutional viewpoint discrimination as well as an impermissible infringement of the students' right to receive information and ideas."[71]

Morse vs. Frederick

In 2007, in *Morse vs. Frederick*,[72] the Court would decide its fourth and most recent student free speech case. In that case, during the Olympic Torch Relay, high school students unfurled a 14-foot banner that read "BONG HiTS 4 JESUS."[73] School officials had permitted students to attend the event as it passed in front of the school during the school day. The principal, perceiving the banner as advocating illegal use of drugs in contravention of school policy, asked the students to furl the banner. One of the students failed to comply, prompting the principal to seize the banner and suspend the student. The student challenged the discipline as violative of his First Amendment free speech rights and sought an injunction and money damages, as well as declaratory judgment.

On the day of the Olympic Torch Relay, the student, who arrived late at school, immediately went across the street to view the event with his classmates. In other words, he did not attend classes before attending the event. Yet the Court characterized the event as a "school-sanctioned and school-supervised event."[74] The Court used this characterization particularly because during the event, school officials "monitored the students' actions." The Court also observed that the school deemed the event as an "approved social event or class trip."[75] Under the school board policy, the same rules that governed student conduct at a "regular school program" governed at a "school-sanctioned and school-supervised event."[76] Noncommercial, consensual student-to-student sexting is clearly not an "approved social event or class trip," distinguishing it from *Morse*.

By extending school authority to an event that occurred outside the physical four corners of the school, the Court expanded the reach of the schoolhouse gate. The Court provided an array of indicia for the expanded schoolhouse gate: (1) the interspersion of administrators and teachers among the students;[77] (2) the fact that the students were "in the midst of ... fellow students, during school hours"[78]; (3) the school's charge to the administrators and teachers to supervise students during the event;[79] (4) the performance of school functions during the event (here, "the high school band and cheerleaders performed");[80] and (5) the fact that the students needed the school's preapproval to attend the event as a "social event or class trip."[81]

The Court made a candid, stunning, but important admission, revealing the judiciary's own uncertainty about the reach of its school-speech jurisprudence: "There is some uncertainty at the *outer boundaries* as to when courts should apply school speech precedents."[82] Given that admission, there should be no rush to judgment to ban or discipline noncommercial, consensual student-to-student sexting, unless there is material and substantial disruption, or the uncertainty in the school-speech jurisprudence is cleared up by the Supreme Court.

The Court gave itself leeway to create a new test in *Morse*, and other tests in the future, when it stated that its creation of a new test in *Fraser* established that "the mode of analysis set forth in *Tinker* is not absolute."[83] The Court also cast a cloud of uncertainty over the reach of *Fraser*—"The mode of analysis employed in *Fraser* is not entirely clear"[84]—which cloud should caution advocates of extending *Fraser* to noncommercial, consensual student-to-student sexting.

Moreover, unlike the banner in *Morse*, which was publicly conveyed, noncommercial, consensual student-to-student sexting, as discussed herein, merely entails privately disseminated communication. Thus, with the uncertainties in the law and the contextual differences between *Morse* and noncommercial, consensual student-to-student sexting, courts should hesitate to blindly extend *Morse* to noncommercial, consensual student-to-student sexting. Indeed, the Court's own statement of the issue before it in *Morse* should highlight the distinction between *Morse* and noncommercial, consensual student-to-student sexting: "*The* question thus becomes whether a principal may, consistent with the First Amendment, restrict student speech at a school event, when that speech is reasonably viewed as promoting illegal drug use."[85]

Despite the disciplined student's assertion that the words on the banner were merely gibberish simply intended to garner media attention, the Supreme Court agreed with school officials that the banner could be interpreted as advocacy of illegal drug use. According to the Court, this advocacy could be interpreted either as an "imperative" to use or a "celebration" of illegal drug use.[86] In ruling that the student did not have a First Amendment right to publicly display the banner, the Court expressed concern about the "severe and permanent damage to the health and well-being of young people" that can result from drug abuse.[87] Certainly, noncommercial, consensual student-to-student sexting is not remotely equivalent to drug use or drug abuse.

The *Morse* test provides that schools can "restrict student expression that they reasonably regard as promoting illegal drug use" without violating the First Amendment.[88] Noncommercial, consensual student-to-student sexting does not advocate illegal use of drugs. In explaining his decision to join the Court's opinion, Justice Alito stated that he did so with the understanding of the *Morse* ruling "as standing at the *far reaches* of what the First Amendment permits."[89] Justice Alito, whose vote made the majority opinion in the case possible, noted: "I join the opinion of the Court on the understanding that the opinion does not hold that the special characteristics of the public schools necessarily justify *any other* speech *restrictions*"[90] besides *Morse*, *Fraser*, and *Tinker*.[91] He added that "the opinion of the Court does not endorse the broad argument advanced by petitioners and the United States that the First Amendment permits public school officials to censor any student speech that interferes with a school's educational mission. This argument can easily be manipulated in dangerous ways, and I would reject it before such abuse occurs."[92]

The Court's creation of the *Morse*, *Fraser*, and *Kuhlmeier* tests, instead of applying the *Tinker* test, which would have provided a straightforward resolution in each of these cases, has merely created confusion in the student speech jurisprudence, particularly when the context of the pertinent case differs from the contexts of the *Morse*, *Fraser*, and *Kuhlmeier* cases. As Justice Thomas aptly stated, "Today, the Court creates another exception. In doing so, we continue to distance ourselves from *Tinker*, but we neither overrule it nor offer an explanation of when it operates and when it does not. I am afraid that our jurisprudence now says that students have a right to speak in schools except when they do not."[93] This highlights the uncertainty in the jurisprudence, providing further reason not to extend a muddled jurisprudence to noncommercial, consensual student-to-student sexting. Even Justice Thomas, who wants to return to the pre-*Tinker* paternalistic era, gave an interesting reason for his decision to join the majority opinion in the case: "I join the Court's opinion because it erodes *Tinker*'s hold in the realm of student speech, even though it does so by adding to the patchwork of exceptions to the *Tinker* standard."[94]

Off-Campus Speech

The U.S. Supreme Court has yet to decide an off-campus student speech case. However, given that the Court has ruled that the free speech rights of students do not end at the schoolhouse gate, this must mean that students have free speech rights that they walk to the schoolhouse gate with. After all, students are persons under the U.S. Constitution and, like all other citizens, should be entitled to constitutional rights outside the schoolhouse gate. As the U.S. Court of Appeals for the Second Circuit declared in a ruling limiting the authority of schools to regulate student off-campus speech, "because school officials have ventured out of the school yard and into the general community where the freedom accorded expression is at its zenith, their actions must be evaluated by the principles that bind government officials in the public arena."[95] Thus, outside the schoolhouse gate, unless there is an established nexus to the school, courts need to respect the constitutional status of students as citizens entitled to First Amendment protection.

Would it not injure our Constitution for a school to discipline a student for a lewd, obscene, plainly offensive, or vulgar comment made by one of its students at his family's party, even though the speech did not occur on school grounds and caused no substantial disruption of the school? Justice Brennan, who provided one of the votes for the judgment in *Fraser*, conceded as much in his concurring opinion, noting that if the student "had given the same speech *outside* of the school environment, he could not have been penalized simply because government officials considered his language to be inappropriate."[96] In fact, he also pointed out that the student's speech—ruled lewd, obscene, plainly offensive, or vulgar in *Fraser*—"may well have been protected had he given it in school but under different circumstances, where the school's legitimate interests in teaching and maintaining civil public discourse were less weighty."[97]

Given that for on-campus student speech, the "school official acts as both prosecutor and judge when he moves against student expression,"[98] it is important that we scrutinize any attempts to regulate off-campus speech where there is insufficient nexus to the school. As the U.S. Court of Appeals for the Second Circuit has stated, when it comes to off-campus student speech, we must not allow even the community to serve as the barometer for punishing such speech;[99] after all, students are citizens like other citizens outside school. In the absence of any contrary test from the U.S. Supreme Court, the requisite nexus should be the *Tinker* test: Does the off-campus student speech cause or is it reasonably forecast to cause material and substantial disruption to the school or infringe rights of other students? As noted earlier, by its nature, noncommercial, consensual student-to-student sexting should pass muster under this test. We concur with the U.S. Court of Appeals for the Ninth Circuit's ruling that "student distribution of non-school-sponsored material cannot be prohibited on the basis of undifferentiated fears of possible disturbances or embarrassment to school officials."[100]

A case often cited when debate arises about the authority of schools to discipline students for off-campus speech is *Beussink vs. Woodland R-IV School District*.[101] In that case, the school district suspended a high school student for 10 days for posting "crude and vulgar" criticism of his school on his personal website.[102] The suspension was imposed despite the fact that the student created the website and posted the comments off-campus, at home, without use of any school resources. Besides, the student himself never intended for the site to be accessed at the school. Instead, the school became aware of the site because a friend of the student brought it to the attention of the school as an act of retaliation against the student after an argument. The friend was the one who accessed the site at the school; she did so without the student's knowledge or authorization.

When the friend showed the homepage comments to a teacher, she was "upset by what she read," as was the principal when he saw the comments.[103] The principal decided to suspend the student "*immediately* upon viewing the homepage ... because he was upset that the homepage's message had been displayed in one of his classrooms."[104] As the Court observed, the principal decided to suspend the student without first determining if other students at the school had viewed the homepage. He also insisted that the student "clean up his homepage or clear it out,"[105] essentially attempting to expand the schoolhouse gate to the student's home; the student complied once he got home. The 10-day suspension impacted the student's grades, causing him to fail several courses. The student sued the district, claiming a violation of his First Amendment rights and seeking a preliminary injunction against the application of the absences to his grades. In granting the injunction, the U.S. District Court for the Eastern District of Missouri relied on the *Tinker* test. The Court found that no material and substantial disruption or infringement of other students' rights resulted from the student's speech; instead, the student was disciplined simply because the principal was upset. As the Court noted, "Disliking or being upset by the content of a student's speech is not an acceptable justification for limiting student speech under *Tinker*."[106]

In its reasoning, the U.S. District Court for the Eastern District of Missouri declared, "Indeed, it is provocative and challenging speech, like Beussink's [the student], which is most in need of the protections of the First Amendment. Popular speech is not likely to provoke censure. It is unpopular speech that invites censure. It is unpopular speech which needs the protection of the First Amendment. The First Amendment was designed for this very purpose."[107]

The Court also emphasized the importance of protecting student speech so that students would have the "opportunity to see the protections of the United States Constitution and the Bill of Rights at work."[108] The Court stated that "the loss of First Amendment freedoms, for even minimal periods of time, unquestionably constitutes irreparable injury."[109] The Court concluded with its own iteration of the *Tinker* test: "Speech within the school that substantially interferes with school discipline may be limited. Individual student speech which is unpopular but does not substantially interfere with school discipline is entitled to protection."[110]

In *Emmett vs. Kent School District No. 415*[111]—another off-campus student speech case—a high school student sought a temporary restraining order against his school for violation of his First Amendment rights after his suspension for comments he made about the school on his personal website and "mock obituaries" on the site. He was also disciplined for infringing the school's copyright by titling the website the "Unofficial Kentlake High Home Page." The mock obituaries were of some of the student's friends and invited people to vote on "who would 'die' next—that is, who would be the subject of the next mock obituary."[112]

A creative writing class the student had taken, which required students to pen their personal obituaries, spurred the idea for the mock obituaries. The U.S. District Court for the Western District of Washington pointed out that the obituaries were "written tongue-in-cheek." The site "included disclaimers warning a visitor that the site was not sponsored by the school, and for entertainment purposes only."[113] The local news learned of the website and reported it as a "hit list of people to be killed, although the words 'hit list' appear nowhere on the web site."[114] The student created the site at home without any school resources. Granting the restraining order, the U.S. District Court for the Western District of Washington stated: "In the present case, Plaintiff's speech was not at a school assembly, as in *Fraser*, and was not in a school-sponsored newspaper, as in *Kuhlmeier*. It was not produced in connection with any class or school project. Although the intended audience was undoubtedly connected to Kentlake High School, the speech was entirely outside of the school's supervision or control."[115] Relying on *Tinker*, the Court found no evidence that the postings on the website presented a threat to the school to create the needed nexus.

Like *Beussink* and *Emmett*, various courts choose to use the *Tinker* test when the other student free speech tests are not clearly applicable.[116] As the U.S. District Court for the Western District of Pennsylvania has observed, "The overwhelming weight of authority has analyzed student speech (whether on or off campus) in accordance with *Tinker*."[117] Recall, *Fraser* dealt with lewd, vulgar, and plainly offensive speech at a school assembly; *Kuhlmeier* dealt with school-sponsored speech; and *Morse* dealt with speech involving advocacy of illegal drug use within an expanded school-house at a school-sanctioned event, so these tests were not directly applicable to the speech in *Beussink* or *Emmett*. In fact, the U.S. Court of Appeals for the Second Circuit admits that "it is not clear, however, that *Fraser* applies to off-campus speech."[118] Additionally, as the U.S. Court of Appeals for the Third Circuit has ruled, "*Fraser* does not allow the School District to punish . . . for expressive conduct which occurred outside of the school context."[119]

We urge courts to embrace the position of the U.S. Court of Appeals for the Second Circuit when dealing with noncommercial, consensual student-to-student sexting: "Our willingness to defer to the schoolmaster's expertise in administering school discipline rests, in large measure, upon the supposition that the arm of authority does not reach beyond the schoolhouse gate. When an educator seeks to extend his dominion beyond these bounds, therefore, he must answer to the same constitutional commands that bind all other institutions of government."[120]

This really is the dictate of *Tinker*'s schoolhouse gate and even *Morse*'s expanded schoolhouse gate. As the U.S. Court of Appeals for the Third Circuit stated in its ruling in 2011, "the First Amendment prohibits the school from reaching beyond the schoolyard to impose what might otherwise be appropriate discipline."[121]

Reflection

Schools eager to regulate student sexting under the anthem of the need for decency would do well to realize the slippery slope it could create. As the U.S. Second Circuit Court of Appeals has eloquently stated, "if the educational interest vindicated by school officials is the need to promote standards of decency and civility among school children, a concept attractive on its face but necessarily elusive if not impossible to apply evenhandedly, it is not apparent why educators would not be permitted to fail a student in an English course for writing a scurrilous letter to the New York Times."[122]

Clearly, "school authority to regulate indecent language aimed at school children can of course be abused."[123] It is important to keep in mind that "school officials are not the final arbiters of their authority [to regulate indecent language], nor do they have limitless discretion to apply their own notions of indecency. Courts have a First Amendment responsibility to insure that robust rhetoric . . . is not suppressed by prudish failures to distinguish the vigorous from the vulgar."[124]

Peter E. Cumming of York University makes the following observation about the cultural disconnect between teens and adults when it comes to sexting:

> There are a few sane voices in the furor over sexting. JSS writes in an online column "Sexting Hysteria," the hysterical and infectious drive to stem sexting among teens and to put it on the level of child pornography has accelerated in just a few weeks. . . . Nothing has actually changed except that the kind of adults who do not engage in sexting, themselves, found out that teen-agers were doing it. . . . Teen-agers fumbling with their sexuality and technology is not something that should scare anyone into legislation, and schools shouldn't be overreacting either. Indeed, one could argue that in some ways virtual sexual activities are safer for teens than actual ones: nobody ever got pregnant or received an STD directly from an online exchange. In "Is 'Sexting' Same as Porn?" Goodman writes, "There is nothing particularly new about young people taking pictures of themselves. It's as old as the Polaroid." In fact, I'd argue it's older than that. Goodman also argues that "The panic not only erases the line between stupid and criminal, it dilutes the real horror of child pornography." Lithwick raises concerns that girls are being punished disproportionately, being charged with producing while boys were merely charged with possessing pornography.[125]

Eager regulators of noncommercial, consensual student-to-student sexting are urged to consider Justice Brennan's admonition in his dissenting opinion in *Kuhlmeier*:

> *Tinker* teaches us that the state educator's undeniable, and undeniably vital, mandate to inculcate moral and political values is not a general warrant to act as "thought police" stifling discussion of all but state-approved topics and advocacy of all but the official position. Otherwise educators could transform students into closed-circuit recipients of only that which the State chooses to communicate, and cast a perverse and impermissible pall of orthodoxy over the classroom. Thus, the State cannot constitutionally prohibit its high school students from recounting in the locker room the particulars of [their] teenage

sexual activity, nor even from advocating irresponsible sex or other presumed abominations of the shared values of a civilized social order. Even in its capacity as educator the State may not assume an Orwellian guardianship of the public mind.[126]

We must realize that schools are not simply filling the role of parents during school hours; instead, they are instruments of the state. As Justice Alito has discerningly stated, "When public school authorities regulate student speech, they act as agents of the State; they do not stand in the shoes of the students' parents. It is a dangerous fiction to pretend that parents simply delegate their authority—including their authority to determine what their children may say and hear—to public school authorities."[127]

Besides, "it is even more dangerous to assume that such a delegation of authority somehow strips public school authorities of their status as agents of the State."[128] We must remember that "most parents, realistically, have no choice but to send their children to a public school and little ability to influence what occurs in the school. It is therefore wrong to treat public school officials, for purposes relevant to the First Amendment, as if they were private, nongovernmental actors standing *in loco parentis*."[129] Now is not the time to "cling to a despotism in the government of schools which has been discarded everywhere else."[130]

Chapter 7

Sexting: Culturally Normal Adolescent Behavior

Introduction

Noncommercial, consensual student-to-student sexting is normal adolescent behavior in our culture; this is not a moral judgment but a statement of cultural fact. As Cole Kazdin and Imaeyen Ibanga rightly note in their report for *ABC News*, "There's nothing coy about this 21st century amorous pursuit."[1] According to educator Dawn Russell, for teens, sexting is "all about immediacy for them, and it's so much about, they're building their hormones and sexuality.... It's so much about getting the opposite sex."[2] As Dr. Elizabeth Schroeder, executive director of Answer (an organization at Rutgers University devoted to sexual education), points out, "Technology is much more far-reaching and permanent, and teenagers are not consequential thinkers.... They are pushing boundaries around sexuality. Years ago they would flash someone or moon someone or write notes or start rumors."[3] As Peggy O'Crowley observes, "Now they can use cell phones and computers to act out sexually."[4]

A few years ago, New York psychologist Susan Lipkins observed a change in adolescents' "thinking about their bodies and sexuality."[5] The advent of cell phones amplifies this change. For example, Anita Modi, a 17-year-old student, expressed how many teens feel about sexting, sexuality, and their bodies: "I guess it's our new way of trying to get attention. It's a measure of your confidence. And the easiest way to display it is how confident you feel in your body." Further, she "believes the preponderance of sexy images of young actresses and models fuels teens to exhibit their sexuality more openly."[6] As another teenager noted, "For young people, sexting is part of their everyday communication system—it's a mating call, a form of gossip."[7]

Legal scholar Robert H. Wood shrewdly captures the essence of sexting as normal adolescent behavior:

> Minors do not suddenly develop their sexuality upon reaching the magic age of eighteen or graduating from high school. It is a process that begins at birth and continues throughout childhood as they go through various physical and mental developments. Sexual behavior that is common among children from ages seven to twelve includes looking at pictures of naked or partially naked people and viewing/listening to sexual content in media. . . . If this is normal behavior in grade school children, our society should not be shocked by the same behavior in high school students who have passed the age of puberty. As far back as 1953, the Kinsey Report found that forty-five percent of women and fifty-seven percent of men had engaged in some kind of sexual play by age twelve. More recent studies found even higher percentages of early sexual activity. Therefore, adopting a zero tolerance approach to such perfectly natural human behavior is irrational and unrealistic.[8]

In her dissertation, Heather K. Hudson points out that "many certified relationship and sexual health experts, counselors, psychologists, and psychiatrists have been promoting sexting as an effective tool for sexual communication. Many of these health professionals have also recommended sexting to couples who have trouble connecting."[9] According to psychology professors Kaveri Subrahmanyam and Patricia Greenfield, "Research shows that adolescents use these communication tools primarily to reinforce existing relationships, both friendships and romantic relationships, and to check out the potential of new entrants into their offline world."[10] Additionally, they emphasize that "finding a romantic partner and establishing a romantic relationship are important adolescent developmental tasks. Related to these tasks are adolescents' developing sexuality and their construction of their sexual selves. Adolescents appear to use electronic media to reinforce existing romantic relationships, just as they do friendships."[11] Subrahmanyam and Greenfield report that "self-disclosure appears to be important for relationship quality in computer-mediated communication."[12]

As we all know, teenagers go through sexual maturation as part of their adolescent development. In their research, Dr. Bonnie L. Halpern-Felsher and Yana Reznik highlight this fact:

> One of the hallmarks of adolescent development is sexual maturation, as pubertal development and hormonal changes result in the development of secondary sexual characteristics, including breasts, pubic hair, and menses.

These newfound physical characteristics often result in the adolescent look-
ing more mature and occur around the same time as the desire for more
autonomy and decision-making opportunities develop, including in the area
of sexual behavior. Adolescents' physical development and increases in their
need for autonomy, coupled with new social influences, yield important *new
attitudes* toward sexual behavior and sexuality.[13]

We should not be bewildered that noncommercial, consensual student-to-
student sexting would be one of those "new attitudes toward sexual behavior
and sexuality."[14] As Subrahmanyam and Greenfield observe, "Society's traditional adolescent issues—intimacy, sexuality, and identity—have all been
transferred to and transformed by the electronic stage."[15]

What is the nature of adolescent sexual behaviors? "Adolescent sexual
behaviors are broadly defined, typically beginning with self-stimulation
(masturbation) and then extending to behaviors involving another person.
These partnered sexual behaviors include kissing, touching, mutual masturbation, oral sex, anal sex, and vaginal sex. The timing of when these
behaviors emerge varies greatly by gender, race/ethnicity, and type of sexual behavior."[16]

Here are some statistics on teen sexuality: "Approximately 47% of all high
school students reported having had sexual intercourse at some point during
high school, ranging from 34% of 9th graders to 63% of 12th graders." Additionally, "adolescents are more likely to initiate and engage in oral sex than
vaginal sex. At least 20% of adolescents have had oral sex by the end of ninth
grade, and over 50% of high school students report having had oral sex at
some point." The statistics also reveal that "among adolescents between the
ages of 15 and 19, 55% of males and 54% of females have had oral sex with
members of the opposite sex."[17] Should it befuddle us that teens would
choose to memorialize these behaviors and exchange the images in noncommercial, consensual student-to-student sexting? And since these are normal
adolescent behaviors, should teens be made criminals for memorializing them
in their noncommercial, consensual student-to-student sexting?

According to Halpern-Felsher and Reznik, "It appears that the trend
toward oral rather than vaginal sex is based in part on sexual attitudes,
namely the desire to avoid risk while still experiencing pleasure."[18] This desire
might also explain the increase in sexting. Besides, research conducted in
2005 found that teens "believed that it was not okay to have vaginal or oral
sex with someone they are not dating, but they did agree that it was okay to
have sex with someone they were dating or with whom they were in love."[19]

In their study on adolescent sexuality, Mary A. Ott and Elizabeth J. Pfeiffer found that "adolescents (all age 14) felt that sex was a normative part of development and recognized that they too would have sex at some point."[20] Craig B. Little and Andrea Rankin report that "several studies indicate that early and steady dating is strongly related to the likelihood of teen sexual activity by both boys and girls."[21] What research further shows is that "clearly the high school years mark the onset of sexual behavior for many youth."[22] W. Andrew Collins of the Institute of Child Development states that "romantic relationships ... have a peculiar intensity and the intensity can be marked by expressions of affection—including physical ones and, perhaps, the expectation of sexual relations, eventually if not now."[23]

The influence of the media on teen sexual culture is certainly indisputable: "Adolescents are constantly exposed to mixed messages about sexuality. On the one hand, adolescents see sex in the media portrayed in a very positive light, with sexual behavior often portrayed as a normal part of adolescent and adult life."[24] As W. Andrew Collins explains, "Adolescents' romantic relationships have inhabited the popular imagination as few other topics have. Popular culture is suffused with images of the dreaminess, preoccupation, shyness, self-consciousness, and sexual awakening of teenagers in love."[25] Les B. Whitbeck and colleagues agree that the teen culture and sexuality have been greatly shaped by the media: "The messages of popular culture as evidenced from popular music, MTV, and movies and television programming aimed at teen audiences essentially reinforce our most robust predictors of early sexual intercourse."[26] Therefore, "it is not surprising then that adolescents' exposure to sex through various media outlets (including television and the Internet) has also been shown to shape adolescents' sexual *attitudes*."[27] According to Whitbeck and colleagues, "An earlier transition to adultlike sexuality is becoming normative. What was [once] an adult behavior has evolved into an acceptable mid- to late-adolescent behavior."[28]

For those who believe adolescent sexuality is wholly inspired by negative teen behaviors, Halpern-Felsher and Reznik point out that adolescent sexual behaviors are "largely influenced by positive motivations, including desires for physical pleasure or excitement, intimate personal relationships, peer approval or peer respect, and self-confidence and exploration."[29] As Sarah Sorenson explains, "Although most adolescent relationships last for only a few weeks or months, these early relationships play a pivotal role in the lives of adolescents and are important to developing the capacity for long-term, committed relationships in adulthood."[30] Also not to be forgotten is the fact that the "quality of adolescent romantic relationships can have long lasting effects on self-esteem and shape personal values regarding romance, intimate relationships, and sexuality."[31]

Adults eager to criminalize sexting are invited to think back to their childhoods. Peter E. Cumming of York University did just that:

> To contextualize youth sexting we should remember our own sexual histories as young people. Apart from digital media's power to disseminate information quickly and broadly, there may be nothing radically new about sexting. The closest I ever came to being expelled from school was in Grade 2, when I was hauled before the authorities for looking up girls' dresses. In 1957, in an Ontario village, as the seven-year-old son of a Protestant clergyman, I was trying my best to learn about sex. At 18, as a don at an Ontario University, I tried to make a political parody of a student council election by posing for the student newspaper—they had cameras then, only the cameras needed film and the newspaper needed to be printed—clad only in a jockstrap; although I was thinly disguised by freckles to make me resemble *Mad* magazine's Alfred E. Neuman, I had to go underground for several days until the Associate Dean cooled off. These events, notably, were *before* television, minicomputers, the Internet, and digital photography.[32]

Cumming continues:

> However, much as contemporary nostalgia might view this as an "earlier, simpler time," and much as current moral panics about youth sexuality might consider children's and youths' current sexting behaviours as depravities signaling the end of civilization, I would suggest that the "innocence" and "experience" of my ancient childhood might actually not be so far separated from the "experience" and "innocence" of many or most sexting exchanges. Perhaps, then, adult alarm about technology and youth sexuality is a red herring—except insofar as it relates to cyber-bullying and sexual harassment.[33]

Cumming asks some very insightful questions that we believe those seeking to prosecute student sexting should strongly consider:

> Are there, for example, significant differences between teens learning to kiss while playing "Spin the Bottle" face-to-face and teen "chicks" and "dudes" going online to "Espin.com" to "spin the bottle and start flirting!" with "Over 4 Million Hotties"? Are there differences between youth playing face-to-face versus online "Strip Poker," or between children investigating each other's

body parts while playing "Doctor" and teens sharing cell phone images of their naked bodies?" As one Macleans [magazine] reader writes, "Young people are showing each other their naked bodies! When did that ever happen before?"[34]

According to Whitbeck and colleagues, the "most basic"[35] characteristic contributing to early sexuality is "pubertal development."[36] They report that "studies incorporating hormonal testing have demonstrated increased sexual interest and activity with the onset of puberty, particularly among adolescent males." Additionally, "for most adolescents, sexual maturation is virtually complete by the 10th grade."[37] The influence of peers is also a contributor to early sexuality. Confirming the influence of teen culture on teens, Whitbeck and colleagues found that students' "perceptions that their friends hold sexually permissive attitudes and are sexually active influence their sexual decision-making. Young people's attributions regarding their friends' sexual activity are more strongly associated with their sexual behaviors than are friends' actual behaviors."[38] The research shows that the "correspondence between adolescents' and close friends' sexual behaviors is well established."[39]

It is no mystery that teens date and will date. The interesting finding about teen dating is that steady dating (*not* unsteady dating) contributes to early sexuality.[40] In fact, "steady dating, *a typical adolescent social activity*, is *consistently* positively associated with early sexuality."[41] Whitbeck and colleagues report that "steady dating increased the likelihood [of early sexual intercourse] five times."[42] They reveal that "the social context of first intercourse, particularly among young women, is most likely a monogamous, love-oriented relationship. The earlier the young person moves into such relationships, the greater the likelihood that he or she will become sexually active."[43] Sorenson reports that "the strongest predictor for having sexual intercourse in 7th through 12th grades is recent involvement in a romantic relationship."[44] Sorenson points out that even though "adults typically dismiss adolescent dating relationships as superficial," it is important to note that "young people do not agree: half of all teens report having been in a dating relationship and nearly one-third of all teens said they have been in a serious relationship."[45] Besides, "as adolescents become more autonomous from their parents, their romantic relationships increasingly become a source of emotional support. One study found that, among tenth graders, only close friends provide more support than romantic partners."[46]

We believe the following research statements from Whitbeck and colleagues apply equally and axiomatically to noncommercial, consensual student-to-student sexting:

> From a life-course developmental perspective, the timing and contexts of life transitions are culturally defined. In U.S. society, what was once considered an early adulthood transition has been evolving into expected behavior in later adolescence. According to life-course theory, as frequency of transitions to adult-like behaviors increase, norms involving the acceptability of such behaviors often change to accommodate the behavioral shift. In this case, the transition to sexual intercourse loses its significance as a marker of young adulthood. Furthermore, as the normative age for this transition shifts, factors limiting sexual expression become less salient as the adolescent approaches the culturally expected ages for this transition. With the age of "acceptable" sexual experimentation gravitating downward, definitions of what is "early" intercourse may change.[47]

Concluding Remarks

"The value of free expression . . . rests on its deep relation to self-respect arising from autonomous self-determination without which the life of the spirit is meager and slavish."[48]

While the U.S. Supreme Court has recognized obscenity, child pornography, true threats, fighting words, and libel as categories of speech unprotected under the First Amendment, the court has never considered sexting. We hope that the ideas we have set forth in this book contribute to the debate so that noncommercial, consensual student-to-student sexting is not automatically lumped in with unprotected speech that can be constitutionally criminalized.

In *Abrams vs. United States*,[49] Justice Holmes brought to our legal consciousness the importance of favoring a marketplace of ideas over censorship of ideas; preserving a marketplace of ideas is vital to the viability of our democratic system and to the First Amendment. Regarding the marketplace of ideas, Justice Holmes declared:

> Men . . . may come to believe . . . that the ultimate good desired is better reached by free trade in ideas—that the best test of truth is the power of the thought to get itself accepted in the competition of the market, and that truth is the only ground upon which their wishes safely can be carried out. That at any rate is the theory of our Constitution. It is an experiment, as all life is an

experiment. Every year if not every day we have to wager our salvation upon
some prophecy based upon imperfect knowledge. While that experiment is
part of our system I think that we should be eternally vigilant against
attempts to check the expression of opinions that we loathe and believe to
be fraught with death, unless they so imminently threaten immediate interference with the lawful and pressing purposes of the law that an immediate
check is required to save the country.[50]

Technological advancements have contributed to the "imperfect knowledge" referenced in Justice Holmes's words—all the more reason we need to
be vigilant against censoring noncommercial, consensual student-to-student
sexting with criminal prosecutions; after all, such sextings are essentially acts
done innocently without criminal intent. Indeed, in enacting Senate Bill 277,
the Nevada legislature observed that "children often act without fully contem-
plating the potential grave consequences of their actions, including, without
limitation, the serious penalties imposed for violating child pornography laws,
the requirement to register as a sex offender for violating such laws, the negative effect on relationships, the loss of educational and employment
opportunities."[51]

Further, the state legislature noted that "it is important to educate children
about the serious consequences of engaging in sexting and to provide an
effective and measured response to children who engage in such behavior
without imposing penalties on these children which will severely, negatively
and, in many cases, permanently alter these children's lives."[52] Besides, "teenagers have no monopoly on foolish choices and devastating consequences.
Think, for example, of the infamous, intercepted cellphone conversation
between the future King of England and his paramour in which he fantasizes
about being a tampon so he can 'live in her trousers': no doubt that would
have been sexting had the technology existed."[53] Moreover, "when, we must
ask, in Western culture, did nudity become pornography, youth sexuality per-
verse, digital technologies the tail wagging the dog, and when and how and
why have we forgotten children's participatory rights as sexual beings?"[54]

We adapt and highlight the words of David A. J. Richards for all to
reflect on in the discourse about censoring noncommercial, consensual
student-to-student sexting:

Within the perspective of the evolving national debate over sexual morality
and the Supreme Court's repeated support of an "uninhibited marketplace
of ideas," it is difficult to see why the [consensual sexting] vision should
not have a place in the marketplace of ideas beside other visions that

celebrate the life of the mind, the sanctity of ascetic piety, or the usefulness of prudent self-discipline. In excluding the [consensual sexting] vision from the marketplace, the [government] fundamentally fails to make a morally neutral judgment . . . of obscene material . . . for in applying the concept of the obscene it affirms one moral and political view and denies another.[55]

As the U.S. Supreme Court has noted, "Even where speech is indecent and enters the home, the objective of shielding children does not suffice to support a blanket ban if the protection can be accomplished by a less restrictive alternative."[56] The use of "blocking and filtering software"[57] on cell phones of students should be encouraged as a less restrictive alternative; after all, "the use of filters does not condemn as criminal any category of speech, and so the potential chilling effect is eliminated, or at least much diminished."[58] With filters, parents can choose to regulate what their children receive and send on their cell phones. Congress has a limited role: "Congress can give strong incentives to schools and libraries to use them [filters]. It could also take steps to promote their development by industry, and their use by parents. . . . By enacting programs to promote use of filtering software, Congress could give parents that ability [to supervise their children] without subjecting protected speech to severe penalties."[59]

Any filter developed for cell phones should be "difficult for children to circumvent . . . because of the technical ability and expertise necessary to do so."[60] Cell phone filters should be designed to match the following description:

One of the features of filtering programs that adds to their effectiveness is that they have built-in mechanisms to prevent children from bypassing or circumventing the filters, including password protection and other devices to prevent children from uninstalling the product or changing the settings. Some products even have a tamper detection feature, by which they can detect when someone is trying to uninstall or disable the product, and then cut off . . . access altogether until it has been properly reconfigured.[61]

The U.S. Supreme Court's reasoning with respect to blocking of cable channels carrying sexually explicit content should apply equally to giving parents, rather than the government, the prerogative to block sexts on their teenagers' phones (or cell phone providers need to be supported in developing sext-blocking technology for parents):

Targeted blocking enables the Government to support parental authority without affecting the First Amendment interests of speakers and willing listeners—listeners for whom, if the speech is unpopular or indecent, the privacy of their own homes may be the optimal place of receipt. Simply put, targeted blocking is less restrictive than banning, and the Government cannot ban speech if targeted blocking is a feasible and effective means of furthering its compelling interests. This is not to say that the absence of an effective blocking mechanism will in all cases suffice to support a law restricting the speech in question; but if a less restrictive means is available for the Government to achieve its goals, the Government must use it.[62]

Congress should encourage cell phone providers to advertise to parents the availability of filtering or blocking technology. These providers could also be required to include inserts with the monthly cell phone bills—inserts designed to educate parents on the need for filters or blocking technology and how to block or filter sexts. Cell phone providers need to ensure that "filters can be programmed or configured in a variety of different ways according to . . . the values of the parents using them and the age and maturity of their children."[63] In this way, filters give parents control, providing them an "appropriate flexible approach" that is different from the "one size fits all approach" of the various criminal statutes that form the basis for prosecuting sexters.[64]

Besides, "if unresponsive [cell phone] operators are a concern . . . a notice statute could give . . . operators ample incentive, through fines or other penalties for noncompliance, to respond to blocking requests in prompt and efficient fashion."[65] To all those prepared to rail against blocking as an inconvenience or as putting the onus on parents, here is the Supreme Court's response: "It is no response that voluntary blocking requires a consumer to take action, or may be inconvenient, or may not go perfectly every time. A court should not assume a plausible, less restrictive alternative would be ineffective; and a court should not presume parents, given full information, will fail to act."[66]

John Gabriel Woodlee notes that the public demand for harsher sentences—which we wholly support—for child pornography criminals and the lack of lobbying power by offenders or potential offenders have effectively ensured very harsh sentencing;[67] we, however, do not believe that teens engaged in noncommercial, consensual student-to-student sexting should be deemed "child pornography criminals." As for Woodlee's point about lack of political power, it is evident that sexting teens have virtually none of the power, such as organization or the right to vote, needed to influence legislators. Moreover, as Woodlee points out, "because offenders often cannot identify themselves as such in advance—and because they may underestimate the risk that they will be caught and convicted—they are unlikely to be motivated to organize lobbying efforts. A desire to avoid the reputational harm of being identified as, or associated with, potential criminals may also discourage lobbying against tough-on-crime legislation."[68]

It is critical to keep in mind that legislators and elected prosecutors do not want to be viewed as "crime softies" by opposing stiffer penalties under child pornography laws; consequently, these laws have passed virtually unanimously. We must also heed the words of Justice Holmes: "It would be a dangerous undertaking for persons trained only to the law to constitute themselves final judges of the worth of pictorial illustrations, outside of the narrowest and most obvious limits."[69]

Justice Stevens's opinion with respect to obscenity is equally applicable to noncommercial, consensual student-to-student sexting, so we will substitute the word "sexting" for "obscenity" to make our point in Justice Stevens's voice: "Criminal prosecutions are, in my view, an inappropriate means to regulate the universe of materials classified as [sexting], since the line between communications which 'offend' and those which do not is too blurred to identify criminal conduct."[70] Recall, the context of our thesis is noncommercial, consensual student-to-student sexting; thus, the sexts are, by definition, not offensive communications to the sexting students.

We call on legislators, judges, and prosecutors to deliberate over Justice Stevens's words when it comes to the various statutes that could be used to prosecute student sexters:

> Criminal penalties are, moreover, strong medicine for the ill that the statute seeks to remedy. To be sure, our cases have recognized a compelling interest in protecting minors from exposure to sexually explicit materials. As a parent, grandparent, and great-grandparent, I endorse that goal without reservation. As a judge, however, I must confess to a growing sense of unease when the interest in protecting children from prurient materials is invoked as a justification for using criminal regulation of speech as a substitute for, or a simple backup to, adult oversight of children's viewing habits.[71]

Criminalizing noncommercial, consensual student-to-student sexting, given its nature as consensual adolescent activity, in order to protect minors is akin to "burn[ing] the house to roast the pig."[72] After all, parents could, for example, simply decline text services on the cell phones of their teenagers if they choose not to allow them to engage in consensual sexting until they are of the age of majority.

FIGURE 7.1. Parental Control versus Parentalist Control.

Source: Cartoon by Kevin Moore of Moore Toons.

As First Amendment scholar Clay Calvert observes in his article "Sex, Cell Phones, Privacy, and the First Amendment: When Children Become Child Pornographers and the Lolita Effect Undermines the Law," "charging kids who sext with criminal offenses carries an unmistakable echo of those fraught, hysteria-filled months in 1692 when magistrates in colonial Massachusetts arrested and charged more than 150 people with the crime of witchcraft."[73] Instead, we must keep the power in the hands of parents. Calvert believes that "the intervention of parents who vigilantly monitor their children's cell phone and text-message usage would seem to be a preferred remedy [to prosecutions] since it keeps the government out of the issue of sexting and away from the intimate (and often embarrassing) activities of minors who are under parental control."[74]

A cartoon by Kevin Moore humorously captures parents censoring student sexting versus governmental control (see Figure 7.1).

The principle of "penal proportionality," which is supposed to underlie criminal statutes, is important when considering the criminalization of noncommercial, consensual student-to-student sexting. This principle states that "fair criminal punishment is measured not only by the amount of harm caused or threatened by the actor but also by his or her blameworthiness."[75] First, we point out that, as discussed earlier, noncommercial, consensual student-to-student sexting does not cause the harm to sexters that the U.S. Supreme Court has looked for in its child pornography jurisprudence, including *Ferber*. Second, in any move to criminalize noncommercial, consensual student-to-student sexting, it is only prudent that policymakers, prosecutors, and judges take into account the extent to which "the immaturity of adolescent offenders is relevant to their blameworthiness."[76] After all, "typical adolescents are less culpable than are adults because adolescent criminal conduct is driven by transitory influences that are constitutive of this development stage."[77] As Laurence Steinberg and Elizabeth S. Scott point out, "It is well established that reasoning capabilities increase through childhood into adolescence and that preadolescents and younger teens differ substantially from adults in their cognitive abilities. . . . [Nonetheless] there is good reason to question whether age differences in decision making disappear by mid-adolescence."[78]

Steinberg and Scott point to "psychosocial immaturity" that influences "decision-making *outcomes*" as an explanation for why "even when teenagers' cognitive capacities come close to those of adults, adolescent judgment and their actual decisions may differ from that of adults."[79] According to Steinberg and Scott, psychosocial immaturity impacts "adolescent values and preferences in ways that drive the cost-benefit calculus in the making of choices. In other words, to the extent that adolescents are less psychologically mature than adults, they are likely to be deficient in their decision-making capacity, even if their cognitive processes are mature."[80]

For minors, "the process of identity formation includes considerable exploration and experimentation over the course of adolescence."[81] Besides, "for most teens, these behaviors are fleeting; they cease with maturity as individual identity becomes settled."[82] Consequently, it would be wrong and unfair to conclude that teens are engaging in noncommercial, consensual student-to-student sexting out of "deep-seated moral deficiency reflective of bad character"; after all, "one reason the typical delinquent youth does not grow up to be an adult criminal is that the developmentally linked values and preferences that drive his or her criminal choices as a teenager change in predictable ways as the youth matures."[83]

There is a reason our country has a judicial system for minors, independent of that for adults, even though oftentimes minors still end up in the criminal justice system when prosecuted as adults. As Joanna S. Markman explains, "The impetus for the creation of a separate juvenile justice system was the acknowledgment that children are not adults, and as such, do not have the capacity for rational thoughts as adults do."[84] As Markman points out, "The juvenile justice system was derived to create a structure whereby rehabilitation would be the ultimate objective in devising juvenile punishment, or, as it is referred to in the language of juvenile law, disposition."[85]

Additionally, the juvenile system was created because of the recognition that minors "are less culpable for conduct and more amenable to rehabilitation. Further, a child's misconduct was believed to be based on factors beyond their control. Those factors included: economic status, home life, environment, genetics, immaturity leading to impulsivity, inability to assess consequences, and lack of experience and judgment."[86] If the recognition that minors are not adults underlies the creation of the separate justice system for minors, we need to also acknowledge this fact when dealing with noncommercial, consensual student-to-student sexting. This is important, particularly because minors have no inclination whatsoever that, based on laws currently on the books, they could become felons (and even be required to register as sex offenders with a conviction) and their lives could be forever damaged, consequent to what they consider to be innocuous consensual sexting.

In its seminal case on the constitutional rights of juveniles, *In re Gault*,[87] the U.S. Supreme Court weighed in on the justifications for treating juveniles differently from adults, which very well should apply to deliberations over noncommercial, consensual student-to-student sexting:

> The early reformers were appalled by adult procedures and penalties, and by the fact that children could be given long prison sentences and mixed in jails with hardened criminals. They were profoundly convinced that society's duty to the child could not be confined by the concept of justice alone. They believed that society's role was not to ascertain whether the child was "guilty" or "innocent," but "What is he, how has he become what he is, and what had best be done in his interest and in the interest of the state to save him from a downward career." The child—essentially good, as they saw it—was to be made "to feel that he is the object of [the state's] care and solicitude," not that he was under arrest or on trial. The rules of criminal procedure were therefore altogether inapplicable. The apparent rigidities, technicalities, and harshness which they observed in both substantive and procedural criminal law were therefore to be discarded. The idea of crime and punishment was to be abandoned. The child was to be "treated" and "rehabilitated" and the

procedures, from apprehension through institutionalization, were to be "clinical" rather than punitive.[88]

Further, in its landmark case *Roper v. Simmons*[89]—holding that the death penalty cannot be applied to persons who were juveniles at the time of their crimes—the U.S. Supreme Court declared that "the reasons why juveniles are not trusted with the privileges and responsibilities of an adult also explain why their irresponsible conduct is not as morally reprehensible as that of an adult."[90] The court identified three key differences between adults and juveniles that justify treating juveniles and adults differently: "First, as any parent knows and as the scientific and sociological studies respondent and his amici cite tend to confirm, [a] lack of maturity and an underdeveloped sense of responsibility are found in youth more often than in adults and are more understandable among the young. These qualities often result in impetuous and ill-considered actions and decisions."[91]

According to the court, "The second area of difference is that juveniles are more vulnerable or susceptible to negative influences and outside pressures, including peer pressure,"[92] and "the third broad difference is that the character of a juvenile is not as well formed as that of an adult. The personality traits of juveniles are more transitory, less fixed."[93]

The U.S. Supreme Court reflected on the typical government decision to set the age of majority at 18: "Drawing the line at 18 years of age is subject, of course, to the objections always raised against categorical rules. The qualities that distinguish juveniles from adults do not disappear when an individual turns 18. . . . For the reasons we have discussed, however, a line must be drawn. . . . The age of 18 is the point where society draws the line for many purposes between childhood and adulthood."[94]

As the court pointed out, however, juveniles' "vulnerability and comparative lack of control over their immediate surroundings mean juveniles have a greater claim than adults to be forgiven for failing to escape negative influences in their whole environment."[95] Besides, "the reality that juveniles still struggle to define their identity means it is less supportable to conclude that even a heinous crime committed by a juvenile is evidence of irretrievably depraved character."[96] The court declared that "from a moral standpoint it would be misguided to equate the failings of a minor with those of an adult, for a greater possibility exists that a minor's character deficiencies will be reformed."[97] In 2010, in *Graham vs. Florida*,[98] the U.S. Supreme Court reaffirmed its conclusions in *Roper*.[99] The court observed that "developments in psychology and brain science continue to show fundamental differences between juvenile and adult minds."[100]

Given the differences between adults and juveniles, should the very fact of being a juvenile not be a mitigating factor against criminally punishing juveniles for noncommercial, consensual student-to-student sexting? As the *Roper* court stated, "The relevance of youth as a mitigating factor derives from the fact that the signature qualities of youth are transient; as individuals mature, the impetuousness and recklessness that may dominate in younger years can subside."[101] For those who argue that deterrence of sexting is a reason to criminally punish minors for noncommercial, consensual student-to-student sexting, keep in mind, as the U.S. Supreme Court has stated, that "the same characteristics that render juveniles less culpable than adults suggest as well that juveniles will be less susceptible to deterrence."[102]

We emphasize that the same reasoning that inspired creation of a juvenile justice system should prevail with respect to noncommercial, consensual student-to-student sexting: "One driving force behind the development of this new juvenile justice system, and thus the need for strict confidentiality, was the minimization of the stigma associated with criminal conduct."[103] We would argue that making students felons (or criminals of any sort) for noncommercial, consensual student-to-student sexting leads to "stigma that could, and most likely would, follow the child throughout the maturation process and consequently impede the process of the child growing into a successful and productive member of society."[104] Indeed, "founders of the juvenile justice system envisioned a process by which disobedient children were to be redirected by a compassionate and knowledgeable judiciary with the assistance of social service agencies. The main objective of this separate system was not punitive, but rather to protect, rehabilitate, and heal the child."[105] This same objective embodying compassion rather than compulsion and penalty should guide the legislative and judicial approach to noncommercial, consensual student-to-student sexting. Let us "heal the child,"[106] not break the child.

The opinion of Justice Kogan of the Florida Supreme Court clearly and incisively supports our thesis about the use of criminal statutes to make criminals of students engaged in noncommercial, consensual student-to-student sexting:

> I also am highly puzzled about who should be regarded as the "aggressor" and who the "victim" when both partners are minors. If both are "chaste,"

then a fair reading of the statute would indicate that both have committed a felony. Yet, this effectively means each child was both aggressor and victim in a single act, which stretches credence to the breaking point. Attempting to brand one as the aggressor and the other as the victim raises very serious questions of equal protection, especially where prosecutors always assume that one type of child—such as "the boy," or the one who is "unchaste"—must be the aggressor. Moreover, still other problems arise in this last situation. Identifying the male or "unchaste" partner as the aggressor will not always be borne out by the facts.[107]

For those who argue that the failure to punish noncommercial, consensual student-to-student sexting could lead to those sexts falling into the wrong hands, Judge Padovano of the Florida Supreme Court has a very erudite and thoughtful response:

The majority concludes that the child in this case did not have a reasonable expectation that the photographs would remain private. To support this conclusion, the majority speculates about the many ways in which the photographs might have been revealed to others. The e-mail transmission might have been intercepted. The relationship might have ended badly. The boyfriend might have wanted to show the photo to someone else to brag about his sexual conquest. With all due respect, I think these arguments are beside the point. Certainly there are circumstances in which the photos might have been revealed unintentionally to third parties, but that would always be the case. . . . The issue is whether the child intended to keep the photos private, not whether it would be possible for someone to obtain the photos against her will and thereby to invade her privacy. The majority states that the child "placed the photos on a computer and then, using the internet, transferred them to another computer," as if to suggest that she left them out carelessly for anyone to find. That is not what happened. She sent the photos to her boyfriend at his personal e-mail address, intending to share them only with him.[108]

Judge Padovano continued:

The method the child used to transmit the photos to her boyfriend carries some danger of disclosure, but so do others. If the child had taken a printed photograph and placed it in her purse, it might have been disclosed to third parties if her purse had been lost or stolen. If she had mailed it to her boyfriend in an envelope, it might have been revealed if the envelope had been delivered to the wrong address and mistakenly opened. As these examples illustrate, there is always a possibility that something a person intends to keep private will eventually be disclosed to others. But we cannot gauge the reasonableness of a person's expectation of privacy merely by speculating about the many ways in which it might be violated. The critical point in this case is that the child intended to keep the photographs private. She did not attempt to exploit anyone or to embarrass anyone. I think her expectation of privacy in the photographs was reasonable. Certainly, an argument could be made that she was foolish to expect that, but the expectation of a sixteen year old cannot be measured by the collective wisdom of appellate judges who have no emotional connection to the event. Perhaps if the child had as much time to reflect on these events, she would have eventually concluded, as the majority did, that there were ways in which these photos might have been unintentionally disclosed. That does not make her expectation of privacy unreasonable. For these reasons, I believe the court has committed a serious error. The statute at issue was designed to protect children, but in this case the court has allowed the state to use it against a child in a way that criminalizes conduct that is protected by constitutional right of privacy.[109]

In the debate about whether criminalization is an appropriate response to noncommercial, consensual student-to-student sexting, as noted earlier, we must remember that sexting is a form of self-expression. Consequently, as free speech, sexting is as critical to the development of adolescents as any other such antediluvian communication sans the technology. The U.S. Supreme Court has earnestly expressed the importance of self-expression to human development; this fully applies to noncommercial, consensual student-to-student sexting:

It is through speech that our convictions and beliefs are influenced, expressed, and tested. It is through speech that we bring those beliefs to bear on Government and on society. It is through speech that our personalities are formed and expressed. The citizen is entitled to seek out or reject certain ideas or influences without Government interference or control. . . . The Constitution exists precisely so that opinions and judgments, including esthetic and moral judgments about art and literature, can be formed, tested, and expressed. What the Constitution says is that these judgments are for the individual to make, not for the Government to decree, even with the mandate or approval of a majority. Technology expands the capacity to choose; and it denies the potential of this revolution if we assume the Government is best positioned to make these choices for us. It is rare that a regulation restricting speech because of its content will ever be permissible. Indeed, were we to give the Government the benefit of the doubt when it attempted to restrict speech, we would risk leaving regulations in place that sought to shape our unique personalities or to silence dissenting ideas.[110]

Even though the Supreme Court has never decided a student sexting case, the court, in its own words, has given us reason to accord First Amendment protection to noncommercial, consensual student-to-student sexting: "A person's inclinations and fantasies . . . are his own and beyond the reach of government."[111] With sexting, teens fantasize consensually; this fantasizing is normal adolescent behavior that should be "beyond the reach of government" and remain within the purview of the parents.

If we want to change teen behavior, we can look at some ideas from Douglas Kirby, senior research scientist at ETR Associates. Kirby, for instance, suggests capitalizing on mass media through such avenues as PSAs (public service announcements) and soap operas to "portray desirable behavior."[112] He suggests that the "programs can use attractive models similar to the targeted group to give reasons for desirable behavior and to model behavior."[113] Instead of criminally penalizing teens for noncommercial, consensual student-to-student sexting, we could use mass media to "mobilize friends and opinion leaders to take a public stance on certain issues."[114] Celebrities, athletes, and others teens look up to could be an important part of that campaign.

Kirby suggests that "sexuality and HIV education programs can use role-playing and small-group activities to reinforce norms";this can be done in and out of school.[115]

Schools can also provide workshops to educate parents on ways to communicate with and help their children with changing their behaviors, if parents choose to discourage noncommercial, consensual student-to-student sexting. Dr. Sameer Hinduja and Dr. Justin W. Patchin suggest that schools share educational information on sexting "through take-home memorandums, student handbooks, newsletters/correspondence to the community, letters to the editor in local newspapers, town hall meetings, and automated phone calls to the families of students." They also suggest the "construction and maintenance of a Facebook Fan Page, a Twitter feed, or a page on the school website that covers sexting."[116]

Lest we take the wrong path that makes felons or criminals of our nation's teens for noncommercial, consensual student-to-student sexting, we must keep in mind that "a cautious expositor of controversy may well choose silence over expression if he knows that his words will be judged by a decisionmaker predisposed to rule against him."[117] "A conviction for a sex crime will arguably cause more damage" to teenagers' "reputations than would their [sext] photos."[118] In essence, prosecution of students for non-commercial, consensual student-to-student sexting is "brutal censorship."[119] It is "unthinking contempt for individual rights [that] is intolerable from any state official. It is particularly insidious from one to whom the public entrusts the task of inculcating in its youth an appreciation for the cherished democratic liberties that our Constitution guarantees."[120] As the U.S. Supreme Court has clearly stated, "Whether viewed as an attempt to express the community's moral outrage or as an attempt to right the balance for the wrong to the victim, the case for retribution is not as strong with a minor as with an adult."[121] The way we treat our children must teach them that "our Constitution is a living reality, not parchment preserved under glass."[122]

We conclude with a letter sent by Jeffrey M. Gamso, legal director of the American Civil Liberties Union of Ohio Foundation, to the prosecutors of all 88 counties in the state of Ohio, which duly captures the essence of our thesis herein (Figure 7.2).

FIGURE 7.2. Letter Sent by ACLU to the Prosecutors of All Ohio Counties.

April 2, 2009

Subject: How to combat "sexting" without criminalizing the victims

Sent to all Ohio County prosecutors

The American Civil Liberties Union of Ohio (ACLU of Ohio) is deeply concerned about the flood of recent prosecutions for "sexting" - the practice, often by teens, of sending a nude or semi-nude picture of themselves via cellphone or Internet.

AMERICAN CIVIL
LIBERTIES UNION
OF OHIO FOUNDATION
4506 CHESTER AVENUE
CLEVELAND, OH 44103-3621
T/216.472.2220
F/216.472.2210
WWW.ACLUOHIO.ORG
contact@acluohio.org

SHARES

We can all agree that minors often do not appreciate the consequences of their actions. This is certainly one of those situations. Teens who send compromising pictures rarely realize those photos will in all probability be shared with others who were not intended to see them.

There are better ways to discourage this behavior than by lashing out and criminalizing the victims for what they have done to themselves. Teens need to be taught the risks and potential consequences of sending nude photos. But that should be done by education, not prosecution. Prosecuting teens who send photos of themselves, in an attempt to protect them from themselves or to serve as a warning to others, could have dire and unintended consequences on these kids.

- The child pornography laws are intended to protect victims from those who do them harm. In these sexting cases, the victim and accused offender are often one and the same. Charging teens for sexting under the child pornography laws is an imperfect fit and inappropriate use of those laws.

- A conviction for sexting does far more than teach a lesson – it can ruin a life. Certainly, any conviction carries with it punishment – fines, a term of imprisonment, community service requirements, et cetera. Findings of delinquency can carry similar consequences. The most onerous of those consequences, applicable both to criminal and delinquency adjudications, are a result of the Adam Walsh Act. The child who foolishly sends a photo of herself or receives a photo (and frankly, even the one who maliciously shares it with friends) can be labeled a "sex offender." The youthful indiscretion then leads, at least potentially, to decades of registration with law enforcement, internet access for the world to the misbehavior, possible community notification, what may be a lifetime of residence and perhaps employment restrictions (and under a bill currently pending in the General Assembly, a prohibition against entering a school). Sexting prosecutions, then, may and likely will limit opportunities for decades if not for the rest of the teens' lives. It is a consequence far beyond any benefit that might flow.

- Even when a teen is arguably harmed by taking, sending, or receiving an inappropriate photo, the intent to harm and the nature of the harm is not the same as that inflicted by those ordinarily charged with child pornography or labeled as sex offenders.

- Ohio, like many states, criminalizes taking or sending nude pictures of a minor. Ohio also places strict prohibitions and requirements on those designated as sex offenders. But those

FIGURE 7.2. (continued)

laws were designed to punish people who victimize others, not to punish teens who naively victimize themselves. Our current laws never contemplated the problem of sexting, nor should they be (mis)used as a substitute for taking the time to address the root problems of sexting. Ohio laws need to be rewritten by the General Assembly to clarify what behavior is punishable by law and what calls for lesser forms of intervention. Until that happens, prosecutors must exercise their discretion to assure that what is designed to protect does not punish. Certainly we can protect our youth without harming them in the process.

- We are aware that in at least some counties prosecutors are attempting to educate teens about the dangers of sexting. Yet we read that in these same counties there will be "zero tolerance" for those who, once put on notice, act anyway. But young people make mistakes, even when they should know better. And lifetime consequences for a teen acting against his or her best interest, even when on notice of that interest, is a consequence entirely out of proportion to the offense.

Naivety is part of adolescence, and we as a society – jurists, educators, and parents – should help protect young people by cautioning them to avoid risky behavior. Threatening teens with criminal prosecution, and all its attendant life-ruining consequences, is not the solution. We need to help our teens better understand the consequences of sexting. We do that through outreach and education, not by causing them further harm.

Thus, we ask for your help in finding a better a solution. Please join us in (A) calling on the General Assembly to clarify the law so that teens caught "sexting" are not subjected to felony sex offense charges, and (B) working with parents and educators to teach young people to respect their own dignity and privacy and the dignity and privacy of others.

Should you have any questions regarding this matter please do not hesitate to contact me directly at (216) 472-2220 or by e-mail at jmgamso@acluohio.org.

Sincerely,

Jeffrey M. Gamso
Legal Director

Source: Jeffrey M. Gamso, "How To Combat 'Sexting' without Criminalizing the Victims," American Civil Liberties Union of Ohio Foundation [April 2, 2009], available at http://www.acluohio.org/issues/juvenilejustice/lettertoohioprosecutors _sexting2009_0402.pdf.

Appendix A

What Do
the Statutes State?

STATE Title of Pertinent Provision *Key definition*	Applicable Statutes and What They Say*
ALABAMA	ALA. CODE § 13A-6-120, et seq. (2009) ALA. CODE § 13A-12-190, et seq. (2006)
Obscene Materials Containing Visual Reproduction of Children	Any person who shall knowingly disseminate or display publicly any obscene matter containing a visual depiction of a person under the age of 17 years engaged in any act of . . . sexual intercourse, sexual excitement, masturbation, breast nudity, genital nudity, or other sexual conduct shall be guilty of a Class B felony.
	Any person who knowingly possesses with intent to disseminate any obscene matter that contains a visual depiction of a person under the age of 17 years engaged in any act of . . . sexual intercourse, sexual excitement, masturbation, breast nudity, genital nudity, or other sexual conduct shall be guilty of a Class B felony. Possession of three or more copies of the same visual depiction contained in obscene matter is prima facie evidence of possession with intent to disseminate the same.
	Any person who knowingly possesses any obscene matter that contains a visual depiction of a person under the age of 17 years engaged in any act of . . . sexual intercourse, sexual excitement, masturbation, genital nudity, or other sexual conduct shall be guilty of a Class C felony.

(continued)

STATE Title of Pertinent Provision *Key definition*	Applicable Statutes and What They Say*
	Any person who knowingly films, prints, records, photographs or otherwise produces any obscene matter that contains a visual depiction of a person under the age of 17 years engaged in any act of . . . sexual intercourse, sexual excitement, masturbation, breast nudity, genital nudity, or other sexual conduct shall be guilty of a Class A felony. . . . Each depiction of each individual less than 17 years of age constitutes a separate offense. . .
Electronic Solicitation of a Child	A person who, knowingly, with the intent to commit an unlawful sex act, entices, induces, persuades, seduces, prevails, advises, coerces, lures, or orders, or attempts to entice, induce, persuade, seduce, prevail, advise, coerce, lure, or order, by means of a computer, . . . cellular phone, . . . or any other electronic communication or storage device, a child who is at least three years younger than the defendant, or another person believed by the defendant to be a child at least three years younger than the defendant to meet with the defendant or any other person for the purpose of engaging in sexual intercourse, sodomy, or to engage in a sexual performance, obscene sexual performance, or sexual conduct for his or her benefit or for the benefit of another, is guilty of electronic solicitation of a child. For purposes of this crime, a child is someone less than 16 years old.
Sexual intercourse	Intercourse, real or simulated, whether genital-genital, oral-genital, anal-genital or oral-anal, whether between persons of the same or opposite sex.
Sexual excitement	The condition of human male or female genitals when in a state of sexual stimulation.
Masturbation	Manipulation, by hand or instrument, of the human genitals, whether one's own or another's for the purpose of sexual stimulation.
Breast nudity	The lewd showing of the post-pubertal human female breasts below a point immediately above the top of the areola.
Genital nudity	The lewd showing of the genitals or pubic area.
Other sexual conduct	Any touching of the genitals, pubic areas or buttocks of the human male or female, or the breasts of the female, whether alone or between members of the same or opposite sex . . . in an act of apparent sexual stimulation or gratification.

STATE Title of Pertinent Provision *Key definition*	Applicable Statutes and What They Say*
ALASKA	ALASKA STAT. § 11.41.455, et seq. (Michie 2008) ALASKA STAT. § 11.46.990(3) (Michie 2010) ALASKA STAT. § 11.61.125, et seq. (Michie 2010)
Unlawful Exploitation of a Minor	A person commits the crime of unlawful exploitation of a minor if, in the state and with the intent of producing a live performance, film, audio, video, electronic, or electromagnetic recording, photograph, negative, slide, book, newspaper, magazine, or other material that visually or aurally depicts the conduct listed in (1)–(7) of this subsection, the person knowingly induces or employs a child under 18 years of age to engage in, or photographs, films, records, or televises a child under 18 years of age engaged in, the following actual or simulated conduct: (1) sexual penetration; (2) the lewd touching of another person's genitals, anus, or breast; (3) the lewd touching by another person of the child's genitals, anus, or breast; (4) masturbation; . . . [or] (6) the lewd exhibition of the child's genitals.
	(Unlawful exploitation of a minor constitutes a class B felony; or a class A felony if the person has been previously convicted of unlawful exploitation of a minor in this jurisdiction or a similar crime in this or another jurisdiction.)
Distribution of Child Pornography	A person commits the crime of distribution of child pornography if the person distributes in this state or advertises, promotes, solicits, or offers to distribute in this state any material that is proscribed under [Alaska Statutes Annotated] 11.61.127.
	(Child pornography distribution is a class B felony; or a class A felony if the person has been previously convicted of distribution of child pornography in this jurisdiction or a similar crime in this or another jurisdiction.)
Possession of Child Pornography	A person commits the crime of possession of child pornography if the person knowingly possesses or knowingly accesses on a computer with intent to view any material that visually depicts conduct described in AS 11.41.455(a) knowing that the production of the material involved the use of a child under 18 years of age who engaged in the conduct.
	[The conduct described in AS 11.41.455(a), as noted above, includes] (1) sexual penetration; (2) the lewd touching of another person's genitals, anus, or breast; (3) the lewd

(*continued*)

	Applicable Statutes and What They Say*

touching by another person of the child's genitals, anus, or breast; (4) masturbation; . . . [or] (6) the lewd exhibition of the child's genitals.

Each film, audio, video, electronic, or electromagnetic recording, photograph, negative, slide, book, newspaper, magazine, or other material that visually or aurally depicts conduct described in AS 11.41.455(a) that is possessed or accessed . . . is a separate violation.

For possession of child pornography, the law provides an affirmative defense if the person possessed or accessed fewer than three depictions and without allowing any person other than a law enforcement agency to view the depictions, either took reasonable steps to destroy the depictions, or reported the matter to a law enforcement agency and allowed the agency access to the depictions.

(Child pornography possession constitutes a class C felony.)

Computer

An electronic device that performs logical, arithmetic, and memory functions by the manipulation of electronic, optical, or magnetic impulses, and includes all input, output, processing, storage, computer software, and communication facilities that are connected or related to a computer.

ARIZONA

ARIZ. REV. STAT. ANN. § 8-309 (West 2010)
ARIZ. REV. STAT. ANN. § 13-3501 (West 2001)
ARIZ. REV. STAT. ANN. § 13-3506.01 (West 2004)
ARIZ. REV. STAT. ANN. § 13-3551, et seq. (West 2001)

Sexual Exploitation of a Minor

A person commits sexual exploitation of a minor by knowingly: 1. Recording, filming, photographing, developing or duplicating any visual depiction in which a minor is engaged in exploitive exhibition or other sexual conduct. 2. Distributing, transporting, exhibiting, receiving, selling, purchasing, electronically transmitting, possessing or exchanging any visual depiction in which a minor is engaged in exploitive exhibition or other sexual conduct.

(Sexual exploitation of a minor is a class 2 felony.)

Luring a Minor for Sexual Exploitation

A person commits luring a minor for sexual exploitation by offering or soliciting sexual conduct with another person knowing or having reason to know that the other person is a minor.

(This is a class 3 felony.)

STATE Title of Pertinent Provision *Key definition*	Applicable Statutes and What They Say*
Aggravated Luring of a Minor for Sexual Exploitation	Both of the following: 1. Knowing the character and content of the depiction, uses an electronic communication device to transmit at least one visual depiction of material that is harmful to minors for the purpose of initiating or engaging in communication with a recipient who the person knows or has reason to know is a minor. 2. By means of the communication, offers or solicits sexual conduct with the minor. The offer or solicitation may occur before, contemporaneously with, after or as an integrated part of the transmission of the visual depiction. (Aggravated luring of a minor for sexual exploitation is a class 2 felony.)
Furnishing Harmful Items to Minors	It is unlawful for any person, with knowledge of the character of the item involved, to intentionally or knowingly transmit or send to a minor by means of electronic mail, personal messaging or any other direct internet communication an item that is harmful to minors when the person knows or believes at the time of the transmission that a minor in this state will receive the item. (Violation of this provision constitutes a class 4 felony.)
Sexting—Unlawful Use of an Electronic Communication Device by a Minor	It is unlawful for a juvenile to intentionally or knowingly use an electronic communication device to transmit or display a visual depiction of a minor that depicts explicit sexual material. (Violation of the above provision constitutes a petty offense if the juvenile transmits or displays the visual depiction to one other person. It constitutes a class 3 misdemeanor if the juvenile transmits or displays the visual depiction to more than one other person. However, violation of the above provision constitutes a class 2 misdemeanor if the defendant has been adjudicated for a prior violation of this provision or if the violation occurred after the defendant's completion of a diversion program as a result of a referral or petition charging a violation of the provision above.) It is unlawful for a juvenile to intentionally or knowingly possess a visual depiction of a minor that depicts explicit sexual material and that was transmitted to the juvenile through the use of an electronic communication device.

(*continued*)

STATE Title of Pertinent Provision *Key definition*	Applicable Statutes and What They Say*
	(Violation of the above provision constitutes a petty offense. However, violation of the above provision constitutes a class 2 misdemeanor if the defendant has been adjudicated for a prior violation of this provision or if the violation occurred after the defendant's completion of a diversion program as a result of a referral or petition charging a violation of the provision above.)
	If all of the following are determined to be applicable, the defendant has not violated the above provision against intentional/knowing possession of a visual depiction of a minor: 1. The juvenile did not solicit the visual depiction. 2. The juvenile took reasonable steps to destroy or eliminate the visual depiction or report the visual depiction to the juvenile's parent, guardian, school official or law enforcement official.)
Sexual conduct	Actual or simulated: (a) Sexual intercourse, including genital-genital, oral-genital, anal-genital or oral-anal, whether between persons of the same or opposite sex. (b) Penetration of the vagina or rectum by any object except when done as part of a recognized medical procedure . . . (d) Masturbation, for the purpose of sexual stimulation of the viewer . . . (f) Defecation or urination for the purpose of sexual stimulation of the viewer.
Simulated	Any depicting of the genitals or rectal areas that gives the appearance of sexual conduct or incipient sexual conduct.
Visual depiction	Each visual image that is contained in an undeveloped film, videotape or photograph or data stored in any form and that is capable of conversion into a visual image.
Minor	A person or persons who were under eighteen years of age at the time a visual depiction was created, adapted or modified.
Exploitive exhibition	Actual or simulated exhibition of the genitals or pubic or rectal areas of any person for the purpose of sexual stimulation of the viewer.
Electronic communication device	Any electronic device that is capable of transmitting visual depictions [including cellphones].
Harmful to minors	That quality of any description or representation, in whatever form, of nudity, sexual activity, sexual conduct, sexual excitement . . . when both: (a) To the average adult applying contemporary state standards with respect to what is suitable

STATE Title of Pertinent Provision *Key definition*	Applicable Statutes and What They Say*
	for minors, it both: (i) Appeals to the prurient interest, when taken as a whole. In order for an item as a whole to be found or intended to have an appeal to the prurient interest, it is not necessary that the item be successful in arousing or exciting any particular form of prurient interest either in the hypothetical average person, in a member of its intended and probable recipient group or in the trier of fact. (ii) Portrays the description or representation in a patently offensive way. (b) Taken as a whole does not have serious literary, artistic, political, or scientific value for minors.
Explicit sexual material	Material that depicts human genitalia or that depicts nudity, sexual activity, sexual conduct, sexual excitement.
ARKANSAS (Arkansas Protection of Children against Exploitation Act of 1979)	ARK. CODE ANN. § 5-27-301, et seq. (Michie 2008) ARK. CODE ANN. § 5-27-401, et seq. (Michie 2009) ARK. CODE ANN. § 5-27-601, et seq. (Michie 2005) ARK. CODE ANN. § 5-27-603 (Michie 2001)
Sexual Exploitation of Children	Any person who employs, uses, persuades, induces, entices, or coerces any child to engage in or who has a child assist any other person to engage in any sexually explicit conduct for the purpose of producing any visual or print medium depicting the sexually explicit conduct is guilty of a: (1) Class B felony for the first offense; and (2) Class A felony for a subsequent offense.
	With knowledge of the character of the visual or print medium involved, no person shall . . . Knowingly solicit, receive, purchase, exchange, possess, view, distribute, or control any visual or print medium depicting a child participating or engaging in sexually explicit conduct.
	(The first violation of this is a Class C felony and any subsequent violation is a Class B felony.)
Distributing, Possessing, or Viewing Matter Depicting Sexually Explicit Conduct Involving a Child	[Distributing, possessing, or viewing matter depicting sexually explicit conduct involving a child occurs when someone knowingly] procures, manufactures, gives, provides, lends, trades, mails, delivers, transfers, publishes, distributes, circulates, disseminates, presents, exhibits, advertises, offers, or agrees to offer through any means, including the internet, any photograph, film, videotape, computer program or file, video game, or any other reproduction or reconstruction that

(continued)

depicts a child or incorporates the image of a child engaging in sexually explicit conduct; [or the person knowingly] possesses or views through any means, including on the internet, any photograph, film, videotape, computer program or file, computer-generated image, video game, or any other reproduction that depicts a child or incorporates the image of a child engaging in sexually explicit conduct.

(For the first offense, the distribution, possession, or viewing of matter depicting sexually explicit conduct involving a child constitutes a Class C felony. Each subsequent violation constitutes a Class B felony.)

Sexually explicit conduct	Actual or simulated: (A) Sexual intercourse, including genital-genital, oral-genital, anal-genital, or oral-anal, whether between persons of the same or opposite sex; . . . (C) Mastur-bation . . .; or (E) Lewd exhibition of: (i) The genitals or pubic area of any person; or (ii) The breast of a female.
Child	Any person under eighteen (18) years of age.
CALIFORNIA	CAL. PENAL CODE § 288.2 (West 2011) CAL. PENAL CODE § 311.1, et seq. (West 2008) CAL. PENAL CODE § 11165.1 (West 2008)
Distribution, Possession, Preparation, Publishing, Producing, Developing, Duplicating, or Printing of Matter Depicting Sexual Conduct by a Minor	Every person who knowingly sends or causes to be sent, or brings or causes to be brought, into this state for sale or distribution, or in this state possesses, prepares, publishes, produces, develops, duplicates, or prints any representation of information, data, or image, including, but not limited to, any film, filmstrip, photograph, negative, slide, photocopy, videotape, video laser disc, computer hardware, computer software, computer floppy disc, data storage media, CD-ROM, or computer-generated equipment or any other computer-generated image that contains or incorporates in any manner, any film or filmstrip, with intent to distribute or to exhibit to, or to exchange with, others, or who offers to dis-tribute, distributes, or exhibits to, or exchanges with, others, any obscene matter, knowing that the matter depicts a person under the age of 18 years personally engaging in or personally simulating sexual conduct, as defined in Section 311.4, shall be punished either by imprisonment in the county jail for up to one year, by a fine not to exceed one thousand dollars

($1,000), or by both the fine and imprisonment, or by imprisonment in the state prison, by a fine not to exceed ten thousand dollars ($10,000), or by the fine and imprisonment. Every person who knowingly sends or causes to be sent, or brings or causes to be brought, into this state for sale or distribution, or in this state possesses, prepares, publishes, produces, or prints, with intent to distribute or to exhibit to others, or who offers to distribute, distributes, or exhibits to others, any obscene matter is for a first offense, guilty of a misdemeanor.

Every person who knowingly sends or causes to be sent, or brings or causes to be brought, into this state for sale or distribution, or in this state possesses, prepares, publishes, produces, develops, duplicates, or prints any representation of information, data, or image, including, but not limited to, any film, filmstrip, photograph, negative, slide, photocopy, videotape, video laser disc, computer hardware, computer software, computer floppy disc, data storage media, CD-ROM, or computer-generated equipment or any other computer-generated image that contains or incorporates in any manner, any film or filmstrip, with intent to distribute or exhibit to, or to exchange with, a person under 18 years of age, or who offers to distribute, distributes, or exhibits to, or exchanges with, a person under 18 years of age any matter, knowing that the matter depicts a person under the age of 18 years personally engaging in or personally simulating sexual conduct, as defined in Section 311.4, is guilty of a felony. It is *not* necessary to prove commercial consideration or that the matter is obscene in order to establish a violation of this subdivision.

Sexual Exploitation of a Child

A person is guilty of sexual exploitation of a child if he or she knowingly develops, duplicates, prints, or exchanges any representation of information, data, or image, including, but not limited to, any film, filmstrip, photograph, negative, slide, photocopy, videotape, video laser disc, computer hardware, computer software, computer floppy disc, data storage media, CD-ROM, or computer-generated equipment or any other computer-generated image that contains or incorporates in any manner, any film or filmstrip that depicts a person under the age of 18 years engaged in an act of sexual conduct.

(continued)

125

STATE Title of Pertinent Provision *Key definition*	**Applicable Statutes and What They Say***
	Sexual exploitation of a child is punishable by a fine of not more than two thousand dollars ($2,000) or by imprisonment in a county jail for not more than one year, or by both that fine and imprisonment.
Harmful Matter Sent with Intent of Seduction of Minor	Every person who, with knowledge that a person is a minor, or who fails to exercise reasonable care in ascertaining the true age of a minor, knowingly distributes, sends, causes to be sent, exhibits, or offers to distribute or exhibit by any means, including, but not limited to, live or recorded telephone messages, any harmful matter, as defined in Section 313, to a minor with the intent of arousing, appealing to, or gratifying the lust or passions or sexual desires of that person or of a minor, and with the intent or for the purpose of seducing a minor, is guilty of a public offense and shall be punished by imprisonment . . . or in a county jail. (A second/subsequent violation constitutes a felony.)
	Every person who, with knowledge that a person is a minor, knowingly distributes, sends, causes to be sent, exhibits, or offers to distribute or exhibit by electronic mail . . . any harmful matter, as defined in Section 313, to a minor with the intent of arousing, appealing to, or gratifying the lust or passions or sexual desires of that person or of a minor, and with the intent, or for the purpose of seducing a minor, is guilty of a public offense and shall be punished by imprisonment . . . or in a county jail. (A second/subsequent violation constitutes a felony punishable by imprisonment.)
Sexual conduct	Actual or simulated: sexual intercourse, oral copulation, anal intercourse, anal oral copulation, masturbation . . . penetration of the vagina or rectum by any object in a lewd or lascivious manner, exhibition of the genitals or pubic or rectal area for the purpose of sexual stimulation of the viewer, any lewd or lascivious sexual act as defined in Section 288, or excretory functions performed in a lewd or lascivious manner, whether or not any of the above conduct is performed alone or between members of the same or opposite sex.
Harmful matter	Matter, taken as a whole, which to the average person, applying contemporary statewide standards, appeals to the prurient interest, and is matter which, taken as a whole, depicts or describes in a patently offensive way sexual conduct

STATE Title of Pertinent Provision *Key definition*	**Applicable Statutes and What They Say***
	and which, taken as a whole, lacks serious literary, artistic, political, or scientific value for minors.
Lewd or lascivious sexual act	[Any act committed] upon or with the body, or any part or member thereof, of a child who is under the age of 14 years, with the intent of arousing, appealing to, or gratifying the lust, passions, or sexual desires of that person or the child. (Committing such an act is punishable by a prison term of three, six or eight years).
Simulation	The appearance of being sexual conduct.
COLORADO	Colo. Rev. Stat. Ann. § 13-21-1001, et seq. (West 2009) Colo. Rev. Stat. Ann. § 18-3-306 (West 2009) Colo. Rev. Stat. Ann. § 18-3-405.4 (West 2009) Colo. Rev. Stat. Ann. § 18-6-403 (West 2004)
Sexual Exploitation of a Child	The general assembly hereby finds and declares: That the sexual exploitation of children constitutes a wrongful invasion of the child's right of privacy and results in social, developmental, and emotional injury to the child. To protect children from sexual exploitation it is necessary to prohibit the production of material which involves or is derived from such exploitation and to exclude all such material from the channels of trade and commerce.
	The mere possession or control of any sexually exploitative material results in continuing victimization of our children by the fact that such material is a permanent record of an act or acts of sexual abuse of a child; that each time such material is shown or viewed, the child is harmed; that such material is used to break down the will and resistance of other children to encourage them to participate in similar acts of sexual abuse; that laws banning the production and distribution of such material are insufficient to halt this abuse; that in order to stop the sexual exploitation and abuse of our children, it is necessary for the state to ban the possession of any sexually exploitative materials; and that the state has a compelling interest in outlawing the possession of any sexually exploitative materials in order to protect society as a whole, and particularly the privacy, health, and emotional welfare of its children.

(continued)

Title of Pertinent
 Provision
Key definition   **Applicable Statutes and What They Say***

Sexual Exploitation of a Child	A person commits sexual exploitation of a child if, for any purpose, he or she knowingly: (a) Causes, induces, entices, or permits a child to engage in, or be used for, any explicit sexual conduct for the making of any sexually exploitative material; or (b) Prepares, arranges for, publishes, including but not limited to publishing through digital or electronic means, produces, promotes, makes, sells, finances, offers, exhibits, advertises, deals in, or distributes, including but not limited to distributing through digital or electronic means, any sexually exploitative material; or (b.5) Possesses or controls any sexually exploitative material for any purpose. . . . (c) Possesses with the intent to deal in, sell, or distribute, including but not limited to distributing through digital or electronic means, any sexually exploitative material; or (d) Causes, induces, entices, or permits a child to engage in, or be used for, any explicit sexual conduct for the purpose of producing a performance. (Sexual exploitation of a child constitutes a class 3 felony.)
Child	A person below the age of eighteen.
Sexually exploitative material	Any photograph, motion picture, video, video tape, print, negative, slide, or other mechanically, electronically, chemically, or digitally reproduced visual material that depicts a child engaged in, participating in, observing, or being used for explicit sexual conduct.
Explicit sexual conduct	Sexual intercourse, erotic fondling, erotic nudity, masturbation . . . or sexual excitement.
Erotic fondling	Touching a person's clothed or unclothed genitals or pubic area, developing or undeveloped genitals or pubic area (if the person is a child), buttocks, breasts, or developing or undeveloped breast area (if the person is a child), for the purpose of real or simulated overt sexual gratification or stimulation of one or more of the persons involved. Erotic fondling shall not be construed to include physical contact, even if affectionate, which is not for the purpose of real or simulated overt sexual gratification or stimulation of one or more of the persons involved.
Erotic nudity	The display of the human male or female genitals or pubic area, the undeveloped or developing genitals or pubic area of the human male or female child, the human breasts, or the undeveloped or developing breast area of the human child, for

STATE Title of Pertinent Provision *Key definition*	Applicable Statutes and What They Say*
	the purpose of real or simulated overt sexual gratification or stimulation of one or more of the persons involved.
Masturbation	The real or simulated touching, rubbing, or otherwise stimulating of a person's own clothed or unclothed genitals or pubic area, developing or undeveloped genitals or pubic area (if the person is a child), buttocks, breasts, or developing or undeveloped breast area (if the person is a child), by manual manipulation or self-induced or with an artificial instrument, for the purpose of real or simulated overt sexual gratification or arousal of the person.
Sexual intercourse	Real or simulated intercourse, whether genital-genital, oral-genital, anal-genital, or oral-anal, between persons of the same or opposite sex ... or with an artificial genital.
Sexual excitement	The real or simulated condition of human male or female genitals when in a state of real or simulated overt sexual stimulation or arousal.
Video tape, video or motion picture	Any material that depicts a moving image of a child engaged in, participating in, observing, or being used for explicit sexual conduct.
CONNECTICUT	CONN. GEN. STAT. ANN. § 53a-90a (West 2007) CONN. GEN. STAT. ANN. § 53a-193, et seq. (West 2007)
Obscenity	A person is guilty of obscenity when, knowing its content and character, he promotes, or possesses with intent to promote, any obscene material or performance. (This is a class B misdemeanor.)
Possession of Child Pornography—First Degree	A person is guilty of possessing child pornography in the first degree when such person knowingly possesses (1) fifty or more visual depictions of child pornography. Possessing child pornography in the first degree is a class B felony and any person found guilty under this section shall be sentenced to a term of imprisonment of which five years of the sentence imposed may not be suspended or reduced by the court.
Possession of Child Pornography—Second Degree	A person is guilty of possessing child pornography in the second degree when such person knowingly possesses twenty or more but fewer than fifty visual depictions of child pornography. Possessing child pornography in the second degree is a class C felony and any person found guilty under this section shall be

(continued)

STATE Title of Pertinent Provision Key definition	Applicable Statutes and What They Say*
	sentenced to a term of imprisonment of which two years of the sentence imposed may not be suspended or reduced by the court.
Possession of Child Pornography—Third Degree	A person is guilty of possessing child pornography in the third degree when such person knowingly possesses fewer than twenty visual depictions of child pornography.
	Possessing child pornography in the third degree is a class D felony and any person found guilty under this section shall be sentenced to a term of imprisonment of which one year of the sentence imposed may not be suspended or reduced by the court.
Possession of Child Pornography by a Minor	No person who is thirteen years of age or older but under eighteen years of age may knowingly possess any visual depiction of child pornography that the subject of such visual depiction knowingly and voluntarily transmitted by means of an electronic communication device to such person and in which the subject of such visual depiction is a person thirteen years of age or older but under sixteen years of age. (This is a class A misdemeanor.)
Transmission of Child Pornography by a Minor	No person who is thirteen years of age or older but under sixteen years of age may knowingly and voluntarily transmit by means of an electronic communication device a visual depiction of child pornography in which such person is the subject of such visual depiction to another person who is thirteen years of age or older but under eighteen years of age. (This is a class A misdemeanor.)
Importing Child Pornography	A person is guilty of importing child pornography when, with intent to promote child pornography, such person knowingly imports or causes to be imported into the state three or more visual depictions of child pornography of known content and character.
	Importing child pornography is a class B felony and any person found guilty under this section shall be sentenced to a term of imprisonment of which five years of the sentence imposed may not be suspended or reduced by the court.
	Affirmative defenses to the first, second and third degree possessing child pornography crimes as well as to the

STATE Title of Pertinent Provision Key definition	Applicable Statutes and What They Say*
	possessing or transmitting of child pornography by a minor crime include either of the following two defenses: Elements of defense #1: (i) the defendant had possession of fewer than three visual depictions of child pornography; and (ii) the defendant did not knowingly purchase, procure, solicit or request such visual depictions or knowingly take any other action to cause such visual depictions to come into the defendant's possession; and (iii) the defendant promptly and in good faith, and without retaining or allowing any person, other than a law enforcement agency, to access any visual depiction or copy thereof, took reasonable steps to destroy each such visual depiction or reported the matter to a law enforcement agency and afforded that agency access to each such visual depiction.
	Elements of defense #2: (i) the defendant possessed a visual depiction of a nude person under sixteen years of age; and (ii) the possession was for a bona fide artistic, medical, scientific, educational, religious, governmental or judicial purpose.
Promote	Manufacture, issue, sell, give, provide, lend, mail, deliver, transfer, transmit, publish, distribute, circulate, disseminate, present, exhibit, advertise, produce, direct or participate in.
Material	Anything tangible which is capable of being used or adapted to arouse prurient, shameful or morbid interest, whether through the medium of reading, observation, sound or in any other manner.
Electronic communication device	Includes cellphones.
Child pornography	Any visual depiction including any photograph, film, videotape, picture or computer-generated image or picture, whether made or produced by electronic, mechanical or other means, of sexually explicit conduct, where the production of such visual depiction involves the use of a person under sixteen years of age engaging in sexually explicit conduct.

(continued)

STATE Title of Pertinent Provision *Key definition*	Applicable Statutes and What They Say*
Sexually explicit conduct	Actual or simulated (A) sexual intercourse, including genital-genital, oral-genital, anal-genital or oral-anal physical contact, whether between persons of the same or opposite sex, or with an artificial genital . . . (C) masturbation . . . or (E) lascivious exhibition of the genitals or pubic area of any person.
DELAWARE	DEL. CODE ANN. tit. 11, § 1103, et seq. (2007)
Sexual Exploitation of a Child	A person is guilty of sexual exploitation of a child when . . . the person knowingly, photographs or films a child engaging in a prohibited sexual act or in the simulation of such an act, or otherwise knowingly creates a visual depiction of a child engaging in a prohibited sexual act or in the simulation of such an act.
	(Sexual exploitation of a child constitutes a class B felony. However, anyone who is convicted of a subsequent or second violation of the sexual exploitation of a child law shall, upon such second or subsequent conviction, be sentenced to life imprisonment.)
Dealing in Child Pornography	[Dealing in child pornography occurs when someone:] (1) knowingly ships, transmits, mails or transports by any means, including by computer or any other electronic or digital method, any book, magazine, periodical, pamphlet, video or film depicting a child engaging in a prohibited sexual act or in the simulation of such an act, or knowingly ships, transmits, mails or transports by any means, including by computer or any other electronic or digital method, any other visual depiction of a child engaging in a prohibited sexual act or in the simulation of such an act; (2) knowingly distributes or disseminates, by means of computer or any other electronic or digital method, or by shows or viewings, any motion picture, video or other visual depiction of a child engaging in a prohibited sexual act or the simulation of such an act. The possession or showing of such motion pictures shall create a rebuttable presumption of ownership thereof for the purposes of distribution or dissemination; (3) intentionally compiles, enters, accesses, transmits, receives, exchanges, disseminates, stores, makes, prints, reproduces or otherwise possesses any photograph, image, file, data or other

STATE Title of Pertinent Provision *Key definition*	**Applicable Statutes and What They Say***
	visual depiction of a child engaging in a prohibited sexual act or in the simulation of such an act; (4) knowingly advertises, promotes, presents, describes, transmits or distributes any visual depiction, exhibition, display or performance with intent to create or convey the impression that such visual depiction, exhibition, display or performance is or contains a depiction of a child engaging in a prohibited sexual act or in the simulation of such an act.
	(Dealing in child pornography constitutes a class B felony.)
Possession of Child Pornography	A person is guilty of possession of child pornography when . . . the person knowingly possesses any visual depiction of a child engaging in a prohibited sexual act or in the simulation of such an act.
	(Possession of child pornography constitutes a class F felony.)
Child	One who is 18 years old or less.
Prohibited sexual act	(1) Sexual intercourse; (2) Anal intercourse; (3) Masturbation; . . . (7) Fellatio; (8) Cunnilingus; (9) Nudity, if such nudity is to be depicted for the purpose of the sexual stimulation or the sexual gratification of any individual who may view such depiction; (10) Sexual contact; (11) Lascivious exhibition of the genitals or pubic area of any child; (12) Any other act which is intended to be a depiction or simulation of any act described in this subsection.
FLORIDA	FLA. STAT. ANN. § 775.0847 (West 2007) FLA. STAT. ANN. § 827.071 (West 2011) FLA. STAT. ANN. § 847.001, et seq. (West 2008) FLA. STAT. ANN. § 847.0135 (West 2009)
Possession or Distribution of Obscenity	[A person commits a misdemeanor of the first degree if he/she] knowingly sells, lends, gives away, distributes, transmits, shows, or transmutes, or offers to sell, lend, give away, distribute, transmit, show, or transmute, or has in his or her possession, custody, or control with intent to sell, lend, give away, distribute, transmit, show, transmute, or advertise in any manner, any obscene . . . picture, drawing, photograph, motion picture film, figure, image, phonograph record, or wire

(*continued*)

Key definition	Applicable Statutes and What They Say*
	or tape or other recording, or any written, printed, or recorded matter of any such character which may or may not require mechanical or other means to be transmuted into auditory, visual, or sensory representations of such character, or any article or instrument for obscene use, or purporting to be for obscene use or purpose; or who knowingly designs, copies, draws, photographs, poses for, writes, prints, publishes, or in any manner whatsoever manufactures or prepares any such material, matter, article, or thing of any such character.
	(It is a felony of the third degree, however, if the violation is based on materials that depict a minor engaged in any act or conduct that is harmful to minors.)
	A person may not knowingly sell, rent, loan, give away, distribute, transmit, or show any obscene material to a minor.
	(Anyone who violates this is guilty of felony of the third degree.)
Possession of Obscenity	[A person commits a misdemeanor of the second degree who] knowingly has in his or her possession, custody, or control any obscene ... picture, drawing, photograph, motion picture film, film, ... any figure, image, phonograph record, or wire or tape or other recording, or any written, printed, or recorded matter of any such character which may or may not require mechanical or other means to be transmuted into auditory, visual, or sensory representations of such character, or any article or instrument for obscene use, or purporting to be for obscene use or purpose, without intent to sell, lend, give away, distribute, transmit, show, transmute, or advertise the same.
	(It is a felony of the third degree, however, if the violation is based on materials that depict a minor engaged in any act or conduct that is harmful to minors.)
Transmission of Child Pornography by Electronic Device or Equipment	Any person in this state who knew or reasonably should have known that he or she was transmitting child pornography ... to another person in this state or in another jurisdiction commits a felony of the third degree.
	Any person in any jurisdiction other than this state who knew or reasonably should have known that he or she was transmitting child pornography ... to any person in this state commits a felony of the third degree.

STATE Title of Pertinent Provision *Key definition*	Applicable Statutes and What They Say*
Transmission of Material Harmful to Minors to a Minor by Electronic Device	Any person who knew or believed that he or she was transmitting an image, information, or data that is harmful to minors . . . to a specific individual known by the defendant to be a minor commits a felony of the third degree.
	Any person in any jurisdiction other than this state who knew or believed that he or she was transmitting an image, information, or data that is harmful to minors, as defined in s. 847.001, to a specific individual known by the defendant to be a minor commits a felony of the third degree.
Sexual Performance by a Child	A person is guilty of the use of a child in a sexual performance if, knowing the character and content thereof, he or she employs, authorizes, or induces a child less than 18 years of age to engage in a sexual performance.
	(Violation of the above provision constitutes a felony of the second degree.)
	A person is guilty of promoting a sexual performance by a child when, knowing the character and content thereof, he or she produces, directs, or promotes any performance which includes sexual conduct by a child less than 18 years of age.
	(Violation of the above provision constitutes a felony of the second degree.)
	It is unlawful for any person to possess with the intent to promote any photograph, motion picture, exhibition, show, representation, or other presentation which, in whole or in part, includes any sexual conduct by a child.
	(Violation of the above provision constitutes a felony of the second degree.)
	It is unlawful for any person to knowingly possess, control, or intentionally view a photograph, motion picture, exhibition, show, representation, image, data, computer depiction, or other presentation which, in whole or in part, he or she knows to include any sexual conduct by a child. The possession, control, or intentional viewing of *each* such photograph, motion picture, exhibition, show, image, data, computer depiction, representation, or presentation is a separate offense.
	(Violation of the above provision constitutes a felony of the third degree.)

(continued)

STATE	
Title of Pertinent	
Provision	
Key definition	**Applicable Statutes and What They Say***

Sexting	A minor commits the offense of sexting if he or she knowingly: (a) Uses a computer, or any other device capable of electronic data transmission or distribution, to transmit or distribute to another minor any photograph or video of any person which depicts nudity . . . and is harmful to minors . . . (b) Possesses a photograph or video of any person that was transmitted or distributed by another minor which depicts nudity . . . and is harmful to minors.
	A minor determined to have violated the above provision:
	(a) Commits a noncriminal violation for a first violation, punishable by 8 hours of community service or, if ordered by the court in lieu of community service, a $60 fine. The court may also order the minor to participate in suitable training or instruction in lieu of, or in addition to, community service or a fine. (b) Commits a misdemeanor of the first degree for a violation that occurs after being found to have committed a noncriminal violation for sexting, punishable as provided in s. 775.082 or s. 775.083, Florida Statutes. (c) Commits a felony of the third degree for a violation that occurs after being found to have committed a misdemeanor of the first degree for sexting, punishable as provided in s. 775.082, s. 775.083, or s. 775.084, Florida Statutes.
	The transmission or distribution of multiple photographs or videos prohibited [under paragraph (a) above constitutes a] single offense if the photographs or videos were transmitted or distributed within the same 24-hour period.
	The possession of multiple photographs or videos that were transmitted or distributed by a minor prohibited under paragraph (b) above constitutes a single offense if the photographs or videos were transmitted or distributed by a minor in the same 24-hour period.
	A minor does not commit the crime of sexting if all the following are applicable:
	1. The minor did not solicit the photograph or video.
	2. The minor took reasonable steps to report the photograph or video to the minor's legal guardian or to a school or law

STATE Title of Pertinent Provision *Key definition*	Applicable Statutes and What They Say*
	enforcement official. 3. The minor did not transmit or distribute the photograph or video to a third party.
	Florida law specifically notes that the prosecution of a minor for sexting does not prohibit the prosecution of a minor for a violation of any law of this state if the photograph or video that depicts nudity also includes the depiction of sexual conduct or sexual excitement.
	(In essence, the law does not prohibit the prosecution of minors for other crimes identified above.)
Child	Someone below the age of 18.
Child pornography	Any image depicting a minor engaged in sexual conduct.
Sexual conduct	Actual or simulated sexual intercourse, deviate sexual intercourse, . . . masturbation . . .; actual lewd exhibition of the genitals; actual physical contact with a person's clothed or unclothed genitals, pubic area, buttocks, or, if such person is a female, breast with the intent to arouse or gratify the sexual desire of either party.
Deviate sexual intercourse	Sexual conduct between persons not married to each other consisting of contact between the penis and the anus, the mouth and the penis, or the mouth and the vulva.
Transmit (with respect to the crime transmission of child pornography by electronic device or equipment)	The act of sending and causing to be delivered any image, information, or data from one or more persons or places to one or more other persons or places over or through any medium, including the Internet, by use of any electronic equipment or device.
Transmit (with respect to the crime transmission of material harmful to minors to a minor by electronic device)	To send to a specific individual known by the defendant to be a minor via electronic mail.
Harmful to minors (other than for the crime transmission of material harmful	Any reproduction, imitation, characterization, description, exhibition, presentation, or representation, of whatever kind or form, depicting nudity, sexual conduct, or sexual excitement when it:

(continued)

STATE Title of Pertinent Provision *Key definition*	Applicable Statutes and What They Say*
to minors to a minor by electronic device)	(a) Predominantly appeals to a prurient, shameful, or morbid interest; (b) Is patently offensive to prevailing standards in the adult community as a whole with respect to what is suitable material or conduct for minors; and (c) Taken as a whole, is without serious literary, artistic, political, or scientific value for minors.
Sexual excitement	The condition of the human male or female genitals when in a state of sexual stimulation or arousal.
Nudity	The showing of the human male or female genitals, pubic area, or buttocks with less than a fully opaque covering; or the showing of the female breast with less than a fully opaque covering of any portion thereof below the top of the nipple; or the depiction of covered male genitals in a discernibly turgid state.
Found to have committed	A determination of guilt that is the result of a plea or trial, or a finding of delinquency that is the result of a plea or an adjudicatory hearing, regardless of whether adjudication is withheld.
Promote	To procure, manufacture, issue, sell, give, provide, lend, mail, deliver, transfer, transmute, publish, distribute, circulate, disseminate, present, exhibit, or advertise or to offer or agree to do the same.
Sexual performance	Any performance or part thereof which includes sexual conduct by a child of less than 18 years of age.
Performance	Any play, motion picture, photograph, or dance or any other visual representation exhibited before an audience.
GEORGIA	GA. CODE ANN. § 16-12-100, et seq. (2003) GA. CODE ANN. § 16-12-101, et seq. (2007)
Sexual Exploitation of Children	It is unlawful for any person knowingly to employ, use, persuade, induce, entice, or coerce any minor to engage in or assist any other person to engage in any sexually explicit conduct for the purpose of producing any visual medium depicting such conduct.
	It is unlawful for any person knowingly to create, reproduce, publish, promote, sell, distribute, give, exhibit, or possess with intent to sell or distribute any visual medium which depicts a

STATE Title of Pertinent Provision *Key definition*	**Applicable Statutes and What They Say***
	minor or a portion of a minor's body engaged in any sexually explicit conduct.
	It is unlawful for any person knowingly to bring or cause to be brought into this state any material which depicts a minor or a portion of a minor's body engaged in any sexually explicit conduct.
	It is unlawful for any person knowingly to possess or control any material which depicts a minor or a portion of a minor's body engaged in any sexually explicit conduct.
	(Sexual exploitation of children is a felony and is punishable by a prison term of not less than five nor more than 20 years and by a fine of not more than $100,000.00. In the event, however, that the person so convicted is a member of the immediate family of the victim, no fine shall be imposed.)
Electronically Furnishing Obscene Materials	A person commits the crime of electronically furnishing obscene materials to minors if: (1) Knowing or having good reason to know the character of the material furnished, the person electronically furnishes to an individual whom the person knows or should have known is a minor: (A) Any picture, photograph, drawing, or similar visual representation or image of a person or portion of a human body which depicts sexually explicit nudity, sexual conduct, . . . and which is harmful to minors; or (B) Any written or aural matter that contains material of the nature described in subparagraph (A) of this paragraph or contains explicit verbal descriptions or narrative accounts of sexual conduct, sexual excitement; . . . (2) The offensive portions of the material electronically furnished to the minor are not merely an incidental part of an otherwise nonoffending whole; (3) The material furnished to the minor, taken as a whole, lacks serious literary, artistic, political, or scientific value; and (4) The material furnished to the minor, taken as a whole, is harmful to minors in that it appeals to and incites prurient interest. (Electronically furnishing obscene materials to minors is a misdemeanor of a high and aggravated nature.)

(*continued*)

STATE Title of Pertinent Provision *Key definition*	Applicable Statutes and What They Say*
Computer or Electronic Pornography and Child Exploitation Prevention Act of 2007	A person commits the offense of computer or electronic pornography if such person intentionally or willfully: (A) Compiles, enters into, or transmits by computer or other electronic device; (B) Makes, prints, publishes, or reproduces by other computer or other electronic device; (C) Causes or allows to be entered into or transmitted by computer or other electronic device; or (D) Buys, sells, receives, exchanges, or disseminates any notice, statement, or advertisement, or any child's name, telephone number, place of residence, physical characteristics, or other descriptive or identifying information for the purpose of offering or soliciting sexual conduct of or with an identifiable child or the visual depiction of such conduct. (A person convicted of computer or electronic pornography shall be punished by a fine of not more than $10,000.00 and by imprisonment for not less than one nor more than 20 years.)
Unlawful Disposition of Material to Minors	It shall be unlawful for any person knowingly to sell or loan for monetary consideration or otherwise furnish or disseminate to a minor . . . any picture, photograph, drawing, sculpture, motion picture film, or similar visual representation or image of a person or portion of the human body which depicts sexually explicit nudity, sexual conduct, . . . and which is harmful to minors. (Violation of this constitutes a misdemeanor of a high and aggravated nature.)
Sexually explicit conduct	Actual or simulated: (A) Sexual intercourse, including genital-genital, oral-genital, anal-genital, or oral-anal, whether between persons of the same or opposite sex; . . . (C) Mastur-bation; (D) Lewd exhibition of the genitals or pubic area of any person; . . . (G) Physical contact in an act of apparent sex-ual stimulation or gratification with any person's unclothed genitals, pubic area, or buttocks or with a female's nude breasts; (H) Defecation or urination for the purpose of sexual stimulation of the viewer; or (I) Penetration of the vagina or rectum by any object except when done as part of a recog-nized medical procedure.

STATE Title of Pertinent Provision *Key definition*	Applicable Statutes and What They Say*
Minor	Someone under the age of 18. However, for purposes of the Computer or Electronic Pornography and Child Exploitation Prevention Act of 2007, minor refers to someone less than 16 years old.
Sexually explicit nudity	A state of undress so as to expose the human male or female genitals, pubic area, or buttocks with less than a full opaque covering, or the showing of the female breast with less than a fully opaque covering of any portion thereof below the top of the nipple, or the depiction of covered or uncovered male genitals in a discernibly turgid state.
Sexual conduct	Human masturbation, sexual intercourse, or any touching of the genitals, pubic areas, or buttocks of the human male or female or the breasts of the female, whether alone or between members of the same or opposite sex . . . in an act of apparent sexual stimulation or gratification.
Sexual excitement	The condition of human male or female genitals or the breasts of the female when in a state of sexual stimulation.
Harmful to minors	That quality of description or representation, in whatever form, of nudity, sexual conduct, sexual excitement, . . . when it: (A) Taken as a whole, predominantly appeals to the prurient, shameful, or morbid interest of minors; (B) Is patently offensive to prevailing standards in the adult community as a whole with respect to what is suitable material for minors; and (C) Is, when taken as a whole, lacking in serious literary, artistic, political, or scientific value for minors.
Electronic device	Any device used for the purpose of communicating with a child for sexual purposes or any device used to visually depict a child engaged in sexually explicit conduct, store any image or audio of a child engaged in sexually explicit conduct, or transmit any audio or visual image of a child for sexual purposes. Such term may include, but shall not be limited to, a computer, cellular phone, thumb drive, video game system, or any other electronic device that can be used in furtherance of exploiting a child for sexual purposes.

(continued)

STATE Title of Pertinent Provision *Key definition*	Applicable Statutes and What They Say*
HAWAII	Haw. Rev. Stat. § 707-750, et seq. (2002) Haw. Rev. Stat. § 708-893 (2006) Stat. § 712-1210, et seq. (2005)
Promoting Child Abuse in the First Degree	A person commits the offense of promoting child abuse in the first degree if, knowing or having reason to know its character and content, the person: (a) Produces or participates in the preparation of child pornography; (b) Produces or participates in the preparation of pornographic material that employs, uses, or otherwise contains a minor engaging in or assisting others to engage in sexual conduct; or (c) Engages in a pornographic performance that employs, uses, or otherwise contains a minor engaging in or assisting others to engage in sexual conduct. (Promoting child abuse in the first degree constitutes a class A felony.)
Promoting Child Abuse in the Second Degree	A person commits the offense of promoting child abuse in the second degree if, knowing or having reason to know its character and content, the person: (a) Disseminates child pornography; (b) Reproduces child pornography with intent to disseminate; (c) Disseminates any book, magazine, periodical, film, videotape, computer disk, or any other material that contains an image of child pornography; or (d) Disseminates any pornographic material which employs, uses, or otherwise contains a minor engaging in or assisting others to engage in sexual conduct. (Promoting child abuse in the second degree constitutes a class B felony.)
Promoting Child Abuse in the Third Degree	A person commits the offense of promoting child abuse in the third degree if, knowing or having reason to know its character and content, the person possesses: (a) Child pornography; (b) Any book, magazine, periodical, film, videotape, computer disk, electronically stored data, or any other material that contains an image of child pornography; or

	Applicable Statutes and What They Say*
	(c) Any pornographic material that employs, uses, or otherwise contains a minor engaging in or assisting others to engage in sexual conduct.
	(Promoting child abuse in the third degree constitutes a class C felony.)
	Hawaii law provides an affirmative defense to promoting child abuse in the third degree if the defendant shows all of the following: (a) Possessed less than three images of child pornography; and (b) Promptly and in good faith, and without retaining or allowing any person, other than a law enforcement agency, to access any image or copy thereof: (i) Took reasonable steps to destroy each such image; or (ii) Reported the matter to a law enforcement agency and afforded that agency access to each such image.
Indecent Electronic Display to a Child	Any person who intentionally masturbates or intentionally exposes the genitals in a lewd or lascivious manner live over a computer online service, internet service, or local bulletin board service and who knows or should know or has reason to believe that the transmission is viewed on a computer or other electronic device by: (a) A minor known by the person to be under the age of eighteen years; (b) Another person, in reckless disregard of the risk that the other person is under the age of eighteen years, and the other person is under the age of eighteen years; or (c) Another person who represents that person to be under the age of eighteen years, is guilty of indecent electronic display to a child.
	(Indecent electronic display to a child constitutes a misdemeanor.)
Promoting Pornography for Minors	A person commits the offense of promoting pornography for minors if . . . knowing its character and content, the person disseminates to a minor material which is pornographic for minors.
	(Promoting pornography for minors constitutes a class C felony.)

(continued)

STATE
Title of Pertinent
Provision
Key definition   Applicable Statutes and What They Say*

Failure to Maintain   A person commits the offense of failure to maintain age
Age Verification   verification records of sexual performers if the person
Records of Sexual   knowingly produces any pornographic performance, book,
Performers   magazine, periodical, film, videotape, computer image, or
                           other matter that contains one or more pornographic visual
                           depictions made after June 30, 2002, of sexual conduct and:
                           (a) Knowingly fails to create and maintain age verification
                           records for each sexual performer;
                           (b) Knowingly makes or causes to be made any false entry into
                           the age verification records of sexual performers required by
                           this section; or
                           (c) Knowingly fails to produce the age verification records of
                           sexual performers required by this section, upon request by a
                           law enforcement officer for the purpose of verifying the age of
                           a sexual performer.

                           (The failure to maintain age verification records of sexual
                           performers constitutes a class C felony.)

Failure to Affix   A person commits the offense of failure to affix information
Information   disclosing location of age verification records of sexual
Disclosing Location   performers if the person knowingly produces any
of Age Verification   pornographic book, magazine, periodical, film, videotape,
Records of Sexual   computer image, or other matter that contains one or more
Performers   pornographic visual depictions made after June 30, 2002, of
                          sexual conduct and fails to affix to each copy a statement
                          describing where any records required by section 712-1218
                          [the age verification records of sexual performers mentioned
                          above] with respect to all performers depicted in that copy of
                          the matter may be located, including the current address and
                          telephone number of the custodian of those records.

                          (The failure to affix information disclosing location of age
                          verification records of sexual performers constitutes a
                          class C felony.)

Disseminating Visual   A person commits the offense of disseminating visual
Depiction of Sexual   depiction of sexual conduct without affixed information
Conduct without   disclosing location of age verification records of sexual
Affixed Information   performers if the person knowingly disseminates, sells, or
Disclosing Location   otherwise transfers, or offers for sale or transfer, any book,
of Age Verification   magazine, periodical, film, videotape, computer image, or

	Applicable Statutes and What They Say*
Records of Sexual Performers	other matter that contains one or more visual depictions made after June 30, 2002, of sexual conduct, and that does not have affixed thereto a statement describing where the age verification records required by section 712-1218 [the age verification records of sexual performers mentioned above] may be located; provided that this section shall not be construed to impose a duty upon any persons to determine the accuracy of the contents of the affixed statement or of the records required to be kept at that location.
	(Disseminating visual depiction of sexual conduct without affixed information disclosing location of age verification records of sexual performers constitutes a misdemeanor.)
Minor	Someone under 18 years old. For purposes of the crimes promoting pornography for minors, failure to maintain age verification records of sexual performers, failure to affix information disclosing location of age verification records of sexual performers, or disseminating visual depiction of sexual conduct without affixed information disclosing location of age verification records of sexual performers, however, minor refers to someone under 16 years old.
Child pornography	Any pornographic visual representation, including any photograph, film, video, picture, or computer or computer-generated image or picture, whether made or produced by electronic, mechanical, or other means, of sexual conduct, if: (a) The pornographic production of such visual representation involves the use of a minor engaging in sexual conduct; or (b) The pornographic visual representation has been created, adapted, or modified to appear that an identifiable minor is engaging in sexual conduct.
Lascivious	Tending to incite lust, to deprave the morals in respect to sexual relations, or to produce voluptuous or lewd emotions in the average person, applying contemporary community standards.
Sexual conduct	Acts of masturbation, homosexuality, lesbianism, . . . sexual penetration, deviate sexual intercourse, . . . or lascivious exhibition of the genital or pubic area of a minor.

(continued)

STATE **Title of Pertinent Provision** *Key definition*	**Applicable Statutes and What They Say***
Disseminate	To publish, sell, distribute, transmit, exhibit, present material, mail, ship, or transport by any means, including by computer, or to offer or agree to do the same.
Pornographic	Any material or performance is pornographic if all of the following coalesce: (a) The average person, applying contemporary community standards would find that, taken as a whole, it appeals to the prurient interest. (b) It depicts or describes sexual conduct in a patently offensive way. (c) Taken as a whole, it lacks serious literary, artistic, political, or scientific merit.
Pornographic for minors	(1) It is primarily devoted to explicit and detailed narrative accounts of sexual excitement, sexual conduct . . .; and: (a) It is presented in such a manner that the average person applying contemporary community standards, would find that, taken as a whole, it appeals to a minor's prurient interest; and (b) Taken as a whole, it lacks serious literary, artistic, political, or scientific value; or (2) It contains any photograph, drawing, or similar visual representation of any person of the age of puberty or older revealing such person with less than a fully opaque covering of his or her genitals and pubic area, or depicting such person in a state of sexual excitement or engaged in acts of sexual conduct . . .; and: (a) It is presented in such a manner that the average person, applying contemporary community standards, would find that, taken as a whole, it appeals to a minor's prurient interest; and (b) Taken as a whole, it lacks serious literary, artistic, political, or scientific value.
Nude	Unclothed or in attire, including but not limited to sheer or see-through attire, so as to expose to view any portion of the pubic hair, anus, cleft of the buttocks, genitals or any portion of the female breast below the top of the areola.
Sexual excitement	Condition of the human male or female genitals when in a state of sexual stimulation or arousal.

STATE Title of Pertinent Provision *Key definition*	**Applicable Statutes and What They Say***
Sexual performer	Any person portrayed in a pornographic visual depiction engaging in, or assisting another person to engage in, sexual conduct.
Age verification records of sexual performers	Individually identifiable records pertaining to every sexual performer portrayed in a visual depiction of sexual conduct, which include:
	(1) Each performer's name and date of birth, as ascertained by the producer's personal examination of a performer's valid driver's license, official state identification card, or passport;
	(2) A certified copy of each performer's valid driver's license, official state identification card, or passport; and
	(3) Any name ever used by each performer including, but not limited to, maiden name, alias, nickname, stage name, or professional name.
IDAHO	Idaho Code Ann. § 18-1507 (Michie 2006) Idaho Code Ann. § 18-1507A (Michie 2006) Idaho Code Ann. § 18-1514, et seq. (Michie 2011)
Idaho Legislature's Strong Statement on Possession of Sexually Exploitative Material for Other Than a Commercial Purpose	It is the policy of the legislature in enacting this section to protect children from the physical and psychological damage caused by their being used in photographic representations of sexual conduct which involves children. It is, therefore, the intent of the legislature to penalize possession of photographic representations of sexual conduct which involves children in order to protect the identity of children who are victimized by involvement in the photographic representations, and to protect children from future involvement in photographic representations of sexual conduct.
Possession of Sexually Exploitative Material for Other Than a Commercial Purpose	Every person who knowingly and willfully has in his possession any sexually exploitative material as defined in section 18-1507, Idaho Code, for other than a commercial purpose, is guilty of a felony, and shall be punished by imprisonment in the state prison for a period not to exceed ten (10) years and by a fine not to exceed ten thousand dollars ($10,000).
Disseminating Material Harmful to Minors	A person is guilty of disseminating material harmful to minors when: 1. He knowingly gives or makes available to a minor or promotes or possesses with intent to promote to minors, or he

(*continued*)

	Applicable Statutes and What They Say*
	knowingly sells or loans to a minor for monetary consideration: (a) Any picture, photograph, drawing, sculpture, motion picture film, or similar visual representation or image of a person or portion of the human body which depicts nudity, sexual conduct . . . and which is harmful to minors; or (b) Any book, pamphlet, magazine, printed matter however reproduced, or sound recording which contains any matter enumerated in paragraph (a) hereof, or explicit and detailed verbal descriptions or narrative accounts of sexual excitement, sexual conduct . . . and which, taken as a whole, is harmful to minors; or (c) Any other material harmful to minors. Disseminating material harmful to minors is a misdemeanor punishable by confinement in the county jail not to exceed one (1) year, or by a fine not to exceed one thousand dollars ($1,000), or by both such fine and jail sentence.
Child or minor	Someone below 18 years old.
Sexually exploitative material	Any photograph, motion picture, videotape, print, negative, slide, or other mechanically, electronically, or chemically reproduced visual material which depicts a child engaged in, participating in, observing, or being used for explicit sexual conduct.
Explicit sexual conduct	Sexual intercourse, erotic fondling, erotic nudity, masturbation, . . . sexual excitement.
Masturbation	Real or simulated touching, rubbing, or otherwise stimulating of a person's own clothed or unclothed genitals or pubic area, developing or undeveloped genitals or pubic area (if the person is a child), buttocks, breasts (if the person is a female), or developing or undeveloped breast area (if the person is a female child), by manual manipulation or self-induced or with an artificial instrument, for the purpose of real or simulated overt sexual gratification or arousal of the person.
Erotic nudity	Display of the human male or female genitals or pubic area, the undeveloped or developing genitals or pubic area of the human male or female child, the human female breasts, or the undeveloped or developing breast area of the human female child, for the purpose of real or simulated overt sexual gratification or stimulation of one (1) or more of the persons involved.

STATE Title of Pertinent Provision *Key definition*	**Applicable Statutes and What They Say***
Nudity	Showing of the human male or female genitals, pubic area or buttocks with less than a full opaque covering, or the showing of the female breast with less than a full opaque covering of any portion thereof below the top of the nipple, or the depiction of covered male genitals in a discernibly turgid state.
Sexual intercourse	Real or simulated intercourse, whether genital-genital, oral-genital, anal-genital, or oral-anal, between persons of the same or opposite sex, . . . or with an artificial genital.
Sexual excitement	Real or simulated condition of human male or female genitals when in a state of real or simulated overt sexual stimulation or arousal.
Erotic fondling	Touching a person's clothed or unclothed genitals or pubic area, developing or undeveloped genitals or pubic area (if the person is a child), buttocks, breasts (if the person is a female), or developing or undeveloped breast area (if the person is a female child), for the purpose of real or simulated overt sexual gratification or stimulation of one (1) or more of the persons involved. Erotic fondling shall not be construed to include physical contact, even if affectionate, which is not for the purpose of real or simulated overt sexual gratification or stimulation of one (1) or more of the persons involved.
Sexual conduct	Any act of masturbation, homosexuality, sexual intercourse, or physical contact with a person's clothed or unclothed genitals, pubic area, buttocks or, if such person be a female, the breast.
Harmful to minors	One or both of the following: (a) The quality of any material or of any performance or of any description or representation, in whatever form, of nudity, sexual conduct, sexual excitement, . . . when it: (1) appeals to the prurient interest of minors as judged by the average person, applying contemporary community standards; and (2) depicts or describes representations or descriptions of nudity, sexual conduct, sexual excitement, . . . which are patently offensive to prevailing standards in the adult community with respect to what is suitable material for minors and includes, but is not limited to, patently offensive representations or descriptions of:

(continued)

149

STATE Title of Pertinent Provision *Key definition*	Applicable Statutes and What They Say*
	(i) intimate sexual acts, normal or perverted, actual or simulated; or (ii) masturbation, excretory functions or lewd exhibition of the genitals or genital area. Nothing herein contained is intended to include or proscribe any matter which, when considered as a whole, and in context in which it is used, possesses serious literary, artistic, political or scientific value for minors, according to prevailing standards in the adult community, with respect to what is suitable for minors. (b) The quality of any material or of any performance, or of any description or representation, in whatever form, which, as a whole, has the dominant effect of substantially arousing sexual desires in persons under the age of eighteen (18) years.
ILLINOIS	705 Ill. Comp. Stat. Ann. 405/3-40b (West 2011) 720 Ill. Comp. Stat. Ann. 5/11-20.1, et seq. (West 2012)
Child Pornography	A person commits child pornography who:
	(1) films, videotapes, photographs, or otherwise depicts or portrays by means of any similar visual medium or reproduction or depicts by computer any child whom he or she knows or reasonably should know to be under the age of 18 and at least 13 years of age or any severely or profoundly mentally retarded person where such child or severely or profoundly mentally retarded person is: (i) actually or by simulation engaged in any act of sexual penetration or sexual conduct with any person . . . .; or (ii) actually or by simulation engaged in any act of sexual penetration or sexual conduct involving the sex organs of the child or severely or profoundly mentally retarded person and the mouth, anus, or sex organs of another person . . .; or which involves the mouth, anus or sex organs of the child or severely or profoundly mentally retarded person and the sex organs of another person . . .; or (iii) actually or by simulation engaged in any act of masturbation; or (iv) actually or by simulation portrayed as being the object of, or otherwise engaged in, any act of lewd fondling, touching, or caressing involving another person . . .; or (v) actually or by simulation engaged in any act of excretion or urination within a sexual context; . . . or (vii) depicted or portrayed in any pose, posture or setting involving a

Key definition	Applicable Statutes and What They Say*
	lewd exhibition of the unclothed or transparently clothed genitals, pubic area, buttocks, or, if such person is female, a fully or partially developed breast of the child or other person; or
(2) with the knowledge of the nature or content thereof, reproduces, disseminates, offers to disseminate, exhibits or possesses with intent to disseminate any film, videotape, photograph or other similar visual reproduction or depiction by computer of any child or severely or profoundly mentally retarded person whom the person knows or reasonably should know to be under the age of 18 and at least 13 years of age or to be a severely or profoundly mentally retarded person, engaged in any activity described in subparagraphs (i) through (vii) of paragraph (1) of this subsection; or
(3) with knowledge of the subject matter or theme thereof, produces any stage play, live performance, film, videotape or other similar visual portrayal or depiction by computer which includes a child whom the person knows or reasonably should know to be under the age of 18 and at least 13 years of age or a severely or profoundly mentally retarded person engaged in any activity described in subparagraphs (i) through (vii) of paragraph (1) of this subsection; or
(4) solicits, uses, persuades, induces, entices, or coerces any child whom he or she knows or reasonably should know to be under the age of 18 and at least 13 years of age or a severely or profoundly mentally retarded person to appear in any stage play, live presentation, film, videotape, photograph or other similar visual reproduction or depiction by computer in which the child or severely or profoundly mentally retarded person is or will be depicted, actually or by simulation, in any act, pose or setting described in subparagraphs (i) through (vii) of paragraph (1) of this subsection; . . . or
(7) solicits, or knowingly uses, persuades, induces, entices, or coerces, a person to provide a child under the age of 18 and at least 13 years of age or a severely or profoundly mentally retarded person to appear in any videotape, photograph, film, stage play, live presentation, or other similar visual reproduction or depiction by computer in which the child or severely or profoundly mentally retarded person will be depicted, actually or by simulation, in any

(continued)

151

Applicable Statutes and What They Say*

act, pose, or setting described in subparagraphs (i) through (vii) of paragraph (1) of this subsection.

If the violation of paragraph (1), (2), (3), (4) or (7) above includes a child engaged in, solicited for, depicted in, or posed in any act of sexual penetration, Illinois law considers the violation a crime of violence.

If the violation does not involve a film, videotape, or other moving depiction," then violating paragraph (1), (4) or (7) above constitutes a Class 1 felony with a mandatory minimum fine of $2,000 and a maximum fine of $100,000.

If the violation involves a film, videotape, or other moving depiction, then violating paragraph (1), (4) or (7) above constitutes a Class X felony with a mandatory minimum fine of $2,000 and a maximum fine of $100,000.

If the violation does not involve a film, videotape, or other moving depiction, a violation of paragraph (3) constitutes a Class 1 felony with a mandatory minimum fine of $1500 and a maximum fine of $100,000.

If the violation involves a film, videotape, or other moving depiction, a violation of paragraph (3) constitutes a Class X felony with a mandatory minimum fine of $1500 and a maximum fine of $100,000.

If the violation does not involve a film, videotape, or other moving depiction, a violation of paragraph (2) constitutes a Class 1 felony with a mandatory minimum fine of $1000 and a maximum fine of $100,000.

If the violation involves a film, videotape, or other moving depiction, a violation of paragraph (2) constitutes a "Class X felony with a mandatory minimum fine of $1000 and a maximum fine of $100,000.

For anyone who within 10 years of a prior conviction has a second conviction for violating the child pornography laws above, the court shall order a presentence psychiatric examination of the person.

STATE **Title of Pertinent** **Provision** *Key definition*	**Applicable Statutes and What They Say***
Aggravated Child Pornography	A person commits aggravated child pornography who: (1) films, videotapes, photographs, or otherwise depicts or portrays by means of any similar visual medium or reproduction or depicts by computer any child whom he or she knows or reasonably should know to be under the age of 13 years where such child is:(i) actually or by simulation engaged in any act of sexual penetration or sexual conduct with any person; . . . or (ii) actually or by simulation engaged in any act of sexual penetration or sexual conduct involving the sex organs of the child and the mouth, anus, or sex organs of another person . . . or which involves the mouth, anus or sex organs of the child and the sex organs of another person; . . . or (iii) actually or by simulation engaged in any act of masturbation; or (iv) actually or by simulation portrayed as being the object of, or otherwise engaged in, any act of lewd fondling, touching, or caressing involving another person; . . . or (v) actually or by simulation engaged in any act of excretion or urination within a sexual context; or . . . (vii) depicted or portrayed in any pose, posture or setting involving a lewd exhibition of the unclothed or transparently clothed genitals, pubic area, buttocks, or, if such person is female, a fully or partially developed breast of the child or other person; or (2) with the knowledge of the nature or content thereof, reproduces, disseminates, offers to disseminate, exhibits or possesses with intent to disseminate any film, videotape, photograph or other similar visual reproduction or depiction by computer of any child whom the person knows or reasonably should know to be under the age of 13 engaged in any activity described in subparagraphs (i) through (vii) of paragraph (1) of this subsection; or (3) with knowledge of the subject matter or theme thereof, produces any stage play, live performance, film, videotape or other similar visual portrayal or depiction by computer which includes a child whom the person knows or reasonably should know to be under the age of 13 engaged in any activity described in subparagraphs (i) through (vii) of paragraph (1) of this subsection; or (4) solicits, uses, persuades, induces, entices, or coerces any child whom he or she knows or reasonably should know to be

(continued)

Applicable Statutes and What They Say*

under the age of 13 to appear in any stage play, live presentation, film, videotape, photograph or other similar visual reproduction or depiction by computer in which the child or severely or profoundly mentally retarded person is or will be depicted, actually or by simulation, in any act, pose or setting described in subparagraphs (i) through (vii) of paragraph (1) of this subsection; . . . or

(6) with knowledge of the nature or content thereof, possesses any film, videotape, photograph or other similar visual reproduction or depiction by computer of any child whom the person knows or reasonably should know to be under the age of 13 engaged in any activity described in subparagraphs (i) through (vii) of paragraph (1) of this subsection.

If the violation of paragraph (1), (2), (3) or (4) above includes a child engaged in, solicited for, depicted in, or posed in any act of sexual penetration, Illinois law considers the violation a crime of violence.

Anyone who violates paragraph (1), (2), (3) or (4) above is guilty of a Class X felony with a mandatory minimum fine of $2,000 and a maximum fine of $100,000.

Anyone who violates paragraph (6) above is guilty of a Class 2 felony with a mandatory minimum fine of $1000 and a maximum fine of $100,000.

A defendant who violates paragraph (1), (2), (3) or (4) above and also has a prior conviction in Illinois or any other state for the offense of child pornography, aggravated child pornography, aggravated criminal sexual abuse, aggravated criminal sexual assault, predatory criminal sexual assault of a child, or any of the offenses formerly known as rape, deviate sexual assault, indecent liberties with a child, or aggravated indecent liberties with a child where the victim was under the age of 18 years or an offense that is substantially equivalent to those offenses, is guilty of a Class X felony for which the person shall be sentenced to a term of imprisonment of not less than 9 years with a mandatory minimum fine of $2,000 and a maximum fine of $100,000.

A defendant who violates paragraph (6) above and has a prior conviction in Illinois or any other state for the offense of child pornography, aggravated child pornography, aggravated criminal sexual abuse, aggravated criminal sexual assault, predatory criminal sexual assault of a child, or any of the offenses formerly known as rape, deviate sexual assault, indecent liberties with a child, or aggravated indecent liberties with a child where the victim was under the age of 18 years or an offense that is substantially equivalent to those offenses, is guilty of a Class 1 felony with a mandatory minimum fine of $1000 and a maximum fine of $100,000.

The court shall order a presentence psychiatric examination of anyone who has a second conviction for aggravated child pornography "within 10 years of a prior conviction.

Distributing Harmful Material to a Minor	A person is guilty of distributing harmful material to a minor when he or she: (1) knowingly sells, lends, distributes, exhibits to, depicts to, or gives away to a minor, knowing that the minor is under the age of 18 or failing to exercise reasonable care in ascertaining the person's true age: (A) any material which depicts nudity, sexual conduct. . . . or which contains explicit and detailed verbal descriptions or narrative accounts of sexual excitement, sexual conduct . . . , and which taken as a whole is harmful to minors; (B) a motion picture, show, or other presentation which depicts nudity, sexual conduct . . . and is harmful to minors.

The predominant appeal to prurient interest of the material shall be judged with reference to *average children of the same general age of the child* to whom such material was sold, lent, distributed or given, unless it appears from the nature of the matter or the circumstances of its dissemination or distribution that it is designed for specially susceptible groups, in which case the predominant appeal of the material shall be judged with reference to its intended or probable recipient group.

(Distributing harmful material to a minor constitutes a Class A misdemeanor. A second violation constitutes a Class 4 felony.)

Sexting—Minors Involved in Electronic Dissemination of	A minor shall not distribute or disseminate an indecent visual depiction of another minor through the use of a computer or electronic communication device.

(continued)

Title of Pertinent
 Provision
 Key definition   **Applicable Statutes and What They Say***

Indecent Visual Depictions	A minor who violates this provision may be subject to a petition for adjudication and adjudged a minor in need of supervision. Additionally a minor found to be in need of supervision under this Section may be: (1) ordered to obtain counseling or other supportive services to address the acts that led to the need for supervision; or (2) ordered to perform community service.
	(Illinois law specifically states that this sexting law does not preclude prosecution for child pornography or for a violation of any other applicable provision of law.)
Disseminate	(i) to sell, distribute, exchange or transfer possession, whether with or without consideration or (ii) to make a depiction by computer available for distribution or downloading through the facilities of any telecommunications network or through any other means of transferring computer programs or data to a computer.
Child pornography	A film, videotape, photograph, or other similar visual medium or reproduction or depiction by computer that is, or appears to be, that of a person, either in part, or in total, under the age of 18 and at least 13 years of age or a severely or profoundly mentally retarded person, regardless of the method by which the film, videotape, photograph, or other similar visual medium or reproduction or depiction by computer is created, adopted, or modified to appear as such.
Minor	Someone below the age of 18.
Harmful to minors	That quality of any description or representation, in whatever form, of nudity, sexual conduct, sexual excitement, . . . when, taken as a whole, it (i) predominately appeals to the prurient interest in sex of minors, (ii) is patently offensive to prevailing standards in the adult community in the State as a whole with respect to what is suitable material for minors, and (iii) lacks serious literary, artistic, political, or scientific value for minors.
Nudity	The showing of the human male or female genitals, pubic area or buttocks with less than a fully opaque covering, or the showing of the female breast with less than a fully opaque covering of any portion below the top of the nipple, or the depiction of covered male genitals in a discernably turgid state.

STATE Title of Pertinent Provision *Key definition*	Applicable Statutes and What They Say*
Sexual excitement	The condition of human male or female genitals when in a state of sexual stimulation or arousal.
Sexual conduct	Acts of masturbation, sexual intercourse, or physical contact with a person's clothed or unclothed genitals, pubic area, buttocks or, if such person be a female, breast.
Electronic communication device	An electronic device, including but not limited to a wireless telephone, personal digital assistant, or a portable or mobile computer, that is capable of transmitting images or pictures.
Indecent visual depiction	A depiction or portrayal in any pose, posture, or setting involving a lewd exhibition of the unclothed or transparently clothed genitals, pubic area, buttocks, or, if such person is female, a fully or partially developed breast of the person.
INDIANA	IND. CODE ANN. § 35-42-4-4 (2004) IND. CODE ANN. § 35-49-1-1, et seq. (2004)
Child Exploitation	A person who knowingly or intentionally: (1) manages, produces, sponsors, presents, exhibits, photographs, films, videotapes, or creates a digitized image of any performance or incident that includes sexual conduct by a child under eighteen (18) years of age; (2) disseminates, exhibits to another person, offers to disseminate or exhibit to another person, or sends or brings into Indiana for dissemination or exhibition matter that depicts or describes sexual conduct by a child under eighteen (18) years of age; . . . commits child exploitation, a Class C felony.
Possession of Child Pornography	A person who knowingly or intentionally possesses: (1) a picture; (2) a drawing; (3) a photograph; (4) a negative image; (5) undeveloped film; (6) a motion picture; (7) a videotape; (8) a digitized image; or (9) any pictorial representation;
	that depicts or describes sexual conduct by a child who the person knows is less than sixteen (16) years of age or who appears to be less than sixteen (16) years of age, and that lacks serious literary, artistic, political, or scientific value commits possession of child pornography, a Class D felony.
	Indiana law provides a strong defense for consensual sexting for anyone charged with violating the parts of the child exploitation

(*continued*)

law or the possession of child pornography law we set
forth above. However, the defendant must show all of the
following:
(1) A cellular telephone, another wireless or cellular
communications device, or a social networking web site was
used to possess, produce, or disseminate the image.
(2) The defendant is not more than four (4) years older or
younger than the person who is depicted in the image or who
received the image.
(3) The relationship between the defendant and the
person who received the image or who is depicted in the
image was a dating relationship or an ongoing personal
relationship. For purposes of this subdivision, the term
"ongoing personal relationship" does not include a family
relationship.
(4) The crime was committed by a person less than twenty-
two (22) years of age.
(5) The person receiving the image or who is depicted in the
image acquiesced in the defendant's conduct.

This defense is not available, however, if:
(1) the person who receives the image disseminates it to a
person other than the person:
(A) who sent the image; or
(B) who is depicted in the image; or
(2) the image is of a person other than the person who sent
the image or received the image.

Obscene Performance	A person who knowingly or intentionally engages in, participates in, manages, produces, sponsors, presents, exhibits, photographs, films, or videotapes any obscene performance commits a Class A misdemeanor. However, the offense is a Class D felony if the obscene performance depicts or describes sexual conduct involving any person who is or appears to be under sixteen (16) years of age.
Dissemination of Matter or Conducting	[Anyone who] knowingly or intentionally disseminates, displays, or makes available the matter [that is obscene or child pornography] through the Internet, computer electronic

STATE Title of Pertinent Provision *Key definition*	**Applicable Statutes and What They Say***
Performance Harmful to Minors	transfer, or a computer network [in any of the following situations] is guilty of a Class D felony: (1) disseminates matter to minors that is harmful to minors; (2) displays matter that is harmful to minors in an area to which minors have visual, auditory, or physical access, unless each minor is accompanied by the minor's parent or guardian; . . . (4) engages in or conducts a performance before minors that is harmful to minors; (5) engages in or conducts a performance that is harmful to minors in an area to which minors have visual, auditory, or physical access, unless each minor is accompanied by the minor's parent or guardian.
	Indiana law provides a defense to the crime of dissemination of matter or conducting performance harmful to minors if all of the following are applicable: (1) A cellular telephone, another wireless or cellular communications device, or a social networking web site was used to disseminate matter to a minor that is harmful to minors. (2) The defendant is not more than four (4) years older or younger than the person who received the matter that is harmful to minors. (3) The relationship between the defendant and the person who received the matter that is harmful to minors was a dating relationship or an ongoing personal relationship. For purposes of this subdivision, the term "ongoing personal relationship" does not include a family relationship. (4) The crime was committed by a person less than twenty-two (22) years of age. (5) The person receiving the matter expressly or implicitly acquiesced in the defendant's conduct.
	This defense is not applicable if the image is disseminated to a person other than the person:
	(A) who sent the image; or (B) who is depicted in the image.
Disseminate	Transfer [of] possession for free or for a consideration.
Sexual conduct	Sexual intercourse, deviate sexual conduct, exhibition of the uncovered genitals intended to satisfy or arouse the sexual desires of any person . . . . or any fondling or touching of a child by another person or of another person by a child intended to arouse or satisfy the sexual desires of either the child or the other person.
Minor	Someone below 18 years old.

(continued)

STATE **Title of Pertinent Provision** *Key definition*	**Applicable Statutes and What They Say***
Matter	(1) Any book, magazine, newspaper, or other printed or written material; (2) any picture, drawing, photograph, motion picture, digitized image, or other pictorial representation; (3) any statue or other figure; (4) any recording, transcription, or mechanical, chemical, or electrical reproduction; or (5) any other articles, equipment, machines, or materials.
Distribute	Transfer [of] possession for a consideration.
Nudity	(1) The showing of the human male or female genitals, pubic area, or buttocks with less than a full opaque covering; (2) the showing of the female breast with less than a fully opaque covering of any part of the nipple; or (3) the depiction of covered male genitals in a discernibly turgid state.
Performance	Any play, motion picture, dance, or other exhibition or presentation, whether pictured, animated, or live, performed before an audience of one (1) or more persons.
Sexual excitement	The condition of human male or female genitals when in a state of sexual stimulation or arousal.
IOWA	Iowa Code Ann. § 728.1 (West 2011) Iowa Code Ann. § 728.12 (West 2011)
Sexual Exploitation of a Minor	It shall be unlawful to employ, use, persuade, induce, entice, coerce, solicit, knowingly permit, or otherwise cause or attempt to cause a minor to engage in a prohibited sexual act or in the simulation of a prohibited sexual act. A person must know, or have reason to know, or intend that the act or simulated act may be photographed, filmed, or otherwise preserved in a negative, slide, book, magazine, computer, computer disk, or other print or visual medium, or be preserved in an electronic, magnetic, or optical storage system, or in any other type of storage system. (Anyone who violates this is guilty of a class C felony. Along with any other sentence, the court could fine the defendant up to $50,000 for each violation.) It shall be unlawful to knowingly promote any material visually depicting a live performance of a minor engaging in a prohibited sexual act or in the simulation of a prohibited sexual act.

Key definition	**Applicable Statutes and What They Say***
	(Anyone who violates this is guilty of a class D felony. Along with any other sentence, the court could fine the defendant up to $25,000 for each violation.)
	It shall be unlawful to knowingly purchase or possess a negative, slide, book, magazine, computer, computer disk, or other print or visual medium, or an electronic, magnetic, or optical storage system, or any other type of storage system which depicts a minor engaging in a prohibited sexual act or the simulation of a prohibited sexual act.
	(Anyone who violates this is guilty of aggravated misdemeanor for a first offense and a class D felony for a second or subsequent offense. Along with any other sentence, the court could fine the defendant up to $25,000 for each violation.)
Minor	Anyone below the age of 18.
Disseminate	To transfer possession, with or without consideration.
Obscene material	Any material depicting or describing the genitals, sex acts, masturbation, excretory functions . . . which the average person, taking the material as a whole and applying contemporary community standards with respect to what is suitable material for minors, would find appeals to the prurient interest and is patently offensive; and the material, taken as a whole, lacks serious literary, scientific, political or artistic value.
Promote	To procure, manufacture, issue, sell, give, provide, lend, mail, deliver, transfer, transmute, transmit, publish, distribute, circulate, disseminate, present, exhibit, or advertise, or to offer or agree to do any of these acts.
Prohibited act	Fondling or touching the pubes or genitals of a minor;fondling or touching the pubes or genitals of a person *by* a minor; nudity of a minor for the purpose of arousing or satisfying the sexual desires of a person who may view a depiction of the nude minor; or sex act.
Sex act (as used in the definition of prohibited act above)	Any sexual contact between two or more persons by: penetration of the penis into the vagina or anus; contact between the mouth and genitalia or by contact between the genitalia of one person and the genitalia or anus of another person; contact between the finger or hand of one person and the genitalia or anus of another person.

(continued)

STATE **Title of Pertinent Provision** *Key definition*	**Applicable Statutes and What They Say***
KANSAS	Kan. Stat. Ann. § 21-5501 (2011) Kan. Stat. Ann. § 21-5509 (2011) Kan. Stat. Ann. § 21-5510 (2011) Kan. Stat. Ann. § 510.155 (2009)
Electronic Solicitation	Electronic solicitation is, by means of communication conducted through the telephone, internet or by other electronic means, enticing or soliciting a person, whom the offender believes to be a child, to commit or submit to an unlawful sexual act. Electronic solicitation is a: (1) Severity level 3, person felony if the offender believes the person to be a child 14 or more years of age but less than 16 years of age; and (2) severity level 1, person felony if the offender believes the person to be a child under 14 years of age.
Sexual Exploitation of a Child	Employing, using, persuading, inducing, enticing or coercing a child under 18 years of age to engage in sexually explicit conduct with the intent to promote any performance [constitutes sexual exploitation of a child]. (This is a severity level 5, person felony.) [The crime of sexual exploitation of a child can also be committed by] possessing any visual depiction of a child under 18 years of age shown or heard engaging in sexually explicit conduct with intent to arouse or satisfy the sexual desires or appeal to the prurient interest of the offender or any other person. (This is a severity level 5, person felony.) [The crime of sexual exploitation of a child can also be committed when a person promotes] any performance that includes sexually explicit conduct by a child under 18 years of age, knowing the character and content of the performance. (This is a severity level 5, person felony.)
Sexual intercourse	Any penetration of the female sex organ by a finger, the male sex organ or any object. Any penetration, however slight, is sufficient to constitute sexual intercourse.

STATE Title of Pertinent Provision *Key definition*	**Applicable Statutes and What They Say***
Electronic solicitation	Communication conducted through the internet or by other electronic means includes, but is not limited to, e-mail, chat-room chats and text messaging.
Sexually explicit conduct	Actual or simulated: Exhibition in the nude; sexual intercourse or sodomy, including genital-genital, oral-genital, anal-genital or oral-anal contact, whether between persons of the same or opposite sex; masturbation; ... or lewd exhibition of the genitals, female breasts or pubic area of any person.
Promoting	Procuring, transmitting, distributing, circulating, presenting, producing, directing, manufacturing, issuing, publishing, displaying, exhibiting ... with intent to arouse or gratify the sexual desire or appeal to the prurient interest of the offender or any other person.
Performance	Any film, photograph, negative, slide, book, magazine or other printed or visual medium, any audio tape recording or any photocopy, video tape, video laser disk, computer hardware, software, floppy disk or any other computer related equipment or computer generated image that contains or incorporates in any manner any film, photograph, negative, photocopy, video tape or video laser disk or any play or other live presentation.
Visual depiction	Any photograph, film, video picture, digital or computer-generated image or picture, whether made or produced by electronic, mechanical or other means.
Nude	Any state of undress in which the human genitals, pubic region, buttock or female breast, at a point below the top of the areola, is less than completely and opaquely covered.
KENTUCKY	KY. REV. STAT. ANN. § 531.010, et seq. (Michie 2009) KY. REV. STAT. ANN. § 531.300, et seq. (Michie 2009)
Use of a Minor in a Sexual Performance	A person is guilty of the use of a minor in a sexual performance if he employs, consents to, authorizes or induces a minor to engage in a sexual performance.
	Use of a minor in a sexual performance is: (a) A Class C felony if the minor so used is less than eighteen (18) years old at the time the minor engages in the prohibited activity; (b) A Class B

(continued)

STATE Title of Pertinent Provision Key definition	Applicable Statutes and What They Say*
	felony if the minor so used is less than sixteen (16) years old at the time the minor engages in the prohibited activity.
Promoting a Sexual Performance by a Minor	A person is guilty of promoting a sexual performance by a minor when, knowing the character and content thereof, he produces, directs or promotes any performance which includes sexual conduct by a minor.
	Promoting a sexual performance by a minor is: (a) A Class C felony if the minor involved in the sexual performance is less than eighteen (18) years old at the time the minor engages in the prohibited activity; (b) A Class B felony if the minor involved in the sexual performance is less than sixteen (16) years old at the time the minor engages in the prohibited activity.
Possession of Matter Portraying a Sexual Performance by a Minor	A person is guilty of possession of matter portraying a sexual performance by a minor when, having knowledge of its content, character, and that the sexual performance is by a minor, he or she knowingly has in his or her possession or control any matter which visually depicts an actual sexual performance by a minor person.
	(Possession of matter portraying a sexual performance by a minor constitutes a Class D felony.)
Distribution of Matter Portraying a Sexual Performance by a Minor	A person is guilty of distribution of matter portraying a sexual performance by a minor when, having knowledge of its content and character, he or she: (a) Sends or causes to be sent into this state for sale or distribution; or (b) Brings or causes to be brought into this state for sale or distribution; or (c) In this state, he or she . . . 2. Distributes; or 3. Offers to distribute; or 4. Has in his or her possession with intent to distribute, exhibit for profit or gain or offer to distribute, any matter portraying a sexual performance by a minor.
	(Distribution of matter portraying a sexual performance by a minor is a Class D felony for the first offense and a Class C felony for each subsequent offense.)
Using Minors to Distribute Material Portraying a Sexual	A person is guilty of using minors to distribute material portraying a sexual performance by a minor when knowing a person to be a minor, or having possession of such facts that he should reasonably know such person is a minor, and

STATE Title of Pertinent Provision	
Key definition	Applicable Statutes and What They Say*
Performance by a Minor	knowing of the content and character of the material, he knowingly . . . uses, a minor to do or assist in doing any of the acts [listed above under the crime of distribution of matter portraying a sexual performance by a minor].
	(Using minors to distribute material portraying a sexual performance by a minor constitutes a Class D felony. However, it is a Class C felony if the defendant has a prior conviction for using minors to distribute material portraying a sexual performance by a minor or for distribution of obscene matter to minors.)
Distribution of Obscene Matter	A person is guilty of distribution of obscene matter when, having knowledge of its content and character, he: (a) Sends or causes to be sent into this state for sale or distribution; or (b) Brings or causes to be brought into this state for sale or distribution; or (c) In this state, he: 1. Prepares, or 2. Publishes, or 3. Prints, or 4. Exhibits, or 5. Distributes, or 6. Offers to distribute, or 7. Has in his possession with intent to distribute, exhibit or offer to distribute, any obscene matter.
	(Distribution of obscene matter is a Class B misdemeanor unless the defendant has in his possession more than one unit of material, in which case it shall be a Class A misdemeanor.)
Distribution of Obscene Matter to Minors	A person is guilty of distribution of obscene material to minors when, knowing a person to be a minor, or having possession of such facts that he should reasonably know that such person is a minor, and with knowledge of the content and character of the material, he knowingly: (a) Sends or causes to be sent; or (b) Exhibits; or (c) Distributes, or offers to distribute,
	obscene material to a minor.
	(Distributing obscene matter to minors constitutes a Class A misdemeanor. However, it is a Class D felony if the defendant has a prior conviction for distribution of obscene matter or for distribution of obscene matter to minors.)

(continued)

STATE **Title of Pertinent Provision** *Key definition*	**Applicable Statutes and What They Say***
Using Minors to Distribute Obscene Material	A person is guilty of using minors to distribute obscene material when knowing a person to be a minor, or having possession of such facts that he should reasonably know such person is a minor, and knowing of the content and character of the material, he knowingly . . . uses, a minor to do or assist in doing any of the acts [listed under the crime of distribution of obscene matter above].
	(Using minors to distribute obscene material constitutes a Class A misdemeanor. However, it is a Class D felony if the defendant has a prior conviction for using minors to distribute obscene material or for distribution of obscene matter to minors.)
Obscene	The predominate appeal of the matter taken as a whole is to a prurient interest in sexual conduct involving minors.
Sexual conduct by a minor	(a) Acts of masturbation, homosexuality, lesbianism, . . . sexual intercourse, or deviant sexual intercourse, actual or simulated; (b) Physical contact with, or willful or intentional exhibition of the genitals; (c) Flagellation or excretion for the purpose of sexual stimulation or gratification; or (d) The exposure, in an obscene manner, of the unclothed or apparently unclothed human male or female genitals, pubic area or buttocks, or the female breast, whether or not subsequently obscured by a mark placed thereon, or otherwise altered, in any resulting motion picture, photograph or other visual representation, exclusive of exposure portrayed in matter of a private, family nature not intended for distribution outside the family.
Performance	Any play, motion picture, photograph or dance.
Sexual performance	Any performance or part thereof which includes sexual conduct by a minor.
Matter	Any book, magazine, newspaper, or other printed or written material or any picture, drawing, photograph, motion picture, live image transmitted over the Internet or other electronic network, or other pictorial representation or any statue or other figure.
Promote	To prepare, publish, print, procure or manufacture, or to offer or agree to do the same.
Sexual conduct	Acts of masturbation, homosexuality, lesbianism, . . . sexual intercourse, or deviant sexual intercourse; or physical contact

STATE **Title of Pertinent** **Provision** *Key definition*	**Applicable Statutes and What They Say***
	with the genitals, flagellation, or excretion for the purpose of sexual stimulation or gratification.
LOUISIANA	LA. REV. STAT. ANN. § 14:81.1 (West 2004) LA. REV. STAT. ANN. § 14:81.1.1(A) (West 2010)
Pornography Involving Juveniles	It shall be unlawful for a person to produce, distribute, possess, or possess with the intent to distribute pornography involving juveniles.
	Whoever intentionally possesses pornography involving juveniles shall be fined not more than ten thousand dollars and shall be imprisoned at hard labor for not less than two years or more than ten years, without benefit of parole, probation, or suspension of sentence.
	Whoever distributes or possesses with the intent to distribute pornography involving juveniles shall be fined not more than ten thousand dollars and shall be imprisoned at hard labor for not less than five years or more than ten years, without benefit of parole, probation, or suspension of sentence.
	If the defendant is at least 17 years old and victim is less than 13 years old, the defendant shall be punished by imprisonment at hard labor for not less than one-half the longest term nor more than twice the longest term of imprisonment listed in (1) or (2) above in this table. Further, the sentence imposed shall be served without benefit of parole, probation, or suspension of sentence. After the defendant has served the prison term, he shall be monitored by the Department of Public Safety and Corrections through the use of electronic monitoring equipment for the remainder of his natural life.
	Whoever engages in the production of pornography involving juveniles shall be fined not more than fifteen thousand dollars and be imprisoned at hard labor for not less than ten years or more than twenty years, without benefit of probation, parole, or suspension of sentence.
	If the defendant is at least 17 years old and victim is less than 13 years old, the defendant shall be punished by imprisonment at hard labor for not less than twenty-five years nor more than ninety-nine years. Further, at least twenty-five

(continued)

STATE Title of Pertinent Provision *Key definition*	Applicable Statutes and What They Say*
	years of the sentence imposed shall be served without benefit of parole, probation, or suspension of sentence. After the defendant has served the prison term, he shall be monitored by the Department of Public Safety and Corrections through the use of electronic monitoring equipment for the remainder of his natural life. The defendant must pay the cost of the electronic monitoring unless the Department of Public Safety and Corrections finds that he cannot afford it.
Sexting	(1) No person under the age of seventeen years shall knowingly and voluntarily use a computer or telecommunication device to transmit an indecent visual depiction of himself to another person. (2) No person under the age of seventeen years shall knowingly possess or transmit an indecent visual depiction that was transmitted by another under the age of seventeen years in violation of the provisions of Paragraph (1) of this Subsection. Penalties for violations of Paragraph (1) are governed the Louisiana Children's Code. (a) For a first offense in violation of Paragraph (A)(2) of this Section, the offender shall be fined not less than one hundred dollars nor more than two hundred fifty dollars, imprisoned for not more than ten days, or both. Imposition or execution of the sentence shall not be suspended unless the offender is placed on probation with a minimum condition that he perform two eight-hour days of court-approved community service. (b) For a second offense in violation of Paragraph (A)(2) of this Section, the offender shall be fined not less than two hundred fifty dollars nor more than five hundred dollars, imprisoned for not less than ten days nor more than thirty days, or both. Imposition or execution of the sentence shall not be suspended unless the offender is placed on probation with a minimum condition that he perform five eight-hour days of court-approved community service. (c) For a third or any subsequent offense in violation of Paragraph (A)(2) of this Section, the offender shall be fined not less than five hundred dollars nor more than seven hundred fifty dollars, imprisoned for not less than thirty days nor more than six months, or both. Imposition or execution of

STATE Title of Pertinent Provision *Key definition*	**Applicable Statutes and What They Say***
	the sentence shall not be suspended unless the offender is placed on probation with a minimum condition that he perform ten eight-hour days of court-approved community service.
Pornography	Any photograph, videotape, film, or other reproduction, whether electronic or otherwise, of any sexual performance involving a child under the age of seventeen.
Sexual performance	Any performance or part thereof that includes actual or simulated sexual intercourse, deviate sexual intercourse, . . . masturbation, . . . or lewd exhibition of the genitals or anus.
Produce	Photograph, videotape, film, or otherwise reproduce pornography involving juveniles, or to solicit, promote, or coerce any child for the purpose of pornography involving juveniles.
Distribute	To issue, sell, give, provide, lend, mail, deliver, transfer, transmute, distribute, circulate, or disseminate by any means.
Indecent visual depiction	Any photograph, videotape, film, or other reproduction of a person under the age of seventeen years engaging in sexually explicit conduct, and includes data stored on any computer, telecommunication device, or other electronic storage media which is capable of conversion into a visual image.
Sexually explicit conduct	Masturbation or lewd exhibition of the genitals, pubic hair, anus, vulva, or female breast nipples of a person under the age of seventeen years.
MAINE	Me. Rev. Stat. Ann. tit. 17-A, § 259 (West 2003) Me. Rev. Stat. Ann. tit. 17-A, § 281, et seq. (West 2006) Me. Rev. Stat. Ann. tit. 17-A, § 284(5) (West 2006)
Solicitation of Child by Computer to Commit a Prohibited Act	A person is guilty of soliciting a child by a computer to commit a prohibited act if: A. The actor: (1) Uses a computer knowingly to solicit, entice, persuade or compel another person to meet with the actor; (2) Is at least 16 years of age; (3) Knows or believes that the other person is less than 14 years of age; and (4) Is at least 3 years older than the expressed age of the other person; and B. The actor has the intent to engage in any one of the following prohibited acts with the other person:

(continued)

Key definition	**Applicable Statutes and What They Say***
	(1) A sexual act; (2) Sexual contact; or (3) Sexual exploitation of a minor.
	(Violating the above provision constitutes a Class D crime.)
	A person is guilty of soliciting a child by a computer to commit a prohibited act if: A. The actor: (1) Uses a computer knowingly to solicit, entice, persuade or compel another person to meet with the actor; (2) Is at least 16 years of age; (3) Knows or believes that the other person is less than 12 years of age; and (4) Is at least 3 years older than the expressed age of the other person; and B. The actor has the intent to engage in any one of the following prohibited acts with the other person: (1) A sexual act; (2) Sexual contact; or (3) Sexual exploitation of a minor.
	(Violating the above provision constitutes a Class C crime.)
Sexual Exploitation of Minors	A person is guilty of sexual exploitation of a minor if: A. Knowing or intending that the conduct will be photographed, the person intentionally or knowingly employs, solicits, entices, persuades, uses or compels another person, not that person's spouse, who is in fact a minor, to engage in sexually explicit conduct. Violation of this paragraph is a Class B crime; B. The person violates paragraph A and, at the time of the offense, the person has one or more prior convictions under this section or for engaging in substantially similar conduct to that contained in this section in another jurisdiction. Violation of this paragraph is a Class A crime; C. The person violates paragraph A and the minor has not in fact attained 12 years of age. Violation of this paragraph is a Class A crime.
	The following mandatory minimum terms of imprisonment apply to sexual exploitation of a minor. A. A court shall impose upon a person convicted under subsection 1, paragraph A . . . a sentencing alternative involving a term of imprisonment of at least 5 years. B. A court shall impose upon a person convicted under subsection 1, paragraph B . . . a sentencing alternative involving a term of imprisonment of at least 10 years.

(Courts are not authorized to suspend minimum prison terms listed above for sexual exploitation of a minor unless the court sets forth in detail, in writing, the reasons for suspending the sentence. The court shall consider the nature and circumstances of the crime, the physical and mental well-being of the minor and the history and character of the defendant and may only suspend the minimum term if the court is of the opinion that the exceptional features of the case justify the imposition of another sentence.)

Dissemination of Sexually Explicit Material

A person is guilty of dissemination of sexually explicit material if:

A. The person intentionally or knowingly disseminates or possesses with intent to disseminate any book, magazine, newspaper, print, negative, slide, motion picture, videotape, computer data file or other mechanically, electronically or chemically reproduced visual image or material that depicts any minor who the person knows or has reason to know is a minor engaging in sexually explicit conduct. Violation of this paragraph is a Class C crime;

B. The person violates paragraph A and, at the time of the offense, has one or more prior convictions under this section or for engaging in substantially similar conduct to that contained in this section in another jurisdiction. Violation of this paragraph is a Class B crime;

C. The person intentionally or knowingly disseminates or possesses with intent to disseminate any book, magazine, newspaper, print, negative, slide, motion picture, videotape, computer data file or other mechanically, electronically or chemically reproduced visual image or material that depicts any minor who is less than 12 years of age who the person knows or has reason to know is a minor less than 12 years of age engaging in sexually explicit conduct. Violation of this paragraph is a Class B crime; or

D. The person violates paragraph C and, at the time of the offense, has one or more prior convictions under this section or for engaging in substantially similar conduct to that contained in this section in another jurisdiction. Violation of this paragraph is a Class A crime.

(continued)

STATE **Title of Pertinent Provision** *Key definition*	**Applicable Statutes and What They Say***
Possession of Sexually Explicit Material	A person is guilty of possession of sexually explicit material if that person: A. Intentionally or knowingly transports, exhibits, purchases, possesses or accesses with intent to view any book, magazine, newspaper, print, negative, slide, motion picture, computer data file, videotape or other mechanically, electronically or chemically reproduced visual image or material that the person knows or should know depicts another person engaging in sexually explicit conduct, and: (1) The other person has not in fact attained 16 years of age; or (2) The person knows or has reason to know that the other person has not attained 16 years of age. Violation of this paragraph is a Class D crime; B. Violates paragraph A and, at the time of the offense, has one or more prior convictions under this section or for engaging in substantially similar conduct to that contained in this section in another jurisdiction. Violation of this paragraph is a Class C crime; C. Intentionally or knowingly transports, exhibits, purchases, possesses or accesses with intent to view any book, magazine, newspaper, print, negative, slide, motion picture, computer data file, videotape or other mechanically, electronically or chemically reproduced visual image or material that the person knows or should know depicts another person engaging in sexually explicit conduct, and: (1) The other person has not in fact attained 12 years of age; or (2) The person knows or has reason to know that the other person has not attained 12 years of age. Violation of this paragraph is a Class C crime; or D. Violates paragraph C and, at the time of the offense, has one or more prior convictions under this section or for engaging in substantially similar conduct to that contained in this section in another jurisdiction. Violation of this paragraph is a Class B crime.

STATE Title of Pertinent Provision *Key definition*	**Applicable Statutes and What They Say***
	(Maine law provides a defense to the crime of possession of sexually-explicit material if the person depicted was the spouse of the person possessing the sexually explicit material at the time the material was produced.)
Computer	Electronic, magnetic, optical, electrochemical, or other high-speed data processing device performing logical, arithmetic, or storage functions, and includes any data storage facility or communications facility directly related to or operating in conjunction with such device.
Minor	Someone below the age of 18.
Sexually explicit conduct	A sexual act; masturbation; lewd exhibition of the genitals, anus or pubic area of a person. An exhibition is considered lewd if the exhibition is designed for the purpose of eliciting or attempting to elicit a sexual response in the intended viewer; or conduct that creates the appearance [of a sexual act, masturbation or lewd exhibition of the genitals, anus or pubic area of a person, which conduct] also exhibits any uncovered or covered portions of the genitals, anus or pubic area.
Photograph	To make, capture, generate or save a print, negative, slide, motion picture, computer data file, videotape or other mechanically, electronically or chemically reproduced visual image or material.
Disseminate	To manufacture, publish, send, promulgate, distribute, exhibit, issue, furnish, sell or transfer or to offer or agree to do any of these acts.
MARYLAND	Mᴅ. Cᴏᴅᴇ Aɴɴ., Cʀɪᴍ. Lᴀᴡ § 11-201, et seq. (2002)
Obscene Matter— Distribution, Exhibition, Importation, and Publication	A person may not: (1) knowingly send or cause to be sent any obscene matter into the State for sale or distribution; (2) knowingly bring or cause to be brought any obscene matter into the State for sale or distribution; (3) in the State prepare, publish, print, exhibit, distribute, or offer to distribute any obscene matter; or (4) possess any obscene matter in the State with the intent to distribute, offer to distribute, or exhibit.
	A person who violates this section is guilty of a misdemeanor and on conviction is subject to:

(continued)

	Applicable Statutes and What They Say*
	(1) for a first violation, imprisonment not exceeding 1 year or a fine not exceeding $1,000 or both; and (2) for each subsequent violation, imprisonment not exceeding 3 years or a fine not exceeding $5,000 or both.
Display of Obscene Item to Minor	A person may not willfully or knowingly display or exhibit to a minor an item: (i) the cover or content of which is principally made up of an obscene description or depiction of illicit sex; or (ii) that consists of an obscene picture of a nude or partially nude figure.
	A violation of this provision constitutes a misdemeanor and upon conviction, the person shall be punished as follows: (1) for a first violation, imprisonment not exceeding 1 year or a fine not exceeding $1,000 or both; and (2) for each subsequent violation, imprisonment not exceeding 3 years or a fine not exceeding $5,000 or both.
Child Pornography	A person may not:
	(1) cause, induce, solicit, or knowingly allow a minor to engage as a subject in the production of obscene matter or a visual representation or performance that depicts a minor engaged as a subject in . . . or sexual conduct; (2) photograph or film a minor engaging in an obscene act, . . . or sexual conduct; (3) use a computer to depict or describe a minor engaging in an obscene act . . . or sexual conduct; (4) knowingly promote, advertise, solicit, distribute, or possess with the intent to distribute any matter, visual representation, or performance: (i) that depicts a minor engaged as a subject in . . . or sexual conduct; or (ii) in a manner that reflects the belief, or that is intended to cause another to believe, that the matter, visual representation, or performance depicts a minor engaged as a subject of . . . or sexual conduct; or (5) use a computer to knowingly compile, enter, transmit, make, print, publish, reproduce, cause, allow, buy, sell, receive, exchange, or disseminate any notice, statement,

STATE Title of Pertinent Provision *Key definition*	Applicable Statutes and What They Say*
	advertisement, or minor's name, telephone number, place of residence, physical characteristics, or other descriptive or identifying information for the purpose of engaging in, facilitating, encouraging, offering, or soliciting . . . sexual conduct of or with a minor.
	A person who violates this section is guilty of a felony and on conviction is subject to:
	(1) for a first violation, imprisonment not exceeding 10 years or a fine not exceeding $25,000 or both; and (2) for each subsequent violation, imprisonment not exceeding 20 years or a fine not exceeding $50,000 or both.
Possession of Visual Representation of Child under 16 Engaged in Certain Sexual Acts	A person may not knowingly possess and intentionally retain a film, videotape, photograph, or other visual representation showing an actual child under the age of 16 years engaged in sexual conduct [or] in a state of sexual excitement. (Anyone who violates this is guilty of a misdemeanor and on conviction is subject to imprisonment not exceeding 5 years or a fine not exceeding $2,500 or both. However, if the person had a prior conviction for possession of visual representation of child under 16 engaged in certain sexual acts, he/she is guilty of a felony and on conviction is subject to imprisonment not exceeding 10 years or a fine not exceeding $10,000 or both.)
Sexual conduct	Maryland law provides an affirmative defense to a defendant who violates the above law on possession of visual representation of child under 16 engaged in certain sexual acts if he or she] promptly and in good faith: (1) took reasonable steps to destroy each visual representation; or (2) reported the matter to a law enforcement agency.
Sexual excitement	Human masturbation; sexual intercourse; [or] whether alone or with another individual . . . any touching of or contact with: (i) the genitals, buttocks, or pubic areas of an individual; or (ii) breasts of a female individual.
Matter	Condition of the human genitals when in a state of sexual stimulation; the condition of the human female breasts when in a state of sexual stimulation; [or] the sensual experiences of individuals engaging in or witnessing sexual conduct or nudity.

(continued)

175

STATE Title of Pertinent Provision *Key definition*	Applicable Statutes and What They Say*
Item	Book, magazine, newspaper, or other printed or written material; picture, drawing, photograph, motion picture, or other pictorial representation; [or] any other article, equipment, machine, or material.
Illicit sex	Still picture or photograph [or] video disc, videotape, video game, film, or computer disc.
Partially nude figure	(i) human genitals in a state of sexual stimulation or arousal; (ii) acts of human masturbation, sexual intercourse, or sodomy; or (iii) fondling or other erotic touching of human genitals. A figure with: (i) less than completely and opaquely covered human genitals, pubic region, buttocks, or female breast below a point immediately above the top of the areola; or (ii) human male genitals in a discernibly turgid state, even if completely and opaquely covered.
MASSACHUSETTS	Mass. Gen. Laws Ann. ch. 272, § 29, et seq. (West 2000)
Dissemination or Possession of Obscene Matter	Whoever disseminates any matter which is obscene, knowing it to be obscene, or whoever has in his possession any matter which is obscene, knowing it to be obscene, with the intent to disseminate the same, shall be punished by imprisonment in the state prison for not more than five years or in a jail or house of correction for not more than two and one-half years or by a fine of not less than one thousand nor more than ten thousand dollars for the first offense, not less than five thousand nor more than twenty thousand dollars for the second offense, or not less than ten thousand nor more than thirty thousand dollars for the third and subsequent offenses, or by both such fine and imprisonment.
Posing or Exhibiting Child in State of Nudity or Sexual Conduct	Whoever, either with knowledge that a person is a child under eighteen years of age or while in possession of such facts that he should have reason to know that such person is a child under eighteen years of age, and with *lascivious intent*, hires, coerces, solicits or entices, employs, procures, uses, causes, encourages, or knowingly permits such child to pose or be exhibited in a state of nudity, for the purpose of representation or reproduction in any visual

	Applicable Statutes and What They Say*
	material, shall be punished by imprisonment in the state prison for a term of not less than ten nor more than twenty years, or by a fine of not less than ten thousand nor more than fifty thousand dollars, or by both such fine and imprisonment.
	Whoever, either with knowledge that a person is a child under eighteen years of age or while in possession of such facts that he should have reason to know that such person is a child under eighteen years of age, hires, coerces, solicits or entices, employs, procures, uses, causes, encourages, or knowingly permits such child to participate or engage in any act that depicts, describes, or represents sexual conduct for the purpose of representation or reproduction in any visual material, or to engage in any live performance involving sexual conduct, shall be punished by imprisonment in the state prison for a term of not less than ten nor more than twenty years, or by a fine of not less than ten thousand nor more than fifty thousand dollars, or by both such fine and imprisonment.
	Massachusetts law also provides that a minor is not capable of consent to posing or exhibiting him or her in a state of nudity or sexual conduct with respect to any of the prohibited acts in (1) or (2) above.
Dissemination of Visual Material of Child in State of Nudity or Sexual Conduct	Whoever, with lascivious intent, disseminates any visual material that contains a representation or reproduction of any posture or exhibition in a *state of nudity* involving the use of a child who is under eighteen years of age, knowing the contents of such visual material or having sufficient facts in his possession to have knowledge of the contents thereof, or has in his possession any such visual material knowing the contents or having sufficient facts in his possession to have knowledge of the contents thereof, with the intent to disseminate the same, shall be punished in the state prison for a term of not less than ten nor more than twenty years or by a fine of not less than ten thousand nor more than fifty thousand dollars or three times the monetary value of any economic gain derived from said dissemination, whichever is greater, or by both such fine and imprisonment.
	Whoever with lascivious intent disseminates any visual material that contains a representation or reproduction of any

(*continued*)

act that depicts, describes, or represents *sexual conduct* participated or engaged in by a child who is under eighteen years of age, knowing the contents of such visual material or having sufficient facts in his possession to have knowledge of the contents thereof, or whoever has in his possession any such visual material knowing the contents or having sufficient facts in his possession to have knowledge of the contents thereof, with the intent to disseminate the same, shall be punished in the state prison for a term of not less than ten nor more than twenty years or by a fine of not less than ten thousand nor more than fifty thousand dollars or three times the monetary value of any economic gain derived from said dissemination, whichever is greater, or by both such fine and imprisonment.

Massachusetts law also provides that a minor is not capable of consent to dissemination of visual material of child in state of nudity or sexual conduct with respect to any of the prohibited acts in (1) or (2) above.

Knowing Possession of Visual Material of Child Depicted in Sexual Conduct

[Anyone who knowingly] possesses a negative, slide, book, magazine, film, videotape, photograph or other similar visual reproduction, or depiction by computer, of any child whom the person knows or reasonably should know to be under the age of 18 years of age and such child is: (i) actually or by simulation engaged in any act of sexual intercourse with any person; . . . (ii) actually or by simulation engaged in any act of sexual contact involving the sex organs of the child and the mouth, anus or sex organs of the child and the sex organs of another person; . . . (iii) actually or by simulation engaged in any act of masturbation; (iv) actually or by simulation portrayed as being the object of, or otherwise engaged in, any act of lewd fondling, touching, or caressing involving another person; . . . (v) actually or by simulation engaged in any act of excretion or urination within a sexual context; . . . or (vii) depicted or portrayed in any pose, posture or setting involving a lewd exhibition of the unclothed genitals, pubic area, buttocks or, if such person is female, a fully or partially developed breast of the child; with knowledge of the nature or content thereof shall be punished by imprisonment in the state prison for not more than five years or in a jail or house of

STATE Title of Pertinent Provision *Key definition*	**Applicable Statutes and What They Say***
	correction for not more than two and one-half years or by a fine of not less than $1,000 nor more than $10,000, or by both such fine and imprisonment for the first offense, not less than five years in a state prison or by a fine of not less than $5,000 nor more than $20,000, or by both such fine and imprisonment for the second offense, not less than 10 years in a state prison or by a fine of not less than $10,000 nor more than $30,000, or by both such fine and imprisonment for the third and subsequent offenses.
Lascivious intent	A state of mind in which the sexual gratification or arousal of any person is an objective. [Evidence for establishing lascivious intent can include any of the following:] whether the circumstances include sexual behavior, sexual relations, infamous conduct of a lustful or obscene nature, deviation from accepted customs and manners, or sexually oriented displays; whether the focal point of a visual depiction is the child's genitalia, pubic area, or breast area of a female child; whether the setting or pose of a visual depiction is generally associated with sexual activity; whether the child is depicted in an unnatural pose or inappropriate attire, considering the child's age; whether the depiction denotes sexual suggestiveness or a willingness to engage in sexual activity; whether the depiction is of a child engaging in or being engaged in sexual conduct, including, but not limited to, sexual intercourse, unnatural sexual intercourse, . . . masturbation, . . . or lewd exhibition of the genitals.
Disseminate	To import, publish, produce, print, manufacture, distribute, sell, lease, exhibit or display.
Minor	Anyone below 18 years old.
Harmful to minors	[Matter that is] obscene or, if taken as a whole, it (1) describes or represents nudity, sexual conduct or sexual excitement, so as to appeal predominantly to the prurient interest of minors; (2) is patently contrary to prevailing standards of adults in the county where the offense was committed as to suitable material for such minors; and (3) lacks serious literary, artistic, political or scientific value for minors.
Matter	Any handwritten or printed material, visual representation, live performance or sound recording including, but not limited to,

(continued)

179

Key definition	Applicable Statutes and What They Say*
	books, magazines, motion picture films, pamphlets, phonographic records, pictures, photographs, figures, statues, plays, dances, or any electronic communication including, but not limited to, electronic mail, instant messages, text messages, and any other communication created by means of use of the Internet or wireless network, whether by computer, telephone, or any other device or by any transfer of signs, signals, writing, images, sounds, data, or intelligence of any nature transmitted in whole or in part by a wire, radio, electromagnetic, photo-electronic or photo-optical system.
Sexual conduct	Human masturbation, sexual intercourse, actual or simulated, normal or perverted, any lewd exhibitions of the genitals, flagellation or torture in the context of a sexual relationship, any lewd touching of the genitals, pubic areas, or buttocks of the human male or female, or the breasts of the female, whether alone or between members of the same or opposite sex, . . . and any depiction or representation of excretory functions in the context of a sexual relationship. Sexual intercourse is simulated when it depicts explicit sexual intercourse which gives the appearance of the consummation of sexual intercourse, normal or perverted.
Sexual excitement	Condition of human male or female genitals or the breasts of the female while in a state of sexual stimulation or the sensual experiences of humans engaging in or witnessing sexual conduct or nudity.
Visual material	Any motion picture film, picture, photograph, videotape, book, magazine, pamphlet that contains pictures, photographs or similar visual representations or reproductions, or depiction by computer, telephone or any other device capable of electronic data storage or transmission.
MICHIGAN	MICH. COMP. LAWS § 750.142 (2004) MICH. COMP. LAWS § 750.145c (2004) MICH. COMP. LAWS § 750.145d (2004)
Child Sexually Abusive Activity or Material	A person who persuades, induces, entices, coerces, causes, or knowingly allows a child to engage in a child sexually abusive activity for the purpose of producing any child sexually

abusive material, or a person who arranges for, produces, makes, or finances, or a person who attempts or prepares or conspires to arrange for, produce, make, or finance any child sexually abusive activity or child sexually abusive material is guilty of a felony, punishable by imprisonment for not more than 20 years, or a fine of not more than $100,000.00, or both, if that person knows, has reason to know, or should reasonably be expected to know that the child is a child or that the child sexually abusive material includes a child or that the depiction constituting the child sexually abusive material appears to include a child, or that person has not taken reasonable precautions to determine the age of the child.

A person who distributes or promotes, or finances the distribution or promotion of, or receives for the purpose of distributing or promoting, or conspires, attempts, or prepares to distribute, receive, finance, or promote any child sexually abusive material or child sexually abusive activity is guilty of a felony, punishable by imprisonment for not more than 7 years, or a fine of not more than $50,000.00, or both, if that person knows, has reason to know, or should reasonably be expected to know that the child is a child or that the child sexually abusive material includes a child or that the depiction constituting the child sexually abusive material appears to include a child, or that person has not taken reasonable precautions to determine the age of the child.

A person who knowingly possesses any child sexually abusive material is guilty of a felony punishable by imprisonment for not more than 4 years or a fine of not more than $10,000.00, or both, if that person knows, has reason to know, or should reasonably be expected to know the child is a child or that the child sexually abusive material includes a child or that the depiction constituting the child sexually abusive material appears to include a child, or that person has not taken reasonable precautions to determine the age of the child.

Obscenity   A person who sells, gives away or in any way furnishes to a person under the age of 18 years a book, pamphlet, or other printed paper or other thing, containing obscene language, or

(continued)

Key definition	Applicable Statutes and What They Say*
	obscene prints, pictures, figures or descriptions tending to corrupt the morals of youth, ... shall be guilty of a misdemeanor.
Child sexually abusive activity	Child engaging in a listed sexual act.
Listed sexual act	Sexual intercourse, erotic fondling, ... masturbation, passive sexual involvement, sexual excitement, or erotic nudity.
Child	Someone below the age of 18.
Erotic nudity	Lascivious exhibition of the genital, pubic, or rectal area of any person. As used in this subdivision, "lascivious" means wanton, lewd, and lustful and tending to produce voluptuous or lewd emotions.
Masturbation	Real or simulated touching, rubbing, or otherwise stimulating of a person's own clothed or unclothed genitals, pubic area, buttocks, or, if the person is female, breasts, or if the person is a child, the developing or undeveloped breast area, either by manual manipulation or self-induced or with an artificial instrument, for the purpose of real or simulated overt sexual gratification or arousal of the person.
Erotic fondling	Touching a person's clothed or unclothed genitals, pubic area, buttocks, or, if the person is female, breasts, or if the person is a child, the developing or undeveloped breast area, for the purpose of real or simulated overt sexual gratification or stimulation of 1 or more of the persons involved. [However, it] does not include physical contact, even if affectionate, that is not for the purpose of real or simulated overt sexual gratification or stimulation of 1 or more of the persons involved.
Passive sexual involvement	[An] act, real or simulated, that exposes another person to or draws another person's attention to an act of sexual intercourse, erotic fondling, ... masturbation, sexual excitement, or erotic nudity because of viewing any of these acts or because of the proximity of the act to that person, for the purpose of real or simulated overt sexual gratification or stimulation of 1 or more of the persons involved.
Child sexually abusive material	Any depiction, whether made or produced by electronic, mechanical, or other means, including a developed or

undeveloped photograph, picture, film, slide, video, electronic visual image, computer diskette, computer or computer-generated image, or picture, or sound recording which is of a child or appears to include a child engaging in a listed sexual act; a book, magazine, computer, computer storage device, or other visual or print or printable medium containing such a photograph, picture, film, slide, video, electronic visual image, computer, or computer-generated image, or picture, or sound recording; or any reproduction, copy, or print of such a photograph, picture, film, slide, video, electronic visual image, book, magazine, computer, or computer-generated image, or picture, other visual or print or printable medium, or sound recording.

Sexual intercourse

Intercourse, real or simulated, whether genital-genital, oral-genital, anal-genital, or oral-anal, whether between persons of the same or opposite sex . . ., or with an artificial genital.

MINNESOTA

MINN. STAT. ANN. § 617.246 (West 2009)
MINN. STAT. ANN. § 617.247 (West 2009)

Use of Minors in Sexual Performance

It is unlawful for a person to promote, employ, use or permit a minor to engage in or assist others to engage minors in posing or modeling alone or with others in any sexual performance or pornographic work if the person knows or has reason to know that the conduct intended is a sexual performance or a pornographic work.

(Anyone who violates this is guilty of a felony and may be sentenced to imprisonment for not more than ten years or to payment of a fine of not more than $20,000 for the first offense and $40,000 for a second or subsequent offense, or both.)

The fact that the minor consented to the sexual performance by the minor is not a defense to a charge of using a minor in a sexual performance.

Possession of Pornographic Work Involving Minors

A person who possesses a pornographic work or a computer disk or computer or other electronic, magnetic, or optical storage system or a storage system of any other type, containing a pornographic work, knowing or with reason to know its content and character, is guilty of a felony and may be sentenced to imprisonment for not more than five years

(*continued*)

STATE Title of Pertinent Provision *Key definition*	Applicable Statutes and What They Say*
	and a fine of not more than $5,000 for a first offense and for not more than ten years and a fine of not more than $10,000 for a second or subsequent offense.
	(Anyone who violates this is guilty of a felony and may be sentenced to imprisonment for not more than ten years if the violation occurs when the person is a registered predatory offender. If the person has a second/subsequent conviction for this crime, within 15 years of the prior conviction, the court shall order a mental examination of the person. The examiner shall report to the court whether treatment of the person is necessary.)
	The fact that the minor consented to the sexual performance by the minor is not a defense to a charge of possession of pornographic work involving minors.
Distribution of Pornographic Work Involving Minors	A person who disseminates pornographic work to an adult or a minor, knowing or with reason to know its content and character, is guilty of a felony and may be sentenced to imprisonment for not more than seven years and a fine of not more than $10,000 for a first offense and for not more than 15 years and a fine of not more than $20,000 for a second or subsequent offense.
	(Anyone who violates this is guilty of a felony and may be sentenced to imprisonment for not more than 15 years if the violation occurs when the person is a registered predatory offender. If the person has a second/subsequent conviction for this crime, within 15 years of the prior conviction, the court shall order a mental examination of the person. The examiner shall report to the court whether treatment of the person is necessary.)
	The fact that the minor consented to the sexual performance by the minor is not a defense to a charge of distribution of pornographic work involving minors.
Sexual performance	Any play, dance or other exhibition presented before an audience or for purposes of visual or mechanical reproduction that uses a minor to depict actual or simulated sexual conduct.
Sexual conduct	An act of sexual intercourse, normal or perverted, including genital-genital, anal-genital, or oral-genital intercourse, whether between human beings; masturbation; lewd exhibitions of the genitals; [or] physical contact with the clothed or

STATE Title of Pertinent Provision *Key definition*	**Applicable Statutes and What They Say***
	unclothed pubic areas or buttocks of a human male or female, or the breasts of the female, whether alone or between members of the same or opposite sex . . . in an act of apparent sexual stimulation or gratification.
Pornographic work	(1) an original or reproduction of a picture, film, photograph, negative, slide, videotape, videodisc, or drawing of a sexual performance involving a minor; or (2) any visual depiction, including any photograph, film, video, picture, drawing, negative, slide, or computer-generated image or picture, whether made or produced by electronic, mechanical, or other means that: (i) uses a minor to depict actual or simulated sexual conduct; (ii) has been created, adapted, or modified to appear that an identifiable minor is engaging in sexual conduct; or (iii) is advertised, promoted, presented, described, or distributed in such a manner that conveys the impression that the material is or contains a visual depiction of a minor engaging in sexual conduct.
Promote	To produce, direct, publish, manufacture, issue, or advertise.
Minor	Someone less than 18 years old.
MISSISSIPPI	Miss. Code Ann. § 97-5-27, et seq. (West 2002)
Depicting Child Engaging in Sexual Conduct	(1) No person shall, by any means including computer, cause, solicit or knowingly permit any child to engage in sexually explicit conduct or in the simulation of sexually explicit conduct for the purpose of producing any visual depiction of such conduct. (2) No person shall, by any means including computer, photograph, film, video tape or otherwise depict or record a child engaging in sexually explicit conduct or in the simulation of sexually explicit conduct. (3) No person shall, by any means including computer, knowingly send, transport, transmit, ship, mail or receive any photograph, drawing, sketch, film, video tape or other visual depiction of an actual child engaging in sexually explicit conduct. (4) No person shall, by any means including computer, receive with intent to distribute, distribute for sale, sell or attempt to sell in any manner any photograph, drawing, sketch, film,

(*continued*)

video tape or other visual depiction of an actual child
engaging in sexually explicit conduct.

(5) No person shall, by any means including computer, possess
any photograph, drawing, sketch, film, video tape or other
visual depiction of an actual child engaging in sexually explicit
conduct.

(6) No person shall, by any means including computer,
knowingly entice, induce, persuade, seduce, solicit, advise,
coerce, or order a child to meet with the defendant or any
other person for the purpose of engaging in sexually explicit
conduct.

(7) No person shall by any means, including computer,
knowingly entice, induce, persuade, seduce, solicit, advise,
coerce or order a child to produce any visual depiction of adult
sexual conduct or any sexually explicit conduct.

Anyone who violates any of the above is guilty of a felony and
upon conviction shall be fined not less than Fifty Thousand
Dollars ($50,000.00) nor more than Five Hundred Thousand
Dollars ($500,000.00) and shall be imprisoned for not less
than five (5) years nor more than forty (40) years. A person
who has a second/subsequent conviction for any of the above
shall be fined not less than One Hundred Thousand Dollars
($100,000.00) nor more than One Million Dollars
($1,000,000.00) and shall be confined in the custody of the
Department of Corrections for life or such lesser term as the
court may determine, but not less than twenty (20) years.

Disseminating Sexual Material to Children	Any person who intentionally and knowingly disseminates sexually oriented material to any person under eighteen (18) years of age shall be guilty of a misdemeanor and upon conviction shall be fined for each offense not less than Five Hundred Dollars ($500.00) nor more than Five Thousand Dollars ($5,000.00) or be imprisoned for not more than one (1) year in the county jail, or be punished by both such fine and imprisonment.

[Dissemination of sexually oriented material occurs when a
person] (a) Sells, delivers or provides, or offers or agrees to
sell, deliver or provide, any sexually oriented writing, picture,
record or other representation or embodiment that is sexually

STATE Title of Pertinent Provision *Key definition*	Applicable Statutes and What They Say*
	oriented; or (b) Presents or directs a sexually oriented play, dance or other performance or participates directly in that portion thereof which makes it sexually oriented; or (c) Exhibits, presents, rents, sells, delivers or provides, or offers or agrees to exhibit, present, rent or to provide any sexually oriented still or motion picture, film, filmstrip or projection slide, or sound recording, sound tape or sound track or any matter or material of whatever form which is a representation, embodiment, performance or publication that is sexually oriented.
Child	Someone less than 18 years old.
Sexually oriented material	Any material is sexually oriented if the material contains representations or descriptions, actual or simulated, of masturbation, sodomy, excretory functions, lewd exhibition of the genitals or female breasts, . . . homosexuality, lesbianism, . . . sexual intercourse, or physical contact with a person's clothed or unclothed genitals, pubic area, buttocks, or the breast or breasts of a female for the purpose of sexual stimulation, gratification or perversion.
Sexually explicit conduct	Actual or simulated: (i) Sexual intercourse, including genital-genital, oral-genital, anal-genital, or oral-anal, whether between persons of the same or opposite sex; . . . (iii) Mastur-bation; . . . (v) Lascivious exhibition of the genitals or pubic area of any person; or (vi) Fondling or other erotic touching of the genitals, pubic area, buttocks, anus or breast.
Simulated	Any depicting of the genitals or rectal areas that gives the appearance of sexual conduct or incipient sexual conduct.
MISSOURI	Mo. Ann. Stat. § 556.061 (West 2008) Mo. Ann. Stat. § 566.010, et seq. (West 2006) Mo. Ann. Stat. § 568.060 (West 2011) Mo. Ann. Stat. § 573.010, et seq. (West 2006)
Sexual Exploitation of a Minor	A person commits the crime of sexual exploitation of a minor if such person knowingly or recklessly photographs, films, videotapes, produces or otherwise creates obscene material with a minor or child pornography. (Sexual exploitation of a minor constitutes a class B felony unless the minor is a child, in which case it is a class A felony.)

(*continued*)

STATE Title of Pertinent Provision *Key definition*	**Applicable Statutes and What They Say***
Promoting Child Pornography in the First Degree	A person commits the crime of promoting child pornography in the first degree if such person possesses with the intent to promote or promotes child pornography of a child less than fourteen years of age or obscene material portraying what appears to be a child less than fourteen years of age. (Promoting child pornography in the first degree constitutes a class B felony unless the person knowingly promotes such material to a minor, in which case it is a class A felony. No person who pleads guilty to or is found guilty of, or is convicted of, promoting child pornography in the first degree shall be eligible for probation, parole, or conditional release for a period of three calendar years.)
Promoting Pornography for Minors or Obscenity in the Second Degree	[The crime of promoting pornography for minors or obscenity in the second degree occurs when someone] promotes, possesses with the purpose to promote, produces, presents, directs or participates in any performance that is pornographic for minors via computer, electronic transfer, Internet or computer network if the person made the matter available to a specific individual known by the defendant to be a minor. (Promoting pornography for minors or obscenity in the second degree constitutes a class A misdemeanor unless the person has pleaded guilty to or has been found guilty of an offense pursuant to this section committed at a different time, in which case it is a class D felony.)
Promoting Child Pornography in the Second Degree	A person commits the crime of promoting child pornography in the second degree if such person possesses with the intent to promote or promotes child pornography of a minor under the age of eighteen or obscene material portraying what appears to be a minor under the age of eighteen. (Promoting child pornography in the second degree is a class C felony unless the person knowingly promotes such material to a minor, in which case it is a class B felony. No person who is found guilty of, pleads guilty to, or is convicted of promoting child pornography in the second degree shall be eligible for probation.)
Possession of Child Pornography	A person commits the crime of possession of child pornography if such person knowingly or recklessly possesses

STATE Title of Pertinent Provision *Key definition*	**Applicable Statutes and What They Say***
	any child pornography of a minor under the age of eighteen or obscene material portraying what appears to be a minor under the age of eighteen.
	(Possession of child pornography constitutes a class C felony unless the person possesses more than twenty still images of child pornography, possesses one motion picture, film, videotape, videotape production, or other moving image of child pornography, or has pleaded guilty to or has been found guilty of an offense under this section, in which case it is a class B felony.)
Furnishing Pornographic Materials to Minors	A person commits the crime of furnishing pornographic material to minors if he or she: (1) Furnishes any material pornographic for minors, knowing that the person to whom it is furnished is a minor or acting in reckless disregard of the likelihood that such person is a minor; or (2) Produces, presents, directs or participates in any performance pornographic for minors that is furnished to a minor knowing that any person viewing such performance is a minor or acting in reckless disregard of the likelihood that a minor is viewing the performance; or (3) Furnishes, produces, presents, directs, participates in any performance or otherwise makes available material that is pornographic for minors via computer, electronic transfer, Internet or computer network if the person made the matter available to a specific individual known by the defendant to be a minor.
	(Furnishing pornographic material to minors or *attempting* to furnish pornographic material to minors is a class A misdemeanor unless the person has pleaded guilty to or has been found guilty of an offense, i.e., a child pornography offense, various sexual offenses or crimes against the family, committed at a different time, in which case it is a class D felony.)
Abuse of a Child	A person commits the crime of abuse of a child if such person . . . photographs or films a child less than eighteen years old engaging in a prohibited sexual act or in the simulation of such an act or who causes or knowingly permits a child to

(continued)

STATE Title of Pertinent Provision *Key definition*	Applicable Statutes and What They Say*
	engage in a prohibited sexual act or in the simulation of such an act for the purpose of photographing or filming the act.
	Abuse of a child is a class C felony, unless: (1) In the course thereof the person inflicts serious emotional injury on the child, or the offense is committed as part of a ritual or ceremony in which case the crime is a class B felony; or (2) A child dies as a result of injuries sustained from conduct chargeable pursuant to the provisions of this section, in which case the crime is a class A felony.
Child	Someone below the age of 14.
Minor	Someone below the age of 18.
Child pornography	(a) Any obscene material or performance depicting sexual conduct, sexual contact, or a sexual performance, . . . and which has as one of its participants or portrays as an observer of such conduct, contact, or performance a minor under the age of eighteen; or (b) Any visual depiction, including any photograph, film, video, picture, or computer or computer-generated image or picture, whether made or produced by electronic, mechanical, or other means, of sexually explicit conduct where: a. The production of such visual depiction involves the use of a minor engaging in sexually explicit conduct; b. Such visual depiction is a digital image, computer image, or computer-generated image that is, or is indistinguishable from, that of a minor engaging in sexually explicit conduct; or c. Such visual depiction has been created, adapted, or modified to show that an identifiable minor is engaging in sexually explicit conduct.
Sexual conduct	Acts of human masturbation; deviate sexual intercourse; sexual intercourse; or physical contact with a person's clothed or unclothed genitals, pubic area, buttocks, or the breast of a female in an act of apparent sexual stimulation or gratification.
Sexual contact	Any touching of the genitals or anus of any person, or the breast of any female person, or any such touching through the clothing, for the purpose of arousing or gratifying sexual desire of any person.

STATE Title of Pertinent Provision Key definition	Applicable Statutes and What They Say*
Sexual performance	Any performance, or part thereof, which includes sexual conduct by a child who is less than seventeen years of age.
Nudity	The showing of postpubertal human genitals or pubic area, with less than a fully opaque covering.
Performance	Any play, motion picture film, videotape, dance or exhibition performed before an audience of one or more.
Sexual excitement	Condition of human male or female genitals when in a state of sexual stimulation or arousal.
Sexually explicit conduct	Actual or simulated: (a) Sexual intercourse, including genital-genital, oral-genital, anal-genital, or oral-anal, whether between persons of the same or opposite sex; . . . (c) Masturbation; . . . or (e) Lascivious exhibition of the genitals or pubic area of any person.
Promote	To manufacture, issue, sell, provide, mail, deliver, transfer, transmute, publish, distribute, circulate, disseminate, present, exhibit, or advertise, or to offer or agree to do the same, by any means including a computer.
Pornographic for minors	Any material or performance is pornographic for minors if the following apply: (a) The average person, applying contemporary community standards, would find that the material or performance, taken as a whole, has a tendency to cater or appeal to a prurient interest of minors; and (b) The material or performance depicts or describes nudity, sexual conduct, sexual excitement, . . . in a way which is patently offensive to the average person applying contemporary adult community standards with respect to what is suitable for minors; and (c) The material or performance, taken as a whole, lacks serious literary, artistic, political, or scientific value for minors.
Explicit sexual material	Any pictorial or three-dimensional material depicting human masturbation, deviate sexual intercourse, sexual intercourse, direct physical stimulation or unclothed genitals, . . . or emphasizing the depiction of postpubertal human genitals; provided, however, that works of art or of anthropological significance shall not be deemed to be within the foregoing definition.
Prohibited sexual act	Any of the following, whether performed or engaged in either with any other person or alone: sexual or anal intercourse, masturbation, . . . fetishism, fellatio, cunnilingus, any other

(continued)

STATE **Title of Pertinent Provision** *Key definition*	**Applicable Statutes and What They Say***
	sexual activity or nudity, if such nudity is to be depicted for the purpose of sexual stimulation or gratification of any individual who may view such depiction.
Fetishism	A condition in which erotic feelings are excited by an object or body part whose presence is psychologically necessary for sexual stimulation or gratification.
MONTANA	MONT. CODE ANN. § 45-5-625 (2009)
Sexual Abuse of Children	A person commits the offense of sexual abuse of children if the person: (a) knowingly employs, uses, or permits the employment or use of a child in an exhibition of sexual conduct, actual or simulated; (b) knowingly photographs, films, videotapes, develops or duplicates the photographs, films, or videotapes, or records a child engaging in sexual conduct, actual or simulated; (c) knowingly, by any means of communication, including electronic communication, persuades, entices, counsels, or procures a child under 16 years of age or a person the offender believes to be a child under 16 years of age to engage in sexual conduct, actual or simulated; (d) knowingly processes, develops, prints, publishes, transports, distributes, sells, exhibits, or advertises any visual or print medium, including a medium by use of electronic communication in which a child is engaged in sexual conduct, actual or simulated; (e) knowingly possesses any visual or print medium, including a medium by use of electronic communication in which a child is engaged in sexual conduct, actual or simulated. Anyone convicted of sexual abuse of children shall be punished by life imprisonment or by imprisonment in the state prison for a term not to exceed 100 years and may be fined not more than $10,000. Here are the exceptions: (A) If the victim is under 16 years of age, a person convicted of the offense of sexual abuse of children shall be punished by life imprisonment or by imprisonment in the state prison for a term of not less than 4 years or more than 100 years and may be fined not more than $10,000. However, if this person has a prior conviction for sexual abuse of children, he or she (a) shall serve the entire sentence; (b) shall serve the sentence in

Key definition	Applicable Statutes and What They Say*
	prison; (c) may not for any reason, except a medical reason, be transferred for any length of time to another type of institution, facility, or program; (d) may not be paroled; and (e) may not be given time off for good behavior or otherwise be given an early release for any reason.; or (B) if the defendant's conviction is for knowingly possessing any visual or print medium, including a medium by use of electronic communication in which a child is engaged in sexual conduct, actual or simulated, he or she shall be fined a maximum of $10,000 or serve a maximum prison term of 10 years or get both this prison term and the $10,000 fine. However, if this person has a prior conviction for sexual abuse of children, he or she (a) shall serve the entire sentence; (b) shall serve the sentence in prison; (c) may not for any reason, except a medical reason, be transferred for any length of time to another type of institution, facility, or program; (d) may not be paroled; and (e) may not be given time off for good behavior or otherwise be given an early release for any reason; or (C) (a) if the victim was 12 years of age or younger and the offender was 18 years of age or older at the time of the offense, the offender: (i) shall be punished by imprisonment in a state prison for a term of 100 years, and during the first 25 years of imprisonment, the offender is not eligible for parole; (ii) may be fined an amount not to exceed $50,000; and (iii) shall be ordered to enroll in and successfully complete the educational phase and the cognitive and behavioral phase of a sexual offender treatment program provided or approved by the department of corrections. (b) If the offender is released after the mandatory minimum period of imprisonment, the offender is subject to supervision by the department of corrections for the remainder of the offender's life and shall participate in the program for continuous, satellite-based monitoring.
Electronic communication	A sign, signal, writing, image, sound, data, or intelligence of any nature transmitted or created in whole or in part by a wire, radio, electromagnetic, photoelectronic, or photo-optical system.

(continued)

STATE Title of Pertinent Provision *Key definition*	**Applicable Statutes and What They Say***
Sexual conduct	(i) Actual or simulated: (A) sexual intercourse, whether between persons of the same or opposite sex; (B) penetration of the vagina or rectum by any object, except when done as part of a recognized medical procedure; . . . (D) masturbation; . . . (F) lewd exhibition of the genitals, breasts, pubic or rectal area, or other intimate parts of any person; or (G) defecation or urination for the purpose of the sexual stimulation of the viewer; or (ii) depiction of a child in the nude or in a state of partial undress with the purpose to abuse, humiliate, harass, or degrade the child or to arouse or gratify the person's own sexual response or desire or the sexual response or desire of any person.
Simulated	Any depicting of the genitals or pubic or rectal area that gives the appearance of sexual conduct or incipient sexual conduct.
NEBRASKA	NEB. REV. STAT. § 28-707 (2010) NEB. REV. STAT. § 28-813.01, et seq. (2009) NEB. REV. STAT. § 28-1463.01, et seq. (2009) NEV. REV. STAT. 200.700, et seq. (2007)
Child Abuse	A person commits child abuse if he or she knowingly, intentionally, or negligently causes or permits a minor child to be . . . placed in a situation to be sexually exploited by allowing, encouraging, or forcing such minor child to solicit for or engage in . . . obscene or pornographic photography, films, or depictions. (Child abuse is a Class I misdemeanor if the offense is committed negligently. Child abuse is a Class IIIA felony if the offense is committed knowingly and intentionally and does not result in serious bodily injury. Child abuse is a Class II felony if the offense is committed knowingly and intentionally and results in serious bodily injury.)
Possession of Visual Depiction of Sexually Explicit Conduct	It shall be unlawful for a person to knowingly possess any visual depiction of sexually explicit conduct . . . which has a child . . . as one of its participants or portrayed observers. (If the defendant is below the age of 19 at the time he/she violates the above provision, the violation constitutes a "Class IV felony for each offense. However, if the defendant has a prior

conviction for the crimes of visual depiction of sexually explicit conduct or visual depiction of sexually explicit acts related to possession under the child Pornography Prevent Act, set forth below, then for *each* offense of possession of sexually explicit conduct for that person, the violation is a Class IC felony.)

Nebraska law provides an affirmative defense to the crime of possession of sexually explicit conduct for consensual sexting if the defendant can show the following: (a) The visual depiction portrays no person other than the defendant; or (b) (i) The defendant was less than nineteen years of age; (ii) the visual depiction of sexually explicit conduct portrays a child who is fifteen years of age or older; (iii) the visual depiction was knowingly and voluntarily generated by the child depicted therein; (iv) the visual depiction was knowingly and voluntarily provided by the child depicted in the visual depiction; (v) the visual depiction contains only one child; (vi) the defendant has not provided or made available the visual depiction to another person except the child depicted who originally sent the visual depiction to the defendant; and (vii) the defendant did not coerce the child in the visual depiction to either create or send the visual depiction.

Child Pornography
Prevention Act:
Visual Depiction of
Sexually Explicit
Conduct

It shall be unlawful for a person to knowingly make, publish, direct, create, provide, or in any manner generate any visual depiction of sexually explicit conduct which has a child as one of its participants or portrayed observers.

The defendant has an affirmative defense if he or she was less than eighteen years of age at the time the visual depiction was created and the visual depiction of sexually explicit conduct includes no person other than the defendant.

It shall be unlawful for a person knowingly to purchase, rent, sell, deliver, distribute, display for sale, advertise, trade, or provide to any person any visual depiction of sexually explicit conduct which has a child as one of its participants or portrayed observers.

Here, Nebraska law provides an affirmative defense if (a) the defendant was less than eighteen years of age, (b) the visual

(*continued*)

depiction of sexually explicit conduct includes no person other than the defendant, (c) the defendant had a reasonable belief at the time the visual depiction was sent to another that it was being sent to a willing recipient, and (d) the recipient was at least fifteen years of age at the time the visual depiction was sent.

It shall be unlawful for a person to knowingly employ, force, authorize, induce, or otherwise cause a child to engage in any visual depiction of sexually explicit conduct which has a child as one of its participants or portrayed observers.

If the violation of (1), (2) or (3) above is by someone less than 19 years old at the time of the violation, the violation constitutes a Class III felony for each offense. Anyone with a prior conviction for (1), (2) or (3) above is instead guilty of a Class IC felony for each violation.

Visual Depiction of Sexually Explicit Acts Related to Possession

It shall be unlawful for a person to knowingly possess with intent to rent, sell, deliver, distribute, trade, or provide to any person any visual depiction of sexually explicit conduct which has a child as one of its participants or portrayed observers.

(If the violation is by someone less than 19 years old at the time of the violation, the violation constitutes a Class IIIA felony for each offense. Anyone with a prior conviction for visual depiction of sexually explicit acts related to possession is guilty of a Class IC felony for each violation.)

Erotic nudity

Display of the human male or female genitals or pubic area, the human female breasts, or the developing breast area of the human female child, for the purpose of real or simulated overt sexual gratification or sexual stimulation of one or more of the persons involved.

Erotic fondling

Touching a person's clothed or unclothed genitals or pubic area, breasts if the person is a female, or developing breast area if the person is a female child, for the purpose of real or simulated overt sexual gratification or sexual stimulation of one or more persons involved. Erotic fondling shall not be construed to include physical contact, even if affectionate, which is not for the purpose of real or simulated overt sexual gratification or sexual stimulation of one or more of the persons involved.

STATE Title of Pertinent Provision *Key definition*	Applicable Statutes and What They Say*
Child	In the case of a participant, means any person under the age of eighteen years and, in the case of a portrayed observer, means any person under the age of sixteen years.
Sexually explicit conduct	(a) Real or simulated intercourse, whether genital-genital, oral-genital, anal-genital, or oral-anal between persons of the same or opposite sex . . . or with an artificial genital; (b) real or simulated masturbation; . . . (d) erotic fondling; (e) erotic nudity; or (f) real or simulated defecation or urination for the purpose of sexual gratification or sexual stimulation of one or more of the persons involved.
Visual depiction	Live performance or photographic representation and includes any undeveloped film or videotape or data stored on a computer disk or by other electronic means which is capable of conversion into a visual image and also includes any photograph, film, video, picture, digital image, or computer-displayed image, video, or picture, whether made or produced by electronic, mechanical, computer, digital, or other means.
NEVADA	NEV. REV. STAT. 200.700, et seq. (2007) Nevada Senate Bill 277
Use of a Minor in Producing Pornography	A person who knowingly uses, encourages, entices or permits a minor to simulate or engage in or assist others to simulate or engage in sexual conduct to produce a performance is guilty of a category A felony.
	[The person shall be punished with a state prison term as follows:]
	If the minor is 14 years of age or older, for life with the possibility of parole, with eligibility for parole beginning when a minimum of 5 years has been served, and shall be further punished by a fine of not more than $100,000.
	If the minor is less than 14 years of age, for life with the possibility of parole, with eligibility for parole beginning when a minimum of 10 years has been served, and shall be further punished by a fine of not more than $100,000.
	(A person who knowingly uses, encourages, entices, coerces or permits a minor to be the subject of a sexual portrayal in a performance is guilty of a category A felony.)

(continued)

STATE **Title of Pertinent Provision** *Key definition*	**Applicable Statutes and What They Say***
Use of a Minor as Subject of Sexual Portrayal in Performance	Regardless of whether the minor is aware that the sexual portrayal is part of a performance, [the defendant shall be punished with a state prison term as follows]: If the minor is 14 years of age or older, for life with the possibility of parole, with eligibility for parole beginning when a minimum of 5 years has been served, and shall be further punished by a fine of not more than $100,000. If the minor is less than 14 years of age, for life with the possibility of parole, with eligibility for parole beginning when a minimum of 10 years has been served, and shall be further punished by a fine of not more than $100,000.
Promotion of Sexual Performance of Minor	A person who knowingly promotes a performance of a minor: 1. Where the minor engages in or simulates, or assists others to engage in or simulate, sexual conduct; or 2. Where the minor is the subject of a sexual portrayal, is guilty of a category A felony. [The person shall be punished with a state prison term as follows:] If the minor is 14 years of age or older, for life with the possibility of parole, with eligibility for parole beginning when a minimum of 5 years has been served, and shall be further punished by a fine of not more than $100,000. If the minor is less than 14 years of age, for life with the possibility of parole, with eligibility for parole beginning when a minimum of 10 years has been served, and shall be further punished by a fine of not more than $100,000.
Distributing Materials Depicting Pornography Involving Minor	A person who knowingly prepares, advertises or distributes any item or material that depicts a minor engaging in, or simulating, or assisting others to engage in or simulate, sexual conduct is guilty of a category B felony and shall be punished by imprisonment in the state prison for a minimum term of not less than 1 year and a maximum term of not more than 15 years, or by a fine of not more than $15,000, or by both fine and imprisonment.
Possession of Visual Presentation Depicting Sexual Conduct of Person	A person who knowingly and willfully has in his or her possession for *any purpose* any film, photograph or other visual presentation depicting a person under the age of 16 years as the subject of a sexual portrayal or engaging in or

STATE Title of Pertinent Provision *Key definition*	Applicable Statutes and What They Say*
under 16 Years of Age	simulating, or assisting others to engage in or simulate, sexual conduct: 1. For the first offense, is guilty of a category B felony and shall be punished by imprisonment in the state prison for a minimum term of not less than 1 year and a maximum term of not more than 6 years, and may be further punished by a fine of not more than $5,000. 2. For any subsequent offense, is guilty of a category A felony and shall be punished by imprisonment in the state prison for a minimum term of not less than 1 year and a maximum term of life with the possibility of parole, and may be further punished by a fine of not more than $5,000. It is critical to note that a child who violates the child pornography laws above may be adjudicated delinquent and subject to registration and community notification as a juvenile sex offender. In 2011, Nevada Senate Bill 277 was signed into law. This law was designed to provide an alternate mechanism for dealing with minors who violate various crimes mentioned above. However, despite this law, prosecutors retain discretion to proceed against the minor under any of the other laws above. The sexting law follows.
Sexting	1. [Subsection 1] A minor shall not knowingly and willfully use an electronic communication device to transmit or distribute a sexual image of himself or herself to another person. 2. [Subsection 2] A minor shall not knowingly and willfully use an electronic communication device to transmit or distribute a sexual image of another minor who is older than, the same age as or not more than 4 years younger than the minor transmitting the sexual image. 3. [Subsection 3] A minor shall not knowingly and willfully possess a sexual image that was transmitted or distributed as described in subsection 1 or 2 if the minor who is the subject of the sexual image is older than, the same age as or not more than 4 years younger than the minor who possesses the sexual image. It is an affirmative defense to a violation charged pursuant to this subsection if the minor who possesses a sexual image:

(*continued*)

(a) Did not knowingly purchase, procure, solicit or request the sexual image or take any other action to cause the sexual image to come into his or her possession; and (b) Promptly and in good faith, and without retaining or allowing any person, other than a law enforcement agency or a school official, to access any sexual image: (1) Took reasonable steps to destroy each image; or (2) Reported the matter to a law enforcement agency or a school official and gave the law enforcement agency or school official access to each image.

A minor who violates subsection 1: (a) For the first violation: (1) Is a child in need of supervision, as that term is used in title 5 of NRS, and is not a delinquent child; and (2) Is not considered a sex offender or juvenile sex offender and is not subject to registration or community notification as a juvenile sex offender pursuant to title 5 of NRS, or as a sex offender pursuant to NRS 179D.010 to 179D.550, inclusive; [and] (b) For the second or a subsequent violation: (1) Commits a delinquent act, and the court may order the detention of the minor in the same manner as if the minor had committed an act that would have been a misdemeanor if committed by an adult; and (2) Is not considered a sex offender or juvenile sex offender and is not subject to registration or community notification as a juvenile sex offender pursuant to title 5 of NRS, or as a sex offender pursuant to NRS 179D.010 to 179D.550, inclusive.

A minor who violates subsection 2: (a) Commits a delinquent act, and the court may order the detention of the minor in the same manner as if the minor had committed an act that would have been a misdemeanor if committed by an adult; and (b) Is not considered a sex offender or juvenile sex offender and is not subject to registration or community notification as a juvenile sex offender pursuant to title 5 of NRS, or as a sex offender pursuant to NRS 179D.010 to 179D.550, inclusive.

A minor who violates subsection 3: (a) Is a child in need of supervision, as that term is used in title 5 of NRS, and is not a delinquent child; and (b) Is not considered a sex offender or juvenile sex offender and is not subject to registration or community notification as a juvenile sex offender pursuant to

STATE Title of Pertinent Provision _Key definition_	Applicable Statutes and What They Say*
	title 5 of NRS, or as a sex offender pursuant to NRS 179D.010 to 179D.550, inclusive.
Sexual portrayal	Depiction of a person in a manner which appeals to the prurient interest in sex and which does not have serious literary, artistic, political or scientific value.
Sexual conduct	Sexual intercourse, lewd exhibition of the genitals, fellatio, cunnilingus, . . . anal intercourse, excretion, . . . masturbation, or the penetration of any part of a person's body or of any object manipulated or inserted by a person into the genital or anal opening of the body of another.
Performance	Any play, film, photograph, computer-generated image, electronic representation, dance or other visual presentation.
Promote	To produce, direct, procure, manufacture, sell, give, lend, publish, distribute, exhibit, advertise or possess for the purpose of distribution.
Minor	Someone below the age of 18.
Electronic communication device	Any electronic device that is capable of transmitting or distributing a sexual image, including, without limitation, a cellular phone, personal digital assistant, computer, computer network and computer system.
School official	Principal, vice principal, school counselor or school police officer.
Sexual image	Any visual depiction, including, without limitation, any photograph or video, of a minor simulating.
NEW HAMPSHIRE	N.H. Rev. Stat. Ann. § 649-A:1, et seq. (2011) N.H. Rev. Stat. Ann. § 649-B:1, et seq. (1999) N.H. Rev. Stat. Ann. § 650:1, et seq. (2011)
New Hampshire Legislature's Strong Policy Statement Supporting Enactment of Its Law	I. The legislature finds that there has been a proliferation of exploitation of children through their use as subjects in sexual performances. The care of children is a sacred trust and should not be abused by those who seek to profit through a commercial network based upon the exploitation of children. The public policy of the state demands the protection of children from exploitation through sexual performances. II. It is the purpose of this chapter to facilitate the prosecution of those who exploit children in the manner specified in

(continued)

STATE Title of Pertinent Provision	
Key definition	**Applicable Statutes and What They Say***
	paragraph I. In accordance with the United States Supreme Court's decision in New York v. Ferber, this chapter makes the dissemination of visual representations of children under the age of 16 engaged in sexual activity illegal irrespective of whether the visual representations are legally obscene; and the legislature urges law enforcement officers to aggressively seek out and prosecute those who violate the provisions of this chapter.
Possession of Child Sexual Abuse Images	No person shall knowingly: (a) Buy, procure, possess, or control any visual representation of a child engaging in sexually explicit conduct; or (b) Bring or cause to be brought into this state any visual representation of a child engaging in sexually explicit conduct.
	(This crime is a class A felony if the defendant has no prior conviction for the same crime in New Hampshire or another state. If the defendant is convicted for the crime above and the indictment alleges that the person has a prior conviction for the same crime, he or she may be sentenced to a maximum sentence not to exceed 20 years and a minimum sentence not to exceed 1/2 of the maximum sentence.)
	New Hampshire law provides an affirmative defense to the crime if the defendant can show that he or she satisfies the following: (i) possessed fewer than three images of the prohibited visual depiction; and (ii) "promptly and in good faith, and without retaining or allowing any person, other than a law enforcement agency, to access any visual depiction or copy thereof: (1) Took reasonable steps to destroy each such visual depiction; or (2) Reported the matter to a law enforcement agency and afforded that agency access to each such visual depiction.
Distribution of Child Sexual Abuse Images	No person shall: (a) Knowingly sell, exchange, or otherwise transfer, or possess with intent to sell, exchange, or otherwise transfer any visual representation of a child engaging in or being engaged in sexually explicit conduct; [or] (b) Knowingly publish, exhibit, or otherwise make available any visual representation of a child engaging in or being engaged in sexually explicit conduct.
	(A defendant who has no prior conviction for the same crime in New Hampshire or another state may be sentenced to a

maximum sentence not to exceed 20 years and a minimum sentence not to exceed 1/2 of the maximum. If the defendant is convicted for the crime above and the indictment alleges that the person has a prior conviction for the same crime, he or she may be sentenced to a maximum sentence not to exceed 30 years and a minimum sentence not to exceed 1/2 of the minimum. Additionally, if a defendant who has no prior conviction for the crime in New Hampshire or another state and is convicted for the knowing exhibition, publication or otherwise making available fewer than three visual representations or images of a child engaging in or being engaged in sexually explicit conduct is guilty of a class B felony.)

Manufacture of Child Sexual Abuse Images

No person shall knowingly create, produce, manufacture, or direct a visual representation of a child engaging in or being engaged in sexually explicit conduct, or participate in that portion of such visual representation that consists of a child engaging in or being engaged in sexually explicit conduct.

(A defendant who has no prior conviction for this crime in New Hampshire or another state may be sentenced to a maximum sentence not to exceed 30 years and a minimum sentence not to exceed 1/2 of the maximum. Additionally, if the defendant is convicted for the crime above and the indictment alleges that the person has a prior conviction for the same crime, he or she may be sentenced to life imprisonment or for such term as the court may order.)

Obscenity

A person is guilty of a misdemeanor if he commits obscenity when, with knowledge of the nature of content thereof [he or she does any of the following acts]: (a) provides or delivers obscene material; or (b) publishes, exhibits or otherwise makes available any obscene material. [Anyone who commits either of these acts] with knowledge that such act involves a child in material deemed obscene . . . is guilty of: (a) A class B felony if such person has had no prior convictions in this state or another state for the conduct; [or] (b) A class A felony if such person has had one or more prior convictions in this state or another state for the conduct.

(continued)

STATE **Title of Pertinent** **Provision** *Key definition*	**Applicable Statutes and What They Say***
	(Each subsequent violation of the obscenity law above constitutes a class B felony.)
	New Hampshire law provides an affirmative defense to prosecution for the obscene acts above if the dissemination was restricted to noncommercial dissemination to personal associates of the accused who are not under 18 years of age.
Computer Pornography and Child Exploitation Prevention Act of 1998:	
Computer Pornography	No person shall knowingly: (a) Compile, enter into, or transmit by means of computer; (b) Make, print, publish, or reproduce by other computerized means;
	(c) Cause or allow to be entered into or transmitted by means of computer; or (d) Buy, sell, receive, exchange, or disseminate by means of computer, any notice, statement, or advertisement, or any minor's name, telephone number, place of residence, physical characteristics, or other descriptive or identifying information, for purposes of facilitating, encouraging, offering, or soliciting sexual conduct of or with any child, or the visual depiction of such conduct.
	(Violation of this provision constitutes a class B felony.)
Child	Someone less than 18 years old. However, for purposes of the Computer Pornography and Child Exploitation Prevention Act of 1998, child refers to someone less than 16 years old.
Visual representation	Any visual depiction, including any photograph, film, video, digital image, picture, or computer or computer-generated image or picture, whether made or produced by electronic, mechanical, or other means, of sexually explicit conduct, where: (a) The production of such visual depiction involves the use of a child engaging in or being engaged in sexually explicit conduct; or (b) Such visual depiction is a digital image, computer image, or computer-generated image of a child engaging in or being engaged in sexually explicit conduct.
Computer	An electronic, magnetic, optical, electrochemical, or other high speed data processing device performing logical, arithmetic, or

STATE Title of Pertinent Provision *Key definition*	Applicable Statutes and What They Say*
	storage functions, and includes any data storage facility or communications facility directly related to or operating in conjunction with such device, but such term does not include an automated typewriter or typesetter, a portable hand held calculator, or other similar device.
Previous conviction or previously convicted	Having been convicted by a jury or a judge, or having plead guilty prior to the commission of the current offense. For purposes of this paragraph, a previous conviction need not have been affirmed on appeal.
Disseminate	To import, publish, produce, print, manufacture, distribute, sell, lease, exhibit, or display.
Sexually explicit conduct	Human masturbation, the touching of the actor's or other person's sexual organs in the context of a sexual relationship, sexual intercourse actual or simulated, normal or perverted, whether alone or between members of the same or opposite sex, . . . or any lewd exhibitions of the buttocks, genitals, flagellation.
Simulated sexual intercourse	[Intercourse that] depicts explicit sexual intercourse that gives the appearance of the consummation of sexual intercourse, normal or perverted.
NEW JERSEY	N.J. Stat. Ann. § 2C:24-4 (West 2005)
Endangering Welfare of Children	[Anyone who] engages in sexual conduct which would impair or debauch the morals of the child, [where the child is less than 16 years old,] is guilty of a crime of the third degree.
	A person commits a crime of the second degree if he causes or permits a child to engage in a prohibited sexual act or in the simulation of such an act if the person knows, has reason to know or intends that the prohibited act may be photographed, filmed, reproduced, or reconstructed in any manner, including on the Internet, or may be part of an exhibition or performance.
	Any person who photographs or films a child in a prohibited sexual act or in the simulation of such an act or who uses any device, including a computer, to reproduce or reconstruct the image of a child in a prohibited sexual act or in the simulation of such an act is guilty of a crime of the second degree.
	[Anyone] who knowingly sells, procures, manufactures, gives, provides, lends, trades, mails, delivers, transfers, publishes,

(*continued*)

Key definition	Applicable Statutes and What They Say*
	distributes, circulates, disseminates, presents, exhibits, advertises, offers or agrees to offer, through any means, including the Internet, any photograph, film, videotape, computer program or file, video game or any other reproduction or reconstruction which depicts a child engaging in a prohibited sexual act or in the simulation of such an act, is guilty of a crime of the second degree.
	Any person who knowingly possesses or knowingly views any photograph, film, videotape, computer program or file, video game or any other reproduction or reconstruction which depicts a child engaging in a prohibited sexual act or in the simulation of such an act, including on the Internet, is guilty of a crime of the fourth degree.
Child	Someone below the age of 16.
Prohibited sexual act	(a) Sexual intercourse; or (b) Anal intercourse; or (c) Masturbation; . . . or (g) Fellatio; or (h) Cunnilingus; [or] (i) Nudity, if depicted for the purpose of sexual stimulation or gratification of any person who may view such depiction; or (j) Any act of sexual penetration or sexual contact.
Sexual penetration	Vaginal intercourse, cunnilingus, fellatio or anal intercourse between persons or insertion of the hand, finger or object into the anus or vagina either by the actor or upon the actor's instruction.
Sexual contact	An intentional touching by the victim or actor, either directly or through clothing, of the victim's or actor's intimate parts for the purpose of degrading or humiliating the victim or sexually arousing or sexually gratifying the actor.
Reproduction	[Refers to,] but is not limited to, computer generated images.
NEW MEXICO	N.M. STAT. ANN. § 30-6A-1, et seq. (Michie 2011) N.M. STAT. ANN. § 30-37-3.2 (Michie 2007)
Sexual Exploitation of Children	It is unlawful for a person to intentionally possess any obscene visual or print medium depicting any prohibited sexual act or simulation of such an act if that person knows or has reason to know that the obscene medium depicts any prohibited sexual act or simulation of such act and if that person knows or has reason to know that one or more of the participants in that act is a child under eighteen years of age.

Applicable Statutes and What They Say*

(Violation of this provision constitutes a fourth degree felony.)

It is unlawful for a person to intentionally distribute any obscene visual or print medium depicting any prohibited sexual act or simulation of such an act if that person knows or has reason to know that the obscene medium depicts any prohibited sexual act or simulation of such act and if that person knows or has reason to know that one or more of the participants in that act is a child under eighteen years of age.

(Violation of this provision constitutes a third degree felony.)

It is unlawful for a person to intentionally cause or permit a child under eighteen years of age to engage in any prohibited sexual act or simulation of such an act if that person knows, has reason to know or intends that the act may be recorded in any obscene visual or print medium or performed publicly.

(Violation of this provision constitutes a third degree felony, unless the child is under the age of thirteen, in which event the person is guilty of a second degree felony.)

It is unlawful for a person to intentionally manufacture any obscene visual or print medium depicting any prohibited sexual act or simulation of such an act if one or more of the participants in that act is a child under eighteen years of age.

(Violation of this provision constitutes a second degree felony.)

It is unlawful for a person to intentionally manufacture any obscene visual or print medium depicting any prohibited sexual act or simulation of such an act if that person knows or has reason to know that the obscene medium depicts a prohibited sexual act or simulation of such an act and if that person knows or has reason to know that a real child under eighteen years of age, who is not a participant, is depicted as a participant in that act.

(Violation of this provision constitutes a fourth degree felony.)

It is unlawful for a person to intentionally distribute any obscene visual or print medium depicting any prohibited sexual act or simulation of such an act if that person knows or has reason to know that the obscene medium depicts a prohibited sexual act or simulation of such an act and if that person knows or has reason to know that a real child under

(continued)

207

STATE Title of Pertinent Provision *Key definition*	Applicable Statutes and What They Say*
	eighteen years of age, who is not a participant, is depicted as a participant in that act.
	(Violation of this provision constitutes a third degree felony.)
Prohibited sexual act	Sexual intercourse, including genital-genital, oral-genital, anal-genital or oral-anal, whether between persons of the same or opposite sex; masturbation; [or] lewd and sexually explicit exhibition with a focus on the genitals or pubic area of any person for the purpose of sexual stimulation.
Visual or print medium	(1) Any film, photograph, negative, slide, computer diskette, videotape, videodisc or any computer or electronically generated imagery; or (2) any book, magazine or other form of publication or photographic reproduction containing or incorporating any film, photograph, negative, slide, computer diskette, videotape, videodisc or any computer generated or electronically generated imagery.
Manufacture	Production, processing, copying by any means, printing, packaging or repackaging of any visual or print medium depicting any prohibited sexual act or simulation of such an act if one or more of the participants in that act is a child under eighteen years of age.
NEW YORK	N.Y. Penal Law § 235.22 (McKinney 2007) N.Y. Penal Law § 263.00, et seq. (McKinney 2008)
Use of a Child in a Sexual Performance	A person is guilty of the use of a child in a sexual performance if knowing the character and content thereof he employs, authorizes or induces a child less than seventeen years of age to engage in a sexual performance. (Use of a child in a sexual performance constitutes a class C felony.)
Promoting an Obscene Sexual Performance by a Child	A person is guilty of promoting an obscene sexual performance by a child when, knowing the character and content thereof, he produces, directs or promotes any obscene performance which includes sexual conduct by a child less than seventeen years of age. (Promoting an obscene sexual performance by a child constitutes a class D felony.)
Possessing an Obscene Sexual	A person is guilty of possessing an obscene sexual performance by a child when, knowing the character and

STATE Title of Pertinent Provision *Key definition*	Applicable Statutes and What They Say*
Performance by a Child	content thereof, he knowingly has in his possession or control any obscene performance which includes sexual conduct by a child less than sixteen years of age. (Possessing an obscene sexual performance by a child constitutes a class E felony.)
Promoting a Sexual Performance By a Child	A person is guilty of promoting a sexual performance by a child when, knowing the character and content thereof, he produces, directs or promotes any performance which includes sexual conduct by a child less than seventeen years of age. (Promoting a sexual performance by a child constitutes a class D felony.)
Possessing a Sexual Performance by a Child	A person is guilty of possessing a sexual performance by a child when, knowing the character and content thereof, he knowingly has in his possession or control any performance which includes sexual conduct by a child less than sixteen years of age. (Possessing a sexual performance by a child constitutes a class E felony.)
Disseminating Indecent Material to Minors in the First Degree	A person is guilty of disseminating indecent material to minors in the first degree when: 1. knowing the character and content of the communication which, in whole or in part, depicts or describes, either in words or images actual or simulated nudity, sexual conduct, . . . and which is harmful to minors, he intentionally uses any computer communication system allowing the input, output, examination or transfer, of computer data or computer programs from one computer to another, to initiate or engage in such communication with a person who is a minor; and 2. by means of such communication he importunes, invites or induces a minor to engage in sexual intercourse, oral sexual conduct or anal sexual conduct, or sexual contact with him, or to engage in a sexual performance, obscene sexual performance, or sexual conduct for his benefit. (Disseminating indecent material to minors in the first degree constitutes a class D felony.)
Sexual conduct	Actual or simulated sexual intercourse, oral sexual conduct, anal sexual conduct, . . . masturbation, . . . or lewd exhibition of the genitals.

(*continued*)

STATE **Title of Pertinent Provision** *Key definition*	**Applicable Statutes and What They Say***
Performance	Any play, motion picture, photograph or dance.
Promote	To procure, manufacture, issue, sell, give, provide, lend, mail, deliver, transfer, transmute, publish, distribute, circulate, disseminate, present, exhibit or advertise, or to offer or agree to do the same.
NORTH CAROLINA	N.C. GEN. STAT. ANN. § 14-190.1, et seq. (2000) N.C. GEN. STAT. ANN. § 14-202.3 (2009)
Obscene Exhibitions	It shall be unlawful for any person, firm or corporation to intentionally disseminate obscenity. A person, firm or corporation disseminates obscenity . . . if he or it: (1) Sells, delivers or provides or offers or agrees to sell, deliver or provide any obscene writing, picture, record or other representation or embodiment of the obscene; or (2) Presents or directs an obscene play, dance or other performance or participates directly in that portion thereof which makes it obscene; or (3) Publishes, exhibits or otherwise makes available anything obscene; or (4) Exhibits, presents, rents, sells, delivers or provides; or offers or agrees to exhibit, present, rent or to provide: any obscene still or motion picture, film, filmstrip, or projection slide, or sound recording, sound tape, or sound track, or any matter or material of whatever form which is a representation, embodiment, performance, or publication of the obscene.
	(Violation of the provisions above constitutes a Class I felony.)
Preparation of Obscene Photographs, Slides and Motion Pictures	Every person who knowingly: (1) Photographs himself or any other person, for purposes of preparing an obscene film, photograph, negative, slide or motion picture for the purpose of dissemination; or (2) Models, poses, acts, or otherwise assists in the preparation of any obscene film, photograph, negative, slide or motion picture for the purpose of dissemination, shall be guilty of a Class 1 misdemeanor.
Disseminating Harmful Material	A person commits the offense of disseminating harmful material to minors if, with or without consideration and knowing the character or content of the material, he: (1) Sells, furnishes, presents, or distributes to a minor material that is harmful to minors; or (2) Allows a minor to review or peruse material that is harmful to minors.

210

Title of Pertinent Provision *Key definition*	Applicable Statutes and What They Say*
	(Disseminating harmful material to minors constitutes a Class 1 misdemeanor.)
Exhibiting Harmful Performance	A person commits the offense of exhibiting a harmful performance to a minor if, with or without consideration and knowing the character or content of the performance, he allows a minor to view a live performance that is harmful to minors.
	(Exhibiting a harmful performance to a minor constitutes a Class 1 misdemeanor.)
	North Carolina law provides an affirmative defense to the crimes of disseminating harmful material to minors or exhibiting a harmful performance to a minor if the defendant can show that the recipient's parent or legal guardian gave prior consent to the dissemination.
First Degree Sexual Exploitation of a Minor	A person commits the offense of first degree sexual exploitation of a minor if, knowing the character or content of the material or performance, he . . . uses, employs, induces, coerces, encourages, or facilitates a minor to engage in or assist others to engage in sexual activity for a live performance or for the purpose of producing material that contains a visual representation depicting this activity.
	(Violation of this provision constitutes a Class C felony.)
Second Degree Sexual Exploitation of a Minor	A person commits the offense of second degree sexual exploitation of a minor if, knowing the character or content of the material, he: (1) Records, photographs, films, develops, or duplicates material that contains a visual representation of a minor engaged in sexual activity; or (2) Distributes, transports, exhibits, receives, sells, purchases, exchanges, or solicits material that contains a visual representation of a minor engaged in sexual activity.
	(Violation of this provision constitutes a Class E felony.)
Third Degree Sexual Exploitation of a Minor	A person commits the offense of third degree sexual exploitation of a minor if, knowing the character or content of the material, he possesses material that contains a visual representation of a minor engaging in sexual activity.
	(Violation of this provision constitutes a Class H felony.)

(continued)

STATE Title of Pertinent Provision *Key definition*	Applicable Statutes and What They Say*
Sexual conduct	Vaginal, anal, or oral intercourse, whether actual or simulated, normal or perverted; [or] masturbation, excretory functions, or lewd exhibition of uncovered genitals.
Obscenity	Obscenity shall be judged with reference to ordinary adults except that it shall be judged with reference to children or other especially susceptible audiences if it appears from the character of the material or the circumstances of its dissemination to be especially designed for or directed to such children or audiences.
Harmful to minors	That quality of any material or performance that depicts sexually explicit nudity or sexual activity and that, taken as a whole, has the following characteristics: a. The average adult person applying contemporary community standards would find that the material or performance has a predominant tendency to appeal to a prurient interest of minors in sex; and b. The average adult person applying contemporary community standards would find that the depiction of sexually explicit nudity or sexual activity in the material or performance is patently offensive to prevailing standards in the adult community concerning what is suitable for minors; and c. The material or performance lacks serious literary, artistic, political, or scientific value for minors.
Material	Pictures, drawings, video recordings, films or other visual depictions or representations but not material consisting entirely of written words.
Minor	Someone who has not reached the age of 18 and who is not married or judicially emancipated.
Sexual activity	Masturbation, whether done alone; vaginal, anal, or oral intercourse; touching, in an act of apparent sexual stimulation or sexual abuse, of the clothed or unclothed genitals, pubic area, or buttocks of another person or the clothed or unclothed breasts of a human female; excretory functions; the insertion of any part of a person's body, other than the male sexual organ, or of any object into another person's anus or vagina, except when done as part of a recognized medical procedure; [or] the lascivious exhibition of the genitals or pubic area of any person.

Key definition	Applicable Statutes and What They Say*
Sexually explicit nudity	Uncovered, or less than opaquely covered, human genitals, pubic area, or buttocks, or the nipple or any portion of the areola of the human female breast [or] covered human male genitals in a discernibly turgid state.
NORTH DAKOTA	N.D. CENT. CODE § 12.1-27.1-01, et seq. (2009) N.D. CENT. CODE § 12.1-27.2-01, et seq. (2009)
Use of a Minor in a Sexual Performance	A person is guilty of a class B felony if, knowing the character and content of a performance, that person employs, authorizes, or induces a minor to engage in sexual conduct during a performance.
Promoting or Directing an Obscene Sexual Performance by a Minor	A person is guilty of a class B felony if, knowing the character and content of a performance, that person produces, directs, or promotes any obscene performance which includes sexual conduct by a person who was a minor at the time of the performance.
Promoting a Sexual Performance by a Minor	A person is guilty of a class C felony if, knowing the character and content of a performance, that person produces, directs, or promotes any performance which includes sexual conduct by a person who was a minor at the time of the performance.
Possession of Material That Includes Sexual Conduct by a Minor	A person is guilty of a class C felony if, knowing of its character and content, that person knowingly possesses any motion picture, photograph, or other visual representation that includes sexual conduct by a minor.
Obscenity	A person is guilty of a class C felony if, knowing of its character, the person disseminates obscene material or if the person produces, transports, or sends obscene material with intent that it be disseminated.
Promoting Obscenity to Minors	It is a class C felony for a person, knowing of its character, to recklessly promote to a minor any material or performance which is harmful to minors.
Minor Performing in Obscene Performance	It is a class C felony to permit a minor to participate in a performance which is harmful to minors.
Sexual conduct	Actual or simulated sexual intercourse, sodomy, . . . masturbation, . . . or lewd exhibition of the buttocks, breasts, or

(continued)

STATE Title of Pertinent Provision *Key definition*	Applicable Statutes and What They Say*
	genitals, including the further definitions of sodomy . . . under section 12.1-27.1-01.
Obscene sexual performance	Any performance which includes sexual conduct by a minor in any obscene material or obscene performance.
Sexual performance	Any performance which includes sexual conduct by a minor.
Performance	Any play, motion picture, photograph, dance, or other visual representation, or any part of a performance.
Promote	To procure, manufacture, issue, sell, give, provide, lend, mail, deliver, transfer, transmit, publish, distribute, circulate, disseminate, present, exhibit.
Simulated	Explicit depiction of any of the conduct set forth in subsection 4 which creates the appearance of actual sexual conduct and which exhibits any nude or partially denuded human figure.
Nude or partially denuded human figures	Less than completely and opaquely covered human genitals, pubic regions, female breasts or a female breast, if the breast or breasts are exposed below a point immediately above the top of the areola, or human buttocks; and includes human male genitals in a discernibly turgid state even if completely and opaquely covered.
Harmful to minors	That quality of any description or representation, in whatever form of sexual conduct or sexual excitement, when such description or representation: a. Considered as a whole, appeals to the prurient sexual interest of minors; b. Is patently offensive to prevailing standards in the adult community in North Dakota as a whole with respect to what is suitable material for minors; and c. Considered as a whole, lacks serious literary, artistic, political, or scientific value for minors.
Sexual excitement	The condition of human male or female genitals when in a state of sexual stimulation or arousal.
OHIO	OHIO REV. CODE ANN. § 2907.01, et seq. (West 2008)
Disseminating Matter Harmful to Juveniles	No person, with knowledge of its character or content, shall recklessly do any of the following: (1) Directly sell, deliver, furnish, disseminate, provide, exhibit, rent, or present to a juvenile, a group of juveniles, a law enforcement officer posing as a juvenile, or a group of law enforcement officers posing as juveniles any material or performance that is obscene or harmful to juveniles; (2) Directly offer or agree to sell, deliver,

	Applicable Statutes and What They Say*

furnish, disseminate, provide, exhibit, rent, or present to a juvenile, a group of juveniles, a law enforcement officer posing as a juvenile, or a group of law enforcement officers posing as juveniles any material or performance that is obscene or harmful to juveniles.

A person directly sells, delivers, furnishes, disseminates, provides, exhibits, rents, or presents or directly offers or agrees to sell, deliver, furnish, disseminate, provide, exhibit, rent, or present material or a performance to a juvenile, a group of juveniles, a law enforcement officer posing as a juvenile, or a group of law enforcement officers posing as juveniles in violation of this section by means of an electronic method of remotely transmitting information if the person knows or has reason to believe that the person receiving the information is a juvenile or the group of persons receiving the information are juveniles.

For the crimes in any of the provisions above: (i) If the material or performance involved is harmful to juveniles, the defendant is guilty of a misdemeanor of the first degree. (ii) If the material or performance involved is obscene, the defendant is guilty of a felony of the fifth degree. (iii) Regardless of (i) and (ii), if the material or performance involved is obscene and the juvenile to whom it is sold, delivered, furnished, disseminated, provided, exhibited, rented, or presented, the juvenile to whom the offer is made or who is the subject of the agreement, or the juvenile who is allowed to review, peruse, or view it is under thirteen years of age, violation of this section is a felony of the fourth degree.

Ohio law provides an affirmative defense to the crimes above if the defendant can show any of the following:
The juvenile was actually married; or
The juvenile involved, at the time of the conduct in question, was accompanied by the juvenile's parent or guardian who, with knowledge of its character, consented to the material or performance being furnished or presented to the juvenile; or
The defendant is the juvenile's spouse; or
The material or performance was furnished or presented for a bona fide medical, scientific, educational, governmental,

(continued)

| STATE
Title of Pertinent
Provision
Key definition	Applicable Statutes and What They Say*

judicial, or *other proper purpose*, by a physician, psychologist, sociologist, scientist, teacher, librarian, clergyman, prosecutor, judge, or *other proper person*.

Pandering Obscenity

No person, with knowledge of the character of the material or performance involved, shall . . . promote or advertise for sale, delivery, or dissemination; sell, deliver, publicly disseminate, publicly display, exhibit, present, rent, or provide; or offer or agree to sell, deliver, publicly disseminate, publicly display, exhibit, present, rent, or provide, any obscene material; . . . or procure, possess, or control any obscene material with purpose to promote or advertise for sale, delivery, or dissemination; sell, deliver, publicly disseminate, publicly display, exhibit, present, rent, or provide; or offer or agree to sell, deliver, publicly disseminate, publicly display, exhibit, present, rent, or provide, any obscene material.

Ohio law provides an affirmative defense to pandering obscenity if the material or performance involved was disseminated or presented for a bona fide medical, scientific, educational, religious, governmental, judicial, or *other proper purpose*, by or to a physician, psychologist, sociologist, scientist, teacher, person pursuing bona fide studies or research, librarian, clergyman, prosecutor, judge, or other person having a *proper interest* in the material or performance.

(Pandering obscenity constitutes a felony of the fifth degree. However, if the defendant has a prior conviction for pandering obscenity or for disseminating matter harmful to juveniles, then pandering obscenity is a felony of the fourth degree.)

Pandering Obscenity Involving a Minor

No person, with knowledge of the character of the material or performance involved, shall do any of the following: (1) Create, reproduce, or publish any obscene material that has a minor as one of its participants or portrayed observers; (2) Promote or advertise for sale or dissemination; sell, deliver, disseminate, display, exhibit, present, rent, or provide; or offer or agree to sell, deliver, disseminate, display, exhibit, present, rent, or provide, any obscene material that has a minor as one of its participants or portrayed observers; . . . (6) Bring or cause to be brought into this state any obscene material that has a minor as one of its participants or portrayed observers.

	Applicable Statutes and What They Say*

(Violation of any of the above provisions constitutes pandering obscenity involving a minor and is a felony of the second degree.)

No person, with knowledge of the character of the material or performance involved, shall . . . buy, procure, possess, or control any obscene material, that has a minor as one of its participants.

(Violation of the above provision constitutes pandering obscenity involving a minor and is a felony of the fourth degree. However, if the defendant has previously pleaded guilty to or has a prior conviction for pandering obscenity involving a minor or for pandering sexually oriented matter involving a minor or for illegal use of a minor in nudity-oriented material or performance, then violation of the above provision instead constitutes a felony of the third degree.)

Pandering Sexually Oriented Matter Involving a Minor

No person, with knowledge of the character of the material or performance involved, shall do any of the following: (1) Create, record, photograph, film, develop, reproduce, or publish any material that shows a minor participating or engaging in sexual activity, masturbation; . . . (2) Advertise for sale or dissemination, sell, distribute, transport, disseminate, exhibit, or display any material that shows a minor participating or engaging in sexual activity, masturbation; . . . (6) Bring or cause to be brought into this state any material that shows a minor participating or engaging in sexual activity, masturbation.

(Violation of any of the above provisions constitutes pandering sexually oriented matter involving a minor and is a felony of the second degree.)

No person, with knowledge of the character of the material or performance involved, shall . . . knowingly solicit, receive, purchase, exchange, possess, or control any material that shows a minor participating or engaging in sexual activity, masturbation.

(Violation of the above provision constitutes pandering sexually oriented matter involving a minor and is a felony of the fourth degree. However, if the defendant has previously

(*continued*)

217

STATE Title of Pertinent Provision *Key definition*	Applicable Statutes and What They Say*
	pleaded guilty to or has a prior conviction for pandering obscenity involving a minor or for pandering sexually oriented matter involving a minor or for illegal use of a minor in nudity-oriented material or performance, then violation of the above provision instead constitutes a felony of the third degree.)
Illegal Use of a Minor in Nudity-Oriented Material or Performance	No person shall ... photograph any minor who is not the person's child or ward in a state of nudity, or create, direct, produce, or transfer any material or performance that shows the minor in a state of nudity, unless both of the following apply: (a) The material or performance is, or is to be, sold, disseminated, displayed, possessed, controlled, brought or caused to be brought into this state, or presented for a bona fide artistic, medical, scientific, educational, religious, governmental, judicial, or other proper purpose, by or to a physician, psychologist, sociologist, scientist, teacher, person pursuing bona fide studies or research, librarian, member of the clergy, prosecutor, judge, or other person having a proper interest in the material or performance; (b) The minor's parents, guardian, or custodian consents in writing to the photographing of the minor, to the use of the minor in the material or performance, or to the transfer of the material and to the specific manner in which the material or performance is to be used.
	No person shall ... consent to the photographing of the person's minor child or ward, or photograph the person's minor child or ward, in a state of nudity or consent to the use of the person's minor child or ward in a state of nudity in any material or performance, or use or transfer a material or performance of that nature, unless the material or performance is sold, disseminated, displayed, possessed, controlled, brought or caused to be brought into this state, or presented for a bona fide artistic, medical, scientific, educational, religious, governmental, judicial, or other proper purpose, by or to a physician, psychologist, sociologist, scientist, teacher, person pursuing bona fide studies or research, librarian, member of the clergy, prosecutor, judge, or other person having a proper interest in the material or performance.

Key definition	Applicable Statutes and What They Say*
	(Violation of either of the above provisions constitutes illegal use of a minor in nudity-oriented material or performance and is a felony of the second degree.)
	No person shall . . . possess or view any material or performance that shows a minor who is not the person's child or ward in a state of nudity, unless one of the following applies: (a) The material or performance is sold, disseminated, displayed, possessed, controlled, brought or caused to be brought into this state, or presented for a bona fide artistic, medical, scientific, educational, religious, governmental, judicial, or other proper purpose, by or to a physician, psychologist, sociologist, scientist, teacher, person pursuing bona fide studies or research, librarian, member of the clergy, prosecutor, judge, or other person having a proper interest in the material or performance. (b) The person knows that the parents, guardian, or custodian has consented in writing to the photographing or use of the minor in a state of nudity and to the manner in which the material or performance is used or transferred.
	(Violation of the above provision constitutes illegal use of a minor in nudity-oriented material or performance and is a felony of the fifth degree. However, if the defendant has previously pleaded guilty to or has a prior conviction for pandering obscenity involving a minor or for pandering sexually oriented matter involving a minor or for illegal use of a minor in nudity-oriented material or performance, then violation of the above provision instead constitutes a felony of the fourth degree.)
Sexual activity	Sexual conduct or sexual contact, or both.
Sexual conduct	Vaginal intercourse between a male and female; anal intercourse, fellatio, and cunnilingus between persons regardless of sex.
Sexual contact	Any touching of an erogenous zone of another, including without limitation the thigh, genitals, buttock, pubic region, or, if the person is a female, a breast, for the purpose of sexually arousing or gratifying either person.
Harmful to juveniles	That quality of any material or performance describing or representing nudity, sexual conduct, sexual excitement, . . . in any form to which all of the following apply: (1) The material

(continued)

STATE Title of Pertinent Provision *Key definition*	Applicable Statutes and What They Say*
	or performance, when considered as a whole, appeals to the prurient interest of juveniles in sex. (2) The material or performance is patently offensive to prevailing standards in the adult community as a whole with respect to what is suitable for juveniles. (3) The material or performance, when considered as a whole, lacks serious literary, artistic, political, and scientific value for juveniles.
Juvenile	Someone less than 18 years old who is not married.
Minor	Someone below 18 years old. The difference between juvenile and minor lies in the fact that, as pertinent for our purposes herein, the state law limits juvenile to one who is not married.
Nudity	Showing, representation, or depiction of human male or female genitals, pubic area, or buttocks with less than a full, opaque covering, or of a female breast with less than a full, opaque covering of any portion thereof below the top of the nipple, or of covered male genitals in a discernibly turgid state.
Material	Any book, magazine, newspaper, pamphlet, poster, print, picture, figure, image, description, motion picture film, phonographic record, or tape, or other tangible thing capable of arousing interest through sight, sound, or touch and includes an image or text appearing on a computer monitor, television screen, liquid crystal display, or similar display device or an image or text recorded on a computer hard disk, computer floppy disk, compact disk, magnetic tape, or similar data storage device.
Performance	Any motion picture, preview, trailer, play, show, skit, dance, or other exhibition performed before an audience.
OKLAHOMA Lewd or Indecent Proposals or Acts as to Child under 16	Okla. Stat. Ann. tit. 21, § 1021, et seq. (West 2011) Okla. Stat. Ann. tit. 21, § 1123(A) (West 2011) Any person who shall knowingly and intentionally: 1. Make any oral, written or electronically or computer-generated lewd or indecent proposal to any child under sixteen (16) years of age for the child to have unlawful sexual relations or sexual intercourse with any person . . . upon conviction, shall be deemed guilty of a felony and shall be punished by

STATE Title of Pertinent Provision *Key definition*	Applicable Statutes and What They Say*
	imprisonment in the State Penitentiary for not less than one (1) year nor more than twenty (20) years.
Obscene Material or Child Pornography	Every person who willfully and knowingly either ... writes, composes, stereotypes, prints, photographs, designs, copies, draws, engraves, paints, molds, cuts, or otherwise prepares, publishes, sells, distributes, keeps for sale, knowingly downloads on a computer, or exhibits any obscene material or child pornography; or ... makes, prepares, cuts, sells, gives, loans, distributes, keeps for sale, or exhibits any disc record, metal, plastic, or wax, wire or tape recording, or any type of obscene material or child pornography, shall be guilty, upon conviction, of a felony and shall be punished by the imposition of a fine of not less than Five Hundred Dollars ($500.00) nor more than Twenty Thousand Dollars ($20,000.00) or by imprisonment for not less than thirty (30) days nor more than ten (10) years, or by both such fine and imprisonment.
Solicitation of Minors	Every person who: 1. Willfully solicits or aids a minor child to perform; or 2. Shows, exhibits, loans, or distributes to a minor child any obscene material or child pornography for the purpose of inducing said minor to participate in [in any of the acts identified above with respect to obscene material or child pornography] ... shall be guilty of a felony, upon conviction, and shall be punished by imprisonment in the custody of the Department of Corrections for not less than ten (10) years nor more than thirty (30) years, except when the minor child is under twelve (12) years of age at the time the offense is committed, and in such case the person shall, upon conviction, be punished by imprisonment in the custody of the Department of Corrections for not less than twenty-five (25) years.

(Anyone who violates any of the provisions above is ineligible for a deferred sentence.) |
| Procuring Minors for Participation in Pornography | Any person who shall procure or cause the participation of any minor under the age of eighteen (18) years in any child pornography or who knowingly possesses, procures, or manufactures, or causes to be sold or distributed any child pornography shall be guilty, upon conviction, of a felony and shall be punished by imprisonment for not more than twenty |

(continued)

221

Key definition	Applicable Statutes and What They Say*
	(20) years or by the imposition of a fine of not more than Twenty-five Thousand Dollars ($25,000.00) or by both said fine and imprisonment.
	(Anyone who violates any of the provisions above is ineligible for a deferred sentence.)
	Oklahoma law specifically notes that the consent of a parent or the minor to any of the acts listed under the crime above—procuring minors for participation in pornography—is not a defense.
Possession or Procurement of Child Pornography	Anyone who possesses or procures child pornography shall, upon conviction, be guilty of a felony and shall be imprisoned for a period of not more than five (5) years or a fine up to, but not exceeding, Five Thousand Dollars ($5,000.00) or by both such fine and imprisonment.
Publication, Distribution or Participation in Preparation of Obscene Material or Child Pornography	No person shall knowingly photograph, act in, pose for, model for, print, sell, offer for sale, give away, exhibit, publish, offer to publish, or otherwise distribute, display, or exhibit any book, magazine, story, pamphlet, paper, writing, card, advertisement, circular, print, picture, photograph, motion picture film, electronic video game or recording, image, cast, slide, figure, instrument, statue, drawing, presentation, or other article which is obscene material or child pornography.
	Any person who violates any provision of this section involving obscene materials, upon conviction, shall be guilty of a misdemeanor and shall be punished by imprisonment in the county jail for not more than one (1) year, or by a fine not exceeding One Thousand Dollars ($1,000.00), or by both such fine and imprisonment.
	Any person who violates any provision of this section involving child pornography, upon conviction, shall be guilty of a felony and shall be punished by imprisonment in the custody of the Department of Corrections for not more than twenty (20) years, or by a fine of not exceeding Ten Thousand Dollars ($10,000.00), or by both such fine and imprisonment. The violator, upon conviction, shall be required to register as a sex offender under the Sex Offenders Registration Act.

STATE Title of Pertinent Provision *Key definition*	**Applicable Statutes and What They Say***
Aggravated Possession of Child Pornography	Any person who, with knowledge of its contents, possesses one hundred (100) or more separate materials depicting child pornography shall be, upon conviction, guilty of aggravated possession of child pornography. The violator shall be punished by imprisonment in the custody of the Department of Corrections for a term not exceeding life imprisonment and by a fine in an amount not more than Ten Thousand Dollars ($10,000.00). The violator, upon conviction, shall be required to register as a sex offender under the Sex Offenders Registration Act. Multiple copies of the same identical material shall each be counted as a separate item.
Facilitating, Encouraging, Offering or Soliciting Sexual Conduct or Engaging in Sexual Communication with a Minor or Person Believed to Be a Minor	It is unlawful for any person to facilitate, encourage, offer or solicit sexual conduct with a minor, or other individual the person believes to be a minor, by use of any technology, or to engage in any communication for sexual or prurient interest with any minor, or other individual the person believes to be a minor, by use of any technology. A person is guilty of violating the provisions of this section if the person knowingly transmits any prohibited communication by use of any technology defined herein, or knowingly prints, publishes or reproduces by use of any technology described herein any prohibited communication, or knowingly buys, sells, receives, exchanges, or disseminates any prohibited communication or any information, notice, statement, website, or advertisement for communication with a minor or access to any name, telephone number, cell phone number, e-mail address, Internet address, text message address, place of residence, physical characteristics or other descriptive or identifying information of a minor, or other individual the person believes to be a minor. Any violation of the provisions of this section shall be a felony, punishable by a fine in an amount not to exceed Ten Thousand Dollars ($10,000.00), or by imprisonment in the custody of the Department of Corrections for a term of not more than ten (10) years, or by both such fine and imprisonment. For purposes of this section, each communication shall constitute a separate offense.

(continued)

STATE Title of Pertinent Provision *Key definition*	Applicable Statutes and What They Say*
Downloads on a computer	Electronically transferring an electronic file from one computer or electronic media to another computer or electronic media.
Child pornography	Any film, motion picture, videotape, photograph, negative, undeveloped film, slide, photographic product, reproduction of a photographic product, CD-ROM, magnetic disk memory, magnetic tape memory, electronic or photo-optical format, play or performance wherein a minor under the age of eighteen (18) years is engaged in any act with a person, other than his or her spouse, of sexual intercourse which is normal or perverted, in any act of anal sodomy, . . . in any act of fellatio or cunnilingus, in any act of excretion in the context of sexual conduct, in any lewd exhibition of the uncovered genitals in the context of masturbation or other sexual conduct, or where the lewd exhibition of the uncovered genitals, buttocks or, if such minor is a female, the breast, has the purpose of sexual stimulation of the viewer, or wherein a person under the age of eighteen (18) years observes such acts or exhibitions.
Explicit child pornography	Material which a law enforcement officer can immediately identify upon first viewing without hesitation as child pornography.
Obscene material	Any representation, performance, depiction or description of sexual conduct, whether in any form or medium including still photographs, undeveloped photographs, motion pictures, undeveloped film, videotape, CD-ROM, magnetic disk memory, magnetic tape memory, electronic or photo-optical format, or a purely photographic product or a reproduction of such product in any book, pamphlet, magazine, or other publication or electronic or photo-optical format, if said items contain the following elements: a. depictions or descriptions of sexual conduct which are patently offensive as found by the average person applying contemporary community standards, b. taken as a whole, have as the dominant theme an appeal to prurient interest in sex as found by the average person applying contemporary community standards, and c. a reasonable person would find the material or performance taken as a whole lacks serious literary, artistic, educational, political, or scientific purposes or value.

Key definition	Applicable Statutes and What They Say*
Sexual conduct	Any of the following: a. acts of sexual intercourse including any intercourse which is normal or perverted, actual or simulated, b. acts of deviate sexual conduct, including oral and anal sodomy, c. acts of masturbation, . . . e. acts of excretion in a sexual context, or f. acts of exhibiting human genitals or pubic areas. [Sexual conduct also] include[s] situations when, if appropriate to the type of conduct, the conduct is performed alone or between members of the same or opposite sex . . . in an act of apparent sexual stimulation or gratification.
Performance	Any display, live or recorded, in any form or medium.
Material	Any book, magazine, newspaper, pamphlet, poster, print, picture, figure, image, description, motion picture film, record, recording tape, CD-ROM disk, Magnetic Disk Memory, Magnetic Tape Memory, video tape, computer software or video game [as well as] all digital and computerized images and depictions.
By use of any technology (as used with respect to the crime of facilitating, encouraging, offering, or soliciting sexual conduct or engaging in sexual communication with a minor or person believed to be a minor)	The use of any telephone or cell phone, computer disk (CD), digital video disk (DVD), recording or sound device, CD-ROM, VHS, computer, computer network or system, Internet or World Wide Web address including any blog site or personal web address, e-mail address, Internet Protocol address (IP), text messaging or paging device, any video, audio, photographic or camera device of any computer, computer network or system, cell phone, any other electrical, electronic, computer or mechanical device, or any other device capable of any transmission of any written or text message, audio or sound message, photographic, video, movie, digital or computer-generated image, or any other communication of any kind by use of an electronic device.
OREGON	OR. REV. STAT. § 163.665, et seq. (2011)
Using Child in Display of Sexually Explicit Conduct	A person commits the crime of using a child in a display of sexually explicit conduct if the person employs, authorizes, permits, compels or induces a child to participate or engage in sexually explicit conduct for any person to observe or to record in a visual recording.

(continued)

STATE Title of Pertinent Provision *Key definition*	Applicable Statutes and What They Say*
	(Using a child in a display of sexually explicit conduct constitutes a Class A felony.)
Encouraging Child Sexual Abuse in the First Degree	A person commits the crime of encouraging child sexual abuse in the first degree if the person: (a)(A) Knowingly develops, duplicates, publishes, prints, disseminates, exchanges, displays, finances, attempts to finance or sells a visual recording of sexually explicit conduct involving a child or knowingly possesses, accesses or views such a visual recording with the intent to develop, duplicate, publish, print, disseminate, exchange, display or sell it; or (B) Knowingly brings into this state, or causes to be brought or sent into this state, for sale or distribution, a visual recording of sexually explicit conduct involving a child; and (b) Knows or is aware of and consciously disregards the fact that creation of the visual recording of sexually explicit conduct involved child abuse.
	(Encouraging child sexual abuse in the first degree constitutes a Class B felony.)
Encouraging Child Sexual Abuse in the Second Degree	A person commits the crime of encouraging child sexual abuse in the second degree if the person: (a)(A)(i) Knowingly possesses or controls, or knowingly accesses with the intent to view, a visual recording of sexually explicit conduct involving a child for the purpose of arousing or satisfying the sexual desires of the person or another person; or (ii) Knowingly pays, exchanges or gives anything of value to obtain or view a visual recording of sexually explicit conduct involving a child for the purpose of arousing or satisfying the sexual desires of the person or another person; and (B) Knows or is aware of and consciously disregards the fact that creation of the visual recording of sexually explicit conduct involved child abuse; or (b)(A) Knowingly pays, exchanges or gives anything of value to observe sexually explicit conduct by a child or knowingly observes, for the purpose of arousing or gratifying the sexual desire of the person, sexually explicit conduct by a child; and (B) Knows or is aware of and consciously disregards the fact that the conduct constitutes child abuse.

STATE Title of Pertinent Provision *Key definition*	Applicable Statutes and What They Say*
Encouraging Child Sexual Abuse in the Third Degree	(Encouraging child sexual abuse in the second degree constitutes a Class C felony.) A person commits the crime of encouraging child sexual abuse in the third degree if the person: (a)(A)(i) Knowingly possesses or controls, or knowingly accesses with the intent to view, a visual recording of sexually explicit conduct involving a child for the purpose of arousing or satisfying the sexual desires of the person or another person; or (ii) Knowingly pays, exchanges or gives anything of value to obtain or view a visual recording of sexually explicit conduct involving a child for the purpose of arousing or satisfying the sexual desires of the person or another person; and (B) Knows or fails to be aware of a substantial and unjustifiable risk that the creation of the visual recording of sexually explicit conduct involved child abuse; or (b)(A) Knowingly pays, exchanges or gives anything of value to observe sexually explicit conduct by a child or knowingly observes, for the purpose of arousing or gratifying the sexual desire of the person, sexually explicit conduct by a child; and (B) Knows or fails to be aware of a substantial and unjustifiable risk that the conduct constitutes child abuse. (Encouraging child sexual abuse in the third degree constitutes a Class A misdemeanor.)
Possession of Materials Depicting Sexually Explicit Conduct of a Child in the First Degree	A person commits the crime of possession of materials depicting sexually explicit conduct of a child in the first degree if the person: (a) Knowingly possesses, accesses or views a visual depiction of sexually explicit conduct involving a child or a visual depiction of sexually explicit conduct that appears to involve a child; and (b) Uses the visual depiction to induce a child to participate or engage in sexually explicit conduct. (Possession of materials depicting sexually explicit conduct of a child in the first degree constitutes a Class B felony.)
Possession of Materials Depicting Sexually Explicit Conduct of a Child in the Second Degree	A person commits the crime of possession of materials depicting sexually explicit conduct of a child in the second degree if the person: (a) Knowingly possesses, accesses or views a visual depiction of sexually explicit conduct involving a child or a visual depiction of sexually explicit conduct that appears to involve a child; and

(continued)

(b) Intends to use the visual depiction to induce a child to participate or engage in sexually explicit conduct.

(Possession of materials depicting sexually explicit conduct of a child in the second degree constitutes a Class C felony.)

Child	A person who is less than 18 years of age, and any reference to a child in relation to a visual recording of the child is a reference to a person who was less than 18 years of age at the time the original image in the visual recording was created and not the age of the person at the time of an alleged offense relating to the subsequent reproduction, use or possession of the visual recording.
Child abuse	Conduct that constitutes, or would constitute if committed in this state, a crime in which the victim is a child.
Sexually explicit conduct	Actual or simulated: (a) Sexual intercourse or deviant sexual intercourse; (b) Genital-genital, oral-genital, anal-genital or oral-anal contact, whether between persons of the same or opposite sex; . . . (c) Penetration of the vagina or rectum by any object other than as part of a medical diagnosis or treatment or as part of a personal hygiene practice; (d) Masturbation; . . .or (f) Lewd exhibition of sexual or other intimate parts.
Visual recording	Includes, but is not limited to, photographs, films, videotapes and computer and other digital pictures, regardless of the manner in which the recording is stored.
Visual depiction	Includes, but is not limited to, visual recordings, pictures and computer-generated images and pictures, whether made or produced by electronic, mechanical or other means.
PENNSYLVANIA	18 PA. CONS. STAT. ANN. § 5903 (West 2000) 18 PA. CONS. STAT. ANN. § 6312 (West 2011) 18 PA. CONS. STAT. ANN. § 6318 (West 2011) 42 PA. CONS. STAT. ANN. § 9795.1 (West 2008)
Obscenity	No person, knowing the obscene character of the materials or performances involved, shall . . . design, copy, draw, photograph, print, utter, publish or in any manner manufacture or prepare any obscene materials; [or] write, print, publish, utter or cause to be written, printed, published or uttered any advertisement or notice of any kind giving information, directly or indirectly, stating or purporting to state

STATE Title of Pertinent Provision *Key definition*	**Applicable Statutes and What They Say***
	where, how, from whom, or by what means any obscene materials can be purchased, obtained or had; [or] produce, present or direct any obscene performance or participate in a portion thereof that is obscene or that contributes to its obscenity; [or] hire, employ, use or permit any minor child to do or assist in doing any act or thing [identified above].
	(Violation of the above provision constitutes a misdemeanor of the first degree. However, a defendant who has a prior conviction for violating the above provision is instead guilty of a felony of the third degree.)
Dissemination of Explicit Sexual Materials to Minors	No person shall knowingly disseminate by sale, loan or otherwise explicit sexual materials to a minor.
	(Violation of the above provision constitutes a felony of the third degree. However, a defendant who has a prior conviction for violating the above provision is instead guilty of a felony of the second degree.)
Unlawful Contact with Minor	[Unlawful contact with a minor is committed when someone is] intentionally in contact with a minor . . . for the purpose of engaging [in sexual abuse of children or obscenity or dissemination of explicit sexual materials to minors, and] either the person initiating the contact or the person being contacted is within this Commonwealth.
	(Unlawful contact with a minor constitutes an offense of the same grade and degree as the most serious underlying offense . . . for which the defendant contacted the minor; or . . . a felony of the third degree; whichever is greater.)
Sexual Abuse of a Child:	
Photographing, Videotaping, Depicting on Computer or Filming Sexual Acts	Any person who causes or knowingly permits a child under the age of 18 years to engage in a prohibited sexual act or in the simulation of such act is guilty of a felony of the second degree if such person knows, has reason to know or intends that such act may be photographed, videotaped, depicted on computer or filmed. Any person who knowingly photographs, videotapes, depicts on computer or films a child under the age of 18 years engaging in a prohibited sexual act or in the

(*continued*)

Key definition	**Applicable Statutes and What They Say***
	simulation of such an act is guilty of a felony of the second degree.
Dissemination of Photographs, Videotapes, Computer Depictions and Films	Any person who knowingly sells, distributes, delivers, disseminates, transfers, displays or exhibits to others, or who possesses for the purpose of sale, distribution, delivery, dissemination, transfer, display or exhibition to others, any book, magazine, pamphlet, slide, photograph, film, videotape, computer depiction or other material depicting a child under the age of 18 years engaging in a prohibited sexual act or in the simulation of such act commits an offense.
	(A first offense under this subsection is a felony of the third degree, and a second or subsequent offense under this subsection is a felony of the second degree.)
Child Pornography	Any person who intentionally views or knowingly possesses or controls any book, magazine, pamphlet, slide, photograph, film, videotape, computer depiction or other material depicting a child under the age of 18 years engaging in a prohibited sexual act or in the simulation of such act commits an offense.
	(A first offense under this subsection is a felony of the third degree, and a second or subsequent offense under this subsection is a felony of the second degree.)
	Anyone convicted for the crime of obscenity, dissemination of explicit sexual materials to minors, unlawful contact with a minor, or sexual abuse of a child, set forth above, must register as a sex offender for 10 years. Anyone convicted of solicitation, conspiracy or attempt to commit any of the crimes above must also register as a sex offender for 10 years. Anyone with two or more convictions for the crime of obscenity, dissemination of explicit sexual materials to minors, unlawful contact with a minor, or sexual abuse of a child, set forth above, must register as a sex offender for his/her lifetime.
Intentionally views	Deliberate, purposeful, voluntary viewing of material depicting a child under 18 years of age engaging in a prohibited sexual act or in the simulation of such act, . . . not includ[ing] the accidental or inadvertent viewing of such material.

STATE Title of Pertinent Provision *Key definition*	**Applicable Statutes and What They Say***
Prohibited sexual act	Masturbation, . . . fellatio, cunnilingus, lewd exhibition of the genitals or nudity if such nudity is depicted for the purpose of sexual stimulation or gratification of any person who might view such depiction [as well as] sexual intercourse.
Explicit sexual materials	Materials which are obscene or: (1) any picture, photograph, drawing, sculpture, motion picture film, video tape or similar visual representation or image of a person or portion of the human body which depicts nudity, sexual conduct, . . . and which is harmful to minors; or (2) any book, pamphlet, magazine, printed matter however reproduced, or sound recording which contains any matter enumerated in paragraph (1), or explicit and detailed verbal descriptions or narrative accounts of sexual excitement, sexual conduct, . . . and which, taken as a whole, is harmful to minors.
Minor	Someone less than 18 years old.
Nudity	Showing of the human male or female genitals, pubic area, or buttocks with less than a fully opaque covering, or the showing of the female breast with less than a fully opaque covering of any portion thereof below the top of the nipple, or the depiction of covered male genitals in a discernibly turgid state.
Sexual conduct	Acts of masturbation, homosexuality, sexual intercourse, sexual bestiality or physical contact with a person's clothed or unclothed genitals, pubic area, buttocks or, if such person be a female, breast.
Sexual excitement	Condition of human male or female genitals when in a state of sexual stimulation or arousal.
Harmful to minors	That quality of any description or representation, in whatever form, of nudity, sexual conduct, sexual excitement, . . . when it: (i) predominantly appeals to the prurient, shameful, or morbid interest of minors; and (ii) is patently offensive to prevailing standards in the adult community as a whole with respect to what is suitable material for minors; and (iii) taken as a whole, lacks serious literary, artistic, political, educational or scientific value for minors.
RHODE ISLAND	R.I. GEN. LAWS § 11-9-1, et seq. (2010) R.I. GEN. LAWS § 11-9-1.4, et seq. (2011)

(continued)

STATE **Title of Pertinent Provision** *Key definition*	**Applicable Statutes and What They Say***
	R.I. GEN. LAWS § 11-9-2 (2011) R.I. GEN. LAWS § 11-37.1-3(a), (c) (2006)
Exploitation for Immoral Purposes	Any person who shall in any manner or under any pretense sell, distribute, let out or otherwise permit any child under eighteen (18) years of age to be used in any book, magazine, pamphlet, or other publication, or in any motion picture film, photograph or pictorial representation, in a setting which taken as a whole suggests to the average person that the child has engaged in, or is about to engage in any sexual act, which shall include, but not be limited to, sodomy, oral copulation, sexual intercourse, masturbation, . . . shall, upon conviction for the first offense be punished by imprisonment for not more than ten (10) years, or a fine of not more than ten thousand dollars ($10,000), or both; upon conviction of a subsequent offense, be punished by imprisonment for not more than fifteen (15) years, a fine of not more than fifteen thousand dollars ($15,000), or both.
	Every person who shall exhibit, use, employ or shall in any manner or under pretense so exhibit, use, or employ any child under the age of eighteen (18) years to any person for the purpose of prostitution or for any other lewd or indecent act shall be imprisoned not exceeding twenty (20) years, or be fined not exceeding twenty thousand dollars ($20,000), or both.
Child Nudity	Every person, firm, association, or corporation which shall publish, sell, offer for sale, loan, give away, or otherwise distribute any book, magazine, pamphlet, or other publication, or any photograph, picture, or film which depicts any child, or children, under the age of eighteen (18) years and known to be under the age of eighteen (18) years of age by the person, firm, association, or corporation in a setting which taken as a whole suggests to the average person that the child, or children, is about to engage in or has engaged in, any sexual act, or which depicts any child under eighteen (18) years of age performing sodomy, oral copulation, sexual intercourse, masturbation, . . . shall, for the first offense, be punished by imprisonment for not more than ten (10) years, or by a fine of not more than ten thousand dollars ($10,000), or both; for

STATE Title of Pertinent Provision	
Key definition	Applicable Statutes and What They Say*
	any subsequent offense, by imprisonment for not more than fifteen (15) years, or by a fine of not more than fifteen thousand dollars ($15,000), or both. Provided, that artistic drawings, sketches, paintings, sculptures, or other artistic renditions, shall be exempt from the provisions of this section.
Child Pornography	[It is a crime to do any of the following:]
	Knowingly produce any child pornography; knowingly mail, transport, deliver or transfer by any means, including by computer, any child pornography; [or] knowingly reproduce any child pornography by any means, including the computer.
	(Violating, attempting or conspiring to violate any of the child pornography provisions above is punishable by a maximum fine of $5,000, or a maximum prison term of 15 years, or both.)
	[The crime of child pornography is also committed if a person] knowingly possess[es] any book, magazine, periodical, film, videotape, computer disk, computer file or any other material that contains an image of child pornography.
	(Violating, attempting or conspiring to violate this child pornography provision is punishable by a maximum fine of $5,000, or a maximum prison term of 5 years, or both.)
	Rhode Island law provides an affirmative defense to violation of this provision if the defendant shows that he or she satisfies the following: (i) Possessed less than three (3) images of child pornography; and (ii) Promptly and in good faith and without retaining or allowing any person, other than a law enforcement agency, to access any image or copy of it: (A) Took reasonable steps to destroy each such image; or (B) Reported the matter to a law enforcement agency and afforded that agency access to each such image.
	If the victim is a minor, conviction for any of the crimes above, requires registration as a sex offender.
Child pornography	Any visual depiction, including any photograph, film, video, picture, or computer or computer-generated image or picture, whether made or produced by electronic, mechanical, or other means, of sexually explicit conduct where:
	(i) The production of such visual depiction involves the use of a minor engaging in sexually explicit conduct; (ii) Such visual

(continued)

STATE Title of Pertinent Provision *Key definition*	**Applicable Statutes and What They Say***
	depiction is a digital image, computer image, or computer-generated image of a minor engaging in sexually explicit conduct; or (iii) Such visual depiction has been created, adapted, or modified to display an identifiable minor engaging in sexually explicit conduct.
Minor	Someone less than 18 years old.
Identifiable minor	(i) [Someone] (A)(I) Who was a minor at the time the visual depiction was created, adapted, or modified; or (II) Whose image as a minor was used in creating, adapting, or modifying the visual depiction; and (ii) Who is recognizable as an actual person by the person's face, likeness, or other distinguishing characteristic, such as a unique birthmark or other recognizable feature; and (B) Shall not be construed to require proof of the actual identity of the identifiable minor.
Sexually explicit conduct	Actual: (i) Graphic sexual intercourse, including genital-genital, oral-genital, anal-genital, or oral-anal, or lascivious sexual intercourse where the genitals, or pubic area of any person is exhibited; . . .(iii) Masturbation; . . . or (v) Graphic or lascivious exhibition of the genitals or pubic area of any person.
Visual depiction	Includes undeveloped film and videotape and data stored on a computer disk or by electronic means, which is capable of conversion into a visual image.
Graphic (when used with respect to a depiction of sexually explicit conduct)	A viewer can observe any part of the genitals or pubic area of any depicted person . . . during any part of the time that the sexually explicit conduct is being depicted.
Sexting—Minor Electronically Disseminating Indecent Material to Another Person	No minor shall knowingly and voluntarily and without threat or coercion use a computer or telecommunication device to transmit an indecent visual depiction of himself or herself to another person. (Rhode Island law classifies this crime as a status offense adjudicated in family court. The state law also specifically excludes those who violate this sexting law from registration as sex offenders.)

STATE Title of Pertinent Provision *Key definition*	**Applicable Statutes and What They Say***
Key Definitions for Rhode Island's Sexting Law: *Minor*	Someone below the age of 18.
Telecommunication device	An analog or digital electronic device which processes data, telephony, video, or sound transmission as part of any system involved in the sending and/or receiving at a distance of voice, sound, data, and/or video transmissions.
Sexually explicit conduct	Actual masturbation or graphic focus on or lascivious exhibition of the nude genitals or pubic area of the minor.
Indecent visual depiction	Any digital image or digital video of the minor engaging in sexually explicit conduct, and includes data stored or any computer, telecommunication device, or other electronic storage media which is capable of conversion into a visual image.
SOUTH CAROLINA	S.C. CODE ANN. § 16-15-305, et seq. (Law. Co-op. 2004)
Disseminating, Procuring or Promoting Obscenity	It is unlawful for any person knowingly to disseminate obscenity. A person disseminates obscenity within the meaning of this article if he: (1) sells, delivers, or provides or offers or agrees to sell, deliver, or provide any obscene writing, picture, record, digital electronic file, or other representation or description of the obscene; (2) presents or directs an obscene play, dance, or other performance, or participates directly in that portion thereof which makes it obscene; (3) publishes, exhibits, or otherwise makes available anything obscene to any group or individual; or (4) exhibits, presents, rents, sells, delivers, or provides; or offers or agrees to exhibit, present, rent, or to provide: any motion picture, film, filmstrip, or projection slide, or sound recording, sound tape, or sound track, video tapes and recordings, or any matter or material of whatever form which is a representation, description, performance, or publication of the obscene. It is unlawful for any person knowingly to create, buy, procure, or process obscene material with the purpose and intent of disseminating it. (Anyone who violates any of the above provisions is guilty of a felony and, upon conviction, must be imprisoned not more

(continued)

	than five years or fined not more than ten thousand dollars, or both.)
	Obscenity must be judged with reference to ordinary adults except that it must be judged with reference to children or other especially susceptible audiences or clearly defined deviant sexual groups if it appears from the character of the material or the circumstances of its dissemination to be especially for or directed to children or such audiences or groups.
First Degree Sexual Exploitation of a Minor	An individual commits the offense of first degree sexual exploitation of a minor if, knowing the character or content of the material or performance, he: (1) uses, employs, induces, coerces, encourages, or facilitates a minor to engage in or assist others to engage in sexual activity for a live performance or for the purpose of producing material that contains a visual representation depicting this activity; . . . or (4) records, photographs, films, develops, duplicates, produces, or creates a digital electronic file for sale or pecuniary gain material that contains a visual representation depicting a minor engaged in sexual activity.
	(Whoever violates the above provision is guilty of a felony and, upon conviction, must be imprisoned for not less than three years nor more than twenty years. No part of the minimum sentence of imprisonment may be suspended nor is the individual convicted eligible for parole until he has served the minimum term of imprisonment. Sentences imposed pursuant to this section must run consecutively with and commence at the expiration of another sentence being served by the person sentenced.)
Second Degree Sexual Exploitation of a Minor	An individual commits the offense of second degree sexual exploitation of a minor if, knowing the character or content of the material, he: (1) records, photographs, films, develops, duplicates, produces, or creates digital electronic file material that contains a visual representation of a minor engaged in sexual activity; or (2) distributes, transports, exhibits, receives, sells, purchases, exchanges, or solicits material that contains a visual representation of a minor engaged in sexual activity.

STATE Title of Pertinent Provision *Key definition*	Applicable Statutes and What They Say*
	(Anyone who violates any of these provisions is guilty of a felony and, upon conviction, must be imprisoned not less than two years nor more than ten years. No part of the minimum sentence may be suspended nor is the individual convicted eligible for parole until he has served the minimum sentence.)
Third Degree Sexual Exploitation of a Minor	An individual commits the offense of third degree sexual exploitation of a minor if, knowing the character or content of the material, he possesses material that contains a visual representation of a minor engaging in sexual activity.
	(Anyone who violates this provision is guilty of a felony and, upon conviction, must be imprisoned not more than ten years.)
Minor	Someone below the age of 18.
Harmful to minors	That quality of any material or performance that depicts sexually explicit nudity or sexual activity and that, taken as a whole, has the following characteristics: (a) the average adult person applying contemporary community standards would find that the material or performance has a predominant tendency to appeal to a prurient interest of minors in sex; and (b) the average adult person applying contemporary community standards would find that the depiction of sexually explicit nudity or sexual activity in the material or performance is patently offensive to prevailing standards in the adult community concerning what is suitable for minors; and (c) to a reasonable person, the material or performance taken as a whole lacks serious literary, artistic, political, or scientific value for minors.
Material	Pictures, drawings, video recordings, films, digital electronic files, or other visual depictions or representations but not material consisting entirely of written words.
Sexual activity	[The following simulations or acts:] masturbation, whether done alone or with another human; vaginal, anal, or oral intercourse; touching, in an act of apparent sexual stimulation or sexual abuse, of the clothed or unclothed genitals, pubic area, or buttocks of another person or the clothed or unclothed breasts of a human female; excretory functions; the

(continued)

STATE Title of Pertinent Provision *Key definition*	Applicable Statutes and What They Say*
	insertion of any part of a person's body, other than the male sexual organ, or of any object into another person's anus or vagina, except when done as part of a recognized medical procedure.
Sexually explicit nudity	The showing of: (a) uncovered, or less than opaquely covered human genitals, pubic area, or buttocks, or the nipple or any portion of the areola of the human female breast; or
	(b) covered human male genitals in a discernibly turgid state.
SOUTH DAKOTA	S.D. CODIFIED LAWS § 22-22-1.3 (Michie 2006) S.D. CODIFIED LAWS § 22-22-24.3 (Michie 2006) S.D. CODIFIED LAWS § 22-24A-2, et seq. (Michie 2011)
Sexual Exploitation of a Minor	A person is guilty of sexual exploitation of a minor if the person causes or knowingly permits a minor to engage in an activity or the simulation of an activity that: (1) Is harmful to minors; (2) Involves nudity; or (3) Is obscene.
	(Violating any of the above provisions constitutes a Class 6 felony. A second/subsequent violation within fifteen years of the prior conviction constitutes a Class 5 felony.)
	Anyone convicted of violating any of the above provisions shall be ordered by the court to undergo a psycho-sexual assessment which includes the following: the offender's sexual history; an identification of precursor activities to sexual offending; intellectual, adaptive and academic functioning; social and emotional functioning; previous legal history; previous treatment history; victim selection and age; risk to the community; and treatment options recommended.
	A minor's consent or the minor's parent's consent to any of the above acts is not a defense.
Possessing, Manufacturing, or Distributing Child Pornography	A person is guilty of possessing, manufacturing, or distributing child pornography if the person: (1) Creates any visual depiction of a minor engaging in a prohibited sexual act, or in the simulation of such an act; (2) Causes or knowingly permits the creation of any visual depiction of a minor engaged in a prohibited sexual act, or in the simulation of such

Key definition	**Applicable Statutes and What They Say***
	an act; or (3) Knowingly possesses, distributes, or otherwise disseminates any visual depiction of a minor engaging in a prohibited sexual act, or in the simulation of such an act.
	(Violating any of the above provisions constitutes a Class 4 felony. A second/subsequent violation within fifteen years of the prior conviction constitutes a Class 3 felony.)
	Anyone convicted of violating any of the above provisions shall be ordered by the court to undergo a psycho-sexual assessment which includes the following: the offender's sexual history; an identification of precursor activities to sexual offending; intellectual, adaptive and academic functioning; social and emotional functioning; previous legal history; previous treatment history; victim selection and age; risk to the community; and treatment options recommended.
	A minor's consent or the minor's parent's consent to any of the above acts is not a defense.
	Anyone convicted of sexual exploitation of a minor or of possessing, manufacturing, or distributing child pornography must register as a sex offender.
Minor or child	Someone less than 18 years old.
Child pornography	Any image or visual depiction of a minor engaged in prohibited sexual acts.
Digital media	Any electronic storage device, including a floppy disk or other magnetic storage device or any compact disc that has memory and the capacity to store audio, video, or written materials.
Harmful to minors	Any reproduction, imitation, characterization, description, visual depiction, exhibition, presentation, or representation, of whatever kind or form, depicting nudity, sexual conduct, or sexual excitement if it: (a) Predominantly appeals to the prurient, shameful, or morbid interest of minors; (b) Is patently offensive to prevailing standards in the adult community as a whole with respect to what is suitable material for minors; and (c) Taken as a whole, is without serious literary, artistic, political, or scientific value for minors.
Computer	Any electronic, magnetic, optical, electrochemical, or other high-speed data processing device performing logical,

(*continued*)

STATE Title of Pertinent Provision *Key definition*	**Applicable Statutes and What They Say***
	arithmetic, or storage functions and includes any data storage facility or communications facility directly related to or operating in conjunction with such device, including wireless communication devices such as cellular phones.
Nudity	Showing or the simulated showing of the human male or female genitals, pubic area, or buttocks with less than a fully opaque covering; or the showing of the female breast with less than a fully opaque covering of any portion thereof below the top of the nipple; or the depiction of covered male genitals in a discernibly turgid state for the purpose of creating sexual excitement.
Prohibited sexual act	Actual or simulated sexual intercourse, . . . masturbation; . . . actual or simulated exhibition of the genitals, the pubic or rectal area, or the bare feminine breasts, in a lewd or lascivious manner; actual physical contact with a person's clothed or unclothed genitals, pubic area, buttocks, or, if such person is a female, breast with the intent to arouse or gratify the sexual desire of either party; defecation or urination for the purpose of creating sexual excitement in the viewer; or any act or conduct which constitutes sexual battery or simulates that sexual battery is being or will be committed. The term includes encouraging, aiding, abetting or enticing any person to commit any such acts as provided in this subdivision.
Sexual battery	Oral, anal, or vaginal penetration by, or union with, the sexual organ of another or the anal or vaginal penetration of another by any other object.
Sexual excitement	Condition of the human male or female genitals if in a state of sexual stimulation or arousal.
Sexually oriented material	Any book, article, magazine, publication, visual depiction or written matter of any kind or any drawing, etching, painting, photograph, motion picture film, or sound recording that depicts sexual activity, actual or simulated, involving human beings, . . . that exhibits uncovered human genitals or the pubic region in a lewd or lascivious manner, or that exhibits human male genitals in a discernibly turgid state, even if completely and opaquely covered.
Visual depiction	Any developed and undeveloped film, photograph, slide and videotape, and any photocopy, drawing, printed or written

STATE Title of Pertinent Provision *Key definition*	**Applicable Statutes and What They Say***
	material, and any data stored on computer disk, digital media, or by electronic means that are capable of conversion into a visual image.
TENNESSEE	TENN. CODE ANN. § 39-17-911, et seq. (2000) TENN. CODE ANN. § 39-17-1001, et seq. (1990)
Tennessee Protection of Children against Sexual Exploitation Act of 1990:	
Sexual Exploitation	It is unlawful for any person to knowingly possess material that includes a minor engaged in: (1) Sexual activity; or (2) Simulated sexual activity that is patently offensive.
	Anyone who violates either of the above provisions may be charged in a separate count for each individual image, picture, drawing, photograph, motion picture film, videocassette tape, or other pictorial representation. However, if the number of materials possessed is greater than fifty (50), the person may be charged in a single count to enhance the class of offense to a Class C or B felony.
	Violation of either of the above provisions constitutes a Class D felony; however, if the number of individual images, materials, or combination of images and materials, that are possessed is more than fifty (50), then the offense shall be a Class C felony. If the number of individual images, materials, or combination of images and materials, exceeds one hundred (100), the offense shall be a Class B felony.
Aggravated Sexual Exploitation	It is unlawful for a person to knowingly promote, sell, distribute, transport, purchase or exchange material, or possess with the intent to promote, sell, distribute, transport, purchase or exchange material, that includes a minor engaged in: (A) Sexual activity; or (B) Simulated sexual activity that is patently offensive.
	Anyone who violates either of the above provisions may be charged in a separate count for each individual image, picture, drawing, photograph, motion picture film, videocassette tape, or other pictorial representation. However, if the number of

(*continued*)

items is greater than twenty-five (25), the person may be charged in a single count to enhance the class of offense to a Class B felony.

Violation of either of the above provisions constitutes a Class C felony; however, if the number of individual images, materials, or combination of images and materials that are promoted, sold, distributed, transported, purchased, exchanged or possessed, with intent to promote, sell, distribute, transport, purchase or exchange, is more than twenty-five (25), then the offense shall be a Class B felony.

It is unlawful for a person to knowingly promote, sell, distribute, transport, purchase or exchange material that is obscene ... or possess material that is obscene, with the intent to promote, sell, distribute, transport, purchase or exchange the material, which includes a minor engaged in: (A) Sexual activity; or (B) Simulated sexual activity that is patently offensive.

Anyone who violates the above provision may be charged in a separate count for each individual image, picture, drawing, photograph, motion picture film, videocassette tape, or other pictorial representation. However, if the number of items is greater than twenty-five (25), the person may be charged in a single count to enhance the class of offense to a Class B felony.

Violation of either of the above provisions constitutes a Class C felony; however, if the number of individual images, materials, or combination of images and materials that are promoted, sold, distributed, transported, purchased, exchanged or possessed, with intent to promote, sell, distribute, transport, purchase or exchange, is more than twenty-five (25), then the offense shall be a Class B felony.

Especially Aggravated Sexual Exploitation

It is unlawful for a person to knowingly promote, employ, use, assist, transport or permit a minor to participate in the performance of, or in the production of, acts or material that includes the minor engaging in: (1) Sexual activity; or (2) Simulated sexual activity that is patently offensive.

Anyone who violates the above provision may be charged in a separate count for each individual performance, image,

STATE Title of Pertinent Provision *Key definition*	**Applicable Statutes and What They Say***
	picture, drawing, photograph, motion picture film, videocassette tape, or other pictorial representation.
	(Violation of either of the above provisions constitutes a Class B felony.)
Obscenity	(a) It is unlawful for any person to knowingly sell or loan for monetary consideration or otherwise exhibit or make available to a minor: (1) Any picture, photograph, drawing, sculpture, motion picture film, video game, computer software game, or similar visual representation or image of a person or portion of the human body, that depicts nudity, sexual conduct, . . . and that is harmful to minors; or (2) Any book, pamphlet, magazine, printed matter, however reproduced, or sound recording, which contains any matter enumerated in subdivision (a)(1), or that contains explicit and detailed verbal descriptions or narrative accounts of sexual excitement, sexual conduct, . . . and that is harmful to minors.
	(Violation of the above provision constitutes a Class A misdemeanor.)
	Tennessee law provides an affirmative defense to the above crime if the minor to whom the material or show was made available or exhibited was, at the time, accompanied by the person's parent or legal guardian, or by an adult with the written permission of the parent or legal guardian.
Minor	Anyone below the age of 18.
Material	(A) Any picture, drawing, photograph, undeveloped film or film negative, motion picture film, videocassette tape or other pictorial representation; . . . (C) Any image stored on a computer hard drive, a computer disk of any type, or any other medium designed to store information for later retrieval; or (D) Any image transmitted to a computer or other electronic media or video screen, by telephone line, cable, satellite transmission, or other method that is capable of further transmission, manipulation, storage or accessing, even if not stored or saved at the time of transmission.
Sexual activity	Any of the following acts:
	(A) Vaginal, anal or oral intercourse, whether done with another person; . . . (B) Masturbation, whether done alone or with

(continued)

STATE Title of Pertinent Provision *Key definition*	Applicable Statutes and What They Say*
	another human; . . . (C) Patently offensive, as determined by contemporary community standards, physical contact with or touching of a person's clothed or unclothed genitals, pubic area, buttocks or breasts in an act of apparent sexual stimulation or sexual abuse; . . . (E) The insertion of any part of a person's body or of any object into another person's anus or vagina, except when done as part of a recognized medical procedure by a licensed professional; (F) Patently offensive, as determined by contemporary community standards, conduct, representations, depictions or descriptions of excretory functions; or (G) Lascivious exhibition of the female breast or the genitals, buttocks, anus or pubic or rectal area of any person.
Patently offensive	That which goes substantially beyond customary limits of candor in describing or representing such matters.
Promote	To finance, produce, direct, manufacture, issue, publish, exhibit or advertise, or to offer or agree to do those things.
Performance	Any play, motion picture, photograph, dance, or other visual representation that can be exhibited before an audience of one (1) or more persons.
TEXAS	TEX. FAM. CODE ANN. § 71.0021(b) (Vernon 2011) TEX. PENAL CODE ANN. § 33.021 (Vernon 2011) TEX. PENAL CODE ANN. § 43.01, et seq. (Vernon 2011) TEX. PENAL CODE ANN. § 43.22, et seq. (Vernon 2011)
Obscene Display or Distribution	A person commits an offense if he intentionally or knowingly displays or distributes an obscene photograph, drawing, or similar visual representation or other obscene material and is reckless about whether a person is present who will be offended or alarmed by the display or distribution. (Violation of the above provision constitutes a Class C misdemeanor.)
Distribution, or Display of Harmful Material to Minor	A person commits an offense if, knowing that the material is harmful: (1) and knowing the person is a minor, he sells, distributes, exhibits, or possesses for sale, distribution, or exhibition to a minor harmful material; (2) he displays harmful material and is reckless about whether a minor is present who will be offended or alarmed by the display; or (3) he hires,

| | employs, or uses a minor to do or accomplish or assist in doing or accomplishing any of the acts prohibited in [(1) or (2)].

Violation of (1) or (2) constitutes a Class A misdemeanor. However, if the violation is committed under (3), the crime is a felony of the third degree.

Texas law provides a defense to the crime of distribution, or display of harmful material to a minor if the defendant was the minor's spouse when the crime was committed. Additionally, the law provides an affirmative defense if the distribution, or exhibition was by a person having scientific, educational, governmental, or other similar justification. |
| Sexual Performance by a Child | A person commits an offense if, knowing the character and content thereof, he employs, authorizes, or induces a child younger than 18 years of age to engage in sexual conduct or a sexual performance. A parent or legal guardian or custodian of a child younger than 18 years of age commits an offense if he consents to the participation by the child in a sexual performance.

(Violation of the above provision constitutes a felony of the second degree, except that the offense is a felony of the first degree if the victim is younger than 14 years of age at the time the offense is committed.)

A person commits an offense if, knowing the character and content of the material, he produces, directs, or promotes a performance that includes sexual conduct by a child younger than 18 years of age.

(Violation of the above provision constitutes a felony of the third degree, except that the offense is a felony of the second degree if the victim is younger than 14 years of age at the time the offense is committed.)

Texas law provides an affirmative defense to prosecution for sexual performance by a child if any of the following is satisfied: (i) the defendant was the spouse of the child at the time of the offense;
(ii) the conduct was for a bona fide educational, medical, psychological, psychiatric, judicial, law enforcement, or legislative purpose; or |

(continued)

STATE **Title of Pertinent Provision** *Key definition*	**Applicable Statutes and What They Say***
	(iii) the defendant is not more than two years older than the child.
Possession or Promotion of Child Pornography	(a) A person commits an offense if: (1) the person knowingly or intentionally possesses visual material that visually depicts a child younger than 18 years of age at the time the image of the child was made who is engaging in sexual conduct; and (2) the person knows that the material depicts the child as described by Subdivision (1).
	(Violation of this subsection constitutes a felony of the third degree.)
	(e) A person commits an offense if: (1) the person knowingly or intentionally promotes or possesses with intent to promote material described by Subsection (a)(1); and (2) the person knows that the material depicts the child as described by Subsection (a)(1).
	(Violation of this subsection constitutes a felony of the second degree.)
Sexting—Electronic Transmission of Certain Visual Material Depicting Minor	A person who is a minor commits an offense if the person intentionally or knowingly: (1) by electronic means promotes to another minor visual material depicting a minor, including the actor, engaging in sexual conduct, if the actor produced the visual material or knows that another minor produced the visual material; or (2) possesses in an electronic format visual material depicting another minor engaging in sexual conduct, if the actor produced the visual material or knows that another minor produced the visual material.
	Violation of subsection (1) above constitutes a Class C misdemeanor, except that the offense is: (1) a Class B misdemeanor if it is shown on the trial of the offense that the actor except as provided by Subdivision (2)(A), has previously been convicted one time of any offense under subsection (1) or (2) above.
	A minor charged under subsection (2) above can avail himself or herself of the following defenses if he or she: (1) did not produce or solicit the visual material; (2) possessed the visual material only after receiving the material from another minor;

STATE Title of Pertinent Provision *Key definition*	**Applicable Statutes and What They Say***
	and (3) destroyed the visual material within a reasonable amount of time after receiving the material from another minor.
	Violation of subsection (2) above constitutes:
	A Class C misdemeanor, except that the offense is: (1) a Class B misdemeanor if it is shown on the trial of the offense that the actor has previously been convicted one time of any offense under subsection (1) or (2) above; or
	A Class A misdemeanor if it is shown on the trial of the offense that the actor has previously been convicted two or more times of any offense under subsection (1) or (2).
	Texas law provides an affirmative defense for consensual sexting if the visual material: (1) depicted only the actor or another minor: (A) who is not more than two years older or younger than the actor and with whom the actor had a dating relationship at the time of the offense; or (B) who was the spouse of the actor at the time of the offense; and (2) was promoted or received only to or from the actor and the other minor.
Minor	Someone less than 18 years old.
Harmful material	Material whose dominant theme taken as a whole: (A) appeals to the prurient interest of a minor, in sex, nudity, or excretion; (B) is patently offensive to prevailing standards in the adult community as a whole with respect to what is suitable for minors; and (C) is *utterly* without redeeming *social* value for minors.
Sexual performance	Any performance or part thereof that includes sexual conduct by a child younger than 18 years of age.
Performance	Any play, motion picture, photograph, dance, or other visual representation that can be exhibited before an audience of one or more persons.
Sexual conduct	Sexual contact, actual or simulated sexual intercourse, deviate sexual intercourse, . . . masturbation, . . . or lewd exhibition of the genitals, the anus, or any portion of the female breast below the top of the areola.
Produce (with respect to a sexual performance)	Any conduct that directly contributes to the creation or manufacture of the sexual performance.

(continued)

STATE Title of Pertinent Provision *Key definition*	Applicable Statutes and What They Say*
Promote	To procure, manufacture, issue, sell, give, provide, lend, mail, deliver, transfer, transmit, publish, distribute, circulate, disseminate, present, exhibit, or advertise or to offer or agree to do any of the above.
Simulated	The explicit depiction of sexual conduct that creates the appearance of actual sexual conduct and during which a person engaging in the conduct exhibits any uncovered portion of the breasts, genitals, or buttocks.
Deviate sexual intercourse	Any contact between the genitals of one person and the mouth or anus of another person.
Sexual contact	Any touching of the anus, breast, or any part of the genitals of another person with intent to arouse or gratify the sexual desire of any person.
Visual material	(A) any film, photograph, videotape, negative, or slide or any photographic reproduction that contains or incorporates in any manner any film, photograph, videotape, negative, or slide; or (B) any disk, diskette, or other physical medium that allows an image to be displayed on a computer or other video screen and any image transmitted to a computer or other video screen by telephone line, cable, satellite transmission, or other method.
Dating relationship	A relationship between individuals who have or have had a continuing relationship of a romantic or intimate nature.
UTAH	UTAH CODE ANN. § 76-4-401 (2008) UTAH CODE ANN. § 76-5b-101, et seq. (2011) UTAH CODE ANN. § 76-10-1201, et seq. (2008)
Utah's forceful legislative statement accompanying its Sexual Exploitation Act	The Legislature of Utah determines that: (a) the sexual exploitation of a minor is excessively harmful to the minor's physiological, emotional, social, and mental development; . . . (c) a minor cannot intelligently and knowingly consent to sexual exploitation; (d) regardless of whether it is classified as legally obscene, material that sexually exploits a minor, . . . is not protected by the First Amendment of the United States Constitution or by the First or Fifteenth sections of Article I of the Utah Constitution and may be prohibited; and (e) prohibition of and punishment for the distribution, possession, possession with intent to distribute, and production of

	Applicable Statutes and What They Say*
	materials that sexually exploit a minor, . . . is necessary and justified to eliminate the market for those materials and to reduce the harm to the minor . . . inherent in the perpetuation of the record of the minor's . . . sexually exploitive activities. (2) It is the purpose of this chapter to prohibit the production, possession, possession with intent to distribute, and distribution of materials that sexually exploit a minor, . . . regardless of whether the materials are classified as legally obscene.
Sexual Exploitation of a Minor (Sexual Exploitation Act)	A person is guilty of sexual exploitation of a minor: (a) when the person: (i) knowingly produces, possesses, or possesses with intent to distribute child pornography; or (ii) intentionally distributes or views child pornography.
	(The law treats each minor depicted in the child pornography as a separate offense. Additionally, each time the same minor is depicted in different child pornography constitutes a separate offense. Sexual exploitation of a minor constitutes a second degree felony.)
Distributing Pornographic Material	A person is guilty of distributing pornographic material when the person knowingly: (a) sends or brings any pornographic material into the state with intent to distribute or exhibit it to others; (b) prepares, publishes, prints, or possesses any pornographic material with intent to distribute or exhibit it to others; (c) distributes or offers to distribute, or exhibits or offers to exhibit, any pornographic material to others; (d) writes, creates, or solicits the publication or advertising of pornographic material; (e) promotes the distribution or exhibition of material the person represents to be pornographic; or (f) presents or directs a pornographic performance in any public place or any place exposed to public view or participates in that portion of the performance which makes it pornographic.
	(Under Utah law, each distributing of pornographic material constitutes a separate offense. If the violation of the above provision is committed by a person 16 or 17 years of age the crime constitutes a class A misdemeanor. If the violation of the above provision is committed by a person younger than 16 years of age the crime constitutes a class B misdemeanor.)

(continued)

STATE Title of Pertinent Provision Key definition	Applicable Statutes and What They Say*
Dealing in Material Harmful to a Minor	A person is guilty of dealing in material harmful to minors when, knowing or believing that a person is a minor, or having negligently failed to determine the proper age of a minor, the person intentionally: (a) distributes or offers to distribute, or exhibits or offers to exhibit, to a minor or a person the actor believes to be a minor, any material harmful to minors; (b) produces, performs, or directs any performance, before a minor or a person the actor believes to be a minor, that is harmful to minors; or (c) participates in any performance, before a minor or a person the actor believes to be a minor, that is harmful to minors.
	(Each separate offense under this section committed by a person 16 or 17 years of age is a class A misdemeanor. If a defendant younger than 18 years of age has been previously convicted or adjudicated to be under the jurisdiction of the juvenile court under this section, each separate subsequent offense is a third degree felony. Each separate offense under this section committed by a person younger than 16 years of age is a class B misdemeanor. If a defendant younger than 18 years of age has been previously convicted or adjudicated to be under the jurisdiction of the juvenile court under this section, each separate subsequent offense is a third degree felony.)
Accessing Pornographic or Indecent Material on School Property	[A] person is guilty of accessing pornographic or indecent material on school property when the person willfully or knowingly creates, views, or otherwise gains access to pornographic or indecent material while present on school property, under circumstances not amounting to an attempted or actual violation [of the crime of distributing pornographic material or the crime of dealing in material harmful to a minor].
	(If the defendant is below the age of 18, each separate offense constitutes a class B misdemeanor.)
Enticing a Minor	(2)(a) A person commits enticement of a minor when the person knowingly uses or attempts to use the Internet or text messaging to solicit, seduce, lure, or entice a minor or another person that the actor believes to be a minor to engage in any sexual activity which is a violation of state criminal law. (b) A person commits enticement of a minor when the person

	Applicable Statutes and What They Say*
	knowingly uses the Internet or text messaging to: (i) initiate contact with a minor or a person the actor believes to be a minor; and (ii) subsequently to the action under Subsection (2)(b)(i), by any electronic or written means, solicits, seduces, lures, or entices, or attempts to solicit, seduce, lure, or entice the minor or a person the actor believes to be the minor to engage in any sexual activity which is a violation of state criminal law. (4) An enticement of a minor under Subsection (2)(a) or (b) with the intent to commit: (a) a first degree felony is a: (i) second degree felony upon the first conviction for violation of this Subsection (4)(a); and (ii) first degree felony punishable by imprisonment for an indeterminate term of not fewer than three years and which may be for life, upon a second or any subsequent conviction for a violation of this Subsection (4)(a); (b) a second degree felony is a third degree felony; (c) a third degree felony is a class A misdemeanor; (d) a class A misdemeanor is a class B misdemeanor; and (e) a class B misdemeanor is a class C misdemeanor. If the defendant has a prior conviction for crime of enticing a minor, the court may not in any way shorten the prison sentence, and the court may not: (i) grant probation; (ii) suspend the execution or imposition of the sentence; (iii) enter a judgment for a lower category of offense; or (iv) order hospitalization.
Minor	Someone below the age of 18.
Child pornography	Any visual depiction, including any live performance, photograph, film, video, picture, or computer or computer-generated image or picture, whether made or produced by electronic, mechanical, or other means, of sexually explicit conduct, where: (a) the production of the visual depiction involves the use of a minor engaging in sexually explicit conduct; [or] (b) the visual depiction is of a minor engaging in sexually explicit conduct.
Distribute	Selling, exhibiting, displaying, wholesaling, retailing, providing, giving, granting admission to, or otherwise transferring or presenting child pornography . . . with or without consideration.

(continued)

STATE Title of Pertinent Provision *Key definition*	Applicable Statutes and What They Say*
Nudity or partial nudity	Any state of dress or undress in which the human genitals, pubic region, buttocks, or the female breast, at a point below the top of the areola, is less than completely and opaquely covered. [For purposes of the crime of distributing pornographic material and the crime of dealing in material harmful to minors as well as the crime of accessing pornographic or indecent material on school property, nudity refers to] (a) the showing of the human male or female genitals, pubic area, or buttocks, with less than an opaque covering; (b) the showing of a female breast with less than an opaque covering, or any portion of the female breast below the top of the areola; or (c) the depiction of covered male genitals in a discernibly turgid state.
Produce	The photographing, filming, taping, directing, producing, creating, designing, or composing of child pornography [or] the securing or hiring of persons to engage in the photographing, filming, taping, directing, producing, creating, designing, or composing of child pornography.
Sexually explicit conduct	Actual or simulated: (a) sexual intercourse, including genital-genital, oral-genital, anal-genital, or oral-anal, whether between persons of the same or opposite sex; (b) masturbation; . . . (e) lascivious exhibition of the genitals or pubic area of any person; (f) the visual depiction of nudity or partial nudity for the purpose of causing sexual arousal of any person; (g) the fondling or touching of the genitals, pubic region, buttocks, or female breast; or (h) the explicit representation of the defecation or urination functions.
Simulated sexually explicit conduct	[A] feigned or pretended act of sexually explicit conduct which duplicates, within the perception of an average person, the appearance of an actual act of sexually explicit conduct.
Harmful to minors	That quality of any description or representation, in whatsoever form, of nudity, sexual conduct, sexual excitement, . . . when it: (i) taken as a whole, appeals to the prurient interest in sex of minors; (ii) is patently offensive to prevailing standards in the adult community as a whole with respect to what is suitable material for minors; and (iii) taken as a whole, does not have serious value for minors.

STATE Title of Pertinent Provision *Key definition*	**Applicable Statutes and What They Say***
Serious value	Includes only serious literary, artistic, political or scientific value for minors.
Performance	Any physical human bodily activity, whether engaged in alone or with other persons, including singing, speaking, dancing, acting, simulating, or pantomiming.
Sexual conduct	Acts of masturbation, sexual intercourse, or any touching of a person's clothed or unclothed genitals, pubic area, buttocks, or, if the person is a female, breast, whether alone or between members of the same or opposite sex . . . in an act of apparent or actual sexual stimulation or gratification.
Sexual excitement	Condition of human male or female genitals when in a state of sexual stimulation or arousal, or the sensual experiences of humans engaging in or witnessing sexual conduct or nudity.
Text messaging	Communication in the form of electronic text or one or more electronic images sent by the actor from a telephone or computer to another person's telephone or computer by addressing the communication to the person's telephone number.
VERMONT	Vt. Stat. Ann. tit. 13, § 2602 (2008) Vt. Stat. Ann. tit. 13, § 2801, et seq. (1999) Vt. Stat. Ann. tit. 13, § 2821, et seq. (1999) Vt. Stat. Ann. tit. 13, § 3251(1) (2005)
Sexual Exploitation of Children:	
Use of a Child in a Sexual Performance	No person shall, with knowledge of the character and content, promote a sexual performance by a child or a performance which contains a lewd exhibition of the genitals, anus or breasts of a child, or hire, employ, procure, use, cause or induce a child to engage in such a performance.
	Anyone charged with violating the above provision has an affirmative defense if he or she can show that before the child participated in the sexual performance, the defendant, in good faith, had a reasonable and factual basis to conclude that the child had in fact attained the age of 16; and the defendant did not rely solely upon the oral allegations or representations of the child as to his or her age.

(continued)

STATE **Title of Pertinent Provision** *Key definition*	**Applicable Statutes and What They Say***
Promoting a Recording of Sexual Conduct	No person may, with knowledge of the character and content, promote any photograph, film or visual recording of sexual conduct by a child, or of a lewd exhibition of a child's genitals or anus. This subsection does not apply to paintings, drawings, or to non-visual or written descriptions of sexual conduct.
	The law provides an affirmative defense to promoting a recording of sexual conduct if the defendant in good faith had a reasonable basis to conclude that the child in fact had attained the age of 16 when the recording was made.
	(Anyone who is convicted of the crime of using a child in a sexual performance or promoting a recording of sexual conduct shall be imprisoned not more than 10 years or fined not more than $20,000.00, or both. A person who has a prior conviction for either of these crimes shall be imprisoned not less than one year nor more than 15 years or fined not more than $50,000.00, or both.)
Possession of Child Pornography	No person shall, with knowledge of the character and content, possess any photograph, film or visual depiction, including any depiction which is stored electronically, of sexual conduct by a child or of a clearly lewd exhibition of a child's genitals or anus.
	[The crime of possession of child pornography does not apply to] paintings, drawings, or nonvisual or written descriptions of sexual conduct.
	(Anyone who commits the crime of possession of child pornography who has a prior conviction for the same crime shall be imprisoned not more than 10 years or fined not more than $50,000.00, or both.)
	(Anyone who commits the crime of possession of child pornography by possessing a photograph, film or visual depiction, including a depiction stored electronically, which constitutes a clearly lewd exhibition of a child's genitals or anus, other than a depiction of sexual conduct by a child, shall be imprisoned not more than two years or fined not more than $5,000.00, or both.)

Key definition	**Applicable Statutes and What They Say***
	(Anyone who commits the crime of possession of child pornography by possessing a photograph, film or visual depiction, including a depiction stored electronically, which constitutes sexual conduct by a child, shall be imprisoned not more than five years or fined not more than $10,000.00, or both.)
	The law provides an affirmative defense to the crime of possession of child pornography if the defendant can show, by a preponderance of the evidence, either of the following: (1) that the defendant in good faith had a reasonable basis to conclude that the child in fact had attained the age of 16 when the depiction was made; (2) that the defendant in good faith took reasonable steps, whether successful or not, to destroy or eliminate the depiction.
Luring a Child	No person shall knowingly solicit, lure, or entice, or to attempt to solicit, lure, or entice, a child under the age of 16 or another person believed by the person to be a child under the age of 16, to engage in a sexual act . . . or engage in lewd and lascivious conduct. [This includes] solicitation, luring, or enticement by any means, including in person, through written or telephonic correspondence or electronic communication.
	(Whoever commits the crime of luring a child shall be imprisoned not more than five years or fined not more than $10,000.00, or both.)
	The crime of luring a child is *not* committed if the person is less than 19 years old, the child is at least 15 years old, and the conduct is consensual.
Obscenity:	
Disseminating Indecent Material to a Minor in the Presence of the Minor	No person may, with knowledge of its character and content, sell, lend, distribute or give away to a minor: (1) Any picture, photograph, drawing, sculpture, motion picture film, or similar visual representation or image, including any such representation or image which is stored electronically, of a person or portion of the human body which depicts nudity, sexual conduct . . . and which is harmful to minors; or (2) Any book, pamphlet, magazine, printed matter however

(*continued*)

reproduced, or sound recording which contains any matter enumerated in subdivision (1) of this subsection, or explicit and detailed verbal descriptions or narrative accounts of sexual excitement, sexual conduct . . . and which, taken as a whole, is harmful to minors.

Distribution of Indecent Material

No person may hire, employ or permit a minor to sell, lend, distribute or give away material, the sale, lending, distribution or giving away of which to minors [violates the above law on disseminating indecent material to a minor in the presence of the minor].

Sexting—Minor Electronically Disseminating Indecent Material to Another Person

No minor shall knowingly and voluntarily and without threat or coercion use a computer or electronic communication device to transmit an indecent visual depiction of himself or herself to another person.

No person shall possess a visual depiction transmitted to the person in violation of subdivision (1) of this subsection. It shall not be a violation of this subdivision if the person took reasonable steps, whether successful or not, to destroy or eliminate the visual depiction.

Any minor who knowingly and voluntarily and without threat or coercion uses a computer or electronic communication device to transmit an indecent visual depiction of himself or herself to another person shall be adjudicated delinquent. The action shall be filed in family court and treated as a juvenile proceeding . . . and may be referred to the juvenile diversion program of the district in which the action is filed. If, however, the minor has previously been adjudicated as in violation of any provision of the sexting law above, he or she may be adjudicated in family court or prosecuted in district court under chapter 64 of this title (sexual exploitation of children) but shall not be subject to the requirements of subchapter 3 of chapter 167 of this title (sex offender registration).

If the minor who violates any provision of the sexting law above has no prior adjudication in violating of the sexting law, he or she shall not be prosecuted under chapter 64 of this title (sexual exploitation of children), and shall not be subject to the

Key definition	Applicable Statutes and What They Say*
	requirements of subchapter 3 of chapter 167 of this title (sex offender registration).
	A minor's record of delinquency adjudications under the sexting law shall be expunged after the minor turns 18.
	(Anyone convicted of the crimes of disseminating indecent material to a minor in the presence of the minor or distribution of indecent material shall be imprisoned not more than one year or fined not more than $1,000.00, or both.)
	Vermont law provides an affirmative defense to the crimes of disseminating indecent material to a minor in the presence of the minor and distribution of indecent material if either of the following applies:
	(i) the defendant was in a parental or guardianship relationship with the minor; or (ii) the minor was accompanied by a parent or legal guardian.
Child	Someone less than 16 years old.
Minor	Someone less than 18 years old.
Sexual conduct	(A) Any conduct involving contact between the penis and the vulva, the penis and the penis, the penis and the anus, the mouth and the penis, the mouth and the anus, the vulva and the vulva or the mouth and the vulva; (B) any intrusion, however slight, by any part of a person's body or any object into the genital or anal opening of another with the intent of arousing, appealing to, or gratifying the lust, passions or sexual desire of any person; (C) any intentional touching, not through the clothing, of the genitals, anus or breasts of another with the intent of arousing, appealing to, or gratifying the lust, passions or sexual desire of any person; [or] (D) masturbation.
Sexual conduct (for purposes of the sexting law)	Acts of masturbation, homosexuality, sexual intercourse, or physical contact with a person's clothed or unclothed genitals, pubic area, buttocks or, if such person be a female, breast.
Sexual performance	Any performance or any part of a performance, which includes sexual conduct by a child.
Performance	(A) An event which is photographed, filmed or visually recorded; or (B) a play, dance or other visual presentation or exhibition before an audience.

(*continued*)

STATE Title of Pertinent Provision *Key definition*	**Applicable Statutes and What They Say***
Promote	To procure, issue, manufacture, publish, sell, give, provide, lend, mail, deliver, distribute, disseminate, circulate, present, exhibit, advertise, or offer to do the same, by any means, including electronic transmission.
Sexual act	Conduct between persons consisting of contact between the penis and the vulva, the penis and the anus, the mouth and the penis, the mouth and the vulva, or any intrusion, however slight, by any part of a person's body or any object into the genital or anal opening of another.
Nudity	The showing of the human male or female genitals, pubic area or buttocks with less than a full opaque covering, or the showing of the female breast with less than a fully opaque covering of any portion thereof below the top of the nipple, or the depiction of covered male genitals in a discernably turgid state.
Sexual excitement	The condition of human male or female genitals when in a state of sexual stimulation or arousal.
Harmful to minors	That quality of any description or representation, in whatever form, of nudity, sexual conduct, sexual excitement, . . . when it: (A) Predominantly appeals to the prurient, shameful or morbid interest of minors; and (B) Is patently offensive to prevailing standards in the adult community in the state of Vermont as a whole with respect to what is suitable material for minors; and (C) Is taken as a whole, lacks serious literary, artistic, political, or scientific value, for minors.
VIRGINIA	VA. CODE ANN. § 18.2-370.01 (Michie 2001) VA. CODE ANN. § 18.2-373 (Michie 2000) VA. CODE ANN. § 18.2-374, et seq. (Michie 2001) VA. CODE ANN. § 19.2-386.31 (Michie 2007)
Indecent Liberties by Children	Any child over the age of thirteen years but under the age of eighteen who, with lascivious intent, knowingly and intentionally exposes his or her sexual or genital parts to any other child under the age of fourteen years who, measured by actual dates of birth, is five or more years the accused's junior, or proposes that any such child expose his or her sexual or genital parts to such person, shall be guilty of a Class 1 misdemeanor.

STATE Title of Pertinent Provision *Key definition*	Applicable Statutes and What They Say*
Production, Publication, Possession, Distribution of Obscene Items	It shall be unlawful for any person knowingly to: (1) Prepare any obscene item for the purposes of sale or distribution; or (2) Print, copy, manufacture, produce, or reproduce any obscene item for purposes of sale or distribution; or (3) Publish, sell, rent, lend, transport in intrastate commerce, or distribute or exhibit any obscene item, or offer to do any of these things; or (4) Have in his possession with intent to sell, rent, lend, transport, or distribute any obscene item.
	(For the first offense, anyone who violates the above provision shall be guilty of a Class 1 misdemeanor. A second/ subsequent violation constitutes a Class 6 felony.)
Production or Participation in Production of Child Pornography	A person shall be guilty of production of child pornography who: 1. Accosts, entices or solicits a person less than 18 years of age with intent to induce or force such person to perform in or be a subject of child pornography; or 2. Produces or makes or attempts or prepares to produce or make child pornography; or 3. Who knowingly takes part in or participates in the filming, photographing, or other production of child pornography by any means.
	(If the subject of the child pornography is a child less than 15 years of age, the person who violates any provision of the child pornography law above shall be punished by not less than five years nor more than 30 years in a state correctional facility. However, if the person is at least seven years older than the subject of the child pornography the person shall be punished by a term of imprisonment of not less than five years nor more than 30 years in a state correctional facility, five years of which shall be a mandatory minimum term of imprisonment.
	For a second or subsequent violation, if the defendant is at least seven years older than the subject, he or she shall be punished by a term of imprisonment of not less than 15 years nor more than 40 years, 15 years of which shall be a mandatory minimum term of imprisonment.
	If the subject of the child pornography is a person at least 15 but less than 18 years of age, the person who violates any provision of the child pornography law shall be punished by not less than one year nor more than 20 years in a state

(continued)

STATE Title of Pertinent Provision *Key definition*	**Applicable Statutes and What They Say***
	correctional facility. However, if the person is at least seven years older than the subject of the child pornography the person shall be punished by term of imprisonment of not less than three years nor more than 30 years in a state correctional facility, three years of which shall be a mandatory minimum term of imprisonment.
	For a second or subsequent violation, if the defendant is at least seven years older than the subject, he or she shall be punished by a term of imprisonment of not less than 10 years nor more than 30 years, 10 years of which shall be a mandatory minimum term of imprisonment.)
Possession, Reproduction, Distribution and Facilitation of Child Pornography	Any person who knowingly possesses child pornography is guilty of a Class 6 felony. [A second/subsequent violation of this provision constitutes a] Class 5 felony.
	Any person who reproduces by any means, including by computer, sells, gives away, distributes, electronically transmits, displays with lascivious intent, purchases, or possesses with intent to sell, give away, distribute, transmit, or display child pornography with lascivious intent shall be punished by not less than five years nor more than 20 years in a state correctional facility. [A second/subsequent violation of this provision] shall be punished by a term of imprisonment of not less than five years nor more than 20 years in a state correctional facility, five years of which shall be a mandatory minimum term of imprisonment.
Use of Communications Systems to Facilitate Certain Offenses Involving Children	It shall be unlawful for any person to use a communications system, including but not limited to computers or computer networks or bulletin boards, or any other electronic means for the purposes of procuring or promoting the use of a minor for any activity in violation of . . . § 18.2-374.1.
	(Violation of this provision constitutes a Class 6 felony.)
Obscene Photographs	Every person who knowingly: (1) Photographs himself or any other person, for purposes of preparing an obscene film, photograph, negative, slide or motion picture for purposes of sale or distribution; or

STATE Title of Pertinent Provision *Key definition*	**Applicable Statutes and What They Say***
	(2) Models, poses, acts, or otherwise assists in the preparation of any obscene film, photograph, negative, slide or motion picture for purposes of sale or distribution; shall be guilty of a Class 3 misdemeanor.
Obscene item	Any obscene leaflet, pamphlet, magazine, booklet, picture, painting, bumper sticker, drawing, photograph, film, negative, slide, motion picture, videotape recording [or] any obscene writing, picture or similar visual representation, or sound recording, stored in an electronic or other medium retrievable in a perceivable form.
Child pornography	Sexually explicit visual material which utilizes or has as a subject an identifiable minor.
Identifiable minor	A person who was a minor at the time the visual depiction was created, adapted, or modified; or whose image as a minor was used in creating, adapting or modifying the visual depiction; and who is recognizable as an actual person by the person's face, likeness, or other distinguishing characteristic, such as a unique birthmark or other recognizable feature.
Sexually explicit visual material	A picture, photograph, drawing, sculpture, motion picture film, digital image, including such material stored in a computer's temporary Internet cache when three or more images or streaming videos are present, or similar visual representation which depicts . . . a lewd exhibition of nudity, . . . or sexual excitement, sexual conduct . . . . or a book, magazine or pamphlet which contains such a visual representation. [Additionally,] an undeveloped photograph or similar visual material may be sexually explicit material notwithstanding that processing or other acts may be required to make its sexually explicit content apparent.
Nudity	[A] state of undress so as to expose the human male or female genitals, pubic area or buttocks with less than a full opaque covering, or the showing of the female breast with less than a fully opaque covering of any portion thereof below the top of the nipple, or the depiction of covered or uncovered male genitals in a discernibly turgid state.
Sexual excitement	Condition of human male or female genitals when in a state of sexual stimulation or arousal.

(continued)

STATE Title of Pertinent Provision *Key definition*	**Applicable Statutes and What They Say***
Sexual conduct	Actual or explicitly simulated acts of masturbation, homosexuality, sexual intercourse, or physical contact in an act of apparent sexual stimulation or gratification with a person's clothed or unclothed genitals, pubic area, buttocks or, if such be female, breast.
WASHINGTON	Wash. Rev. Code Ann. § 9.68A.001, et seq. (West 2010)
The Washington legislature's strong statement in support of its law	The legislature finds that the prevention of sexual exploitation and abuse of children constitutes a government objective of surpassing importance. The care of children is a sacred trust and should not be abused by those who seek commercial gain or personal gratification based on the exploitation of children. The legislature further finds that the protection of children from sexual exploitation can be accomplished without infringing on a constitutionally protected activity. . . . By amending current statutes governing depictions of a minor engaged in sexually explicit conduct, it is the intent of the legislature to ensure that intentional viewing of and dealing in child pornography over the internet is subject to a criminal penalty without limiting the scope of existing prohibitions on the possession of or dealing in child pornography, including the possession of electronic depictions of a minor engaged in sexually explicit conduct.
	The legislature explicitly notes that its law on sexual exploitation of children does not apply to lawful conduct between spouses.
Sexual Exploitation of Children: Sexual Exploitation of a Minor	A person is guilty of sexual exploitation of a minor if the person . . . aids, invites, employs, authorizes, or causes a minor to engage in sexually explicit conduct, knowing that such conduct will be photographed or part of a live performance.
	(Sexual exploitation of a minor constitutes a class B felony.)
Dealing in Depictions of Minor Engaged in Sexually Explicit Conduct in the First Degree	A person commits the crime of dealing in depictions of a minor engaged in sexually explicit conduct in the first degree when he or she: (i) Knowingly develops, duplicates, publishes, prints, disseminates, exchanges, finances, attempts to finance, or sells a visual or printed matter that depicts a minor engaged in an act of sexually explicit conduct; . . . or (ii) Possesses with intent

Key definition	**Applicable Statutes and What They Say***
	to develop, duplicate, publish, print, disseminate, exchange, or sell any visual or printed matter that depicts a minor engaged in an act of sexually explicit conduct.
	(Dealing in depictions of a minor engaged in sexually explicit conduct in the first degree constitutes a class B felony.)
	Each depiction or image of visual or printed matter constitutes a separate offense.
Dealing in Depictions of Minor Engaged in Sexually Explicit Conduct in the Second Degree	A person commits the crime of dealing in depictions of a minor engaged in sexually explicit conduct in the second degree when he or she: (i) Knowingly develops, duplicates, publishes, prints, disseminates, exchanges, finances, attempts to finance, or sells any visual or printed matter that depicts a minor engaged in an act of sexually explicit conduct; . . . or (ii) Possesses with intent to develop, duplicate, publish, print, disseminate, exchange, or sell any visual or printed matter that depicts a minor engaged in an act of sexually explicit conduct.
	(Dealing in depictions of a minor engaged in sexually explicit conduct in the second degree constitutes a class C felony.)
	Each incident of dealing in one or more depictions or images of visual or printed matter constitutes a separate offense.
Sending, Bringing into State Depictions of Minor Engaged in Sexually Explicit Conduct in the First Degree	A person commits the crime of sending or bringing into the state depictions of a minor engaged in sexually explicit conduct in the first degree when he or she knowingly sends or causes to be sent, or brings or causes to be brought, into this state for sale or distribution, a visual or printed matter that depicts a minor engaged in sexually explicit conduct.
	(Sending or bringing into the state depictions of a minor engaged in sexually explicit conduct in the first degree constitutes a class B felony.)
	Each depiction or image of visual or printed matter constitutes a separate offense.
Sending, Bringing into State Depictions of Minor Engaged In Sexually Explicit Conduct in the Second Degree	A person commits the crime of sending or bringing into the state depictions of a minor engaged in sexually explicit conduct in the second degree when he or she knowingly sends or causes to be sent, or brings or causes to be brought, into this state for sale or distribution, any visual or printed matter that depicts a minor engaged in sexually explicit conduct.

(*continued*)

Key definition	**Applicable Statutes and What They Say***
	(Sending or bringing into the state depictions of a minor engaged in sexually explicit conduct in the second degree constitutes a class C felony.)
	Each incident of sending or bringing into the state one or more depictions or images of visual or printed matter constitutes a separate offense.
Possession of Depictions of Minor Engaged in Sexually Explicit Conduct in the First Degree	A person commits the crime of possession of depictions of a minor engaged in sexually explicit conduct in the first degree when he or she knowingly possesses a visual or printed matter depicting a minor engaged in sexually explicit conduct. (Possession of depictions of a minor engaged in sexually explicit conduct in the first degree constitutes a class B felony.)
	Each depiction or image of visual or printed matter constitutes a separate offense.
Possession of Depictions of Minor Engaged in Sexually Explicit Conduct in the Second Degree	A person commits the crime of possession of depictions of a minor engaged in sexually explicit conduct in the second degree when he or she knowingly possesses any visual or printed matter depicting a minor engaged in sexually explicit conduct.
	(Possession of depictions of a minor engaged in sexually explicit conduct in the second degree constitutes a class C felony.)
	Each incident of possession of one or more depictions or images of visual or printed matter constitutes a separate offense.
Reporting of Depictions of Minor Engaged in Sexually Explicit Conduct	A person who, in the course of processing or producing visual or printed matter either privately or commercially, has reasonable cause to believe that the visual or printed matter submitted for processing or producing depicts a minor engaged in sexually explicit conduct shall immediately report such incident, or cause a report to be made, to the proper law enforcement agency.
	(Violation of this provision constitutes a gross misdemeanor.)
Communication with Minor for Immoral Purposes	A person who communicates with a minor for immoral purposes, or a person who communicates with someone the person believes to be a minor for immoral purposes, is guilty of a gross misdemeanor.

	(A person who communicates with a minor for immoral purposes is guilty of a class C felony if the person has previously been convicted of communication with a minor for immoral purposes or if the person communicates with a minor or with someone the person believes to be a minor for immoral purposes through the sending of an electronic communication.)
Minor	Someone below the age of 18.
Visual or printed matter	Any photograph or other material that contains a reproduction of a photograph.
Sexually explicit conduct	Actual or simulated: (a) Sexual intercourse, including genital-genital, oral-genital, anal-genital, or oral-anal, whether between persons of the same or opposite sex; . . . (b) Penetration of the vagina or rectum by any object; (c) Masturbation; . . . (e) Defecation or urination for the purpose of sexual stimulation of the viewer; (f) Depiction of the genitals or unclothed pubic or rectal areas of any minor, or the unclothed breast of a female minor, for the purpose of sexual stimulation of the viewer; . . . and (g) Touching of a person's clothed or unclothed genitals, pubic area, buttocks, or breast area for the purpose of sexual stimulation of the viewer.
Live performance	Any play, show, skit, dance, or other exhibition performed or presented to or before an audience of one or more, with or without consideration.
Photograph	To make a print, negative, slide, digital image, motion picture, or videotape.
WEST VIRGINIA	W. Va. Code § 61-8C-1, et seq. (2011)
Use of Minors in Filming Sexually Explicit Conduct	Any person who causes or knowingly permits, uses, persuades, induces, entices or coerces such minor to engage in or uses such minor to do or assist in any sexually explicit conduct shall be guilty of a felony when such person has knowledge that any such act is being photographed or filmed. Upon conviction thereof, such person shall be fined not more than ten thousand dollars, or imprisoned in the penitentiary not more than ten years, or both fined and imprisoned.
	Any person who photographs or films such minor engaging in any sexually explicit conduct shall be guilty of a felony, and,

(continued)

	upon conviction thereof, shall be fined not more than ten thousand dollars, or imprisoned in the penitentiary not more than ten years, or both fined and imprisoned.
Distribution and Exhibiting of Material Depicting Minors Engaged in Sexually Explicit Conduct	Any person who, with knowledge, sends or causes to be sent, or distributes, exhibits, possesses or displays or transports any material visually portraying a minor engaged in any sexually explicit conduct is guilty of a felony, and, upon conviction thereof, shall be imprisoned in the penitentiary not more than two years, and fined not more than two thousand dollars.
Minor	Someone less than 18 years old.
Sexually explicit conduct	Any of the following, whether actually performed or simulated:
	(1) Genital to genital intercourse; (2) Fellatio; (3) Cunnilingus; (4) Anal intercourse; (5) Oral to anal intercourse; . . . (7) Masturbation; . . . (9) Excretory functions in a sexual context; or (10) Exhibition of the genitals, pubic or rectal areas of any person in a sexual context.
WISCONSIN	Wis. Stat. Ann. § 948.01, et seq. (West 2005)
Sexual Exploitation of a Child	[A person commits the crime of sexual exploitation of a child if he or she] with knowledge of the character and content of the sexually explicit conduct involving the child [either] employs, uses, persuades, induces, entices, or coerces any child to engage in sexually explicit conduct for the purpose of recording or displaying in any way the conduct [or] records or displays in any way a child engaged in sexually explicit conduct.
	(Violation of any provision above constitutes a Class C felony. However, it is a Class F felony if the person is under 18 years of age when the offense occurs.)
	[The crime of sexual exploitation of a child is committed when someone who] knows the character and content of the sexually explicit conduct involving the child [and] knows or reasonably should know [that such child is below the age of 18] produces, performs in, profits from, promotes, imports into the state, reproduces, advertises, sells, distributes, or possesses with intent to sell or distribute, any recording of a child engaging in sexually explicit conduct.

STATE Title of Pertinent Provision *Key definition*	Applicable Statutes and What They Say*
	(Violation of any provision above constitutes a Class C felony. However, it is a Class F felony if the person is under 18 years of age when the offense occurs.)
Causing a Child to View or Listen to Sexual Activity	[A person commits the crime of causing a child to view or listen to sexual activity if he or she] intentionally causes a child who has not attained 18 years of age to view or listen to sexually explicit conduct [and] the viewing or listening is for the purpose of sexually arousing or gratifying the actor or humiliating or degrading the child. (Violation of the above provision constitutes a Class F felony if the child is less than 13 years old. However, it is a Class H felony if the child is at least 13 years old but less than 18 years old.)
Child Enticement	[Anyone who] causes or attempts to cause any child who has not attained the age of 18 years to go into any vehicle, building, room or secluded place [with the intent of] recording the child engaging in sexually explicit conduct [commits the crime of child enticement]. (Child enticement constitutes a Class D felony.)
Exposing Genitals or Pubic Area	[A person commits the crime exposing genitals or pubic area, if] for purposes of sexual arousal or sexual gratification, [he or she] causes a child to expose genitals or pubic area or exposes genitals or pubic area to a child. (Exposing genitals or pubic area constitutes a Class I felony. It is, however, a Class A misdemeanor if the defendant was a child at the time of the violation and was less than 19 years old and not more than 4 years older than the child at the time of the violation.) Wisconsin excludes a defendant from the crime exposing genitals or public area if he or she is married to the child.
Exposing a Child to Harmful Material or Harmful Descriptions or Narrations	Whoever, with knowledge of the character and content of the material, sells, rents, exhibits, plays, distributes, or loans to a child any harmful material, with or without monetary consideration, is guilty of a Class I felony if any of the following applies: 1. The person knows or reasonably should know that the child has not attained the age of 18 years. 2.

(*continued*)

Key definition	**Applicable Statutes and What They Say***
	The person has face-to-face contact with the child before or during the sale, rental, exhibit, playing, distribution, or loan.
	Any person who has attained the age of 17 and who, with knowledge of the character and content of the description or narrative account, verbally communicates, by any means, a harmful description or narrative account to a child, with or without monetary consideration, is guilty of a Class I felony if any of the following applies: 1. The person knows or reasonably should know that the child has not attained the age of 18 years. 2. The person has face-to-face contact with the child before or during the communication.
	Whoever, with knowledge of the character and content of the material, possesses harmful material with the intent to sell, rent, exhibit, play, distribute, or loan the material to a child is guilty of a Class A misdemeanor if any of the following applies: 1. The person knows or reasonably should know that the child has not attained the age of 18 years. 2. The person has face-to-face contact with the child.
Possession of Child Pornography	[Possession of child pornography crime is committed by anyone who] possesses any undeveloped film, photographic negative, photograph, motion picture, videotape, or other recording of a child engaged in sexually explicit conduct [if all the following situations apply]: (a) The person knows that he or she possesses the material. (b) The person knows the character and content of the sexually explicit conduct in the material. (c) The person knows or reasonably should know that the child engaged in sexually explicit conduct has not attained the age of 18 years.
	(Violation of this provision constitutes a Class D felony. However, if the defendant is less than 18 years old at the time of the violation, it is a Class I felony.)
	[The crime of possession of child pornography is committed by anyone who] exhibits or plays a recording of a child engaged in sexually explicit conduct, [if all of the following are satisfied]:
	(a) The person knows that he or she has exhibited or played the recording. (b) Before the person exhibited or played the recording, he or she knew the character and content of the

	sexually explicit conduct. (c) Before the person exhibited or played the recording, he or she knew or reasonably should have known that the child engaged in sexually explicit conduct had not attained the age of 18 years.
	(Violation of this provision constitutes a Class D felony. However, if the defendant is less than 18 years old at the time of the violation, it is a Class I felony.)
Child	Someone less than 18 years old.
Sexually explicit conduct	Actual or simulated: (a) Sexual intercourse, meaning vulvar penetration as well as cunnilingus, fellatio or anal intercourse between persons or any other intrusion, however slight, of any part of a person's body or of any object into the genital or anal opening either by a person or upon the person's instruction. The emission of semen is not required; . . . (c) Masturbation; . . . or
	(e) Lewd exhibition of intimate parts.
Sexual intercourse	Vulvar penetration as well as cunnilingus, fellatio or anal intercourse between persons or any other intrusion, however slight, of any part of a person's body or of any object into the genital or anal opening either by the defendant or upon the defendant's instruction. The emission of semen is not required.
Harmful to children	That quality of any description, narrative account or representation, in whatever form, of nudity, sexually explicit conduct, sexual excitement, . . . when it: 1. Predominantly appeals to the prurient, shameful or morbid interest of children; 2. Is patently offensive to prevailing standards in the adult community as a whole with respect to what is suitable for children; and 3. Lacks serious literary, artistic, political, scientific or educational value for children, when taken as a whole.
Harmful material	1. Any picture, photograph, drawing, sculpture, motion picture film or similar visual representation or image of a person or portion of the human body that depicts nudity, sexually explicit conduct, . . . and that is harmful to children; or 2. Any book, pamphlet, magazine, printed matter however reproduced or recording that contains any matter enumerated in subd. 1., or explicit and detailed verbal descriptions or

(*continued*)

STATE Title of Pertinent Provision *Key definition*	Applicable Statutes and What They Say*
	narrative accounts of sexual excitement, sexually explicit conduct, . . . and that, taken as a whole, is harmful to children.
Harmful description or narrative account	Any explicit and detailed description or narrative account of sexual excitement, sexually explicit conduct, . . . that, taken as a whole, is harmful to children.
Sexual excitement	Condition of human male or female genitals when in a state of sexual stimulation or arousal.
Nudity	Showing of the human male or female genitals, pubic area or buttocks with less than a full opaque covering, or the showing of the female breast with less than a fully opaque covering of any portion thereof below the top of the nipple, or the depiction of covered male genitals in a discernibly turgid state.
WYOMING	Wyo. Stat. Ann. § 6-4-301, et seq. (Michie 2011)
Promoting Obscenity	A person commits the crime of promoting obscenity if he: (i) Produces or reproduces obscene material with the intent of disseminating it; (ii) Possesses obscene material with the intent of disseminating it; or (iii) Knowingly disseminates obscene material.
	Promoting obscenity to a minor constitutes a misdemeanor. For each violation, the defendant shall be punished by a fine not to exceed six thousand dollars ($6,000.00) or by imprisonment for not to exceed one (1) year, or both.
Sexual Exploitation of a Child	A person is guilty of sexual exploitation of a child if, for any purpose, he knowingly: (i) Causes, induces, entices, coerces or permits a child to engage in, or be used for, the making of child pornography; (ii) Causes, induces, entices or coerces a child to engage in, or be used for, any explicit sexual conduct; [or] (iii) Manufactures, generates, creates, receives, distributes, reproduces, delivers or possesses with the intent to deliver, including through digital or electronic means, whether or not by computer, any child pornography.
	Violation of any of the above provisions constitutes a felony punishable by imprisonment for not less than five (5) years nor more than twelve (12) years, a fine of not more than ten thousand dollars ($10,000.00), or both. A second/subsequent violation constitutes a felony punishable by imprisonment for not less than seven (7) years nor more than twelve (12) years,

STATE Title of Pertinent Provision *Key definition*	**Applicable Statutes and What They Say***
	a fine of not more than ten thousand dollars ($10,000.00), or both.
	Knowingly possessing child pornography, for any purpose, constitutes sexual exploitation of a child.
	Violation of the above provision constitutes a felony punishable by imprisonment for not more than ten (10) years, a fine of not more than ten thousand dollars ($10,000.00), or both. A second/subsequent violation constitutes a felony punishable by imprisonment for not less than seven (7) years nor more than twelve (12) years, a fine of not more than ten thousand dollars ($10,000.00), or both.
Sexual conduct	Patently offensive representations or descriptions of ultimate sexual acts, normal or perverted, actual or simulated [or] patently offensive representations or descriptions of masturbation, excretory functions or lewd exhibitions of the genitals.
Disseminate	To sell, distribute, deliver, provide, exhibit or otherwise make available to another.
Material	Any form of human expression or communication intended for, or capable of, visual, auditory or sensory perception.
Produce or reproduce	To bring into being regardless of the process or means employed. Undeveloped photographs, films, molds, casts, printing plates and like articles may be obscene notwithstanding that further processing or other acts are necessary to make the obscenity patent or to disseminate or exhibit the obscene material.
Child	Someone less than 18 years old.
Child pornography	Any visual depiction, including any photograph, film, video, picture, computer or computer-generated image or picture, whether or not made or produced by electronic, mechanical or other means, of explicit sexual conduct, where: (A) The production of the visual depiction involves the use of a child engaging in explicit sexual conduct; (B) The visual depiction is of explicit sexual conduct involving a child or an individual virtually indistinguishable from a child; or (C) The visual depiction has been created, adapted or modified to depict

(continued)

STATE Title of Pertinent Provision *Key definition*	Applicable Statutes and What They Say*
	explicit sexual conduct involving a child or an individual virtually indistinguishable from a child.
Explicit sexual conduct	Actual or simulated sexual intercourse, including genital-genital, oral-genital, anal-genital or oral-anal, between persons of the same or opposite sex, . . . masturbation, . . . or lascivious exhibition of the genitals or pubic area of any person.
Visual depiction	Developed and undeveloped film and videotape, and data stored on computer disk or by electronic means which is capable of conversion into a visual image.

* Internal quotation marks omitted; emphasis added.

Diverse Statutory Punishments for Felonies and Misdemeanors

State	Punishments for Felonies and Misdemeanors
Alabama	(a) Sentences for felonies shall be for a definite term of imprisonment, which imprisonment includes hard labor, within the following limitations: (1) For a Class A felony, for life or not more than 99 years or less than 10 years. (2) For a Class B felony, not more than 20 years or less than 2 years. (3) For a Class C felony, not more than 10 years or less than 1 year and 1 day. (5) For a Class B or C felony in which a firearm or deadly weapon was used or attempted to be used in the commission of the felony, or a Class B felony criminal sex offense involving a child as defined in Section 15-20-21(5), not less than 10 years. (c) In addition to any penalties heretofore or hereafter provided by law, in all cases where an offender is designated as a sexually violent predator pursuant to Section 15-20-25.3, or where an offender is convicted of a Class A felony criminal sex offense involving a child as defined in Section 15-20-21(5), and is sentenced to a county jail or the Alabama Department of Corrections, the sentencing judge shall impose an additional penalty of not less than 10 years of post-release supervision to be served upon the defendant's release from incarceration. (d) In addition to any penalties heretofore or hereafter provided by law, in all cases where an offender is convicted of a sex offense pursuant to Section 13A-6-61, 13A-6-63, or 13A-6-65.1, when the defendant was 21 years of age or older and the victim was six years of age or less at the time the offense was committed, the defendant shall be sentenced to life imprisonment without the possibility of parole.[1]
Alaska	(a) Upon conviction of an offense, a defendant may be sentenced to pay a fine as authorized in this section or as otherwise authorized by law. (b) Upon conviction of an offense, a defendant who is not an organization may be sentenced to pay, unless otherwise specified in the provision of law defining the offense, a fine of no more than (1) $500,000 for murder in the first or second degree, attempted murder in the first degree, murder of an unborn child, sexual assault in the first degree, sexual abuse of a minor in the first degree, kidnapping, promoting prostitution in the first degree under AS 11.66.110(a)(2), or misconduct involving a controlled substance in the first degree; (2) $250,000 for a class A felony; (3) $100,000 for a class B felony; (4) $50,000 for a class C felony; (5) $10,000 for a class A misdemeanor; (6) $2,000 for a class B misdemeanor; (7) $500 for a violation.[2]

Except as provided in (i) of this section, a defendant convicted of a class A felony may be sentenced to a definite term of imprisonment of not more than 20 years, and shall be sentenced to a definite term within the following presumptive ranges, subject to adjustment as provided in AS 12.55.155—12.55.175:

(1) if the offense is a first felony conviction and does not involve circumstances described in (2) of this subsection, five to eight years;

(2) if the offense is a first felony conviction (A) and the defendant possessed a firearm, used a dangerous instrument, or caused serious physical injury or death during the commission of the offense, or knowingly directed the conduct constituting the offense at a uniformed or otherwise clearly identified peace officer, firefighter, correctional employee, emergency medical technician, paramedic, ambulance attendant, or other emergency responder who was engaged in the performance of official duties at the time of the offense, seven to 11 years; (B) and the conviction is for manufacturing related to methamphetamine under AS 11.71.020(a)(2)(A) or (B), seven to 11 years, if (i) the manufacturing occurred in a building with reckless disregard that the building was used as a permanent or temporary home or place of lodging for one or more children under 18 years of age or the building was a place frequented by children; or (ii) in the course of manufacturing or in preparation for manufacturing, the defendant obtained the assistance of one or more children under 18 years of age or one or more children were present;

(3) if the offense is a second felony conviction, 10 to 14 years;

(4) if the offense is a third felony conviction and the defendant is not subject to sentencing under (l) of this section, 15 to 20 years. [3]

Except as provided in (i) of this section, a defendant convicted of a class B felony may be sentenced to a definite term of imprisonment of not more than 10 years, and shall be sentenced to a definite term within the following presumptive ranges, subject to adjustment as provided in AS 12.55.155—12.55.175:

(1) if the offense is a first felony conviction and does not involve circumstances described in (2) of this subsection, one to three years; a defendant sentenced under this paragraph may, if the court finds it appropriate, be granted a suspended imposition of sentence under AS 12.55.085 if, as a condition of probation under AS 12.55.086, the defendant is required to serve an active term of imprisonment within the range specified in this paragraph, unless the court finds that a mitigation factor under AS 12.55.155 applies;

(continued)

State	Punishments for Felonies and Misdemeanors

(2) if the offense is a first felony conviction,

   (A) the defendant violated AS 11.41.130, and the victim was a child under 16 years of age, two to four years;

   (B) two to four years if the conviction is for an attempt, solicitation, or conspiracy to manufacture related to methamphetamine under AS 11.31 and AS 11.71.020(a)(2)(A) or (B), and

     (i) the attempted manufacturing occurred, or the solicited or conspired offense was to have occurred, in a building with reckless disregard that the building was used as a permanent or temporary home or place of lodging for one or more children under 18 years of age or the building was a place frequented by children; or

……….(ii) in the course of an attempt to manufacture, the defendant obtained the assistance of one or more children under 18 years of age or one or more children were present;

(3) if the offense is a second felony conviction, four to seven years;

(4) if the offense is a third felony conviction, six to 10 years.[4]

Except as provided in (i) of this section, a defendant convicted of a class C felony may be sentenced to a definite term of imprisonment of not more than five years, and shall be sentenced to a definite term within the following presumptive ranges, subject to adjustment as provided in AS 12.55.155—12.55.175:

(1) if the offense is a first felony conviction and does not involve circumstances described in (4) of this subsection, zero to two years; a defendant sentenced under this paragraph may, if the court finds it appropriate, be granted a suspended imposition of sentence under AS 12.55.085, and the court may, as a condition of probation under AS 12.55.086, require the defendant to serve an active term of imprisonment within the range specified in this paragraph;

(2) if the offense is a second felony conviction, two to four years;

(3) if the offense is a third felony conviction, three to five years;

(4) if the offense is a first felony conviction, and the defendant violated AS 08.54.720(a)(15), one to two years.[5]

If a defendant is sentenced under (c), (d), (e), or (i) of this section, except to the extent permitted under AS 12.55.155—12.55.175, (1) imprisonment may not be suspended under AS 12.55.080 below the low end of the presumptive range; (2) and except as provided in (d)(1) or (e)(1) of this section, imposition of sentence may not be suspended under AS 12.55.085; (3) terms of imprisonment may not be otherwise reduced.[6]

Nothing in this section or AS 12.55.135 limits the discretion of the sentencing judge except as specifically provided.[7]

A defendant convicted of

(1) sexual assault in the first degree, sexual abuse of a minor in the first degree, or promoting prostitution in the first degree under AS 11.66.110(a)(2) may be sentenced to a definite term of imprisonment of not more than 99 years and shall be sentenced to a definite term within the following presumptive ranges, subject to adjustment as provided in AS 12.55.155—12.55.175:

(A) if the offense is a first felony conviction, the offense does not involve circumstances described in (B) of this paragraph, and the victim was

(i) less than 13 years of age, 25 to 35 years;

(ii) 13 years of age or older, 20 to 30 years;

(B) if the offense is a first felony conviction and the defendant possessed a firearm, used a dangerous instrument, or caused serious physical injury during the commission of the offense, 25 to 35 years;

(C) if the offense is a second felony conviction and does not involve circumstances described in (D) of this paragraph, 30 to 40 years;

(D) if the offense is a second felony conviction and the defendant has a prior conviction for a sexual felony, 35 to 45 years;

(E) if the offense is a third felony conviction and the defendant is not subject to sentencing under (F) of this paragraph or (l) of this section, 40 to 60 years;

(F) if the offense is a third felony conviction, the defendant is not subject to sentencing under (l) of this section, and the defendant has two prior convictions for sexual felonies, 99 years;

(2) unlawful exploitation of a minor under AS 11.41.455(c)(2), online enticement of a minor under AS 11.41.452(e), or attempt, conspiracy, or solicitation to commit sexual assault in the first degree, sexual abuse of a minor in the first degree, or promoting prostitution in the first degree under AS 11.66.110(a)(2) may be sentenced to a definite term of imprisonment of not more than 99 years and shall be sentenced to a definite term within the following presumptive ranges, subject to adjustment as provided in AS 12. 55.155—12.55.175:

(continued)

State	Punishments for Felonies and Misdemeanors
	(A) if the offense is a first felony conviction, the offense does not involve circumstances described in (B) of this paragraph, and the victim was
	(i) under 13 years of age, 20 to 30 years;
	(ii) 13 years of age or older, 15 to 30 years;
	(B) if the offense is a first felony conviction and the defendant possessed a firearm, used a dangerous instrument, or caused serious physical injury during the commission of the offense, 25 to 35 years;
	(C) if the offense is a second felony conviction and does not involve circumstances described in (D) of this paragraph, 25 to 35 years;
	(D) if the offense is a second felony conviction and the defendant has a prior conviction for a sexual felony, 30 to 40 years;
	(E) if the offense is a third felony conviction, the offense does not involve circumstances described in (F) of this paragraph, and the defendant is not subject to sentencing under (l) of this section, 35 to 50 years;
	(F) if the offense is a third felony conviction, the defendant is not subject to sentencing under (l) of this section, and the defendant has two prior convictions for sexual felonies, 99 years;
	(3) sexual assault in the second degree, sexual abuse of a minor in the second degree, online enticement of a minor under AS 11.41.452(d), unlawful exploitation of a minor under AS 11.41.455(c)(1), or distribution of child pornography under AS 11.61.125(e)(2) may be sentenced to a definite term of imprisonment of not more than 99 years and shall be sentenced to a definite term within the following presumptive ranges, subject to adjustment as provided in AS 12.55.155—12.55.175:
	(A) if the offense is a first felony conviction, five to 15 years;
	(B) if the offense is a second felony conviction and does not involve circumstances described in (C) of this paragraph, 10 to 25 years;
	(C) if the offense is a second felony conviction and the defendant has a prior conviction for a sexual felony, 15 to 30 years;
	(D) if the offense is a third felony conviction and does not involve circumstances described in (E) of this paragraph, 20 to 35 years;

278

(E) if the offense is a third felony conviction and the defendant has two prior convictions for sexual felonies, 99 years;

(4) sexual assault in the third degree, incest, indecent exposure in the first degree, possession of child pornography, distribution of child pornography under AS 11.61.125(e)(1), or attempt, conspiracy, or solicitation to commit sexual assault in the second degree, sexual abuse of a minor in the second degree, unlawful exploitation of a minor, or distribution of child pornography, may be sentenced to a definite term of imprisonment of not more than 99 years and shall be sentenced to a definite term within the following presumptive ranges, subject to adjustment as provided in AS 12.55.155—12.55.175:

(A) if the offense is a first felony conviction, two to 12 years;

(B) if the offense is a second felony conviction and does not involve circumstances described in (C) of this paragraph, eight to 15 years;

(C) if the offense is a second felony conviction and the defendant has a prior conviction for a sexual felony, 12 to 20 years;

(D) if the offense is a third felony conviction and does not involve circumstances described in (E) of this paragraph, 15 to 25 years;

(E) if the offense is a third felony conviction and the defendant has two prior convictions for sexual felonies, 99 years.[8]

Notwithstanding any other provision of law, a defendant convicted of an unclassified or class A felony offense ... shall be sentenced to a definite term of imprisonment of 99 years when the defendant has been previously convicted of two or more most serious felonies. If a defendant is sentenced to a definite term under this subsection,

(1) imprisonment for the prescribed definite term may not be suspended under AS 12.55.080;

(2) imposition of sentence may not be suspended under AS 12.55.085;

(3) imprisonment for the prescribed definite term may not be reduced, except as provided in (j) of this section.[9]

Other than for convictions subject to a mandatory 99-year sentence, the court shall impose, in addition to an active term of imprisonment imposed under (i) of this section, a minimum period of (1) suspended imprisonment of five years and a minimum period of probation supervision of 15 years for conviction of an unclassified felony,

(continued)

279

State	Punishments for Felonies and Misdemeanors
	(2) suspended imprisonment of three years and a minimum period of probation supervision of 10 years for conviction of a class A or class B felony, or (3) suspended imprisonment of two years and a minimum period of probation supervision of five years for conviction of a class C felony. The period of probation is in addition to any sentence received under (i) of this section and may not be suspended or reduced. Upon a defendant's release from confinement in a correctional facility, the defendant is subject to this probation requirement and shall submit and comply with the terms and requirements of the probation.[10]
Arizona	Unless a specific sentence is otherwise provided, the term of imprisonment for a first felony offense shall be the presumptive sentence determined pursuant to subsection D of this section. Except for those felonies involving a dangerous offense or if a specific sentence is otherwise provided, the court may increase or reduce the presumptive sentence within the ranges set by subsection D of this section. Any reduction or increase shall be based on the aggravating and mitigating circumstances listed in § 13-701, subsections D and E and shall be within the ranges prescribed in subsection D of this section. B. If a person is convicted of a felony without having previously been convicted of any felony and if at least two of the aggravating factors listed in § 13-701, subsection D apply, the court may increase the maximum term of imprisonment otherwise authorized for that offense to an aggravated term. If a person is convicted of a felony without having previously been convicted of any felony and if the court finds at least two mitigating factors listed in § 13-701, subsection E apply, the court may decrease the minimum term of imprisonment otherwise authorized for that offense to a mitigated term. C. The aggravated or mitigated term imposed pursuant to subsection D of this section may be imposed only if at least two of the aggravating circumstances are found beyond a reasonable doubt to be true by the trier of fact or are admitted by the defendant, except that an aggravating circumstance under § 13-701, subsection D, paragraph 11 shall be found to be true by the court, or in mitigation of the crime are found to be true by the court, on any evidence or information introduced or submitted to the court or the trier of fact before sentencing or any evidence presented at trial, and factual findings and reasons in support of these findings are set forth on the record at the time of sentencing.

D. The term of imprisonment for a presumptive, minimum, maximum, mitigated or aggravated sentence shall be within the range prescribed under this subsection. The terms are as follows:

Felony	Mitigated	Minimum	Presumptive	Maximum	Aggravated
Class 2	3 years	4 years	5 years	10 years	12.5 years
Class 3	2 years	2.5 years	3.5 years	7 years	8.75 years
Class 4	1 year	1.5 years	2.5 years	3 years	3.75 years
Class 5	.5 years	.75 years	1.5 years	2 years	2.5 years
Class 6	.33 years	.5 years	1 year	1.5 years	2 years

E. The court shall inform all of the parties before sentencing occurs of its intent to increase or decrease a sentence to the aggravated or mitigated sentence pursuant this section. If the court fails to inform the parties, a party waives its right to be informed unless the party timely objects at the time of sentencing.

(1) For the purposes of this section, "trier of fact" means a jury, unless the defendant and the state waive a jury in which case the trier of fact means the court.[11]

Arkansas

(a) A defendant convicted of a felony may be sentenced to pay a fine:

(1) Not exceeding fifteen thousand dollars ($15,000) if the conviction is of a Class A felony or Class B felony;

(2) Not exceeding ten thousand dollars ($10,000) if the conviction is of a Class C felony or Class D felony;

(3) In accordance with a limitation of the statute defining the felony if the conviction is of an unclassified felony.

(b) A defendant convicted of a misdemeanor may be sentenced to pay a fine:

(1) Not exceeding two thousand five hundred dollars ($2,500) if the conviction is of a Class A misdemeanor,

(2) Not exceeding one thousand dollars ($1,000) if the conviction is of a Class B misdemeanor;

(3) Not exceeding five hundred dollars ($500) if the conviction is of a Class C misdemeanor; or

(4) In accordance with a limitation of the statute defining the misdemeanor if the conviction is of an unclassified misdemeanor.[12]

(continued)

State	Punishments for Felonies and Misdemeanors
	(a) A defendant convicted of a felony shall receive a determinate sentence according to the following limitations: (1) For a Class Y felony, the sentence shall be not less than ten (10) years and not more than forty (40) years, or life; (2) For a Class A felony, the sentence shall be not less than six (6) years nor more than thirty (30) years; (3) For a Class B felony, the sentence shall be not less than five (5) years nor more than twenty (20) years; (4) For a Class C felony, the sentence shall be not less than three (3) years nor more than ten (10) years; (5) For a Class D felony, the sentence shall not exceed six (6) years; and (6) For an unclassified felony, the sentence shall be in accordance with a limitation of the statute defining the felony. (b) A defendant convicted of a misdemeanor may be sentenced according to the following limitations: (1) For a Class A misdemeanor, the sentence shall not exceed one (1) year; (2) For a Class B misdemeanor, the sentence shall not exceed ninety (90) days; (3) For a Class C misdemeanor, the sentence shall not exceed thirty (30) days; and (4) For an unclassified misdemeanor, the sentence shall be in accordance with a limitation of the statute defining the misdemeanor.[13]
California	(a) Every person who violates subdivision (a) of Section 311.2 or Section 311.5 is punishable by fine of not more than one thousand dollars ($1,000) plus five dollars ($5) for each additional unit of material coming within the provisions of this chapter, which is involved in the offense, not to exceed ten thousand dollars ($10,000), or by imprisonment in the county jail for not more than six months plus one day for each additional unit of material coming within the provisions of this chapter, and which is involved in the offense, not to exceed a total of 360 days in the county jail, or by both that fine and imprisonment. If that person has previously been convicted of any offense in this chapter, or of a violation of Section 313.1, a violation of subdivision (a) of Section 311.2 or Section 311.5 is punishable as a felony. (b) Every person who violates subdivision (a) of Section 311.4 is punishable by fine of not more than two thousand dollars ($2,000) or by imprisonment in the county jail for not more than one year, or by both that fine and imprisonment, or by imprisonment in the state prison. If that person has been previously convicted of a violation of former Section 311.3 or Section 311.4 he or she is punishable by imprisonment in the state prison.

(c) Every person who violates Section 311.7 is punishable by fine of not more than one thousand dollars ($1,000) or by imprisonment in the county jail for not more than six months, or by both that fine and imprisonment. For a second and subsequent offense he or she shall be punished by a fine of not more than two thousand dollars ($2,000), or by imprisonment in the county jail for not more than one year, or by both that fine and imprisonment. If the person has been twice convicted of a violation of this chapter, a violation of Section 311.7 is punishable as a felony.[14]

Colorado

(III)(A) As to any person sentenced for a felony committed on or after July 1, 1985, except as otherwise provided in sub-subparagraph (E) of this subparagraph (III), in addition to, or in lieu of, any sentence to imprisonment, probation, community corrections, or work release, a fine within the following presumptive ranges may be imposed for the specified classes of felonies:

Class	Minimum Sentence	Maximum Sentence
1	No fine	No fine
2	Five thousand dollars	One million dollars
3	Three thousand dollars	Seven hundred fifty thousand dollars
4	Two thousand dollars	Five hundred thousand dollars
5	One thousand dollars	One hundred thousand dollars
6	One thousand dollars	One hundred thousand dollars

(V)(A) As to any person sentenced for a felony committed on or after July 1, 1993, felonies are divided into six classes which are distinguished from one another by the following presumptive ranges of penalties which are authorized upon conviction:

Class	Minimum Sentence	Maximum Sentence	Mandatory Period of Parole
1	Life imprisonment	Death	None
2	Eight years imprisonment	Twenty-four years imprisonment	Five years
3	Four years imprisonment	Twelve years imprisonment	Five years
4	Two years imprisonment	Six years imprisonment	Three years

(continued)

State	Punishments for Felonies and Misdemeanors
	5 One year imprisonment Three years imprisonment Two years 6 One year imprisonment Eighteen months imprisonment One year (C.7) Any person sentenced for a felony committed on or after July 1, 2002, involving unlawful sexual behavior, as defined in section 16-22-102(9), C.R.S., or for a felony, committed on or after July 1, 2002, the underlying factual basis of which involved unlawful sexual behavior, and who is not subject to the provisions of part 10 of this article, shall be subject to the mandatory period of parole specified in sub-subparagraph (A) of this subparagraph (V). (II.5) Notwithstanding anything in this section to the contrary, any person sentenced for a sex offense, as defined in section 18-1.3-1003(5), committed on or after November 1, 1998, may be sentenced to pay a fine in addition to, but not instead of, a sentence for imprisonment or probation pursuant to section 18-1.3-1004.[15]
Connecticut	For any felony committed on or after July 1, 1981, the sentence of imprisonment shall be a definite sentence and, unless the section of the general statutes that defines the crime specifically provides otherwise, the term shall be fixed by the court as follows: . . . (3) for the class A felony of aggravated sexual assault of a minor under section 53a-70c, a term not less than twenty-five years or more than fifty years; (4) for a class A felony other than an offense specified in subdivision (2) or (3) of this section, a term not less than ten years nor more than twenty-five years; . . . (7) for a class C felony, a term not less than one year nor more than ten years; (8) for a class D felony, a term not less than one year nor more than five years; and (9) for an unclassified felony, a term in accordance with the sentence specified in the section of the general statutes that defines the crime.[16] A fine for the conviction of a felony shall be fixed by the court as follows: (1) For a class A felony, an amount not to exceed twenty thousand dollars; (2) for a class B felony, an amount not to exceed fifteen thousand dollars; (3) for a class C felony, an amount not to exceed ten thousand dollars; (4) for a class D felony, an amount not to exceed five thousand dollars; (5) for an unclassified felony, an amount in accordance with the fine specified in the section of the general statutes that defines the crime.[17] A sentence of imprisonment for a misdemeanor shall be a definite sentence and, unless the section of the general statutes that defines the crime specifically provides otherwise, the term shall be fixed by the court as follows: (1) For

a class A misdemeanor, a term not to exceed one year; (2) for a class B misdemeanor, a term not to exceed six months; (3) for a class C misdemeanor, a term not to exceed three months; and (4) for an unclassified misdemeanor, a term in accordance with the sentence specified in the section of the general statutes that defines the crime.[18]

A fine for the conviction of a misdemeanor shall be fixed by the court as follows: (1) For a class A misdemeanor, an amount not to exceed two thousand dollars; (2) for a class B misdemeanor, an amount not to exceed one thousand dollars; (3) for a class C misdemeanor, an amount not to exceed five hundred dollars; (4) for an unclassified misdemeanor, an amount in accordance with the fine specified in the section of the general statutes that defines the crime.[19]

Delaware	

(a) A sentence of incarceration for a felony shall be a definite sentence.

(b) The term of incarceration which the court may impose for a felony is fixed as follows:

(1) For a class A felony not less than 15 years up to life imprisonment to be served at Level V except for conviction of first-degree murder in which event § 4209 of this title shall apply.

(2) For a class B felony not less than 2 years up to 25 years to be served at Level V.

(3) For a class C felony up to 15 years to be served at Level V.

(4) For a class D felony up to 8 years to be served at Level V.

(5) For a class E felony up to 5 years to be served at Level V.

(6) For a class F felony up to 3 years to be served at Level V.

(7) For a class G felony up to 2 years to be served at Level V.

(c) In the case of the conviction of any felony, the court shall impose a sentence of Level V incarceration where a minimum sentence is required by subsection (b) of this section and may impose a sentence of Level V incarceration up to the maximum stated in subsection (b) of this section for each class of felony.

(d) Where a minimum, mandatory, mandatory minimum or minimum mandatory sentence is required by subsection (b) of this section, such sentence shall not be subject to suspension by the court.

(e) Where no minimum sentence is required by subsection (b) of this section, or with regard to any sentence in excess of the minimum required sentence, the court may suspend that part of the sentence for probation or any other punishment set forth in § 4204 of this title.

(continued)

State	Punishments for Felonies and Misdemeanors
	(f) Any term of Level V incarceration imposed under this section must be served in its entirety at Level V, reduced only for earned 'good time' as set forth in § 4381 of this title.
	(g) No term of Level V incarceration imposed under this section shall be served in other than a full custodial Level V institutional setting unless such term is suspended by the court for such other level sanction.
	(h) The Department of Correction, the remainder of this section notwithstanding, may house Level V inmates at a Level IV work release center or halfway house during the last 180 days of their sentence; provided, however, that the first 5 days of any sentence to Level V, not suspended by the court, must be served at Level V.
	(i) The Department of Correction, the remainder of this section notwithstanding, may grant Level V inmates 48-hour furloughs during the last 120 days of their sentence to assist in their adjustment to the community.
	(j) No sentence to Level V incarceration imposed pursuant to this section is subject to parole.
	(k) In addition to the penalties set forth above, the court may impose such fines and penalties as it deems appropriate.
	(l) In all sentences for less than 1 year the court may order that more than 5 days be served in Level V custodial setting before the Department may place the offender in Level IV custody.[20]
Florida	(3) A person who has been convicted of any other designated felony may be punished as follows:
	… (b) For a felony of the first degree, by a term of imprisonment not exceeding 30 years or, when specifically provided by statute, by imprisonment for a term of years not exceeding life imprisonment.
	(c) For a felony of the second degree, by a term of imprisonment not exceeding 15 years. (d) For a felony of the third degree, by a term of imprisonment not exceeding 5 years.
	(4) A person who has been convicted of a designated misdemeanor may be sentenced as follows:
	(a) For a misdemeanor of the first degree, by a definite term of imprisonment not exceeding 1 year;
	(b) For a misdemeanor of the second degree, by a definite term of imprisonment not exceeding 60 days.
	(5) Any person who has been convicted of a noncriminal violation may not be sentenced to a term of imprisonment nor to any other punishment more severe than a fine, forfeiture, or other civil penalty, except as provided in chapter 316 or by ordinance of any city or county.

(6) Nothing in this section shall be construed to alter the operation of any statute of this state authorizing a trial court, in its discretion, to impose a sentence of imprisonment for an indeterminate period within minimum and maximum limits as provided by law, except as provided in subsection (1).

(7) This section does not deprive the court of any authority conferred by law to decree a forfeiture of property, suspend or cancel a license, remove a person from office, or impose any other civil penalty. Such a judgment or order may be included in the sentence.

(8)(a) The sentencing guidelines that were effective October 1, 1983, and any revisions thereto, apply to all felonies, except capital felonies, committed on or after October 1, 1983, and before January 1, 1994, and to all felonies, except capital felonies and life felonies, committed before October 1, 1983, when the defendant affirmatively selects to be sentenced pursuant to such provisions.

(b) The 1994 sentencing guidelines, that were effective January 1, 1994, and any revisions thereto, apply to all felonies, except capital felonies, committed on or after January 1, 1994, and before October 1, 1995.

(c) The 1995 sentencing guidelines that were effective October 1, 1995, and any revisions thereto, apply to all felonies, except capital felonies, committed on or after October 1, 1995, and before October 1, 1998.

(d) The Criminal Punishment Code applies to all felonies, except capital felonies, committed on or after October 1, 1998. Any revision to the Criminal Punishment Code applies to sentencing for all felonies, except capital felonies, committed on or after the effective date of the revision.

(e) Felonies, except capital felonies, with continuing dates of enterprise shall be sentenced under the sentencing guidelines or the Criminal Punishment Code in effect on the beginning date of the criminal activity.....

(10) If a defendant is sentenced for an offense committed on or after July 1, 2009, which is a third degree felony but not a forcible felony as defined in s. 776.08, and excluding any third degree felony violation under chapter 810, and if the total sentence points pursuant to s. 921.0024 are 22 points or fewer, the court must sentence the offender to a nonstate prison sanction. However, if the court makes written findings that a nonstate prison sanction could present a danger to the public, the court may sentence the offender to a state correctional facility pursuant to this section.

(11) The purpose of this section is to provide uniform punishment for those crimes made punishable under this

(continued)

State	Punishments for Felonies and Misdemeanors
	section and, to this end, a reference to this section constitutes a general reference under the doctrine of incorporation by reference.[21] A person who has been convicted of an offense other than a capital felony may be sentenced to pay a fine in addition to any punishment described in s. 775.082; when specifically authorized by statute, he or she may be sentenced to pay a fine in lieu of any punishment described in s. 775.082. A person who has been convicted of a noncriminal violation may be sentenced to pay a fine. Fines for designated crimes and for noncriminal violations shall not exceed: . . . (b) $10,000, when the conviction is of a felony of the first or second degree. (c) $5,000, when the conviction is of a felony of the third degree. (d) $1,000, when the conviction is of a misdemeanor of the first degree. (e) $500, when the conviction is of a misdemeanor of the second degree or a noncriminal violation. (f) Any higher amount equal to double the pecuniary gain derived from the offense by the offender or double the pecuniary loss suffered by the victim. (g) Any higher amount specifically authorized by statute.[22]
Georgia	As used in this Code section, the term "sexual offense" means: . . . (6) Enticing a child for indecent purposes, as defined in Code Section 16-6-5, unless subject to the provisions of subsection (c) of Code Section 16-6-5; . . . or (10) Sexual exploitation of children, as defined in Code Section 16-12-100.[23] Except as provided in subsection (c) of this Code section, and notwithstanding any other provisions of law to the contrary, any person convicted of a sexual offense shall be sentenced to a split sentence which shall include the minimum term of imprisonment specified in the Code section applicable to the offense. No portion of the mandatory minimum sentence imposed shall be suspended, stayed, probated, deferred, or withheld by the sentencing court and such sentence shall include, in addition to the mandatory imprisonment, an additional probated sentence of at least one year. No person convicted of a sexual offense shall be sentenced as a first offender pursuant to Article 3 of Chapter 8 of Title 42, relating to probation for first offenders, or any other provision of Georgia law relating to the sentencing of first offenders.[24] In the court's discretion, the court may deviate from the mandatory minimum sentence as set forth in subsection (b) of this Code section, or any portion thereof, provided that: (A) The defendant has no prior conviction of an offense prohibited by Chapter 6 of Title 16 or Part 2 of Article 3 of Chapter 12 of Title 16, nor a prior conviction for any offense under federal law or the laws of another

state or territory of the United States which consists of the same or similar elements of offenses prohibited by Chapter 6 of Title 16 or Part 2 of Article 3 of Chapter 12 of Title 16;

(B) The defendant did not use a deadly weapon or any object, device, or instrument which when used offensively against a person would be likely to or actually did result in serious bodily injury during the commission of the offense;

(C) The court has not found evidence of a relevant similar transaction;

(D) The victim did not suffer any intentional physical harm during the commission of the offense;

(E) The offense did not involve the transportation of the victim; and

(F) The victim was not physically restrained during the commission of the offense.

(2) If the court deviates in sentencing pursuant to this subsection, the judge shall issue a written order setting forth the judge's reasons. Any such order shall be appealable by the defendant pursuant to Code Section 5-6-34, or by the State of Georgia pursuant to Code Section 5-7-1.[25]

If the court imposes a probated sentence, the defendant shall submit to review by the Sexual Offender Registration Review Board for purposes of risk assessment classification within ten days of being sentenced and shall otherwise comply with Article 2 of Chapter 1 of Title 42.[26]

Hawaii

A person who has been convicted of an offense may be sentenced to pay a fine not exceeding: (a) $50,000, when the conviction is of a class A felony . . . ; (b) $25,000, when the conviction is of a class B felony; (c) $10,000, when the conviction is of a class C felony; (d) $2,000, when the conviction is of a misdemeanor; (e) $1,000, when the conviction is of a petty misdemeanor or a violation; . . . (g) Any higher or lower amount specifically authorized by statute.[27]

Notwithstanding part II; sections 706-605, 706-606, 706-606.5, 706-660.1, 706-661, and 706-662; and any other law to the contrary, a person who has been convicted of a class A felony, except class A felonies defined in chapter 712, part IV, shall be sentenced to an indeterminate term of imprisonment of twenty years without the possibility of suspension of sentence or probation. The minimum length of imprisonment shall be determined by the Hawaii paroling authority in accordance with section 706-669. A person who has been convicted of a class A felony defined in chapter 712, part IV, may be sentenced to an indeterminate term of imprisonment, except as

(continued)

State	Punishments for Felonies and Misdemeanors
	provided for in section 706-660.1 relating to the use of firearms in certain felony offenses and section 706-606.5 relating to repeat offenders. When ordering such a sentence, the court shall impose the maximum length of imprisonment which shall be twenty years. The minimum length of imprisonment shall be determined by the Hawaii paroling authority in accordance with section 706-669.[28]
	A person who has been convicted of a class B or class C felony may be sentenced to an indeterminate term of imprisonment except as provided for in section 706-660.1 relating to the use of firearms in certain felony offenses and section 706-606.5 relating to repeat offenders. When ordering such a sentence, the court shall impose the maximum length of imprisonment which shall be as follows:
	(1) For a class B felony—10 years; and
	(2) For a class C felony—5 years.
	The minimum length of imprisonment shall be determined by the Hawaii paroling authority in accordance with section 706-669.[29]
Idaho	Except in cases where a different punishment is prescribed by this code, every offense declared to be a felony is punishable by imprisonment in the state prison not exceeding five (5) years, or by fine not exceeding fifty thousand dollars ($50,000), or by both such fine and imprisonment.[30]
Illinois	SENTENCE PROVISIONS; ALL FELONIES. Except as otherwise provided, for all felonies:
	(a) NO SUPERVISION. The court, upon a plea of guilty or a stipulation by the defendant of the facts supporting the charge or a finding of guilt, may not defer further proceedings and the imposition of a sentence and may not enter an order for supervision of the defendant.
	(b) FELONY FINES. An offender may be sentenced to pay a fine not to exceed, for each offense, $25,000 or the amount specified in the offense, whichever is greater. . . . A fine may be imposed in addition to a sentence of conditional discharge, probation, periodic imprisonment, or imprisonment. See Article 9 of Chapter V (730 ILCS 5/Ch. V, Art. 9) for imposition of additional amounts and determination of amounts and payment.[31]
	CLASS 1 FELONIES; SENTENCE. For a Class 1 felony: (a) TERM. The sentence of imprisonment, other than for second degree murder, shall be a determinate sentence of not less than 4 years and not more than 15 years. . . . The sentence of

imprisonment for an extended term Class 1 felony, as provided in Section 5-8-2 (730 ILCS 5/5-8-2), shall be a term not less than 15 years and not more than 30 years.[32]

CLASS 2 FELONIES; SENTENCE. For a Class 2 felony: (a) TERM. The sentence of imprisonment shall be a determinate sentence of not less than 3 years and not more than 7 years. The sentence of imprisonment for an extended term Class 2 felony, as provided in Section 5-8-2 (730 ILCS 5/5-8-2), shall be a term not less than 7 years and not more than 14 years.[33]

CLASS 3 FELONIES; SENTENCE. For a Class 3 felony: (a) TERM. The sentence of imprisonment shall be a determinate sentence of not less than 2 years and not more than 5 years. The sentence of imprisonment for an extended term Class 3 felony, as provided in Section 5-8-2 (730 ILCS 5/5-8-2), shall be a term not less than 5 years and not more than 10 years.[34]

CLASS X FELONIES; SENTENCE. For a Class X felony: (a) TERM. The sentence of imprisonment shall be a determinate sentence of not less than 6 years and not more than 30 years. The sentence of imprisonment for an extended term Class X felony, as provided in Section 5-8-2 (730 ILCS 5/5-8-2), shall be not less than 30 years and not more than 60 years.[35]

Indiana

Sec. 7. (a) A person who commits a Class D felony shall be imprisoned for a fixed term of between six (6) months and three (3) years, with the advisory sentence being one and one-half (1 1/2) years. In addition, the person may be fined not more than ten thousand dollars ($10,000).

(b) Notwithstanding subsection (a), if a person has committed a Class D felony, the court may enter judgment of conviction of a Class A misdemeanor and sentence accordingly. However, the court shall enter a judgment of conviction of a Class D felony if:

(1) the court finds that:

(A) the person has committed a prior, unrelated felony for which judgment was entered as a conviction of a Class A misdemeanor; and

(B) the prior felony was committed less than three (3) years before the second felony was committed;

(2) the offense is domestic battery as a Class D felony under IC 35-42-2-1.3; or

(3) the offense is possession of child pornography (IC 35-42-4-4(c)).

(continued)

291

State	Punishments for Felonies and Misdemeanors
	The court shall enter in the record, in detail, the reason for its action whenever it exercises the power to enter judgment of conviction of a Class A misdemeanor granted in this subsection.[36]
	Sec. 6. (a) A person who commits a Class C felony shall be imprisoned for a fixed term of between two (2) and eight (8) years, with the advisory sentence being four (4) years. In addition, the person may be fined not more than ten thousand dollars ($10,000).[37]
Iowa	The maximum sentence for any person convicted of a felony shall be that prescribed by statute or, if not prescribed by statute, if other than a class A felony shall be determined as follows:
	1. A felon sentenced for a first conviction for a violation of section 124.401D, shall be confined for no more than ninety-nine years.
	2. A class B felon shall be confined for no more than twenty-five years.
	3. An habitual offender shall be confined for no more than fifteen years.
	4. A class C felon, not an habitual offender, shall be confined for no more than ten years, and in addition shall be sentenced to a fine of at least one thousand dollars but not more than ten thousand dollars.
	5. A class D felon, not an habitual offender, shall be confined for no more than five years, and in addition shall be sentenced to a fine of at least seven hundred fifty dollars but not more than seven thousand five hundred dollars. The surcharges required by sections 911.1, 911.2, and 911.3 shall be added to a fine imposed on a class C or class D felon, as provided by those sections, and are not a part of or subject to the maximums set in this section.[38]
Kansas	(a) A person who has been convicted of a felony may, in addition to the sentence authorized by law, be ordered to pay a fine which shall be fixed by the court as follows:
	(1) For any off-grid felony crime or any felony ranked in severity level 1 of the drug grid as provided in K.S.A. 21-6805, and amendments thereto, a sum not exceeding $500,000;
	(2) for any felony ranked in severity levels 1 through 5 of the nondrug grid as provided in K.S.A. 21-6804 and amendments thereto, or in severity levels 2 or 3 of the drug grid as provided in K.S.A. 21-6805, and amendments thereto, a sum not exceeding $300,000; and

(3) for any felony ranked in severity levels 6 through 10 of the nondrug grid as provided in K.S.A. 21-6804, and amendments thereto, or in severity level 4 of the drug grid as provided in K.S.A. 21-6805, and amendments thereto, a sum not exceeding $100,000.[39]

(b) A person who has been convicted of a misdemeanor, in addition to or instead of the imprisonment authorized by law, may be sentenced to pay a fine which shall be fixed by the court as follows:

(1) For a class A misdemeanor, a sum not exceeding $2,500;

(2) for a class B misdemeanor, a sum not exceeding $1,000;

(3) for a class C misdemeanor, a sum not exceeding $500; and

(4) for an unclassified misdemeanor, any sum authorized by the statute that defines the crime. If no penalty is provided in such law, the fine shall not exceed the fine provided herein for a class C misdemeanor.[40]

(c) As an alternative to any of the above fines, the fine imposed may be fixed at any greater sum not exceeding double the pecuniary gain derived from the crime by the offender.[41]

| Kentucky | (1) A sentence of imprisonment for a felony shall be an indeterminate sentence, the maximum of which shall be fixed within the limits provided by subsection (2), and subject to modification by the trial judge pursuant to KRS 532.070. |

(2) Unless otherwise provided by law, the authorized maximum terms of imprisonment for felonies are:

(a) For a Class A felony, not less than twenty (20) years nor more than fifty (50) years, or life imprisonment;

(b) For a Class B felony, not less than ten (10) years nor more than twenty (20) years;

(c) For a Class C felony, not less than five (5) years nor more than ten (10) years; and

(d) For a Class D felony, not less than one (1) year nor more than five (5) years.

(3) For any felony specified in KRS Chapter 510, KRS 530.020, 530.064(1)(a), or 531.310, the sentence shall include an additional five (5) year period of postincarceration supervision which shall be added to the maximum sentence rendered for the offense. During this period of postincarceration supervision, if a defendant violates the provisions of postincarceration supervision, the defendant may be reincarcerated for:

(a) The remaining period of his initial sentence, if any is remaining; and

(continued)

State	Punishments for Felonies and Misdemeanors
	(b) The entire period of postincarceration supervision, or if the initial sentence has been served, for the remaining period of postincarceration supervision.
	(4) In addition to the penalties provided in this section, for any person subject to a period of postincarceration supervision pursuant to KRS 532.400 his or her sentence shall include an additional one (1) year period of postincarceration supervision following release from incarceration upon expiration of sentence if the offender is not otherwise subject to another form of postincarceration supervision. During this period of postincarceration supervision, if an offender violates the provisions of supervision, the offender may be reincarcerated for the remaining period of his or her postincarceration supervision.
	(5) The actual time of release within the maximum established by subsection (1), or as modified pursuant to KRS 532.070, shall be determined under procedures established elsewhere by law.[42]
Louisiana	When a defendant has been convicted of a felony or misdemeanor, the court should impose a sentence of imprisonment if any of the following occurs: (1) There is an undue risk that during the period of a suspended sentence or probation the defendant will commit another crime. (2) The defendant is in need of correctional treatment or a custodial environment that can be provided most effectively by his commitment to an institution. (3) A lesser sentence will deprecate the seriousness of the defendant's crime.[43]
	The following grounds, while not controlling the discretion of the court, shall be accorded weight in its determination of suspension of sentence or probation: ... (2) The offender knew or should have known that the victim of the offense was particularly vulnerable or incapable of resistance due to extreme youth. ... (3) The offender offered or has been offered or has given or received anything of value for the commission of the offense.... (12) The offender was persistently involved in similar offenses not already considered as criminal history or as a part of a multiple offender adjudication.... (21) Any other relevant aggravating circumstances. (22) The defendant's criminal conduct neither caused nor threatened serious harm. (23) The defendant did not contemplate that his criminal conduct would cause or threaten serious harm. ... (25) There were substantial grounds tending to excuse or justify the defendant's criminal conduct, though failing to establish a defense. (26) The victim of the defendant's criminal conduct induced or facilitated its commission.... (28) The defendant has no history of prior delinquency or criminal activity or has led a

law-abiding life for a substantial period of time before the commission of the instant crime. (29) The defendant's criminal conduct was the result of circumstances unlikely to recur. (30) The defendant is particularly likely to respond affirmatively to probationary treatment. (31) The imprisonment of the defendant would entail excessive hardship to himself or his dependents.... (33) Any other relevant mitigating circumstance.[44]

Maine

1. In the case of a person convicted of a crime other than murder, the court may sentence to imprisonment for a definite term as provided for in this section, unless the statute which the person is convicted of violating expressly provides that the fine and imprisonment penalties it authorizes may not be suspended, in which case the convicted person shall be sentenced to imprisonment and required to pay the fine authorized therein. Except as provided in subsection 7, the place of imprisonment must be as follows.

A. For a Class D or Class E crime the court must specify a county jail as the place of imprisonment. B. For a Class A, Class B or Class C crime the court must: (1) Specify a county jail as the place of imprisonment if the term of imprisonment is 9 months or less; or (2) Commit the person to the Department of Corrections if the term of imprisonment is more than 9 months....

2. The court shall set the term of imprisonment as follows:

A. In the case of a Class A crime, the court shall set a definite period not to exceed 30 years; B. In the case of a Class B crime, the court shall set a definite period not to exceed 10 years; C. In the case of a Class C crime, the court shall set a definite period not to exceed 5 years; D. In the case of a Class D crime, the court shall set a definite period of less than one year; or E. In the case of a Class E crime, the court shall set a definite period not to exceed 6 months....

4-D. If the State pleads and proves that a crime under section 282 was committed against a person who had not attained 12 years of age, the court, in exercising its sentencing discretion, shall give the age of the victim serious consideration.[45]

Maryland

A person who violates this section [child pornography law] is guilty of a felony and on conviction is subject to: (1) for a first violation, imprisonment not exceeding 10 years or a fine not exceeding $25,000 or both; and (2) for each subsequent violation, imprisonment not exceeding 20 years or a fine not exceeding $50,000 or both.[46]

(continued)

State	Punishments for Felonies and Misdemeanors
	(b)(1) Except as provided in paragraph (2) of this subsection, a person who violates this section [possession of visual representation of child under 16] is guilty of a misdemeanor and on conviction is subject to imprisonment not exceeding 5 years or a fine not exceeding $2,500 or both. (2) A person who violates this section, having previously been convicted under this section, is guilty of a felony and on conviction is subject to imprisonment not exceeding 10 years or a fine not exceeding $10,000 or both.[47]
Massachusetts	Whoever disseminates any matter which is obscene, or whoever has in his possession any matter which is obscene, knowing it to be obscene, with the intent to disseminate the same, shall be punished by imprisonment in the state prison for not more than five years or in a jail or house of correction for not more than two and one-half years or by a fine of not less than one thousand nor more than ten thousand dollars for the first offense, not less than five thousand nor more than twenty thousand dollars for the second offense, or not less than ten thousand nor more than thirty thousand dollars for the third and subsequent offenses, or by both such fine and imprisonment.[48]

Whoever, either with knowledge that a person is a child under eighteen years of age or while in possession of such facts that he should have reason to know that such person is a child under eighteen years of age, and with lascivious intent, hires, coerces, solicits or entices, employs, procures, uses, causes, encourages, or knowingly permits such child to pose or be exhibited in a state of nudity, for the purpose of representation or reproduction in any visual material, shall be punished by imprisonment in the state prison for a term of not less than ten nor more than twenty years, or by a fine of not less than ten thousand nor more than fifty thousand dollars, or by both such fine and imprisonment. (b) Whoever, either with knowledge that a person is a child under eighteen years of age or while in possession of such facts that he should have reason to know that such person is a child under eighteen years of age, hires, coerces, solicits or entices, employs, procures, uses, causes, encourages, or knowingly permits such child to participate or engage in any act that depicts, describes, or represents sexual conduct for the purpose of representation or reproduction in any visual material, or to engage in any live performance involving sexual conduct, shall be punished by imprisonment in the state prison for a term of not less than ten nor more than twenty years, or by a fine of not less than ten thousand nor more than fifty thousand dollars, or by both such fine and imprisonment.[49] |

Whoever, with lascivious intent, disseminates any visual material that contains a representation or reproduction of any posture or exhibition in a state of nudity involving the use of a child who is under eighteen years of age, knowing the contents of such visual material or having sufficient facts in his possession to have knowledge of the contents thereof, or has in his possession any such visual material knowing the contents or having sufficient facts in his possession to have knowledge of the contents thereof, with the intent to disseminate the same, shall be punished in the state prison for a term of not less than ten nor more than twenty years or by a fine of not less than ten thousand nor more than fifty thousand dollars or three times the monetary value of any economic gain derived from said dissemination, whichever is greater, or by both such fine and imprisonment.[50]

Whoever with lascivious intent disseminates any visual material that contains a representation or reproduction of any act that depicts, describes, or represents sexual conduct participated or engaged in by a child who is under eighteen years of age, knowing the contents of such visual material or having sufficient facts in his possession to have knowledge of the contents thereof, or whoever has in his possession any such visual material knowing the contents or having sufficient facts in his possession to have knowledge of the contents thereof, with the intent to disseminate the same, shall be punished in the state prison for a term of not less than ten nor more than twenty years or by a fine of not less than ten thousand nor more than fifty thousand dollars or three times the monetary value of any economic gain derived from said dissemination, whichever is greater, or by both such fine and imprisonment.[51]

Michigan

(2) A person who persuades, induces, entices, coerces, causes, or knowingly allows a child to engage in a child sexually abusive activity for the purpose of producing any child sexually abusive material, or a person who arranges for, produces, makes, or finances, or a person who attempts or prepares or conspires to arrange for, produce, make, or finance any child sexually abusive activity or child sexually abusive material is guilty of a felony, punishable by imprisonment for not more than 20 years, or a fine of not more than $100,000.00, or both, if that person knows, has reason to know, or should reasonably be expected to know that the child is a child or that the child sexually abusive material includes a child or that the depiction constituting the child sexually abusive material appears to include a child, or that person has not taken reasonable precautions to determine the age of the child.

(3) A person who distributes or promotes, or finances the distribution or promotion of, or receives for the purpose

(continued)

State	Punishments for Felonies and Misdemeanors
	of distributing or promoting, or conspires, attempts, or prepares to distribute, receive, finance, or promote any child sexually abusive material or child sexually abusive activity is guilty of a felony, punishable by imprisonment for not more than 7 years, or a fine of not more than $50,000.00, or both, if that person knows, has reason to know, or should reasonably be expected to know that the child is a child or that the child sexually abusive material includes a child or that the depiction constituting the child sexually abusive material appears to include a child, or that person has not taken reasonable precautions to determine the age of the child. This subsection does not apply to the persons described in section 7 of 1984 PA 343, MCL 752.367.
	(4) A person who knowingly possesses any child sexually abusive material is guilty of a felony punishable by imprisonment for not more than 4 years or a fine of not more than $10,000.00, or both, if that person knows, has reason to know, or should reasonably be expected to know the child is a child or that the child sexually abusive material includes a child or that the depiction constituting the child sexually abusive material appears to include a child, or that person has not taken reasonable precautions to determine the age of the child.[52]
Minnesota	Subd. 2. Use of minor. It is unlawful for a person to promote, employ, use or permit a minor to engage in or assist others to engage minors in posing or modeling alone or with others in any sexual performance or pornographic work if the person knows or has reason to know that the conduct intended is a sexual performance or a pornographic work. Any person who violates this subdivision is guilty of a felony and may be sentenced to imprisonment for not more than ten years or to payment of a fine of not more than $20,000 for the first offense and $40,000 for a second or subsequent offense, or both.[53]
Mississippi	Any person who intentionally and knowingly disseminates sexually oriented material to any person under eighteen (18) years of age shall be guilty of a misdemeanor and upon conviction shall be fined for each offense not less than Five Hundred Dollars ($500.00) nor more than Five Thousand Dollars ($5,000.00) or be imprisoned for not more than one (1) year in the county jail, or be punished by both such fine and imprisonment.[54]
	Any person who violates any provision of Section 97-5-33 shall be guilty of a felony and upon conviction shall be fined not less than Fifty Thousand Dollars ($50,000.00) nor more than Five Hundred Thousand Dollars ($500,000.00) and shall be imprisoned for not less than five (5) years nor more than forty (40) years. Any person convicted of a second or subsequent violation of Section 97-5-33 shall be fined not less than One Hundred

Thousand Dollars ($100,000.00) nor more than One Million Dollars ($1,000,000.00) and shall be confined in the custody of the Department of Corrections for life or such lesser term as the court may determine, but not less than twenty (20) years.[55]

Missouri

1. This section shall not be construed to affect the powers of the governor under article IV, section 7, of the Missouri Constitution. This statute shall not affect those provisions of section 565.020, RSMo, section 558.018 or section 571.015, RSMo, which set minimum terms of sentences, or the provisions of section 559.115, RSMo, relating to probation.

2. The provisions of subsections 2 to 5 of this section shall be applicable to all classes of felonies except those set forth in chapter 195, RSMo, and those otherwise excluded in subsection 1 of this section. For the purposes of this section, "prison commitment" means and is the receipt by the department of corrections of an offender after sentencing. For purposes of this section, prior prison commitments to the department of corrections shall not include commitment to a regimented discipline program established pursuant to section 217.378, RSMo. Other provisions of the law to the contrary notwithstanding; any offender who has pleaded guilty to or has been found guilty of a felony other than a dangerous felony as defined in section 556.061, RSMo, and is committed to the department of corrections shall be required to serve the following minimum prison terms:

(1) If the offender has one previous prison commitment to the department of corrections for a felony offense, the minimum prison term which the offender must serve shall be forty percent of his or her sentence or until the offender attains seventy years of age, and has served at least thirty percent of the sentence imposed, whichever occurs first;

(2) If the offender has two previous prison commitments to the department of corrections for felonies unrelated to the present offense, the minimum prison term which the offender must serve shall be fifty percent of his or her sentence or until the offender attains seventy years of age, and has served at least forty percent of the sentence imposed, whichever occurs first;

(3) If the offender has three or more previous prison commitments to the department of corrections for felonies unrelated to the present offense, the minimum prison term which the offender must serve shall be eighty percent of his or her sentence or until the offender attains seventy years of age, and has served at least forty percent of the sentence imposed, whichever occurs first. . . .

(continued)

299

State	Punishments for Felonies and Misdemeanors
	4. For the purpose of determining the minimum prison term to be served, the following calculations shall apply:
	(1) A sentence of life shall be calculated to be thirty years;
	(2) Any sentence either alone or in the aggregate with other consecutive sentences for crimes committed at or near the same time which is over seventy-five years shall be calculated to be seventy-five years.
	5. For purposes of this section, the term "minimum prison term" shall mean time required to be served by the offender before he or she is eligible for parole, conditional release or other early release by the department of corrections....
	8. If the imposition or execution of a sentence is suspended, the court may order any or all of the following restorative justice methods, or any other method that the court finds just or appropriate:
	(1) Restitution to any victim or a statutorily created fund for costs incurred as a result of the offender's actions;
	(2) Offender treatment programs;
	(3) Mandatory community service;
	(4) Work release programs in local facilities; and
	(5) Community-based residential and nonresidential programs.
	9. The provisions of this section shall apply only to offenses occurring on or after August 28, 2003.
	10. Pursuant to subdivision (1) of subsection 8 of this section, the court may order the assessment and payment of a designated amount of restitution to a county law enforcement restitution fund established by the county commission pursuant to section 50.565, RSMo. Such contribution shall not exceed three hundred dollars for any charged offense. Any restitution moneys deposited into the county law enforcement restitution fund pursuant to this section shall only be expended pursuant to the provisions of section 50.565, RSMo.
	11. A judge may order payment to a restitution fund only if such fund had been created by ordinance or resolution of a county of the state of Missouri prior to sentencing. A judge shall not have any direct supervisory authority or administrative control over any fund to which the judge is ordering a defendant to make payment.
	12. A defendant who fails to make a payment to a county law enforcement restitution fund may not have his or her probation revoked solely for failing to make such payment unless the judge, after evidentiary hearing, makes a finding supported by a preponderance of the evidence that the defendant either willfully refused to make the payment

or that the defendant willfully, intentionally, and purposefully failed to make sufficient bona fide efforts to acquire the resources to pay.[56]

1. The authorized terms of imprisonment, including both prison and conditional release terms, are:

(1) For a class A felony, a term of years not less than ten years and not to exceed thirty years, or life imprisonment;

(2) For a class B felony, a term of years not less than five years and not to exceed fifteen years;

(3) For a class C felony, a term of years not to exceed seven years;

(4) For a class D felony, a term of years not to exceed four years;

(5) For a class A misdemeanor, a term not to exceed one year;

(6) For a class B misdemeanor, a term not to exceed six months;

(7) For a class C misdemeanor, a term not to exceed fifteen days.

2. In cases of class C and D felonies, the court shall have discretion to imprison for a special term not to exceed one year in the county jail or other authorized penal institution, and the place of confinement shall be fixed by the court. If the court imposes a sentence of imprisonment for a term longer than one year upon a person convicted of a class C or D felony, it shall commit the person to the custody of the department of corrections for a term of years not less than two years and not exceeding the maximum authorized terms provided in subdivisions (3) and (4) of subsection 1 of this section.

3. (1) When a regular sentence of imprisonment for a felony is imposed, the court shall commit the person to the custody of the department of corrections for the term imposed under section 557.036, RSMo, or until released under procedures established elsewhere by law.

(2) A sentence of imprisonment for a misdemeanor shall be for a definite term and the court shall commit the person to the county jail or other authorized penal institution for the term of his or her sentence or until released under procedure established elsewhere by law.

4. (1) A sentence of imprisonment for a term of years for felonies other than dangerous felonies as defined in section 556.061, RSMo, and other than sentences of imprisonment which involve the individual's fourth or subsequent remand to the department of corrections shall consist of a prison term and a conditional release term. The conditional

(continued)

State	Punishments for Felonies and Misdemeanors
	release term of any term imposed under section 557.036, RSMo, shall be: (a) One-third for terms of nine years or less; (b) Three years for terms between nine and fifteen years; (c) Five years for terms more than fifteen years; and the prison term shall be the remainder of such term. The prison term may be extended by the board of probation and parole pursuant to subsection 5 of this section. (2) "Conditional release" means the conditional discharge of an offender by the board of probation and parole, subject to conditions of release that the board deems reasonable to assist the offender to lead a law-abiding life, and subject to the supervision under the state board of probation and parole. The conditions of release shall include avoidance by the offender of any other crime, federal or state, and other conditions that the board in its discretion deems reasonably necessary to assist the releasee in avoiding further violation of the law. 5. The date of conditional release from the prison term may be extended up to a maximum of the entire sentence of imprisonment by the board of probation and parole. The director of any division of the department of corrections except the board of probation and parole may file with the board of probation and parole a petition to extend the conditional release date when an offender fails to follow the rules and regulations of the division or commits an act in violation of such rules. Within ten working days of receipt of the petition to extend the conditional release date, the board of probation and parole shall convene a hearing on the petition. The offender shall be present and may call witnesses in his or her behalf and cross-examine witnesses appearing against the offender. The hearing shall be conducted as provided in section 217.670, RSMo. If the violation occurs in close proximity to the conditional release date, the conditional release may be held for a maximum of fifteen working days to permit necessary time for the division director to file a petition for an extension with the board and for the board to conduct a hearing, provided some affirmative manifestation of an intent to extend the conditional release has occurred prior to the conditional release date. If at the end of a fifteen-working-day period a board decision has not been reached, the offender shall be released conditionally. The decision of the board shall be final.[57]
Montana	Except as provided in subsection (3), if an offender convicted of one of the following offenses was previously convicted of one of the following offenses or of an offense under the laws of another state or of the United

States that, if committed in this state, would be one of the following offenses, the offender must be sentenced to life in prison, unless the death penalty is applicable and imposed: . . . (iv) 45-5-625, sexual abuse of children.[58]

Nebraska

(1) For purposes of the Nebraska Criminal Code and any statute passed by the Legislature after the date of passage of the code, felonies are divided into nine classes which are distinguished from one another by the following penalties which are authorized upon conviction:

Class I felony

Death

Class IA felony
Life imprisonment

Class IB felony
Maximum—life imprisonment

Minimum—twenty years imprisonment

Class IC felony
Maximum—fifty years imprisonment

Mandatory minimum—five years imprisonment

Class ID felony
Maximum—fifty years imprisonment

Mandatory minimum—three years imprisonment

Class II felony
Maximum—fifty years imprisonment

Minimum—one year imprisonment

Class III felony
Maximum—twenty years imprisonment, or twenty-five thousand dollars fine, or both

Minimum—one year imprisonment

Class IIIA felony
Maximum—five years imprisonment, or ten thousand dollars fine, or both

Minimum—none

Class IV felony
Maximum—five years imprisonment, or ten thousand dollars fine, or both

Minimum—none

(continued)

State	Punishments for Felonies and Misdemeanors
	(2) All sentences of imprisonment for Class IA, IB, IC, ID, II, and III felonies and sentences of one year or more for Class IIIA and IV felonies shall be served in institutions under the jurisdiction of the Department of Correctional Services. Sentences of less than one year shall be served in the county jail except as provided in this subsection. If the department certifies that it has programs and facilities available for persons sentenced to terms of less than one year, the court may order that any sentence of six months or more be served in any institution under the jurisdiction of the department. Any such certification shall be given by the department to the State Court Administrator, who shall forward copies thereof to each judge having jurisdiction to sentence in felony cases. (3) Nothing in this section shall limit the authority granted in sections 29-2221 and 29-2222 to increase sentences for habitual criminals. (4) A person convicted of a felony for which a mandatory minimum sentence is prescribed shall not be eligible for probation.[59] For purposes of the Nebraska Criminal Code and any statute passed by the Legislature after the date of passage of the code, misdemeanors are divided into seven classes which are distinguished from one another by the following penalties which are authorized upon conviction: **Class I misdemeanor** Maximum—not more than one year imprisonment, or one thousand dollars fine, or both Minimum—none **Class II misdemeanor** Maximum—six months imprisonment, or one thousand dollars fine, or both Minimum—none **Class III misdemeanor** Maximum—three months imprisonment, or five hundred dollars fine, or both Minimum—none **Class IIIA misdemeanor** Maximum—seven days imprisonment, five hundred dollars fine, or both

Minimum—none

Class IV misdemeanor

Maximum—no imprisonment, five hundred dollars fine

Minimum—one hundred dollars fine

Class V misdemeanor

Maximum—no imprisonment, one hundred dollars fine

Minimum—none

Class W misdemeanor

Driving under the influence or implied consent

First conviction

Maximum—sixty days imprisonment and five hundred dollars fine

Mandatory minimum—seven days imprisonment and four hundred dollars fine

Second conviction

Maximum—six months imprisonment and five hundred dollars fine

Mandatory minimum—thirty days imprisonment and five hundred dollars fine

Third conviction

Maximum—one year imprisonment and six hundred dollars fine

Mandatory minimum—ninety days imprisonment and six hundred dollars fine.[60]

Sentences of imprisonment in misdemeanor cases shall be served in the county jail, except that in the following circumstances the court may, in its discretion, order that such sentences be served in institutions under the jurisdiction of the Department of Correctional Services:

(a) If the sentence is for a term of one year upon conviction of a Class I misdemeanor;

(b) If the sentence is to be served concurrently or consecutively with a term for conviction of a felony; or

(c) If the Department of Correctional Services has certified as provided in section 28-105 as to the availability of facilities and programs for short-term prisoners and the sentence is for a term of six months or more.[61]

(continued)

State	Punishments for Felonies and Misdemeanors
Nevada	1. Except when a person is convicted of a category A felony, and except as otherwise provided by specific statute, a person convicted of a felony shall be sentenced to a minimum term and a maximum term of imprisonment which must be within the limits prescribed by the applicable statute, unless the statute in force at the time of commission of the felony prescribed a different penalty. The minimum term of imprisonment that may be imposed must not exceed 40 percent of the maximum term imposed.
	2. Except as otherwise provided by specific statute, for each felony committed on or after July 1, 1995:
	(a) A category A felony is a felony for which a sentence of death or imprisonment in the state prison for life with or without the possibility of parole may be imposed, as provided by specific statute.
	(b) A category B felony is a felony for which the minimum term of imprisonment in the state prison that may be imposed is not less than 1 year and the maximum term of imprisonment that may be imposed is not more than 20 years, as provided by specific statute.
	(c) A category C felony is a felony for which a court shall sentence a convicted person to imprisonment in the state prison for a minimum term of not less than 1 year and a maximum term of not more than 5 years. In addition to any other penalty, the court may impose a fine of not more than $10,000, unless a greater fine is authorized or required by statute.
	(d) A category D felony is a felony for which a court shall sentence a convicted person to imprisonment in the state prison for a minimum term of not less than 1 year and a maximum term of not more than 4 years. In addition to any other penalty, the court may impose a fine of not more than $5,000, unless a greater fine is authorized or required by statute.
	(e) A category E felony is a felony for which a court shall sentence a convicted person to imprisonment in the state prison for a minimum term of not less than 1 year and a maximum term of not more than 4 years. Except as otherwise provided in paragraph (b) of subsection 1 of NRS 176A.100, upon sentencing a person who is found guilty of a category E felony, the court shall suspend the execution of the sentence and grant probation to the person upon such conditions as the court deems appropriate. Such conditions of probation may include, but are not limited to, requiring the person to serve a term of confinement of not more than 1 year in the county jail. In

New Hampshire

addition to any other penalty, the court may impose a fine of not more than $5,000, unless a greater penalty is authorized or required by statute.[62]

I. The provisions of this section govern the classification of every offense, whether defined within this code or by any other statute.

II. Every offense is either a felony, misdemeanor or violation.

(a) Felonies and misdemeanors are crimes. (b) A violation does not constitute a crime and conviction of a violation shall not give rise to any disability or legal disadvantage based on conviction of a criminal offense.

III. A felony is murder or a crime so designated by statute within or outside this code or a crime defined by statute outside of this code where the maximum penalty provided is imprisonment in excess of one year; . . . .

(a) Felonies other than murder are either class A felonies or class B felonies when committed by an individual. . . .

(1) Class A felonies are crimes so designated by statute within or outside this code and any crime defined by statute outside of this code for which the maximum penalty, exclusive of fine, is imprisonment in excess of 7 years. (2) Class B felonies are crimes so designated by statute within or outside this code and any crime defined outside of this code for which the maximum penalty, exclusive of fine, is imprisonment in excess of one year but not in excess of 7 years.

IV. Misdemeanors are either class A misdemeanors or class B misdemeanors when committed by an individual. . . .

(a) A class A misdemeanor is any crime so designated by statute within or outside this code and any crime defined outside of this code for which the maximum penalty, exclusive of fine, is imprisonment not in excess of one year. (b) A class B misdemeanor is any crime so designated by statute within or outside this code and any crime defined outside of this code for which the maximum penalty does not include any term of imprisonment or any fine in excess of the maximum provided for a class B misdemeanor in RSA 651:2, IV(a). (c) Any crime designated within or outside this code as a misdemeanor without specification of the classification shall be presumed to be a class B misdemeanor unless: (1) An element of the offense involves an 'act of violence' or 'threat of violence' as defined in paragraph VII; or (2) The state files a notice of intent to seek class A misdemeanor penalties on or before the date of arraignment. Such notice shall be on a form approved in accordance with RSA 490:26-d. (d) Nothing in this paragraph shall prohibit the state from reducing any offense

(continued)

State	Punishments for Felonies and Misdemeanors
	originally charged as a class A misdemeanor to a class B misdemeanor at any time with the agreement of the person charged.

V. A violation is an offense so designated by statute within or outside this code and, except as provided in this paragraph, any offense defined outside of this code for which there is no other penalty provided other than a fine or fine and forfeiture or other civil penalty.....

V-a. The violation of any requirement created by statute or by municipal regulation enacted pursuant to an enabling statute, where the statute neither specifies the penalty or offense classification, shall be deemed a violation, and the penalties to be imposed by the court shall be those provided for a violation under RSA 651:2.

VI. Prior to or at the time of arraignment, the state may, in its discretion, charge any offense designated a misdemeanor, as defined by paragraph IV, as a violation. At such time, the prosecutor shall make an affirmative statement to the court as to whether he intends to proceed under this paragraph. In such cases the penalties to be imposed by the court shall be those provided for a violation under RSA 651:2. This paragraph shall not apply to any offense for which a statute prescribes an enhanced penalty for a subsequent conviction of the same offense.

VII. The state may change any offense designated or defined as a class A misdemeanor as defined by paragraph IV to a class B misdemeanor, so long as no element of the offense involves an act of violence or threat of violence. The term 'act of violence' means attempting to cause or purposely or recklessly causing bodily injury or serious bodily injury with or without a deadly weapon; and the term 'threat of violence' means placing or attempting to place another in fear of imminent bodily injury either by physical menace or by threats to commit a crime against the person of the other. The state may change an offense pursuant to this paragraph if such change is in the interest of public safety and welfare and is not inconsistent with the societal goals of deterrence and prevention of recidivism, as follows:

(a) In its own discretion prior to or at the time of arraignment in the district court;

(b) In its own discretion following an entry of appeal in the superior court or within 20 days thereafter;

(c) With the agreement of the person charged at any other time; or

(d) In its own discretion, following entry of a complaint at a regional jury trial court or within 21 days thereafter.

VIII. If a person convicted of a class A misdemeanor has been sentenced and such sentence does not include any period of actual incarceration or a suspended or deferred jail sentence or any fine in excess of the maximum provided for a class B misdemeanor in RSA 651:2, IV(a), the court shall record such conviction and sentence as a class B misdemeanor.[63]

I. A person convicted of a felony or a Class A misdemeanor may be sentenced to imprisonment, probation, conditional or unconditional discharge, or a fine.

II. If a sentence of imprisonment is imposed, the court shall fix the maximum thereof which is not to exceed:

(a) Fifteen years for a class A felony,

(b) Seven years for a class B felony,

(c) One year for a class A misdemeanor,

(d) Life imprisonment for murder in the second degree, and, in the case of a felony only, a minimum which is not to exceed 1/2 of the maximum, or if the maximum is life imprisonment, such minimum term as the court may order.[64]

New Jersey
A person who has been convicted of an offense may be sentenced to pay a fine, to make restitution, or both, such fine not to exceed:

a. (1) $200,000.00 when the conviction is of a crime of the first degree;

(2) $150,000.00 when the conviction is of a crime of the second degree;

b. (1) $15,000.00 when the conviction is of a crime of the third degree;

(2) $10,000.00 when the conviction is of a crime of the fourth degree;

c. $1,000.00, when the conviction is of a disorderly persons offense;

d. $500.00, when the conviction is of a petty disorderly persons offense.[65]

Except as otherwise provided, a person who has been convicted of a crime may be sentenced to imprisonment, as follows:

(1) In the case of a crime of the first degree, for a specific term of years which shall be fixed by the court and shall be between 10 years and 20 years;

(2) In the case of a crime of the second degree, for a specific term of years which shall be fixed by the court and shall be between five years and 10 years;

(continued)

309

State	Punishments for Felonies and Misdemeanors
	(3) In the case of a crime of the third degree, for a specific term of years which shall be fixed by the court and shall be between three years and five years;
	(4) In the case of a crime of the fourth degree, for a specific term which shall be fixed by the court and shall not exceed 18 months. [66]
New Mexico	If a person is convicted of a noncapital felony, the basic sentence of imprisonment is as follows:
	(1) for a first degree felony resulting in the death of a child, life imprisonment;
	(2) for a first degree felony for aggravated criminal sexual penetration, life imprisonment;
	(3) for a first degree felony, eighteen years imprisonment;
	(4) for a second degree felony resulting in the death of a human being, fifteen years imprisonment;
	(5) for a second degree felony for a sexual offense against a child, fifteen years imprisonment;
	(6) for a second degree felony, nine years imprisonment;
	(7) for a third degree felony resulting in the death of a human being, six years imprisonment;
	(8) for a third degree felony for a sexual offense against a child, six years imprisonment;
	(9) for a third degree felony, three years imprisonment; or
	(10) for a fourth degree felony, eighteen months imprisonment. [67]
	The court may, in addition to the imposition of a basic sentence of imprisonment, impose a fine not to exceed:
	(1) for a first degree felony resulting in the death of a child, seventeen thousand five hundred dollars ($17,500);
	(2) for a first degree felony for aggravated criminal sexual penetration, seventeen thousand five hundred dollars ($17,500);
	(3) for a first degree felony, fifteen thousand dollars ($15,000);
	(4) for a second degree felony resulting in the death of a human being, twelve thousand five hundred dollars ($12,500);
	(5) for a second degree felony for a sexual offense against a child, twelve thousand five hundred dollars ($12,500);
	(6) for a second degree felony, ten thousand dollars ($10,000);
	(7) for a third degree felony resulting in the death of a human being, five thousand dollars ($5,000);

(8) for a third degree felony for a sexual offense against a child, five thousand dollars ($5,000); or

(9) for a third or fourth degree felony, five thousand dollars ($5,000).[68]

New York

Maximum term of sentence. The maximum term of an indeterminate sentence shall be at least three years and the term shall be fixed as follows:

(a) For a class A felony, the term shall be life imprisonment;

(b) For a class B felony, the term shall be fixed by the court, and shall not exceed twenty-five years;

(c) For a class C felony, the term shall be fixed by the court, and shall not exceed fifteen years;

(d) For a class D felony, the term shall be fixed by the court, and shall not exceed seven years; and

(e) For a class E felony, the term shall be fixed by the court, and shall not exceed four years.[69]

1. Indeterminate sentence. A sentence of imprisonment for a felony committed by a juvenile offender shall be an indeterminate sentence. . . .

2. Maximum term of sentence. The maximum term of an indeterminate sentence for a juvenile offender shall be at least three years and the term shall be fixed as follows:

(a) For the class A felony of murder in the second degree, the term shall be life imprisonment;

(b) For the class A felony of arson in the first degree, or for the class A felony of kidnapping in the first degree the term shall be fixed by the court, and shall be at least twelve years but shall not exceed fifteen years;

(c) For a class B felony, the term shall be fixed by the court, and shall not exceed ten years;

(d) For a class C felony, the term shall be fixed by the court, and shall not exceed seven years; and

(e) For a class D felony, the term shall be fixed by the court and shall not exceed four years.[70]

[Eff. until Sept. 1, 2013. See, also, subdivision 3 below.] Maximum term of sentence. Except as provided in subdivision five or six of this section, or as provided in subdivision five of section 70.80 of this article, the maximum term of an indeterminate sentence for a second felony offender must be fixed by the court as follows:

(a) For a class A-II felony, the term must be life imprisonment;

(b) For a class B felony, the term must be at least nine years and must not exceed twenty-five years;

(c) For a class C felony, the term must be at least six years and must not exceed fifteen years;

(d) For a class D felony, the term must be at least four years and must not exceed seven years; and

(continued)

State	Punishments for Felonies and Misdemeanors
	(e) For a class E felony, the term must be at least three years and must not exceed four years; provided, however, that where the sentence is for the class E felony offense specified in section 240.32 of this chapter, the maximum term must be at least three years and must not exceed five years.[71] [Eff. Sept. 1, 2013. See, also, subdivision 3 above.] Maximum term of sentence. Except as provided in subdivision five of this section, or as provided in subdivision five of section 70.80 of this article, the maximum term of an indeterminate sentence for a second felony offender must be fixed by the court as follows: (a) For a class A-II felony, the term must be life imprisonment; (b) For a class B felony, the term must be at least nine years and must not exceed twenty-five years; (c) For a class C felony, the term must be at least six years and must not exceed fifteen years; (d) For a class D felony, the term must be at least four years and must not exceed seven years; and (e) For a class E felony, the term must be at least three years and must not exceed four years.[72]
North Carolina	(a) Offense Classification; Default Classifications.—The offense classification is as specified in the offense for which the sentence is being imposed. If the offense is a felony for which there is no classification, it is a Class I felony. (b) Fines.—Any judgment that includes a sentence of imprisonment may also include a fine. If a community punishment is authorized, the judgment may consist of a fine only. Additionally, when the defendant is other than an individual, the judgment may consist of a fine only. Unless otherwise provided, the amount of the fine is in the discretion of the court. (c) Punishments for Each Class of Offense and Prior Record Level; Punishment Chart Described.—The authorized punishment for each class of offense and prior record level is as specified in the chart below. Prior record levels are indicated by the Roman numerals placed horizontally on the top of the chart. Classes of offense are indicated by the letters placed vertically on the left side of the chart. Each cell on the chart contains the following components: (1) A sentence disposition or dispositions: "C" indicates that a community punishment is authorized; "I" indicates that an intermediate punishment is authorized; "A" indicates that an active punishment is authorized; and "Life Imprisonment Without Parole" indicates that the defendant shall be imprisoned for the remainder of the prisoner's natural life. (2) A presumptive range of minimum durations, if the sentence of

imprisonment is neither aggravated or mitigated; any minimum term of imprisonment in that range is permitted unless the court finds pursuant to G. S. 15A-1340.16 that an aggravated or mitigated sentence is appropriate. The presumptive range is the middle of the three ranges in the cell. (3) A mitigated range of minimum durations if the court finds pursuant to G.S. 15A-1340.16 that a mitigated sentence of imprisonment is justified; in such a case, any minimum term of imprisonment in the mitigated range is permitted. The mitigated range is the lower of the three ranges in the cell. (4) An aggravated range of minimum durations if the court finds pursuant to G.S. 15A-1340.16 that an aggravated sentence of imprisonment is justified; in such a case, any minimum term of imprisonment in the aggravated range is permitted. The aggravated range is the higher of the three ranges in the cell.

	PRIOR RECORD LEVEL						
	I 0-1 Pt	II 2-5 Pts	III 6-9 Pts	IV 10-13 Pts	V 14-17 Pts	VI 18+ Pts	DISPOSITION
A	A	Life Imprisonment Without Parole or Death as Established by Statute					
	A	A	A	A	A	A	DISPOSITION
B1	240-300	276-345	317-397	365-456	Life Imprisonment Without Parole		Aggravated
	192-240	221-276	254-317	292-365	336-420	386-483	PRESUMPTIVE
	144-192	166-221	190-254	219-292	252-336	290-386	Mitigated
	A	A	A	A	A	A	DISPOSITION
B2	157-196	180-225	207-258	238-297	273-342	314-393	Aggravated
	125-157	144-180	165-207	190-238	219-273	251-314	PRESUMPTIVE
	94-125	108-144	124-165	143-190	164-219	189-251	Mitigated
	A	A	A	A	A	A	DISPOSITION
C	73-92	83-104	96-120	110-138	127-159	146-182	Aggravated
	58-73	67-83	77-96	88-110	101-127	117-146	PRESUMPTIVE

(continued)

State	Punishments for Felonies and Misdemeanors						
	44-58	50-67	58-77	66-88	76-101	87-117	Mitigated
D	A	A	A	A	A	A	DISPOSITION
	64-80	73-92	84-105	97-121	111-139	128-160	Aggravated
	51-64	59-73	67-84	78-97	89-111	103-128	PRESUMPTIVE
	38-51	44-59	51-67	58-78	67-89	77-103	Mitigated
E	I/A	I/A	A	A	A	A	DISPOSITION
	25-31	29-36	33-41	38-48	44-55	50-63	Aggravated
	20-25	23-29	26-33	30-38	35-44	40-50	PRESUMPTIVE
	15-20	17-23	20-26	23-30	26-35	30-40	Mitigated
F	I/A	I/A	A	A	A	A	DISPOSITION
	16-20	19-23	21-27	25-31	28-36	33-41	Aggravated
	13-16	15-19	17-21	20-25	23-28	26-33	PRESUMPTIVE
	10-13	11-15	13-17	15-20	17-23	20-26	Mitigated
G	I/A	I/A	I/A	I/A	A	A	DISPOSITION
	13-16	14-18	17-21	19-24	22-27	25-31	Aggravated
	10-13	12-14	13-17	15-19	17-22	20-25	PRESUMPTIVE
	8-10	9-12	10-13	11-15	13-17	15-20	Mitigated
H	C/I/A	I/A	I/A	I/A	I/A	A	DISPOSITION
	6-8	8-10	10-12	11-14	15-19	20-25	Aggravated
	5-6	6-8	8-10	9-11	12-15	16-20	PRESUMPTIVE
	4-5	4-6	6-8	7-9	9-12	12-16	Mitigated
I	C	C/I	I	I/A	I/A	I/A	DISPOSITION
	6-8	6-8	6-8	8-10	9-11	10-12	Aggravated
	4-6	4-6	5-6	6-8	7-9	8-10	PRESUMPTIVE
	3-4	3-4	4-5	4-6	5-7	6-8	Mitigated

(d) Maximum Sentences Specified for Class F through Class I Felonies.—Unless provided otherwise in a statute establishing a punishment for a specific crime, for each minimum term of imprisonment in the chart in subsection (c) of this section, expressed in months, the corresponding maximum term of imprisonment, also expressed in months, is as specified in the table below for Class F through Class I felonies. The first figure in each cell in the table is the minimum term and the second is the maximum term.

3-13	4-14	5-15	6-17	7-18	8-19	9-20	10-21
11-23	12-24	13-25	14-26	15-27	16-29	17-30	18-31
19-32	20-33	21-35	22-36	23-37	24-38	25-39	26-41
27-42	28-43	29-44	30-45	31-47	32-48	33-49	34-50
35-51	36-53	37-54	38-55	39-56	40-57	41-59	42-60
43-61	44-62	45-63	46-65	47-66	48-67	49-68	

(e) Maximum Sentences Specified for Class B1 through Class E Felonies for Minimum Terms up to 339 Months.—Unless provided otherwise in a statute establishing a punishment for a specific crime, for each minimum term of imprisonment in the chart in subsection (c) of this section, expressed in months, the corresponding maximum term of imprisonment, also expressed in months, is as specified in the table below for Class B1 through Class E felonies. The first figure in each cell of the table is the minimum term and the second is the maximum term.

15-30	16-32	17-33	18-34	19-35	20-36	21-38	22-39
23-40	24-41	25-42	26-44	27-45	28-46	29-47	30-48
31-50	32-51	33-52	34-53	35-54	36-56	37-57	38-58
39-59	40-60	41-62	42-63	43-64	44-65	45-66	46-68
47-69	48-70	49-71	50-72	51-74	52-75	53-76	54-77
55-78	56-80	57-81	58-82	59-83	60-84	61-86	62-87
63-88	64-89	65-90	66-91	67-93	68-94	69-95	70-96
71-98	72-99	73-100	74-101	75-102	76-104	77-105	78-106
79-107	80-108	81-110	82-111	83-112	84-113	85-114	86-115

(continued)

State	Punishments for Felonies and Misdemeanors							
	87-117	88-118	89-119	90-120	91-122	92-123	93-124	94-125
	95-126	96-128	97-129	98-130	99-131	100-132	101-134	102-135
	103-136	104-137	105-138	106-140	107-141	108-142	109-143	110-144
	111-146	112-147	113-148	114-149	115-150	116-152	117-153	118-154
	119-155	120-156	121-158	122-159	123-160	124-161	125-162	126-164
	127-165	128-166	129-167	130-168	131-170	132-171	133-172	134-173
	135-174	136-176	137-177	138-178	139-179	140-180	141-182	142-183
	143-184	144-185	145-186	146-188	147-189	148-190	149-191	150-192
	151-194	152-195	153-196	154-197	155-198	156-200	157-201	158-202
	159-203	160-204	161-206	162-207	163-208	164-209	165-210	166-212
	167-213	168-214	169-215	170-216	171-218	172-219	173-220	174-221
	175-222	176-224	177-225	178-226	179-227	180-228	181-230	182-231
	183-232	184-233	185-234	186-236	187-237	188-238	189-239	190-240
	191-242	192-243	193-244	194-245	195-246	196-248	197-249	198-250
	199-251	200-252	201-254	202-255	203-256	204-257	205-258	206-260
	207-261	208-262	209-263	210-264	211-266	212-267	213-268	214-269
	215-270	216-271	217-273	218-274	219-275	220-276	221-278	222-279
	223-280	224-281	225-282	226-284	227-285	228-286	229-287	230-288
	231-290	232-291	233-292	234-293	235-294	236-296	237-297	238-298
	239-299	240-300	241-302	242-303	243-304	244-305	245-306	246-308
	247-309	248-310	249-311	250-312	251-314	252-315	253-316	254-317
	255-318	256-320	257-321	258-322	259-323	260-324	261-326	262-327
	263-328	264-329	265-330	266-332	267-333	268-334	269-335	270-336
	271-338	272-339	273-340	274-341	275-342	276-344	277-345	278-346
	279-347	280-348	281-350	282-351	283-352	284-353	285-354	286-356
	287-357	288-358	289-359	290-360	291-362	292-363	293-364	294-365

295-366	296-368	297-369	298-370	299-371	300-372	301-374	302-375
303-376	304-377	305-378	306-380	307-381	308-382	309-383	310-384
311-386	312-387	313-388	314-389	315-390	316-392	317-393	318-394
319-395	320-396	321-398	322-399	323-400	324-401	325-402	326-404
327-405	328-408	329-407	330-408	331-410	332-411	333-412	334-413
335-414	336-416	337-417	338-418	339-419			

(e1) Maximum Sentences Specified for Class B1 through Class E Felonies for Minimum Terms of 340 Months or More.—Unless provided otherwise in a statute establishing a punishment for a specific crime, when the minimum sentence is 340 months or more, the corresponding maximum term of imprisonment shall be equal to the sum of the minimum term of imprisonment and twenty percent (20%) of the minimum term of imprisonment, rounded to the next highest month, plus 12 additional months.[73]

Except as provided in subsections (b) and (c), every person who shall be convicted of any misdemeanor for which no specific classification and no specific punishment is prescribed by statute shall be punishable as a Class 1 misdemeanor. Any misdemeanor that has a specific punishment, but is not assigned a classification by the General Assembly pursuant to law is classified as follows, based on the maximum punishment allowed by law for the offense as it existed on the effective date of Article 81B of Chapter 15A of the General Statutes: (1) If that maximum punishment is more than six months imprisonment, it is a Class 1 misdemeanor; (2) If that maximum punishment is more than 30 days but not more than six months imprisonment, it is a Class 2 misdemeanor; and (3) If that maximum punishment is 30 days or less imprisonment or only a fine, it is a Class 3 misdemeanor. Misdemeanors that have punishments for one or more counties or cities pursuant to a local act of the General Assembly that are different from the generally applicable punishment are classified pursuant to this subsection if not otherwise specifically classified.[74]

(a) Generally—The prior record level of a felony offender is determined by calculating the sum of the points assigned to each of the offender's prior convictions that the court, or with respect to subdivision (b)(7) of this section, the jury, finds to have been proved in accordance with this section.

(continued)

State	Punishments for Felonies and Misdemeanors
	(b) Points—Points are assigned as follows:

(1) For each prior felony Class A conviction, 10 points.

(1a) For each prior felony Class B1 conviction, 9 points.

(2) For each prior felony Class B2, C, or D conviction, 6 points.

(3) For each prior felony Class E, F, or G conviction, 4 points.

(4) For each prior felony Class H or I conviction, 2 points.

(5) For each prior misdemeanor conviction as defined in this subsection, 1 point. For purposes of this subsection, misdemeanor is defined as any Class A1 and Class 1 nontraffic misdemeanor offense, impaired driving (G.S. 20-138.1), impaired driving in a commercial vehicle (G.S. 20-138.2), and misdemeanor death by vehicle (G.S. 20-141.4(a2)), but not any other misdemeanor traffic offense under Chapter 20 of the General Statutes.

(6) If all the elements of the present offense are included in any prior offense for which the offender was convicted, whether or not the prior offense or offenses were used in determining prior record level, 1 point.

(7) If the offense was committed while the offender was on supervised or unsupervised probation, parole, or post-release supervision, or while the offender was serving a sentence of imprisonment, or while the offender was on escape from a correctional institution while serving a sentence of imprisonment, 1 point.

For purposes of determining prior record points under this subsection, a conviction for a first degree rape or a first degree sexual offense committed prior to the effective date of this subsection shall be treated as a felony Class B1 conviction, and a conviction for any other felony Class B offense committed prior to the effective date of this subsection shall be treated as a felony Class B2 conviction. G.S. 15A-1340.16(a5) specifies the procedure to be used to determine if a point exists under subdivision (7) of this subsection. The State must provide a defendant with written notice of its intent to prove the existence of the prior record point under subdivision (7) of this subsection as required by G.S. 15A-1340.16(a6).

(c) Prior Record Levels for Felony Sentencing.—The prior record levels for felony sentencing are:

(1) Level I—Not more than 1 point.

(2) Level II—At least 2, but not more than 5 points.

(3) Level III—At least 6, but not more than 9 points.

(4) Level IV—At least 10, but not more than 13 points.

(5) Level V—At least 14, but not more than 17 points.

(6) Level VI—At least 18 points.

In determining the prior record level, the classification of a prior offense is the classification assigned to that offense at the time the offense for which the offender is being sentenced is committed.[75]

North Dakota

Offenses are divided into seven classes, which are denominated and subject to maximum penalties, as follows:

1. Class AA felony, for which a maximum penalty of life imprisonment without parole may be imposed. The court must designate whether the life imprisonment sentence imposed is with or without an opportunity for parole. Notwithstanding the provisions of section 12-59-05, a person found guilty of a class AA felony and who receives a sentence of life imprisonment with parole, shall not be eligible to have that person's sentence considered by the parole board for thirty years, less sentence reduction earned for good conduct, after that person's admission to the penitentiary.

2. Class A felony, for which a maximum penalty of twenty years' imprisonment, a fine of ten thousand dollars, or both, may be imposed.

3. Class B felony, for which a maximum penalty of ten years' imprisonment, a fine of ten thousand dollars, or both, may be imposed.

4. Class C felony, for which a maximum penalty of five years' imprisonment, a fine of five thousand dollars, or both, may be imposed.

5. Class A misdemeanor, for which a maximum penalty of one year's imprisonment, a fine of two thousand dollars, or both, may be imposed.

6. Class B misdemeanor, for which a maximum penalty of thirty days' imprisonment, a fine of one thousand dollars, or both, may be imposed.

7. Infraction, for which a maximum fine of five hundred dollars may be imposed. Any person convicted of an infraction who has, within one year prior to commission of the infraction of which the person was convicted, been previously convicted of an offense classified as an infraction may be sentenced as though convicted of a class B

(continued)

State	Punishments for Felonies and Misdemeanors
	misdemeanor. If the prosecution contends that the infraction is punishable as a class B misdemeanor, the complaint shall specify that the offense is a misdemeanor.[76]
Ohio	If a child is adjudicated a delinquent child or a juvenile traffic offender, the court may order any of the following dispositions, in addition to any other disposition authorized or required by this chapter:
(1) Impose a fine in accordance with the following schedule:
(a) For an act that would be a minor misdemeanor or an unclassified misdemeanor if committed by an adult, a fine not to exceed fifty dollars;
(b) For an act that would be a misdemeanor of the fourth degree if committed by an adult, a fine not to exceed one hundred dollars;
(c) For an act that would be a misdemeanor of the third degree if committed by an adult, a fine not to exceed one hundred fifty dollars;
(d) For an act that would be a misdemeanor of the second degree if committed by an adult, a fine not to exceed two hundred dollars;
(e) For an act that would be a misdemeanor of the first degree if committed by an adult, a fine not to exceed two hundred fifty dollars;
(f) For an act that would be a felony of the fifth degree or an unclassified felony if committed by an adult, a fine not to exceed three hundred dollars;
(g) For an act that would be a felony of the fourth degree if committed by an adult, a fine not to exceed four hundred dollars;
(h) For an act that would be a felony of the third degree if committed by an adult, a fine not to exceed seven hundred fifty dollars;
(i) For an act that would be a felony of the second degree if committed by an adult, a fine not to exceed one thousand dollars;
(j) For an act that would be a felony of the first degree if committed by an adult, a fine not to exceed one thousand five hundred dollars; . . .
(2) Require the child to pay costs.[77]

(A) Except as provided in division (B)(1), (B)(2), (B)(3), (B)(4), (B)(5), (B)(6), (B)(7), (B)(8), (E), (G), (H), or (J) of this section or in division (D)(6) of section 2919.25 of the Revised Code and except in relation to an offense for which a sentence of death or life imprisonment is to be imposed, if the court imposing a sentence upon an offender for a felony elects or is required to impose a prison term on the offender pursuant to this chapter, the court shall impose a definite prison term that shall be one of the following:

(1) For a felony of the first degree, the prison term shall be three, four, five, six, seven, eight, nine, ten, or eleven years.

(2) For a felony of the second degree, the prison term shall be two, three, four, five, six, seven, or eight years.

(3)(a) For a felony of the third degree that is a violation of section 2903.06, 2903.08, 2907.03, 2907.04, or 2907.05 of the Revised Code or that is a violation of section 2911.02 or 2911.12 of the Revised Code if the offender previously has been convicted of or pleaded guilty in two or more separate proceedings to two or more violations of section 2911.01, 2911. 02, 2911.11, or 2911.12 of the Revised Code, the prison term shall be twelve, eighteen, twenty-four, thirty, thirty-six, forty-two, forty-eight, fifty-four, or sixty months.

(b) For a felony of the third degree that is not an offense for which division (A)(3)(a) of this section applies, the prison term shall be nine, twelve, eighteen, twenty-four, thirty, or thirty-six months.

(4) For a felony of the fourth degree, the prison term shall be six, seven, eight, nine, ten, eleven, twelve, thirteen, fourteen, fifteen, sixteen, seventeen, or eighteen months.

(5) For a felony of the fifth degree, the prison term shall be six, seven, eight, nine, ten, eleven, or twelve months.[78]

Except as otherwise provided in this division and in addition to imposing court costs pursuant to section 2947.23 of the Revised Code, the court imposing a sentence upon an offender for a felony may sentence the offender to any financial sanction or combination of financial sanctions authorized under this section or, in the circumstances specified in section 2929.32 of the Revised Code, may impose upon the offender a fine in accordance with that section. Finan-cial sanctions that may be imposed pursuant to this section include, but are not limited to, the following: . . . . (3) Except as provided in division (B)(1), (3), or (4) of this section, a fine payable by the offender to the state, to a politi-cal subdivision when appropriate for a felony, or as described in division (B)(2) of this section to one or more law enforcement agencies, in the following amount:

(continued)

State	Punishments for Felonies and Misdemeanors
	(a) For a felony of the first degree, not more than twenty thousand dollars; (b) For a felony of the second degree, not more than fifteen thousand dollars; (c) For a felony of the third degree, not more than ten thousand dollars; (d) For a felony of the fourth degree, not more than five thousand dollars; (e) For a felony of the fifth degree, not more than two thousand five hundred dollars.[79]
Oklahoma	Any violation of the provisions of this section [facilitating, encouraging, offering or soliciting sexual conduct or engaging in sexual communication with a minor or person believed to be a minor] shall be a felony, punishable by a fine in an amount not to exceed Ten Thousand Dollars ($10,000.00), or by imprisonment in the custody of the Department of Corrections for a term of not more than ten (10) years, or by both such fine and imprisonment. For purposes of this section, each communication shall constitute a separate offense. Except for persons sentenced to life or life without parole, any person sentenced to imprisonment for two (2) years or more for a violation of this section shall be required to serve a term of post-imprisonment supervision pursuant to sub-paragraph f of paragraph 1 of subsection A of Section 991a of Title 22 of the Oklahoma Statutes under conditions determined by the Department of Corrections. The jury shall be advised that the mandatory post-imprisonment supervision shall be in addition to the actual imprisonment.[80] Any person who, with knowledge of its contents, possesses one hundred (100) or more separate materials depicting child pornography shall be, upon conviction, guilty of aggravated possession of child pornography. The violator shall be punished by imprisonment in the custody of the Department of Corrections for a term not exceeding life imprisonment and by a fine in an amount not more than Ten Thousand Dollars ($10,000.00). The violator, upon conviction, shall be required to register as a sex offender under the Sex Offenders Registration Act.[81]
Oregon	(1) Notwithstanding ORS 161.605, when a person is convicted of one of the offenses listed in subsection (2)(a) of this section and the offense was committed on or after April 1, 1995, or of one of the offenses listed in subsection (2)(b) of this section and the offense was committed on or after October 4, 1997, or of the offense described in subsection (2)(c) of this section and the offense was committed on or after January 1, 2008, the court shall impose, and the person shall serve, at least the entire term of imprisonment listed in subsection (2) of this section. The person is not, during the service of the term of imprisonment, eligible for release on post-prison supervision

or any form of temporary leave from custody. The person is not eligible for any reduction in, or based on, the minimum sentence for any reason whatsoever under ORS 421.121 or any other statute. The court may impose a greater sentence if otherwise permitted by law; but may not impose a lower sentence than the sentence specified in subsection (2) of this section.

(2) The offenses to which subsection (1) of this section applies and the applicable mandatory minimum sentences are:

(a)(P) Sexual abuse in the first degree, as defined in ORS 163.427   75 months

(b)(B) Using a child in a display of sexually explicit conduct, as defined in ORS 163.670.   70 months.[82]

The maximum term of an indeterminate sentence of imprisonment for a felony is as follows:

(1) For a Class A felony, 20 years. (2) For a Class B felony, 10 years. (3) For a Class C felony, 5 years. (4) For an unclassified felony as provided in the statute defining the crime. [83]

A sentence to pay a fine for a felony shall be a sentence to pay an amount, fixed by the court, not exceeding: . . . (b) $375,000 for a Class A felony. (c) $250,000 for a Class B felony. (d) $125,000 for a Class C felony. [84]

A sentence to pay a fine for a misdemeanor shall be a sentence to pay an amount, fixed by the court, not exceeding: (a) $6,250 for a Class A misdemeanor. (b) $2,500 for a Class B misdemeanor. (c) $1,250 for a Class C misdemeanor. [85]

Pennsylvania

(b) Classification of crimes—(2) A crime is a felony of the first degree if it is so designated in this title or if a person convicted thereof may be sentenced to a term of imprisonment, the maximum of which is more than ten years.

(3) A crime is a felony of the second degree if it is so designated in this title or if a person convicted thereof may be sentenced to a term of imprisonment, the maximum of which is not more than ten years.

(4) A crime is a felony of the third degree if it is so designated in this title or if a person convicted thereof may be

(continued)

State	Punishments for Felonies and Misdemeanors
	sentenced to a term of imprisonment, the maximum of which is not more than seven years.
	(5) A crime declared to be a felony, without specification of degree, is of the third degree.
	(6) A crime is a misdemeanor of the first degree if it is so designated in this title or if a person convicted thereof may be sentenced to a term of imprisonment, the maximum of which is not more than five years.
	(7) A crime is a misdemeanor of the second degree if it is so designated in this title or if a person convicted thereof may be sentenced to a term of imprisonment, the maximum of which is not more than two years.
	(8) A crime is a misdemeanor of the third degree if it is so designated in this title or if a person convicted thereof may be sentenced to a term of imprisonment, the maximum of which is not more than one year.
	(9) A crime declared to be a misdemeanor, without specification of degree, is of the third degree. [86]
	Except as provided in 42 Pa.C.S. § 9714 (relating to sentences for second and subsequent offenses), a person who has been convicted of a felony may be sentenced to imprisonment as follows:
	(1) In the case of a felony of the first degree, for a term which shall be fixed by the court at not more than 20 years.
	(2) In the case of a felony of the second degree, for a term which shall be fixed by the court at not more than ten years.
	(3) In the case of a felony of the third degree, for a term which shall be fixed by the court at not more than seven years. [87]
	A person who has been convicted of a misdemeanor may be sentenced to imprisonment for a definite term which shall be fixed by the court and shall be not more than:
	(1) Five years in the case of a misdemeanor of the first degree.
	(2) Two years in the case of a misdemeanor of the second degree.
	(3) One year in the case of a misdemeanor of the third degree. [88]
Rhode Island	Every person, firm, association, or corporation which shall publish, sell, offer for sale, loan, give away, or otherwise distribute any book, magazine, pamphlet, or other publication, or any photograph, picture, or film which depicts any child, or children, under the age of eighteen (18) years and known to be under the age of eighteen (18) years of age by the person, firm, association, or corporation in a setting which taken as a whole

suggests to the average person that the child, or children, is about to engage in or has engaged in, any sexual act, or which depicts any child under eighteen (18) years of age performing sodomy, oral copulation, sexual intercourse, masturbation . . . shall, for the first offense, be punished by imprisonment for not more than ten (10) years, or by a fine of not more than ten thousand dollars ($10,000), or both; for any subsequent offense, by imprisonment for not more than fifteen (15) years, or by a fine of not more than fifteen thousand dollars ($15,000), or both. Provided, that artistic drawings, sketches, paintings, sculptures, or other artistic renditions, shall be exempt from the provisions of this section.[89]

South Carolina

A person convicted of classified offenses, must be imprisoned as follows:

(1) for a Class A felony, not more than thirty years;

(2) for a Class B felony, not more than twenty-five years;

(3) for a Class C felony, not more than twenty years;

(4) for a Class D felony, not more than fifteen years;

(5) for a Class E felony, not more than ten years;

(6) for a Class F felony, not more than five years;

(7) for a Class A misdemeanor, not more than three years;

(8) for a Class B misdemeanor, not more than two years;

(9) for a Class C misdemeanor, not more than one year.[90]

(C) The following offenses are Class C felonies and the maximum terms established for a Class C felony, as set forth in Section 16-1-20(A), apply: . . .

16-15-395   Sexual exploitation of a minor . . .

(D) The following offenses are Class D felonies and the maximum terms established for a Class D felony, as set forth in Section 16-1-20(A), apply: . . .

16-15-355   Disseminating obscene material to a minor 12 years or younger . . .

(continued)

325

State	Punishments for Felonies and Misdemeanors
	(E) The following offenses are Class E felonies and the maximum terms established for a Class E felony, as set forth in Section 16-1-20(A), apply: . . . .
	16-3-820 — Promoting, producing, or directing a sexual performance by a child under 18 . . . .
	16-15-345 — Unlawful to disseminate obscene material to any person under 18 years of age
	16-15-385 — Dissemination of obscene material to minors is unlawful
	16-15-405(D) — Sexual exploitation of a minor Second degree
	16-15-410 — Sexual exploitation of a minor Third degree. [91]
South Dakota	Except as otherwise provided by law, felonies are divided into the following nine classes which are distinguished from each other by the following maximum penalties which are authorized upon conviction:
	(1) Class A felony: death or life imprisonment in the state penitentiary. A lesser sentence than death or life imprisonment may not be given for a Class A felony. In addition, a fine of fifty thousand dollars may be imposed;
	(2) Class B felony: life imprisonment in the state penitentiary. A lesser sentence may not be given for a Class B felony. In addition, a fine of fifty thousand dollars may be imposed;
	(3) Class C felony: life imprisonment in the state penitentiary. In addition, a fine of fifty thousand dollars may be imposed;
	(4) Class 1 felony: fifty years imprisonment in the state penitentiary. In addition, a fine of fifty thousand dollars may be imposed;
	(5) Class 2 felony: twenty-five years imprisonment in the state penitentiary. In addition, a fine of fifty thousand dollars may be imposed;
	(6) Class 3 felony: fifteen years imprisonment in the state penitentiary. In addition, a fine of thirty thousand dollars may be imposed;

(7) Class 4 felony: ten years imprisonment in the state penitentiary. In addition, a fine of twenty thousand dollars may be imposed;

(8) Class 5 felony: five years imprisonment in the state penitentiary. In addition, a fine of ten thousand dollars may be imposed; and

(9) Class 6 felony: two years imprisonment in the state penitentiary or a fine of four thousand dollars, or both. The court, in imposing sentence on a defendant who has been found guilty of a felony, shall order in addition to the sentence that is imposed pursuant to the provisions of this section, that the defendant make restitution to any victim in accordance with the provisions of chapter 23A-28.[92]

Tennessee   A sentence for a felony is a determinate sentence.... The authorized terms of imprisonment and fines for felonies are: (1) Class A felony, not less than fifteen (15) nor more than sixty (60) years. In addition, the jury may assess a fine not to exceed fifty thousand dollars ($50,000), unless otherwise provided by statute;

(2) Class B felony, not less than eight (8) nor more than thirty (30) years. In addition, the jury may assess a fine not to exceed twenty-five thousand dollars ($25,000), unless otherwise provided by statute;

(3) Class C felony, not less than three (3) years nor more than fifteen (15) years. In addition, the jury may assess a fine not to exceed ten thousand dollars ($10,000), unless otherwise provided by statute;

(4) Class D felony, not less than two (2) years nor more than twelve (12) years. In addition, the jury may assess a fine not to exceed five thousand dollars ($5,000), unless otherwise provided by statute; and

(5) Class E felony, not less than one (1) year nor more than six (6) years. In addition, the jury may assess a fine not to exceed three thousand dollars ($3,000), unless otherwise provided by statute.[93]

A sentence for a misdemeanor is a determinate sentence.... The authorized terms of imprisonment and fines for misdemeanors are: (1) Class A misdemeanor, not greater than eleven (11) months, twenty-nine (29) days or a fine not to exceed two thousand five hundred dollars ($2,500), or both, unless otherwise provided by statute; (2) Class B misdemeanor, not greater than six (6) months or a fine not to exceed five hundred dollars ($500), or both, unless otherwise provided by statute; and (3) Class C misdemeanor, not greater than thirty (30) days or a fine not to exceed fifty dollars ($50.00), or both, unless otherwise provided by statute.[94]

(continued)

327

State	Punishments for Felonies and Misdemeanors
Texas	An individual adjudged guilty of a Class A misdemeanor shall be punished by: (1) a fine not to exceed $4,000; (2) confinement in jail for a term not to exceed one year; or (3) both such fine and confinement.[95] An individual adjudged guilty of a Class B misdemeanor shall be punished by: (1) a fine not to exceed $2,000; (2) confinement in jail for a term not to exceed 180 days; or (3) both such fine and confinement.[96] An individual adjudged guilty of a Class C misdemeanor shall be punished by a fine not to exceed $500.[97] (a) Except as provided by Subsection (c)(2), if it is shown on the trial of a felony of the third degree that the defendant has previously been finally convicted of a felony other than a state jail felony punishable under Section 12.35(a), on conviction the defendant shall be punished for a felony of the second degree. (b) Except as provided by Subsection (c)(2) or (c)(4), if it is shown on the trial of a felony of the second degree that the defendant has previously been finally convicted of a felony other than a state jail felony punishable under Section 12.35(a), on conviction the defendant shall be punished for a felony of the first degree. (c)(1) If it is shown on the trial of a felony of the first degree that the defendant has previously been finally convicted of a felony other than a state jail felony punishable under Section 12.35(a), on conviction the defendant shall be punished by imprisonment in the Texas Department of Criminal Justice for life, or for any term of not more than 99 years or less than 15 years. In addition to imprisonment, an individual may be punished by a fine not to exceed $10,000.[98] (a) An individual adjudged guilty of a felony of the first degree shall be punished by imprisonment in the Texas Department of Criminal Justice for life or for any term of not more than 99 years or less than 5 years. (b) In addition to imprisonment, an individual adjudged guilty of a felony of the first degree may be punished by a fine not to exceed $10,000.[99]

(a) An individual adjudged guilty of a felony of the second degree shall be punished by imprisonment in the Texas Department of Criminal Justice for any term of not more than 20 years or less than 2 years.

(b) In addition to imprisonment, an individual adjudged guilty of a felony of the second degree may be punished by a fine not to exceed $10,000.[100]

(a) An individual adjudged guilty of a felony of the third degree shall be punished by imprisonment in the Texas Department of Criminal Justice for any term of not more than 10 years or less than 2 years.

(b) In addition to imprisonment, an individual adjudged guilty of a felony of the third degree may be punished by a fine not to exceed $10,000.[101]

(a) If it is shown on the trial of a Class A misdemeanor that the defendant has been before convicted of a Class A misdemeanor or any degree of felony, on conviction he shall be punished by:

(1) a fine not to exceed $4,000;

(2) confinement in jail for any term of not more than one year or less than 90 days; or

(3) both such fine and confinement.

(b) If it is shown on the trial of a Class B misdemeanor that the defendant has been before convicted of a Class A or Class B misdemeanor or any degree of felony, on conviction he shall be punished by:

(1) a fine not to exceed $2,000;

(2) confinement in jail for any term of not more than 180 days or less than 30 days; or

(3) both such fine and confinement.

(c) If it is shown on the trial of an offense punishable as a Class C misdemeanor under Section 42.01 or 49.02 that the defendant has been before convicted under either of those sections three times or three times for any combination of those offenses and each prior offense was committed in the 24 months preceding the date of commission of the instant offense, the defendant shall be punished by:

(1) a fine not to exceed $2,000;

(2) confinement in jail for a term not to exceed 180 days; or

(3) both such fine and confinement.

(continued)

329

State	Punishments for Felonies and Misdemeanors
	(d) If the punishment scheme for an offense contains a specific enhancement provision increasing punishment for a defendant who has previously been convicted of the offense, the specific enhancement provision controls over this section. [102]
Utah	A person who has been convicted of a felony may be sentenced to imprisonment for an indeterminate term as follows:
	(1) In the case of a felony of the first degree, unless the statute provides otherwise, for a term of not less than five years and which may be for life.
	(2) In the case of a felony of the second degree, unless the statute provides otherwise, for a term of not less than one year nor more than 15 years.
	(3) In the case of a felony of the third degree, unless the statute provides otherwise, for a term not to exceed five years. [103]
	A person convicted of an offense may be sentenced to pay a fine, not exceeding:
	(a) $10,000 for a felony conviction of the first degree or second degree;
	(b) $5,000 for a felony conviction of the third degree;
	(c) $2,500 for a class A misdemeanor conviction;
	(d) $1,000 for a class B misdemeanor conviction;
	(e) $750 for a class C misdemeanor conviction or infraction conviction; and
	(f) any greater amounts specifically authorized by statute. [104]
Vermont	(c) A person who violates section 2827 of this title by possessing a photograph, film or visual depiction, including a depiction stored electronically, which constitutes:
	(1) a clearly lewd exhibition of a child's genitals or anus, other than a depiction of sexual conduct by a child, shall be imprisoned not more than two years or fined not more than $5,000.00, or both;
	(2) sexual conduct by a child, shall be imprisoned not more than five years or fined not more than $10,000.00, or both.

(d) A person who violates section 2827 of this title after being convicted of a previous violation of the same section shall be imprisoned not more than 10 years or fined not more than $50,000.00, or both.[105]

| Virginia | The authorized punishments for conviction of a misdemeanor are: |

(a) For Class 1 misdemeanors, confinement in jail for not more than twelve months and a fine of not more than $2,500, either or both.

(b) For Class 2 misdemeanors, confinement in jail for not more than six months and a fine of not more than $1,000, either or both.

(c) For Class 3 misdemeanors, a fine of not more than $500.

(d) For Class 4 misdemeanors, a fine of not more than $250.

For a misdemeanor offense prohibiting proximity to children as described in subsection A of § 18.2-370.2, the sentencing court is authorized to impose the punishment set forth in subsection B of that section in addition to any other penalty provided by law.[106]

The authorized punishments for conviction of a felony are:

(a) For Class 1 felonies, death, if the person so convicted was 18 years of age or older at the time of the offense and is not determined to be mentally retarded pursuant to § 19.2-264.3:1.1, or imprisonment for life and, subject to subdivision (g), a fine of not more than $100,000. If the person was under 18 years of age at the time of the offense or is determined to be mentally retarded pursuant to § 19.2-264.3:1.1, the punishment shall be imprisonment for life and, subject to subdivision (g), a fine of not more than $100,000.

(b) For Class 2 felonies, imprisonment for life or for any term not less than 20 years and, subject to subdivision (g), a fine of not more than $100,000.

(c) For Class 3 felonies, a term of imprisonment of not less than five years nor more than 20 years and, subject to subdivision (g), a fine of not more than $100,000.

(d) For Class 4 felonies, a term of imprisonment of not less than two years nor more than 10 years and, subject to subdivision (g), a fine of not more than $100,000.

(continued)

State	Punishments for Felonies and Misdemeanors
	(e) For Class 5 felonies, a term of imprisonment of not less than one year nor more than 10 years, or in the discretion of the jury or the court trying the case without a jury, confinement in jail for not more than 12 months and a fine of not more than $2,500, either or both.
	(f) For Class 6 felonies, a term of imprisonment of not less than one year nor more than five years, or in the discretion of the jury or the court trying the case without a jury, confinement in jail for not more than 12 months and a fine of not more than $2,500, either or both.[107]
Washington	For a felony defined by a statute of this state that is not in Title 9A RCW, unless otherwise provided:
	(1) If the maximum sentence of imprisonment authorized by law upon a first conviction of such felony is twenty years or more, such felony shall be treated as a class A felony for purposes of this chapter;
	(2) If the maximum sentence of imprisonment authorized by law upon a first conviction of such felony is eight years or more, but less than twenty years, such felony shall be treated as a class B felony for purposes of this chapter;
	(3) If the maximum sentence of imprisonment authorized by law upon a first conviction of such felony is less than eight years, such felony shall be treated as a class C felony for purposes of this chapter.[108]
	Maximum sentences for crimes committed July 1, 1984, and after:
	(1) Felony. Unless a different maximum sentence for a classified felony is specifically established by a statute of this state, no person convicted of a classified felony shall be punished by confinement or fine exceeding the following:
	(a) For a class A felony, by confinement in a state correctional institution for a term of life imprisonment, or by a fine in an amount fixed by the court of fifty thousand dollars, or by both such confinement and fine;
	(b) For a class B felony, by confinement in a state correctional institution for a term of ten years, or by a fine in an amount fixed by the court of twenty thousand dollars, or by both such confinement and fine;
	(c) For a class C felony, by confinement in a state correctional institution for five years, or by a fine in an amount fixed by the court of ten thousand dollars, or by both such confinement and fine. . . .[109]
	(4) This section applies to only those crimes committed on or after July 1, 1984.
	Unless otherwise provided by a statute of this state, on all sentences under this chapter the court may impose fines according to the following ranges:

	Class A felonies	$0–50,000
	Class B felonies	$0–20,000
	Class C felonies	$0–10,000[110]
West Virginia	Any person who, with knowledge, sends or causes to be sent, or distributes, exhibits, possesses or displays or transports any material visually portraying a minor engaged in any sexually explicit conduct is guilty of a felony, and, upon conviction thereof, shall be imprisoned in the penitentiary not more than two years, and fined not more than two thousand dollars.[111]	
Wisconsin	Penalties for felonies are as follows:	
	(a) For a Class A felony, life imprisonment.	
	(b) For a Class B felony, imprisonment not to exceed 60 years.	
	(c) For a Class C felony, a fine not to exceed $ 100,000 or imprisonment not to exceed 40 years, or both.	
	(d) For a Class D felony, a fine not to exceed $ 100,000 or imprisonment not to exceed 25 years, or both.	
	(e) For a Class E felony, a fine not to exceed $ 50,000 or imprisonment not to exceed 15 years, or both.	
	(f) For a Class F felony, a fine not to exceed $25,000 or imprisonment not to exceed 12 years and 6 months, or both.	
	(g) For a Class G felony, a fine not to exceed $25,000 or imprisonment not to exceed 10 years, or both.	
	(h) For a Class H felony, a fine not to exceed $10,000 or imprisonment not to exceed 6 years, or both.	
	(i) For a Class I felony, a fine not to exceed $10,000 or imprisonment not to exceed 3 years and 6 months, or both.[112]	
	Penalties for misdemeanors are as follows:	
	(a) For a Class A misdemeanor, a fine not to exceed $10,000 or imprisonment not to exceed 9 months, or both.	
	(b) For a Class B misdemeanor, a fine not to exceed $1,000 or imprisonment not to exceed 90 days, or both.	
	(c) For a Class C misdemeanor, a fine not to exceed $500 or imprisonment not to exceed 30 days, or both.[113]	
Wyoming	(c) The sexual exploitation of a child pursuant to paragraphs (b)(i) through (iii) of this section is a felony punishable by imprisonment for not less than five (5) years nor more than twelve (12) years, a fine of not more	

(continued)

State	Punishments for Felonies and Misdemeanors
	than ten thousand dollars ($10,000.00), or both. (d) The sexual exploitation of a child by possession of sexually exploitive material pursuant to paragraph (b)(iv) of this section is a felony punishable by imprisonment for not more than ten (10) years, a fine of not more than ten thousand dollars ($10,000.00), or both. (e) A second or subsequent conviction pursuant to paragraphs (b)(i) through (iv) of this section, or of a substantially similar law of any other jurisdiction, is a felony punishable by imprisonment for not less than seven (7) years nor more than twelve (12) years, a fine of not more than ten thousand dollars ($10,000.00), or both.[114]

(b) Promoting obscenity is a misdemeanor punishable upon conviction as follows:
(i) If to an adult, by a fine not to exceed one thousand dollars ($1,000.00) or by imprisonment for not to exceed one (1) year, or both;
(ii) If to a minor, for each violation, by a fine not to exceed six thousand dollars ($6,000.00) or by imprisonment for not to exceed one (1) year, or both.[115] |

Notes

Chapter 1

1. Amanda Lenhart, Rich Ling, Scott Campbell, and Kristen Purcell, "Teens and Mobile Phones," *Pew Internet and American Life Project* (Washington, DC: Pew Research Center, 2010), 71, http://pewinternet.org/Reports/2010/Teens-and-Mobile-Phones/Summary-of-findings.aspx. In the Pew study, 66 percent of the students had cell phones before the age of 14, while approximately 75 percent of high school students had cell phones.

2. Ibid.

3. Ibid. The study also found that more than four out of every five teenagers sleep with their cell phones. Further, the study revealed that "the biggest driver of whether a teen sleeps with their phone is texting. Teens who use their cellphones to text are 42% more likely to sleep with their phones than cell-owning teens that do not text" (p. 73).

4. Ibid.

5. Lenhart et al., "Teens and Mobile Phones."

6. Ibid.

7. Ibid.

8. Ibid.

9. "Facts," *Text Ed* (a study conducted by TRU Research on behalf of LG Mobile Comm, 2010), http://www.lg.com/us/mobile-phones/text-education/facts.jsp.

10. Lenhart et al., "Teens and Mobile Phones."

11. Mary E. Muscari, "Sexting: New Technology, Old Problem," *Medscape Today News*, last modified October 25, 2010, http://www.medscape.com/viewarticle/702078.

12. "Policy Statement on Sexting," National Center for Missing & Exploited Children, last modified September 21, 2009, http://www.missingkids.com/missingkids/servlet/NewsEventServlet?LanguageCountry=en_US&PageId=4130.

13. Lenhart et al., "Teens and Mobile Phones," 3.

14. Terri Day, "The New Digital Dating Behavior—Sexting: Teens' Explicit Love Letters: Criminal Justice or Civil Liability," *Hastings Communications and Entertainment Law Journal* 33, no. 1 (2010): 73. For an alternative characterization of sexting, see Sharma Howard, "Parenting Teens: 'Sexting' Is This Generation's Streaking, Skinny-Dipping," *Norwich Bulletin*, May 3, 2009, http://www.norwich bulletin.com/living/x1393558689/Parenting-teens-Sexting-is-this-generation-s -streaking-skinny-dipping#axzz1Xn6CZINw.

15. Missy Diaz, "Sexting Is Nothing to LOL About; Teens Who Text Nude Pictures Could Be Guilty of a Felony," *Florida Sun-Sentinel*, July 28, 2009, http:// articles.sun-sentinel.com/2009-07-28/news/0907270634_1_sexting-nude-photos -child-pornography.

16. Judith Levine, "What's the Matter with Teen Sexting?" *American Prospect*, January 30, 2009, http://prospect.org/cs/articles?article=whats_the_matter_with _teen_sexting.

17. Day, *New Digital Dating Behavior*, 73. See also David Rosen, "Obama's First Amendment Challenge? Sexting: The Latest Innovation in Porn," *CounterPunch*, March 25, 2009, http://www.counterpunch.org/2009/03/25/sexting-the-latest -innovation-in-porn/. "Each generation re-imagines the erotic. In this process, notions of the pornographic or the obscene are challenged and changed. And in the process, the generation is changed, its erotic sensibility remade, thus shifting the sexual landscape. The eroticism of today's teens is not that of their grandparents, let alone their parents."

18. "Naked Photos, E-Mail Get Teens in Trouble," *Associated Press*, June 5, 2008, http://www.foxnews.com/story/0,2933,363438,00.html.

19. Olympia Meola, "Legislators Look Into How Va. Laws Cover 'Sexting,' " *Richmond Times-Dispatch*, May 20, 2009.

20. We liked the idea of including a cartoon because we felt Heather K. Hudson, in her dissertation "Factors Affecting Sexting Behaviors among Selected Undergraduate Students," available at http://web.coehs.siu.edu/public/her/ sitebefore2012/grad/new/siu/hed/hed_597/hudson/H.%20Hudson%20Prospectus. pdf, made effective use of a cartoon in conveying her dissertation research.

21. Alex Branch, "When Is Sexting Just a Huge Mistake, and When Is It a Crime?" *Fort-Worth Star Telegram*, December 30, 2009, http://sexoffender research.blogspot.com/2009/12/when-is-sexting-just-huge-mistake-and.html.

22. Day, *New Digital Dating Behavior*, 77.

23. Deborah Feyerick and Sheila Steffen, " 'Sexting' Lands Teen on Sex Offender List," *CNN's American Morning*, April 7, 2009, http://articles.cnn.com/ 2009-04-07/justice/sexting.busts_1_phillip-alpert-offender-list-offender-registry ?_s=PM:CRIME.

24. Dionne Searcey, "A Lawyer, Some Teens and a Fight Over 'Sexting,' " *Wall Street Journal*, April 21, 2009, http://online.wsj.com/article/SB1240261155283 36397.html. Bill Albert of the National Campaign to Prevent Teen and

Unplanned Pregnancy characterized it as "an awfully heavy sword" (Alex Branch, "When Is Sexting Just a Huge Mistake?").

25. Mike Brunker, " 'Sexting' Surprise: Teens Face Child Porn Charges," *MSNBC.com*, January 15, 2009, http://www.msnbc.msn.com/id/28679588/ns/technology_and_science-tech_and_gadgets/t/sexting-surprise-teens-face-child-porn-charges/#.TmvSONRcCnk.

26. Meola, "Legislators Look Into How Va. Laws Cover 'Sexting.' " In other words, the law has not caught up with the technology. See Feyerick and Steffen, " 'Sexting' Lands Teen on Sex Offender List."

27. John A. Humbach, " 'Sexting' and the First Amendment," *Hastings Constitutional Law Quarterly* 37 (2010): 438.

28. *Texas v. Johnson*, 491 U.S. 397, 404 (1989).

29. *Johnson*, 491 U.S. at 404 (citing *Spence v. Washington*, 418 U.S. 405, 410–11 [1974]).

30. *Spence*, 418 U.S. at 410–11.

31. *Id.* at 411.

32. Feyerick and Steffen, " 'Sexting' Lands Teen on Sex Offender List."

Chapter 2

1. Amanda Lenhart, "Teens and Sexting," *Pew Internet and American Life Project* (Washington, DC: Pew Research Center, 2009), http://pewinternet.org/~/media//Files/Reports/2009/PIP_Teens_and_Sexting.pdf.

2. Ibid.

3. Ibid.

4. Ibid.

5. Amanda Lenhart, "Teens and Sexting," *Pew Internet and American Life Project* (Washington, DC: Pew Research Center, 2009), http://pewinternet.org/~/media//Files/Reports/2009/PIP_Teens_and_Sexting.pdf. In the study, a high schooler comparing sex to sexting stated that "Most people are too shy to have sex. Sexting is not as bad" (8).

6. Ibid.

7. Ibid.

8. Ibid.

9. Ibid.

10. Ibid.

11. Ibid.

12. Ibid.

13. "Sex and Tech: Results from a Survey of Teens and Young Adults" (Washington, DC: The National Campaign to Prevent Teen and Unplanned Pregnancy, 2008), http://www.thenationalcampaign.org/sextech/PDF/SexTech_Summary.pdf (hereafter referred to as the "National Campaign study").

14. Ibid.

15. Ibid.

16. Ibid. (internal quotation marks omitted).

17. "Facts," Text Ed (a study conducted by TRU Research on behalf of LG Mobile Comm, 2010), http://www.lg.com/us/mobile-phones/text-education/facts.jsp.

18. Charles Sophy, "The Download on Sexting," *TextEd*, http://www.lg.com/us/mobile-phones/text-education/articles/the-download-on-sexting.jsp.

19. Ibid.

20. Sameer Hinduja and Justin W. Patchin, "Sexting: A Brief Guide for Educators and Parents" (Cyberbullying Research Center, 2010), http://www.scribd.com/doc/58793571/Sexting-A-Brief-Guide-For-Educators-Parents-Hinduja-Patchin.

21. "MTV-Associated Press Poll Digital Abuse Survey" (Menlo Park, CA: Knowledge Networks, September 23, 2009), www.athinline.org/MTV-AP_Digital_Abuse_Study_Full.pdf. The adults were between the ages of 18 and 24 years old.

22. Ibid. Twelve percent of the study's respondents described their sexting of naked pictures or videos of themselves to others as "flirty," 10 percent described these sexts as "hot," 11 percent as "exciting," 10 percent as "fun," 9 percent as "entertaining," 5 percent as "funny," 4 percent as "loving," 5 percent as "passionate," 10 percent as "trusting," and 14 percent as "sexy" (18).

23. Lenhart, "Teens and Sexting." This study examined only sexting of pictures or videos, not sexting of sexually suggestive messages.

24. "Teen Online & Wireless Safety Survey" (Cox Communications/National Center for Missing and Exploited Children, 2009), http://www.cox.com/takecharge/safe_teens_2009/research.html.

25. Ibid., 33 (these numbers for sexting reflect both sending and receiving of sexts).

26. The study also found that time spent online every week by the teen sexter exceeds that of the average teenager. Eighty percent of teen sexters are also likely to have posted pictures of themselves on social networking sites or public blogs. Eighty-six percent of teen sexters have a social networking profile.

27. Ibid., 33.

28. Ibid., 12.

29. Ibid., 33.

30. Scott Michels, "Teen Charged with Sending Nude Pics of Herself," *ABCNews.Com*, October 10, 2008, http://abcnews.go.com/TheLaw/story?id=5995084&page=1&page=1; Russ Zimmer, "Hottinger: Law Didn't Anticipate Cell Phone Photo Case," *Newark Advocate*, October 8, 2008, http://www.newarkadvocate.com/apps/pbcs.dll/article?AID=/20081008/NEWS01/810080302&s=d.

31. Kim Zetter, "Teen Girl Faced Child Porn Charges for E-Mailing Nude Pictures of Herself to Friends—Update," *Wired Blog Network*, October 22, 2008, http://www.wired.com/threatlevel/2008/10/teen-girl-faces.

32. Zimmer, "Cell Phone Photo Case."

33. Ibid.

34. Zetter, "Teen Girl Faced Child Porn Charges."

35. Russ Zimmer, "Student to Admit to 1 Charge in Cell-Phone Nudity Case," *Newark Advocate*, November 11, 2008, http://www.newarkadvocate.com/article/20081111/NEWS01/811110350/Student-admit-1-charge-cell-phone-nudity-case.

36. Kelli Wynn, "Do U Know if UR Kids R Sexting?" *Dayton Daily News*, March 26, 2009, http://www.statesman.com/blogs/content/oh/story/news/local/neighbors/2009/03/26/ddn032609dzsextinside.html.

37. Zetter, "Teen Girl Faced Child Porn Charges."

38. Geoffrey Fattah, "Prosecutors Charge Teen with Felony in Nude Cell Phone Pictures Case," *Deseret News* (Utah), April 17, 2008, http://www.deseretnews.com/article/695271368/Prosecutors-charge-teen-with-felony-in-nude-cell-phone-pictures-case.html.

39. Dahlia Lithwick, "Teens, Nude Photos and the Law," *Daily Beast*, February 23, 2009, http://www.thedailybeast.com/newsweek/2009/02/13/teens-nude-photos-and-the-law.html.

40. Gigi Stone, " 'Sexting' Teens Can Go Too Far," *ABC News*, March 13, 2009, http://abcnews.go.com/Technology/WorldNews/sexting-teens/story?id=6456834.

41. "Cell Phone 'Sexting' Leads to Arrest of 2 Va. High School Students on Child Porn Charges," *TimesNews.Net*, March 11, 2009, http://www.timesnews.net/article.php?id=9012350.

42. Kristen Schorsch, "Sexting May Spell Court for Children: Kids Trading Photos Seen as Child Porn, Which Is a Felony," *Chicago Tribune*, January 29, 2010, http://articles.chicagotribune.com/2010-01-29/news/1001280853_1_sexting-cell-phones-nude.

43. Nancy Rommelmann, "Anatomy of a Child Pornographer," *Reason*, July 2009, http://reason.com/archives/2009/06/04/anatomy-of-a-child-pornographe.

44. Ibid.

45. Ibid.

46. Ibid.

47. Grant Schulte, "Iowa Court Upholds Sexting Conviction," *USA Today*, September 18, 2009, http://www.usatoday.com/news/nation/2009-09-18-iowa-sexting_N.htm.

48. "Davis County Seeing Influx of 'Sexting' Crimes," *ABC4.com*, March 29, 2010, http://www.abc4.com/news/local/story/Davis-County-seeing-influx-of-sexting-crimes/a6fb1z-SFkelvn-YWvWhoA.cspx.

49. Ibid.

50. The age of consent for other countries can be found on AVERT's website. See AVERT, Worldwide Ages of Consent, http://www.avert.org/age-of-consent.htm.

Chapter 3

1. 18 U.S.C.A. § 2251, et seq.

2. See generally 18 U.S.C.A. § 2251, et seq. (referring to "visual depictions").

3. 18 U.S.C.A. § 2251(a) (emphasis added).

4. 18 U.S.C.A. § 2251(e).

5. See 18 U.S.C.A. § 2251(a).

6. Pub.L. 108-21, Title V, § 501(2), Apr. 30, 2003, 117 Stat. 676 (cited in annotations to 18 U.S.C.A. § 2251).

7. See also Congressional Findings, Pub.L. 104-208, Div. A, Title I, § 101(a) [Title I, § 121, subsec. 1], Sept. 30, 1996, 110 Stat. 3009-26 (noting that "child pornography is often used by pedophiles and child sexual abusers to stimulate and whet their own sexual appetites, and as a model for sexual acting out with children; such use of child pornography can desensitize the viewer to the pathology of sexual abuse or exploitation of children, so that it can become acceptable to and even preferred by the viewer").

8. See, for example, Pub.L. 110-358, § 102, October 8, 2008, 122 Stat. 4001 (cited in annotations to 18 U.S.C.A. § 2251): "Congress finds the following: (1) Child pornography is estimated to be a multibillion dollar industry of global proportions, facilitated by the growth of the Internet; (2) data has shown that 83 percent of child pornography possessors had images of children younger than 12 years old, 39 percent had images of children younger than 6 years old, and 19 percent had images of children younger than 3 years old; (3) Child pornography is a permanent record of a child's abuse and the distribution of child pornography images revictimizes the child each time the image is viewed."

9. Pub.L. 110-358, § 102(1), October 8, 2008, 122 Stat. 4001.

10. See, for example, Pub.L. 109-248, Title V, § 501, July 27, 2006, 120 Stat. 623 (cited in annotations to 18 U.S.C.A. § 2251).

11. See, for example, Pub.L. 109-248, Title V, § 501(1)(B), July 27, 2006, 120 Stat. 623; Pub.L. 104-208, Div. A, Title I, § 101(a) [Title I, § 121, subsec. 1], September 30, 1996, 110 Stat. 3009-26 (cited in annotations to 18 U.S.C.A. § 2251).

12. Pub.L. 110-358, § 102(3). See also Pub.L. 104-208, Div. A, Title I, § 101(a) [Title I, § 121, subsec. 1], September 30, 1996, 110 Stat. 3009-26 (cited in annotations to 18 U.S.C.A. § 2251).

13. Like subsection 2251 of the CPPA, subsection 2252A comes under Chapter 110 of the U.S. Code titled "Sexual Exploitation and Other Abuse of Children," 18 U.S.C.A. § 2252A. For the federal sentencing guidelines and enhancements applicable to child pornography cases, see U.S. Sentencing Guidelines (USSG) Manual §2G2.2 (2010). For a great discussion of the background of USSG §2G2.2, see Jesse P. Basbaum, "Inequitable Sentencing for Possession of Child Pornography: A Failure to Distinguish Voyeurs from Pederasts," *Hastings Law Journal* 61 (2010): 1281–1305.

14. 18 U.S.C.A. § 2252A(a)(1) (2009). The history of the child pornography sentencing guidelines reveals that, rightly so, the sentencing enhancements for child pornography possession, distribution, and receipt have consistently increased over the years. See United States Sentencing Commission, *The History of the Child Pornography Guidelines* (Washington, DC: United States Sentencing Commission, 2009), http://www.ussc.gov/Research/Research_Projects/Sex_Offenses/20091030 _History_Child_Pornography_Guidelines.pdf. Over the past thirty years, Congress has established increasing mandatory sentencing minimums and issued directives to the United States Sentencing Commission designed to minimize the "incidence of downward departures" from sentencing requirements (6). See also Stephen F. Smith, "Proportionality and Federalization," *Virginia Law Review* 91, no. 4 (2005): 879–903. While the stringent sentencing requirements are justified for adults and others involved in child pornography, they are too stringent for consensual noncommercial teen sexting. Indeed, sentencing courts have recognized the guidelines as severe and have sought lower sentences, even for criminals who *should* be severely punished; there is no justice in subjecting consensual teen sexters to such severe penalties. "Sentencing courts have also expressed comment on the perceived severity of the child pornography guidelines through increased below-guidelines variance and downward departure rates" (United States Sentencing Commission, *History of the Child Pornography Guidelines*, 54). John Gabriel Woodlee notes that "district court judges are increasingly unwilling to follow the advisory Federal Sentencing Guidelines when imposing sentences for possession of child pornography. In 2009, they issued below-Guidelines sentences in 43 percent of the cases governed by Section 2G2.2, the Guideline for child pornography possession, compared with 15.9 percent of all cases. Many district judges have apparently concluded not only that Section 2G2.2 is too harsh, but also that it warrants little deference—that they should be free to favor their own judgment over the policy choices embodied in that Guideline" ("Congressional Manipulation of the Sentencing Guideline for Child Pornography Possession: An Argument for or against Deference?" *Duke Law Journal* 60 [2011]: 1015–1016). Woodlee further states, "Because the child pornography Guideline reflects extensive congressional intervention rather than the Commission's empirical analysis, many district courts have concluded that this Guideline warrants little or no deference" (1032). Yet in fiscal year 2009, in 1,496 cases, sentences were imposed over the sentencing guideline range (United States Sentencing Commission, *Final Quarterly Data Report* [Washington, DC: United States Sentencing Commission, 2009], 1, http://www.ussc.gov/Data_and_Statistics/Federal _Sentencing_Statistics/Quarterly_Sentencing_Updates/USSC_2009_Quarter_Report _Final.pdf).

15. 18 U.S.C.A. § 2252A(a)(2). For a description of how judges calculate sentences under the sentences guidelines, see Woodlee, "Congressional Manipulation of Sentencing Guideline": "Under the Guidelines, judges determine sentences using a grid called the Sentencing Table. Each box in the grid contains a range of

sentences; within each range, the longest sentence is 25 percent longer than the shortest. The appropriate box is selected by calculating the offense level, a y-axis variable that measures the severity of the offender's conduct, and the criminal history category, an x-axis variable that reflects the offender's conviction record. To calculate the offense level, a court identifies the base offense level, which is determined by the crime of conviction, and adjusts it based on specific offense characteristics prescribed for each offense and adjustments applicable to all offenses" (1020).

16. 18 U.S.C.A. § 2252A(b)(1).

17. 18 U.S.C.A. § 2251A(a)(5).

18. 18 U.S.C.A. § 2252A(b)(2).

19. 18 U.S.C.A. § 2257(a).

20. 18 U.S.C.A. § 2257(a)-(b).

21. See generally 18 U.S.C.A. § 2257.

22. 18 U.S.C.A. § 2257(a).

23. 18 U.S.C.A. § 2257(h)(2)(A)(i).

24. 18 U.S.C.A. § 2257(a)-(b).

25. 18 U.S.C.A. § 2257(h)(1).

26. 18 U.S.C.A. § 2256(2)(A)(i) (2006).

27. 18 U.S.C.A. § 2256(2)(A)(iii).

28. 18 U.S.C.A. § 2256(2)(A)(iv).

29. 18 U.S.C.A. § 2257(a) (emphasis added).

30. 18 U.S.C.A. § 2257(h)(3).

31. 636 F. Supp. 828 (S.D. Cal. 1986) aff'd sub nom, United States vs. Wiegand, 812 F.2d 1239 (9th Cir. 1987), cert. denied, 484 U.S. 856 (1987).

32. United States vs. Dost, 636 F. Supp. at 832.

33. For federal courts relying on or discussing the *Dost* factors see, for example, United States vs. Knox, 32 F.3d 733 (3d Cir. 1992); United States vs. Wolf, 890 F.2d 241 (10th Cir.1989); United States vs. Nolan, 818 F.2d 1015 (1st Cir.1987); United States vs. Arvin, 900 F.2d 1385 (9th Cir.1990), cert. denied, 498 U.S. 1024 (1991); United States vs. Rubio, 834 F.2d 442 (5th Cir.1987); United States vs. Frabizio, 459 F.3d 80 (1st Cir. 2006); United States vs. Villasenor, 236 F.3d 220 (5th Cir. 2000); United States vs. Overton, 573 F.3d 679 (9th Cir. 2009); United States vs. Horn, 187 F.3d 781 (8th Cir. 1999); United States vs. Rivera, 546 F.3d 245 (2d Cir. 2008). Some states have also relied on the Dost factors to interpret lasciviousness in their statute. See, for example, State vs. Saulsbury, 498 N.W.2d 338 (Neb. 1993).

34. *Dost*, 636 F. Supp. at 832.

35. Ibid.

36. Ibid. (internal quotation marks omitted).

37. United States vs. Kemmerling, 285 F.3d 644, 645-46 (8th Cir. 2002) (internal citations and quotation marks omitted).

38. 18 U.S.C.A. § 2257(b)(1),(3). The CPPA expects persons who produce "actual sexually explicit conduct" to be aware of any regulations that might be implemented to enforce the recordkeeping requirements. This is evident in the CPPA's further requirement that such persons "require the performer to provide such other indicia of his or her identity as may be prescribed by regulations."

39. 18 U.S.C.A. § 2257(b)(2),(3).

40. 18 U.S.C.A. § 2257(c) (emphasis added). While there is very little good news for student sexters in the CPPA, this section of the CPPA does provide the little there is, stating that "no information or evidence obtained from records required to be created or maintained by this section shall, except as provided in this section, directly or indirectly, be used as evidence against any person with respect to any violation of law" (18 U.S.C.A. § 2257[d][1]). However, any evidence or information from the records can, of course, be used to prosecute violations of the CPPA and to prosecute sexters for "furnishing of false information" (18 U.S.C.A. § 2257[d][2]).

41. 18 U.S.C.A. § 2257(e)(1).

42. 18 U.S.C.A. § 2257(f)(1).

43. 18 U.S.C.A. § 2257(i). Additionally, anyone who has been convicted of a crime that is punishable under the CPPA's recordkeeping requirements would face a maximum 10-year prison term and/or a fine.

44. For an excellent analysis of the sex offender registration laws and community notification requirements that could apply to minors convicted for the sex crimes set forth in Table 6, see Elizabeth Garfinkle, "Coming of Age in America: The Misapplication of Sex-Offender Registration and Community-Notification Laws to Juveniles," *California Law Review* 91, no. 1 (2003): 163 and Jacqueline Canlas-LaFlam, "Has Georgia Gone Too Far—Or Will Sex Offenders Have To?" *Hastings Constitutional Law Quarterly* 35, no. 2 (2008): 309–44. Garfinkle observes that "in a misguided effort to protect potential child and adolescent victims from the special crime of sexual assault, many states require registration and notification for child and adolescent offenders who have traditionally been viewed as needing special protections themselves" (163–64). See also page 204: "Community notification can deny a child the opportunity to grow up normally by subjecting him or her to false labels of sexual dysfunction, ostracism, reduced life chances, and harassment." For a thoughtful discussion of the history of sex offender notification statutes, see Joanna S. Markman, "Community Notification and the Perils of Mandatory Juvenile Sex Offender Registration: The Dangers Faced by Children and Their Families," *Seton Hall Legislative Journal* 32 (2008): 261, 275.

45. For a discussion of "prosecutorial overkill," see Clay Calvert et al., "Judicial Erosion of Protection for Defendants in Obscenity Prosecutions? When Courts Say, Literally, Enough Is Enough and when Internet Availability Does Not Mean Acceptance," *Harvard Journal of Sports & Entertainment Law* 1 (2010): 7. See also

Miller vs. Mitchell, 598 F.3d 139 (3d Cir. 2010), addressing a district's attorney's threat to prosecute minors for child pornography unless they participated in a prescribed education program. In one of the pictures that the district attorney was relying on for the child pornography prosecution in *Miller*, the girls could be seen "from the waist up wearing white, opaque bras" (144) while one of them was on the phone and the other flashed the peace sign. Even though the mother of one of the girls "protests that her daughter and friend were merely being 'goof balls' and were not naked, Skumanick [the district attorney] claimed the image constituted child pornography because they were posed 'provocatively.' He promised to prosecute them on felony child pornography charges if they did not agree to his conditions and attend the proposed program." In the district attorney's letter to the parents of the students, he stated in pertinent part:

> [Child's name] has been identified in a police investigation involving the possession and/or dissemination of child pornography. In consultation with the Victims Resource Center and the Juvenile Probation Department, we have developed a six to nine month program which focuses on education and counseling. If you[r] son/daughter successfully completes this program no charges will be filed and no record of his/her involvement will be maintained. We have scheduled a meeting with all of the identified juveniles and their parents to discuss the program in more detail and to answer your questions. Following the meeting you will be asked to participate in the program. Participation in the program is voluntary. Please note, however, charges will be filed against those that do not participate or those that do not successfully complete the program. (143–44)

> The U.S. Circuit Court of Appeals for the Third Circuit characterized the "choice" the district attorney presented the students as "Hobson's choice" and stated that "the Does would have to choose either to assert their constitutional rights and face a prosecution of Nancy Doe based not on probable cause but as punishment for exercising their constitutional rights, or forgo those rights and avoid prosecution. On the facts before us, this Hobson's Choice is unconstitutional" (155).

46. Ashcroft vs. American Civil Liberties Union, 542 U.S. 656, 660 (2004).

47. Reno vs. American Civil Liberties Union, 521 U.S. 844, 872 (1997).

48. For pending legislation on sexting, see "2011 Legislation Related to 'Sexting,'" National Conference of State Legislatures, January 23, 2012, http://www.ncsl.org/default.aspx?tabid=22127.

Chapter 4

1. Amy Adler, "All Porn All the Time," *New York University Review of Law & Social Change* 31 (2007): 695, 700.

2. Ibid. (internal quotation marks omitted).

3. Ibid., 701.

4. Ibid. (emphasis added).

5. Ibid., 703.

6. Ibid., 695, 705 (internal quotation marks omitted).

7. Shannon Creasy, "Defending Against a Charge of Obscenity in the Internet Age: How Google Searches Can Illuminate *Miller*'s 'Contemporary Community Standards,'" *Georgia State University Law Review* 16 (2010): 1029, 1035.

8. David A. J. Richards, "Free Speech and Obscenity Law: Toward a Moral Theory of the First Amendment," *University of Pennsylvania Law Review* 123 (1974): 76.

9. Queen vs. Hicklin (1868) L.R. 3 Q.B. 360, 368.

10. Shannon Creasy, "Defending Against a Charge of Obscenity," 1035 (internal quotation marks omitted).

11. Eric Handelman, "Obscenity and the Internet: Does the Current Obscenity Standard Provide Individuals with the Proper Constitutional Safeguards?" *Albany Law Review* 59 (1995): 718.

12. United States vs. Kennerley, 209 F. 119, 121 (S.D.N.Y. 1913).

13. Id.

14. Id.

15. Id.

16. *Kennerley*, 209 F. at 120.

17. Handelman, "Obscenity and the Internet," 719.

18. United States vs. One Book Entitled Ulysses by James Joyce, 72 F.2d 705, 707 (2d Cir. 1934) and United States vs. One Book Called "Ulysses," 5 F. Supp. 182 (S.D.N.Y. 1933).

19. Handelman, "Obscenity and the Internet," 719 (citing United States vs. One Book Called "Ulysses," 5 F. Supp. at 184–85).

20. *Kennerley*, 209 F. at 121.

21. 354 U.S. 476 (1957).

22. Id. at 481 ("Although this is the first time the question has been squarely presented to this Court, either under the First Amendment or under the Fourteenth Amendment, expressions found in numerous opinions indicate that this Court has always assumed that obscenity is not protected by the freedoms of speech and press").

23. Id. at 488–89 ("The early leading standard of obscenity allowed material to be judged merely by the effect of an isolated excerpt upon particularly susceptible persons. Regina vs. Hicklin, [1868] L.R. 3 Q.B. 360. Some American courts adopted this standard but later decisions have rejected it and substituted this test: whether to the average person, applying contemporary community standards, the dominant theme of the material taken as a whole appeals to prurient interest. The *Hicklin* test, judging obscenity by the effect of isolated passages upon the most

susceptible persons, might well encompass material legitimately treating with sex, and so it must be rejected as unconstitutionally restrictive of the freedoms of speech and press").

24. The federal statute stated:

> Every obscene, lewd, lascivious, or filthy book, pamphlet, picture, paper, letter, writing, print, or other publication of an indecent character; and . . . every written or printed card, letter, circular, book, pamphlet, advertisement, or notice of any kind giving information, directly or indirectly, where, or how, or from whom, or by what means any of such mentioned matters, articles, or things may be obtained or made, . . . whether sealed or unsealed . . . is declared to be nonmailable matter and shall not be conveyed in the mails or delivered from any post office or by any letter carrier. Whoever knowingly deposits for mailing or delivery, anything declared by this section to be nonmailable, or knowingly takes the same from the mails for the purpose of circulating or disposing thereof, or of aiding in the circulation or disposition thereof, shall be fined not more than $5,000 or imprisoned not more than five years, or both. (at 479, note 1)

25. The federal and state statutes were also challenged under the Due Process Clause; however, that is not a focus of our discussion. The state statute provided:

> Every person who wilfully and lewdly, either: 3. Writes, composes, stereotypes, prints, publishes, sells, distributes, keeps for sale, or exhibits any obscene or indecent writing, paper, or book; or designs, copies, draws, engraves, paints, or otherwise prepares any obscene or indecent picture or print; or molds, cuts, casts, or otherwise makes any obscene or indecent figure; or, 4. Writes, composes, or publishes any notice or advertisement of any such writing, paper, book, picture, print or figure; . . . is guilty of a misdemeanor. (at 480, note 2 [internal quotation marks omitted])

26. Duncan vs. Louisiana, 391 U.S. 145 (1968); Gitlow vs. New York, 268 U.S. 652 (1925). The Due Process Clause provides in pertinent part: "nor shall any State deprive any person of life, liberty, or property, without due process of law" (U.S. Const. Amend. XIV).

27. *Roth*, 354 U.S. at 481.

28. Id. at 485 (emphasis added).

29. Id. at 487–88 (quoting Thornhill vs. State of Alabama, 310 U.S. 88, 101–102 [1940]).

30. *Roth*, 354 U.S. at 481 (emphasis added). Justice Douglas characterized this reference to history as "fictionalized assertions of constitutional history" (A Book Named 'John Cleland's Memoirs of a Woman of Pleasure' vs. Attorney General

of Com. of Mass., 383 U.S. 413, 431 [1966] [Douglas, J., concurring]). Additionally, he pointed out that "neither reason nor history warrants exclusion of any particular class of expression from the protection of the First Amendment on nothing more than a judgment that it is utterly without merit" (at 430).

31. *Roth*, 354 U.S. at 481 (emphasis added).

32. Richards, "Free Speech and Obscenity Law," 76.

33. *Roth*, 354 U.S. at 485.

34. Id. at 484. In its rationale for the *Roth* decision, the Court cited the Model Penal Code's 1957 definition of obscenity: "A thing is obscene if, considered as a whole, its predominant appeal is to prurient interest, *i.e.*, a *shameful or morbid* interest in nudity, sex, or excretion, and if it goes *substantially beyond* customary limits of candor in description or representation of such matters" (at 488, note 20 [emphasis added], citing A.L.I., Model Penal Code, § 207.10[2] [Tentative Draft No. 6, 1957]). How could one argue that consensual sexting is a "shameful or morbid interest in nudity, sex, or excretion"? How could one argue that consensual sexting "goes substantially beyond customary limits of candor in description or representation of such matters," given that consensual sexting is normal adolescent behavior?

35. Id. at 484 (emphasis added).

36. Id. at 489.

37. Id. at 509 (Douglas, J., dissenting).

38. Id. at 509–10 (internal citations omitted).

39. 378 U.S. 184 (1964).

40. Id. at 195–96.

41. Id. at 197 (Stewart, J., concurring).

42. Id. (Stewart, J., concurring).

43. 383 U.S. 413 (1966).

44. *A Book Named 'John Cleland's Memoirs of a Woman of Pleasure,'* 383 U.S. at 418.

45. Id. (emphasis added).

46. Id. at 419. ("A book cannot be proscribed unless it is found to be utterly without redeeming social value. This is so even though the book is found to possess the requisite prurient appeal and to be patently offensive. Each of the three federal constitutional criteria is to be applied independently.")

47. Id. at 419–20 (emphasis added).

48. *A Book Named 'John Cleland's Memoirs of a Woman of Pleasure,'* 383 U.S. at 421.

49. Id. at 432, note 11 (Douglas, J., concurring). See also Smith vs. United States, 431 U.S. 291 (1977).

50. *A Book Named 'John Cleland's Memoirs of a Woman of Pleasure,'* 383 U.S. at 427–28 (Douglas, J., concurring).

51. Id. at 431–32 (Douglas, J., concurring) (internal citations omitted).

52. Id. at 431–32, note 10 (Douglas, J., concurring).

53. Id.

54. Miller vs. California, 413 U.S. 15, 21–22 (1973) (emphasis added) (citing *A Book Named 'John Cleland's Memoirs of a Woman of Pleasure,'* 383 U.S. at 459 [Harlan, J., dissenting]).

55. 390 U.S. 629 (1968).

56. Id. at 631.

57. Id. at 632.

58. *Ginsberg,* 390 U.S. at 632.

59. Id. at 633.

60. Id. at 636.

61. Id.

62. *Ginsberg,* 390 U.S. at 637, note 5 (emphasis added). See also Id. at 640.

63. Id. at 639–41.

64. *Ginsberg,* 390 U.S. at 640–41 (emphasis added) (internal quotation marks omitted).

65. Id. at 641.

66. Id. (emphasis added). Despite this telling statement, the Court immediately and summarily stated: "But obscenity is not protected expression and may be suppressed without a showing of the circumstances which lie behind the phrase 'clear and present danger' in its application to protected speech. To sustain state power to exclude material defined as obscenity by § 484-h requires only that we be able to say that it was not irrational for the legislature to find that exposure to material condemned by the statute is harmful to minors" (internal citations omitted). The Court added: "To be sure, there is no lack of 'studies' which purport to demonstrate that obscenity is or is not 'a basic factor in impairing the ethical and moral development of youth and a clear and present danger to the people of the state.' But the growing consensus of commentators is that 'while these studies all agree that a causal link has not been demonstrated, they are equally agreed that a causal link has not been disproved either.' We do not demand of legislatures 'scientifically certain criteria of legislation' " (Id. at 641–43).

67. Id. at 640 (internal citations omitted).

68. *Ginsberg,* 390 U.S. at 640 (emphasis added).

69. Id. at 674 (Fortas, J., dissenting).

70. 394 U.S. 557 (1969).

71. Id. at 558 (emphasis added).

72. Id. at 559–60.

73. Id. at 560–61.

74. *Stanley,* 394 U.S. at 560 (emphasis added).

75. Id. at 560–61 (emphasis added).

76. Id. at 563 (emphasis added).

77. Id. at 563–64 (emphasis added; internal citations omitted).

78. Id. at 563.

79. Id. at 564 (emphasis added; internal citations omitted).

80. Id. at 564. ("For also fundamental is the right to be free, except in very limited circumstances, from unwanted governmental intrusions into one's privacy.") Indeed, the Court characterized the state of Georgia's prosecution of the appellant for the mere possession of the films as "a drastic invasion of personal liberties guaranteed by the First and Fourteenth Amendments" (Id. at 565).

81. Id. at 565 (emphasis added).

82. Id.

83. Id. at 565–66 (emphasis added) (internal citations omitted).

84. Id. at 566.

85. Id.

86. Id.

87. Id. at 566–67.

88. United States vs. Playboy Entertainment Group, Inc., 529 U.S. 803, 816–17, 823–24 (2000).

89. 413 U.S. 15 (1973).

90. Id. at 18.

91. Id. at 16 (internal quotation marks omitted). The statutory section that formed the basis of the conviction stated: "Sending or bringing into state for sale or distribution; printing, exhibiting, distributing or possessing within state: (a) Every person who knowingly: sends or causes to be sent, or brings or causes to be brought, into this state for sale or distribution, or in this state prepares, publishes, prints, exhibits, distributes, or offers to distribute, or has in his possession with intent to distribute or to exhibit or offer to distribute, any obscene matter is guilty of a misdemeanor" (Id. at 17, note 1).

92. Id. at 18.

93. Id.

94. *Miller*, 413 U.S. at 18 (emphasis added).

95. Id. at 16 (internal quotation marks omitted).

96. Id. at 18–19.

97. Id. at 18, note 2 (emphasis added).

98. Id.

99. Id. The Court also pointed out that obscene pornographic material "forms a subgroup of all 'obscene' expression, but not the whole, at least as the word 'obscene' is now used in our language."

100. See id. at 19–20 ("It is in this context that we are called on to define the standards which must be used to identify obscene material that a State may regulate without infringing on the First Amendment as applicable to the States through the Fourteenth Amendment").

101. Id. at 22. See also id. at 29 ("It is certainly true that the absence, since *Roth*, of a single majority view of this Court as to proper standards for testing obscenity

has placed a strain on both state and federal courts. But today, for the first time since *Roth* was decided in 1957, a majority of this Court has agreed on concrete guidelines to isolate 'hard core' pornography from expression protected by the First Amendment").

102. Id. (internal quotation marks omitted) (citing Interstate Circuit, Inc. vs. Dallas, 390 U.S. 676, 704–05 [1968] [Harlan, J., concurring and dissenting]).

103. Id. at 22.

104. Ontario vs. Quon, 130 S.Ct. 2619, 2629 (2010).

105. Id. at 2629.

106. *Miller*, 413 U.S. at 23–24 (emphasis added).

107. Id. at 24 (internal quotation marks omitted).

108. Id. at 24.

109. Id. at 33–34.

110. *Quon*, 130 S.Ct. at 2629.

111. Id.

112. *Miller*, 413 U.S. at 40–41 (Douglas, J., dissenting). In his critique of the majority opinion in *Miller*, Justice Douglas pointed out that the word "obscenity" does not appear in the Constitution. ("The difficulty is that we do not deal with constitutional terms, since 'obscenity' is not mentioned in the Constitution or Bill of Rights. And the First Amendment makes no such exception from 'the press' which it undertakes to protect nor, as I have said on other occasions, is an exception necessarily implied, for there was no recognized exception to the free press at the time the Bill of Rights was adopted which treated 'obscene' publications differently from other types of papers, magazines, and books. So there are no constitutional guidelines for deciding what is and what is not 'obscene.' The Court is at large because we deal with tastes and standards of literature.") Similarly, sexting does not appear in the Constitution.

113. Smith vs. United States, 431 U.S. 291, 319–21 (1977) (Stevens, J., dissenting).

114. Cohen vs. California, 403 U.S. 15 (1971).

115. Id. at 25.

116. *Miller*, 413 U.S. at 24.

117. Brockett vs. Spokane Arcades, Inc., 472 U.S. 491, 504 (1985).

118. *Miller*, 413 U.S. at 24.

119. Id.

120. Id.

121. Id. at 44–45 (Douglas, J., dissenting).

122. Id. at 34 (emphasis added) (citing Breard vs. Alexandria, 341 U.S. 622, 645 [1951]).

123. Id.

124. Id. at 34–35 (emphasis added; internal citations omitted).

125. Id. at 24.

126. Edward J. Eberle, "Art as Speech," *University of Pennsylvania Journal of Law & Social Change* 11 (2007–08): 1.

127. Ibid.

128. Ibid.

129. Ibid.

130. Ibid.

131. Ibid.

132. *Miller*, 413 U.S. at 40 (Douglas, J., dissenting) (internal citations omitted).

133. H. Franklin Robbins, Jr. and Steven G. Mason, "The Law of Obscenity—or Absurdity?" *St. Thomas Law Review* 15 (2003): 531.

134. Ibid.

135. *Miller*, 413 U.S. at 36.

136. Id. at 46 (Douglas, J., dissenting).

137. 413 U.S. 49 (1973).

138. Id. at 51.

139. Id. at 73 (Brennan, J., dissenting)

140. Id. at 84 (Brennan, J., dissenting) (internal citations omitted).

141. 418 U.S. 153 (1974).

142. Id. (emphasis added).

143. Id.

144. *Jenkins*, 418 U.S. at 161.

145. Id.

146. 422 U.S. 205 (1975).

147. Id. at 206. The ordinance provided:

Drive-In Theaters, Films Visible From Public Streets or Public Places. It shall be unlawful and it is hereby declared a public nuisance for any ticket seller, ticket taker, usher, motion picture projection machine operator, manager, owner, or any other person connected with or employed by any drive-in theater in the City to exhibit, or aid or assist in exhibiting, any motion picture, slide, or other exhibit in which the human male or female bare buttocks, human female bare breasts, or human bare public areas are shown, if such motion picture, slide, or other exhibit is visible from any public street or public place. Violation of this section shall be punishable as a Class C offense. (Id. at 206–07)

148. Id. (internal quotation marks omitted).

149. Id. at 212.

150. Id. at 212–13.

151. *Erznoznik*, 422 U.S. at 213.

152. Id. at 213–14 (emphasis added; internal citations omitted). The Court also noted that "in *Miller v. California*, supra, we abandoned the *Roth-Memoirs* test for

judging obscenity with respect to adults. We have not had occasion to decide what effect *Miller* will have on the *Ginsberg* formulation. It is clear, however, that under any test of obscenity as to minors not all nudity would be proscribed" (Id. at 213, note 10).

153. 535 U.S. 234 (2002).

154. Id. at 240 (emphasis added).

Chapter 5

1. Amy Adler, "Inverting the First Amendment," *University of Pennsylvania Law Review* 149 (2001): 922. See also pages 922–23:

> The First Amendment as we understand it was born amid grave concern for our national security. The nation was at war. The Supreme Court's first significant free speech cases arose in prosecutions under the 1917 Espionage Act for agitation against the war and the draft. Those cases begot the fabled "clear and present danger" test; they also eventually gave us the ringing dissents of Holmes and Brandeis that still inform our "liberal nostalgia" for that era. When we think of the First Amendment, we think of this history: battles over subversive advocacy, and later, socialist or communist ideology. Yet, as John Hart Ely points out, our nostalgia for that period in the Court's history ignores the harsh results of the cases. For example, all of the defendants in the first three "clear and present danger" cases ended up in prison for ten years "for quite tame and ineffectual expression." Ely recounts a history of free speech jurisprudence, understood through the subversive advocacy cases, in which the Justices acquiesced to the vexing political pressures of this century, and in particular to McCarthyism. In his view, our commitment to the First Amendment fluctuates in response to cultural anxiety. Thus, the greatest threats to free speech, and the most crucial need for First Amendment vigilance, arise in times of social crisis.

2. Ibid., 922.

3. Ibid., 925.

4. 458 U.S. 747 (1982).

5. Id. at 752.

6. *Ferber*, 458 U.S. at 752.

7. Id. at 751.

8. Id.

9. Id.

10. Id.

11. Id. (internal quotation marks omitted).

12. Id. at 753.

13. Id. at 768.

14. Id. at 756 (emphasis added).

15. Id. at 756–58.

16. Id.at 759–60.

17. Id. at 761–62.

18. Id. at 762–63.

19. Id. at 763–64.

20. Id. at 756–57 (emphasis added; internal quotation marks omitted) (citing Globe Newspaper Co. vs. Superior Court, 457 U.S. 596, 607 [1982]).

21. Id. at 757 (citing Prince vs. Massachusetts, 321 U.S. 158, 168 [1944]).

22. Id.

23. Id. (emphasis added).

24. Id. at 758.

25. Id. at 757, note 8 (emphasis added).

26. Id. at 759.

27. Id. at 760 (emphasis added).

28. Id.

29. Id. at 776 (Brennan, J., concurring) (internal quotation marks omitted).

30. Id. at 760, note 10.

31. Id. at 761.

32. Id. at 761–62.

33. Id.

34. Ashcroft vs. Free Speech Coalition, 535 U.S. 234, 254 (2002).

35. 906 N.E.2d 212, 213 (Ind. Ct. App. 2009).

36. Id. at 223 (internal citations and quotation marks omitted).

37. Id.

38. 758 A.2d 301 (Vt. 2000).

39. Id. at 302 ("The two had been friends, but had never had sexual contact with each other prior to the incident in question. One night in October 1995, while G. T. and M. N. were watching a television movie in M. N.'s house, G. T. began kissing M. N. on the mouth. G. T. then pulled M. N.'s legs out straight, pulled her shorts down, pulled his pants down, and got on top of her. He continued kissing her with his hands on her shoulders. M. N., who had never previously had intercourse, felt what she believed was G. T.'s penis in her vagina. G. T. asked if it hurt, but did not stop when M. N. said it hurt. Although she was not afraid of him, M. N. was not sure what G. T. would have done if she had pushed him off of her").

40. Id. at 302–9.

41. Id. at 305.

42. Id. at 303. Further, under the state's law, specified persons must report the acts to the Department of Social and Rehabilitation Services or face prosecution (id. at 305). The Court called attention to the "the irony of maintaining

confidential the fact and detail of a juvenile delinquency adjudication, while placing and disseminating information about the same juvenile in the child abuse
registry." The Court noted that in this case, "the tension goes beyond irony."

43. *In re G. T.*, 758 A.2d at 306.

44. Id.

45. Id. at 306–7 (citing Sanford H. Kadish, "Legal Norm and Discretion in the
Police and Sentencing Processes," *Harvard Law Review* 75 [1962]: 909–11).

46. Id. at 309.

47. 165 P.3d 1206 (Utah 2007).

48. Id. at 1209 (internal quotation marks omitted) (citing Savage vs. Utah
Youth Village, 104 P.3d 1242 [Utah 2004]). See also State ex rel. Z.C., 165 P.3d
at 1212 note 9 ("The primary fail-safe against the absurd application of criminal
law is the wise employment of prosecutorial discretion, a quality that is starkly
absent in this case. While the State makes no attempt to defend the prosecution's
charging decision, it suggests that the particular offense selected by the prosecutor
as the basis for the delinquency petition is not significant because a juvenile delinquency adjudication is not a criminal conviction, but merely a means to bring
the juvenile within the guiding supervision of the juvenile court. If this is
truly the case, it begs the question of why the prosecutor could not have accomplished the intended result by basing the delinquency petition on a victimless
offense that more accurately fits the conduct at issue").

49. Id. at 1207. We do not in any way advocate sexual relations between 13- and
12-year-olds. We are simply iterating the facts of the case.

50. Id.

51. State ex rel. Z.C., 165 P.3d at 1208. For further explanation of the absurd
results canon of statutory interpretation, see id. at 1210 (internal quotation marks
and citations omitted):

> In one of its earliest applications of the absurd result doctrine, the Supreme
> Court was called upon to interpret a federal statute that made it a crime to
> knowingly and willfully obstruct or retard the passage of the mail. The stat-
> ute was applied to a sheriff and his posse who had boarded a steamboat
> and executed an arrest warrant for murder against a mail carrier who was
> in the process of transporting the mail. The Court held that in order to avoid
> such an absurd result, it is presumed that the legislature intended exceptions
> to its language. As such, general terms should be so limited in their applica-
> tion as not to lead to injustice, oppression, or an absurd consequence. The
> Court supported this proposition with two frequently cited historical illustra-
> tions of the principle: The common sense of man approves the judgment
> mentioned by Puffendorf, that the Bolognian law which enacted, that who-
> ever drew blood in the streets should be punished with the utmost severity,
> did not extend to the surgeon who opened the vein of a person that fell down

in the street in a fit. The same common sense accepts the ruling, cited by Plowden, that the statute of 1st Edward II, which enacts that a prisoner who breaks prison shall be guilty of felony, does not extend to a prisoner who breaks out when the prison is on fire—for he is not to be hanged because he would not stay to be burnt. And we think that a like common sense will sanction the ruling we make, that the act of Congress which punishes the obstruction or retarding of the passage of the mail, or of its carrier, does not apply to a case of temporary detention of the mail caused by the arrest of the carrier upon an indictment for murder.

52. Id. at 1211.

53. Id.

54. Id. at 1212.

55. Id. at 1212, note 8.

56. Id. at 1213.

57. Id. See also id. at 1213, note 10 ("Our analysis would likewise apply to all cases similar to Z. C.'s even if the State elected to charge only one of the minors involved. We hold that the application of Utah Code section 76–5–404.1 is absurd where no true perpetrator or victim exists. And the State may not create a perpetrator and a victim through selective prosecution").

58. *Ferber*, 458 U.S. at 762.

59. Id. at 776–77 (Brennan, J., concurring) (internal quotation marks omitted).

60. Id. at 762.

61. Id. at 763.

62. Id.

63. Id. at 763–64 (emphasis added).

64. Id. at 764.

65. Id. (emphasis added).

66. Id.

67. Id. at 765.

68. Id. at 764. See also id. at 761 (rejecting the *Miller* test for child pornography cases).

69. Id. at 773.

70. See id. at 775 (O'Connor, J., concurring) ("It is quite possible that New York's statute is overbroad because it bans depictions that do not actually threaten the harms identified by the Court. For example, clinical pictures of adolescent sexuality, such as those that might appear in medical textbooks, might not involve the type of sexual exploitation and abuse targeted by New York's statute. Nor might such depictions feed the poisonous 'kiddie porn' market that New York and other States have attempted to regulate. Similarly, pictures of children engaged in rites widely approved by their cultures, such as those that might appear in issues of the *National Geographic*, might not trigger the compelling interests identified by the Court").

71. 130 S.Ct. 1577 (2010).

72. Id. at 1582.

73. Id. at 1591 (internal quotations marks and citations omitted).

74. Id.

75. *Ferber*, 458 U.S. at 778 (Stevens, J., concurring).

76. 495 U.S. 103 (1990).

77. Id. at 107.

78. Id. at 106–07 (internal quotations marks omitted).

79. Id. at 109.

80. Id. (emphasis added).

81. Id. at 110.

82. Id. at 111 (emphasis added).

83. *Stevens*, 130 S.Ct. 1577, 1599 (2010) (Alito, J., dissenting) (internal citations and quotation marks omitted).

84. *Osborne*, 495 U.S. at 111.

85. Id. at 111, note 7.

86. Ashcroft vs. Free Speech Coalition, 535 U.S. 234 (2002) (internal citations omitted) (citing Kingsley International Pictures Corporation vs. Regents of University of New York, 360 U.S. 684, 689 [1959]).

87. Id.

88. Id. at 114. See also id. at 112, note 9: Such "innocuous" viewing or possession which the Court highlighted under the Ohio statute in the case included "material or performance ... sold, disseminated, displayed, possessed, controlled, brought or caused to be brought into this state, or presented for a bona fide artistic, medical, scientific, educational, religious, governmental, judicial, or other proper purpose, by or to a physician, psychologist, sociologist, scientist, teacher, person pursuing bona fide studies or research, librarian, clergyman, prosecutor, judge, or other person having a proper interest in the material or performance." The Court noted that under the Ohio law, "innocuous" viewing or possession could arise if "the person knows that the parents, guardian, or custodian has consented in writing to the photographing or use of the minor in a state of nudity and to the manner in which the material or performance is used or transferred." Additionally, the Court observed the following about the Ohio statute: "It is true that, despite the statutory exceptions, one might imagine circumstances in which the statute, by its terms, criminalizes constitutionally protected conduct. If, for example, a parent gave a family friend a picture of the parent's infant taken while the infant was unclothed, the statute would apply. But, given the broad statutory exceptions and the prevalence of child pornography, it is far from clear that the instances where the statute applies to constitutionally protected conduct are significant enough to warrant a finding that the statute is overbroad."

89. Id. at 111, note 11.

90. 535 U.S. 234 (2002).

91. Id. at 234 (syllabus).

92. Id. at 246.

93. Id. at 247.

94. Id.

95. Id.

96. *Free Speech Coalition*, 535 U.S. at 247.

97. Id. (internal citation omitted).

98. Id. at 247–48 (internal citations omitted).

99. Id. at 250 (emphasis added; internal citations omitted).

100. Id.

101. Id.

102. Id. (internal citations omitted).

103. Id. at 250–51 (emphasis added; internal citations omitted). Additionally, in 2010, in United States vs. Stevens, 130 S.Ct. 1577 (2010), the U.S. Supreme Court reaffirmed the fact that *Ferber* dealt with abuse and had a commercial undertone:

> When we have identified categories of speech as fully outside the protection of the First Amendment, it has not been on the basis of a simple cost-benefit analysis. In *Ferber*, for example, we classified child pornography as such a category. We noted that the State of New York had a compelling interest in protecting children from abuse, and that the value of using children in these works (as opposed to simulated conduct or adult actors) was de minimis. But our decision did not rest on this "balance of competing interests" alone. We made clear that *Ferber* presented a special case: The market for child pornography was "intrinsically related" to the underlying abuse, and was therefore "an integral part of the production of such materials, an activity illegal throughout the Nation." As we noted, "It rarely has been suggested that the constitutional freedom for speech and press extends its immunity to speech or writing used as an integral part of conduct in violation of a valid criminal statute." *Ferber* thus grounded its analysis in a previously recognized, long-established category of unprotected speech, and our subsequent decisions have shared this understanding. *See* Osborne v. Ohio, 495 U.S. 103, 110, 110 S.Ct. 1691, 109 L.Ed.2d 98 (1990) (describing *Ferber* as finding "persuasive" the argument that the advertising and sale of child pornography was "an integral part" of its unlawful production [internal quotation marks omitted]); Ashcroft vs. Free Speech Coalition, 535 U.S. 234, 249–250, 122 S.Ct. 1389, 152 L.Ed.2d 403 (2002) (noting that distribution and sale "were intrinsically related to the sexual abuse of children," giving the speech at issue "a proximate link to the crime from which it came." Our decisions in Ferber and other cases cannot be taken as establishing a freewheeling authority to declare new categories of speech outside the scope of the First

Amendment. (*Stevens*, 130 S.Ct. at 1586 [internal citations and quotation marks omitted]).

104. *Free Speech Coalition*, 535 U.S. at 251–52 (emphasis added; internal citations omitted).

105. Id. at 253.

106. Id. (internal citations and quotation marks omitted) (citing Hess vs. Indiana, 414 U.S. 105, 108 [1973] [per curiam]).

107. Id. at 253–54.

108. Id. at 255 (citing Broadrick vs. Oklahoma, 413 U.S. 601, 612 [1973]).

Chapter 6

1. Amanda Lenhart, Rich Ling, Scott Campbell, and Kristen Purcell, "Teens and Mobile Phones," Pew Internet and American Life Project (Washington, DC: Pew Research Center, 2010), http://pewinternet.org/Reports/2010/Teens-and -Mobile-Phones/Summary-of-findings.aspx.

2. Ibid. (emphasis added).

3. Ibid. (internal quotation marks omitted).

4. Ibid.

5. Ibid.

6. Tinker vs. Des Moines Independent Community School District, 393 U.S. 503, 506 (1969).

7. Lenhart et al., "Teens and Mobile Phones."

8. Ibid. (emphasis added).

9. Ibid.

10. Ibid. ("Perhaps heartening to administrators is the finding that about a third of teens text frequently in class [31%], another third of teens [33%] text in class occasionally and a third [36%] say they never send text messages during class. These findings mostly hold regardless of the regulatory environment, although there are exceptions in the extremes of behavior").

11. *Tinker*, 393 U.S.

12. Id. at 508.

13. Id. at 508–09 (emphasis added; internal citations omitted).

14. Id. at 507 (citing West Virginia State Board of Education vs. Barnette, 319 U.S. 624, 637 [1943]).

15. Id. at 509 (emphasis added).

16. Id. at 511.

17. Id. at 509. (Additionally, "an official memorandum prepared after the suspension that listed the reasons for the ban on wearing the armbands made no reference to the anticipation of such disruption.")

18. Id. at 508.

19. Id. at 510, 514. See id. at 510 ("In the present case, the District Court made no such finding, and our independent examination of the record fails to yield evidence that the school authorities had reason to anticipate that the wearing of the armbands would substantially interfere with the work of the school or impinge upon the rights of other students").

20. Id.

21. Id. at 510–11.

22. Id. at 511.

23. Id. at 511 (emphasis added). Justice Thomas articulates this paternalistic attitude toward students very well. See, for example, Morse vs. Frederick, 551 U.S. 393, 410–22 (2007) (Thomas, J., concurring).

24. Id. at 511.

25. Id. (emphasis added).

26. Id. (emphasis added; internal quotation marks omitted) (citing Burnside vs. Byars, 363 F.2d 744, 749 [5th Cir. 1966]).

27. Id. at 512 (citing Meyer vs. Nebraska, 262 U.S. 390, 402 [1923]).

28. Id. (internal quotation marks omitted).

29. Id. (internal quotation marks omitted).

30. Id. (internal quotation marks omitted) (citing Shelton vs. Tucker, 364 U.S. 479, 487 [1960]).

31. Id. (internal quotation marks omitted).

32. Id. (internal quotation marks omitted).

33. Id. at 506.

34. Id. at 512.

35. Id. (emphasis added).

36. Id.

37. Id. at 512–13 (emphasis added; internal quotation marks omitted) (citing *Burnside*, 363 F.2d at 749).

38. Id. at 513.

39. 478 U.S. 675 (1986).

40. Id. at 677.

41. Id. The Court confirmed this in Hazelwood School District vs. Kuhlmeier, 484 U.S. 260, 272, note 4 (1988) ("The decision in Fraser rested on the 'vulgar,' 'lewd,' and 'plainly offensive' character of a speech delivered at an official school assembly").

42. Id. at 678. Justice Stevens described the student as "an outstanding young man with a fine academic record" (id. at 692 [Stevens, J., dissenting]).

43. Id. at 687 (Brennan, J., concurring) (internal quotation marks omitted). In his concurrence, Justice Brennan observed that if the student gave "the same speech outside of the school environment, he could not have been penalized simply because government officials considered his language to be inappropriate" (id. at 688 [Brennan, J., concurring]). Justice Stevens expressed his thoughts on

the offensiveness of the speech by comparing it to another colorful speech: " 'Frankly, my dear, I don't give a damn.' When I was a high school student, the use of those words in a public forum shocked the Nation. Today Clark Gable's four-letter expletive is less offensive than it was then" (id. at 691 [Stevens, J., dissenting]).

44. Id. at 681.

45. *Fraser*, 478 U.S. at 681 (emphasis added).

46. Id. at 683.

47. Id. See id. at 689, note 2 (Brennan, J., concurring) (internal citations omitted) for Justice Brennan's reaction to this characterization by the Court ("The Court speculates that the speech was 'insulting' to female students, and 'seriously damaging' to 14-year-olds, so that school officials could legitimately suppress such expression in order to protect these groups. There is no evidence in the record that any students, male or female, found the speech 'insulting.' And while it was not unreasonable for school officials to conclude that respondent's remarks were inappropriate for a school-sponsored assembly, the language respondent used does not even approach the sexually explicit speech regulated in Ginsberg v. New York, 390 U.S. 629, 88 S.Ct. 1274, 20 L.Ed.2d 195 [1968], or the indecent speech banned in FCC v. Pacifica Foundation, 438 U.S. 726, 98 S.Ct. 3026, 57 L.Ed.2d 1073 [1978]. Indeed, to my mind, respondent's speech was no more 'obscene,' 'lewd,' or 'sexually explicit' than the bulk of programs currently appearing on prime time television or in the local cinema. Thus, I disagree with the Court's suggestion that school officials could punish respondent's speech out of a need to protect younger students").

48. Id. at 688 (Brennan, J., concurring).

49. Id.

50. Id. at 689, note 2 (Brennan, J., concurring).

51. Id. at 683.

52. Id. at 684.

53. Id.

54. Id. at 685.

55. Id. at 692 (Stevens, J., dissenting).

56. Id. at 692, note 2 (Stevens, J., dissenting) (citing Bender vs. Williamsport Area School District, 475 U.S. 534 [1986] [dissenting opinions]). Additionally, Justice Stevens pointed out the lack of "evidence in the record indicating that any students found the speech to be offensive" (citing Fraser vs. Bethel School District No. 403, 755 F.2d 1356, 1361, note 4 [9th Cir. 1985]).

57. Id.

58. Id. at 696 (Stevens, J., dissenting) (internal citations and quotation marks omitted).

59. 484 U.S. 260 (1988).

60. Id. at 262.

61. Id. at 263.

62. Id.

63. Id. at 267 (internal citations omitted) (citing Perry Education Association vs. Perry Local Educators' Association, 460 U.S. 37, 46, note 7, 47 [1983]).

64. Id.

65. Id.

66. Id.

67. Id.

68. Id. at 273.

69. Id. at 279–80 (Brennan, J., dissenting) (internal citations and quotation marks omitted).

70. Id. at 280 (Brennan, J., dissenting) (internal citations and quotation marks omitted).

71. Id. at 286–87 (Brennan, J., dissenting) (internal citations and quotation marks omitted).

72. 551 U.S. 393 (2007).

73. Id. at 397.

74. Id. at 396.

75. Id. at 397.

76. Id. at 396.

77. Id. at 401.

78. Id. In this case, the Court stated that the disciplined student "cannot stand in the midst of his fellow students, during school hours, at a school-sanctioned activity and claim he is not at school" (internal quotation marks omitted).

79. Id. at 397, 401.

80. Id. at 401.

81. Id. at 400–1.

82. Id. at 401 (emphasis added).

83. Id. at 405.

84. Id.

85. Id. at 403 (emphasis added).

86. Id. at 402.

87. Id. at 407–8.

88. Id. at 408–9.

89. Id. at 425 (Alito, J., concurring) (emphasis added).

90. Id. (emphasis added).

91. Id.

92. Id. at 423 (Alito, J., concurring) (internal citations omitted).

93. Id. at 418 (Thomas, J., concurring).

94. Id. at 422 (Thomas, J., concurring).

95. Thomas vs. Granville Central School District, 607 F.2d 1043, 1050 (2d Cir. 1979).

96. *Fraser*, 478 U.S. at 688 (Brennan, J., concurring) (emphasis added).

97. Id. at 689 (Brennan, J., concurring).

98. *Thomas*, 607 F.2d at 1043, 1053.

99. See id. at 1051 ("We may not permit school administrators to seek approval of the community-at-large by punishing students for expression that took place off school property. Nor may courts endorse such punishment because the populace would approve. The First Amendment will not abide the additional chill on protected expression that would inevitably emanate from such a practice. Indeed, experience teaches that future communications would be inhibited regardless of the intentions of well meaning school officials").

100. Emmett vs. Kent School District No. 415, 92 F.Supp.2d 1088, 1090 (W.D.Wash. 2000) (internal quotation marks omitted) (citing Burch vs. Barker, 861 F.2d 1149 [9th Cir.1988]).

101. 30 F.Supp.2d 1175 (E.D. Mo. 1998).

102. Id. at 1177.

103. Id.

104. Id. at 1178, 1180 (emphasis added).

105. *Beussink*, 30 F.Supp.2d at 1179 (internal quotation marks omitted).

106. Id. at 1181.

107. Id. at 1182.

108. Id.

109. Id. at 1180 (citing Elrod vs. Burns, 427 U.S. 347, 373 [1976] [plurality opinion]).

110. Id. at 1182.

111. 92 F.Supp.2d 1088 (W.D. Wash. 2000).

112. Id. at 1089.

113. Id. at 1089.

114. Id. (internal quotation marks omitted).

115. Id. at 1090.

116. See, for example, Chandler vs. McMinnville School District, 978 F.2d 524 (9th Cir. 1992) (pointing out the pre-*Morse* approach of many courts).

117. Killion vs. Franklin Regional School District, 136 F.Supp.2d 446, 455 (W.D. Pa. 2001).

118. Doninger vs. Niehoff, 527 F.3d 41, 49 (2d Cir. 2008). See also Saxe vs. State College Area School District, 240 F.3d 200, 213 (3d Cir. 2001) ("According to *Fraser*, then, there is no First Amendment protection for 'lewd,' 'vulgar,' 'indecent,' and 'plainly offensive' speech in school"); and Layshock ex rel. Layshock vs. Hermitage School District, 650 F.3d 205, 212–19 (3d Cir. 2011) for the U.S. Third Circuit Court of Appeals' limitation of Fraser to on-campus student speech.

119. *Layshock ex rel. Layshock*, 650 F.3d at 219.

120. *Thomas*, 607 F.2d at 1044–45.

121. *Layshock ex rel. Layshock*, 650 F.3d at 207.

122. *Thomas*, 607 F.2d at 1053, note 18 (internal citation omitted).

123. Id. at 1057.

124. Id.

125. Peter E. Cumming, "Children's Rights, Voices, Technology, Sexuality" (Roundtable on Youth, Sexuality, Technology, Congress of the Humanities and Social Sciences 2009, Carleton University, Ottawa, May 26, 2009), 7–8 (internal citation and quotation marks omitted), http://www.yorku.ca/cummingp/documents/TeenSextingbyPeterCummingMay262009.pdf.

126. *Kuhlmeier*, 484 U.S. at 286 (Brennan, J., dissenting) (internal citations and quotation marks omitted).

127. *Morse*, 551 U.S. at 424 (Alito, J., concurring).

128. Id.

129. Id.

130. Cooper vs. McJunkin, 4 Ind. 290, 291 (Ind. 1853).

Chapter 7

1. Cole Kazdin and Imaeyen Ibanga, "The Truth about Teens Sexting," *Good Morning America*, April 15, 2009, http://abcnews.go.com/GMA/Parenting/truth-teens-sexting/story?id=7337547#.Tu4V7PLEI_g.

2. Ibid.

3. Peggy O'Crowley, "The Sexting Generation," *Real Psychology*, August 13, 2009, http://www.realpsychology.com/content/tags/sexting-generation.

4. Ibid.

5. Ibid.

6. Ibid.

7. Ibid.

8. Robert H. Wood, "The First Amendment Implications of Sexting at Public Schools: A Quandary for Administrators Who Intercept Visual Love Notes," *Journal of Law & Policy* 18 (2010): 733–34 (internal quotation marks omitted). See Garfinkle, "Coming of Age in America," 185 (internal citations and quotation marks omitted):

> Over fifty years ago, Alfred Kinsey shocked the nation by revealing that what is still considered deviant sexual behavior was far more common than deviant. A well-respected entomologist, Kinsey applied his careful, detailed, scientific methodology to a massive government-sponsored study of human sexual behavior. The result proved far more titillating and controversial to the public than his insect studies had been. Among other things, Kinsey found that childhood sexual activity was extremely common. Infants and toddlers demonstrated sexual response, and most children engaged in some sort of sexual play. More specifically, Kinsey found that 40% of preadolescent

boys had engaged in heterosexual play and 60% had engaged in homosexual play, with the average age of onset for such activity being 8.8 and 9.2 years respectively. Kinsey's colleague found that 66% of boys in 1943 had had some heterosexual play experience by the time they were thirteen years old. However, far from being grateful for his thorough studies, Congress interrogated Kinsey and the Rockefeller Foundation defunded his work. The political climate could not permit research dollars to go to a subject as morally depraved as normative sexual behavior. Although Kinsey's studies remain the most thorough on the subject to date, many modern studies have corroborated his findings that adolescent and preadolescent sexual activity is a common facet of American childhoods.

9. Heather K. Hudson, "Factors Affecting Sexting Behaviors among Selected Undergraduate Students" (dissertation, Southern Illinois University–Carbondale, 2008), http://web.coehs.siu.edu/public/her/sitebefore2012/grad/new/siu/hed/hed_597/hudson/H.%20Hudson%20Prospectus.pdf.

10. Kaveri Subrahmanyam and Patricia Greenfield, "Online Communication and Adolescent Relationships," *Future of Children* 18, no. 1 (2008), 120, http://www.futureofchildren.org/futureofchildren/publications/docs/18_01_06.pdf. See also Amanda Lenhart, discussing statistics on various teenage phone habits, "Teens and Mobile Phones over the Past Five Years: Pew Internet Looks Back," *Pew Internet and American Life Project* (Washington, DC: Pew Research Center, 2009), http://www.pewinternet.org/~/media/Files/Reports/2009/PIP%20Teens%20and%20Mobile%20Phones%20Data%20Memo.pdf.

11. Ibid., 128.

12. Ibid., 131.

13. Bonnie L. Halpern-Felsher and Yana Reznik, "Adolescent Sexual Attitudes and Behaviors: A Developmental Perspective," *Prevention Researcher* 16, no. 4 (2009): 3 (emphasis added).

14. Ibid.

15. Subrahmanyam and Greenfield, "Online Communication and Adolescent Relationships."

16. Halpern-Felsher and Reznik, "Adolescent Sexual Attitudes," 3.

17. Ibid. ("Additionally, between 14% and 50% of adolescents had oral sex prior to vaginal sex, and both sexual behaviors are more prevalent than anal sex.") See also Les B. Whitbeck, Kevin A. Yoder, Dan R. Hoyt, and Rand D. Conger, "Early Adolescent Sexual Activity: A Developmental Study," *Journal of Marriage & the Family* 61 (1999): 934 (Reporting that among eighth-grade students, 11% admit that they have experienced coitus. Among tenth-grade students, "between 40% and 50% . . . have been sexually active").

18. Halpern-Felsher and Reznik, "Adolescent Sexual Attitudes," 3.

19. Ibid., 4–5. In the 2005 study, teens reported that "it was more acceptable to have oral than vaginal sex, and that oral sex was less against their moral values than was vaginal sex." Teens could very well take this attitude toward noncommercial, consensual student-to-student sexting—seeing it as a more moral way to express their sexuality without engaging in vaginal sex.

20. Ibid., 5 (citing Mary A. Ott and Elizabeth J. Pfeiffer, " 'That's Nasty' to Curiosity: Early Adolescent Cognitions about Sexual Abstinence," *Journal of Adolescent Health* 44, no. 6 [2009]: 575–81). For more statistics on teenage sexuality, see Craig B. Little and Andrea Rankin, "Why Do They Start It? Explaining Reported Early-Teen Sexual Activity," *Sociological Forum* 16, no. 4 (2001): 703–29.

21. Little and Rankin, "Why Do They Start It?" 710. See also page 724 ("Based on these results, combined with our findings from teen focus groups in the community, we have hypothesized that boys may be inclined to initiate sex as a mechanism of status-seeking while girls do so more as a way of attaining approval and love in an intimate, dating (boyfriend) relationship. We believe that this hypothesis is certainly in accord with our data, that some recent work points in the same direction").

22. Halpern-Felsher and Reznik, "Adolescent Sexual Attitudes," 6. See also Sarah Sorenson, "Adolescent Romantic Relationships" (ACT for Youth Center of Excellence Research Facts and Findings, 2007), 1 (internal citations omitted), http://www.actforyouth.net/resources/rf/rf_romantic_0707.pdf ("Romantic relationships are central to social life during middle to late adolescence [ages 15–19]. Three-fourths of teens age 16–18 report having had a relationship, dated, or 'hooked up' with someone and half of these youth have had a serious boyfriend or girlfriend. Many youth in middle to late adolescence report spending more time with their romantic partner than with friends and family"). This report was a collaboration of University of Rochester, Cornell University, Cornell Cooperative Extension of New York City, and the New York State Center for School Safety.

23. W. Andrew Collins, "More Than Myth: The Developmental Significance of Romantic Relationships during Adolescence," *Journal of Research on Adolescence* 13, no. 1 (2003): 2, http://www.fed.cuhk.edu.hk/~lchang/material/adol/Reading%20List/Collins.pdf.

24. Halpern-Felsher and Reznik, "Adolescent Sexual Attitudes," 5.

25. Collins, "More than Myth," 1. See also Lawrence G. Walters, "How to Fix the Sexting Problem: An Analysis of the Legal and Policy Considerations for Sexting Legislation," *First Amendment Law Review* 9 (2010): 106 (internal citations omitted) ("Miley Cyrus, Vanessa Hudgens, and other celebrity teens have made headlines by taking nude photos which later appeared on the Internet. The attention these images generate may spur other young girls to engage in similar behavior").

26. Whitbeck et al., "Early Adolescent Sexual Activity," 944.

27. Halpern-Felsher and Reznik, "Adolescent Sexual Attitudes," 5 (emphasis added). See also pages 5–6 ("Adolescents' bonding with school and relationships with peers also shapes their sexual attitudes. Bersamin and colleagues [2006] showed that adolescents who were more bonded to school were less likely to have vaginal or oral sex. Adolescents are also more likely to have favorable attitudes toward sex if they believe their friends are accepting of sexual behavior and if they believe more of their friends are having sex").

28. Whitbeck et al., "Early Adolescent Sexual Activity," 944.

29. Halpern-Felsher and Reznik, "Adolescent Sexual Attitudes," 4.

30. Sorenson, "Adolescent Romantic Relationships," 1.

31. Ibid. ("Romantic relationships become increasingly significant in the lives of young people as they move from early to late adolescence. Although dating has not yet begun, in early adolescence [ages 10–14] most youth are very preoccupied with romantic issues. Youth at this age spend significant amounts of time in mixed-gender groups that intensify their romantic interest and may eventually lead to romantic relationships").

32. Cumming, "Children's Rights, Voices, Technology, Sexuality," 8–9.

33. Ibid., 9. See also Douglas Kirby et al., "School-Based Programs to Reduce Sexual Risk Behaviors: A Review of Effectiveness," *Public Health Reports* 109, no. 3 (1994): 339 ("We are sexual human beings from birth, but during adolescence, sexual feelings change and intensify. Those sexual feelings can add a vital dimension to the lives of adolescents, a dimension that has many positive elements. There can be those wonderful and intense feelings of being attracted to someone else, there can be great caring and great pleasure, and there can be the opportunity for growth that comes from an intimate relationship with another person. These positive elements should not be forgotten or ignored").

34. Cumming, "Children's Rights, Voices, Technology, Sexuality," 9.

35. Whitbeck et al., "Early Adolescent Sexual Activity," 934.

36. Ibid., 935. See also Clay Calvert, "Sex, Cell Phones, Privacy, and the First Amendment: When Children become Child Pornographers and the Lolita Effect Undermines the Law," *CommLaw Conspectus* 18 (2009): 1 (pointing out that teen sexuality is on the rise and that sexting is "normal" behavior for teenagers).

37. Whitbeck et al., "Early Adolescent Sexual Activity," 935.

38. Ibid.

39. Ibid.

40. Whitbeck et al., "Early Adolescent Sexual Activity," 936.

41. Ibid. (emphasis added).

42. Ibid., 943.

43. Ibid., 936.

44. Sorenson, "Adolescent Romantic Relationships," 2.

45. Ibid., 1.

46. Ibid., 2.

47. Whitbeck et al., "Early Adolescent Sexual Activity," 936.

48. Richards, "Free Speech and Obscenity Law," 62.

49. Abrams vs. United States, 250 U.S. 616 (1919).

50. Id. at 630 (Holmes, J., dissenting).

51. Senate Bill No. 277, at 2, http://www.leg.state.nv.us/Session/76th2011/Bills/SB/SB277_EN.pdf.

52. Id. at 3.

53. Cumming, "Children's Rights, Voices, Technology, Sexuality," 10 (internal citation and quotation marks omitted).

54. Ibid., 10–11.

55. Richards, "Free Speech and Obscenity Law," 81–82 (internal quotation marks omitted) (quoting Paris Adult Theatre I vs. Slaton, 413 U.S. 49, 69 [1973]).

56. United States vs. Playboy Entertainment Group, Inc., 529 U.S. 803, 814 (2000).

57. *Ashcroft*, 542 U.S. at 667. Justice Stevens wrote a concurrence in which he emphasized the importance of filters rather than criminal law as the way to regulate minors' access to obscene materials on the Internet. The same reasoning should apply to sexting: "Encouraging deployment of user-based controls, such as filtering software, would serve Congress' interest in protecting minors from sexually explicit Internet materials as well or better than attempting to regulate the vast content of the World Wide Web at its source, and at a far less significant cost to First Amendment values" (id. at 674 [Stevens, J., concurring]).

58. *Ashcroft*, 542 U.S. at 667.

59. Id. at 669–70 (internal citations omitted). See also id. at 670 (internal citations omitted) for more on use of filters ("The closest precedent on the general point is our decision in *Playboy Entertainment Group. Playboy Entertainment Group*, like this case, involved a content-based restriction designed to protect minors from viewing harmful materials. The choice was between a blanket speech restriction and a more specific technological solution that was available to parents who chose to implement it. Absent a showing that the proposed less restrictive alternative would not be as effective, we concluded, the more restrictive option preferred by Congress could not survive strict scrutiny").

60. *Gonzales*, 478 F.Supp.2d at 795.

61. Id. The cell phone providers should "actively take steps to make sure that children are not able to come up with ways to circumvent their filters. Filtering companies monitor . . . to identify any methods for circumventing filters, and when such methods are found, the filtering companies respond by putting in extra protections in an attempt to make sure that those methods do not succeed with their products."

62. *Playboy Entertainment Group, Inc.*, 529 U.S. at 815.

63. American Civil Liberties Union vs. Mukasey, 534 F.3d 181, 199 (3d Cir. 2008).

64. Id. at 203.

65. *Playboy Entertainment Group, Inc.*, 529 U.S. at 824.

66. Id. This was the U.S. Supreme Court's response to the government's contention in *Playboy Entertainment Group, Inc.* that parents might fail to use blocking or filtering technology because of parental "inertia, indifference, or distraction" (id. at 825). In *Mukasey*, the U.S. Court of Appeals for the Third Circuit stated that "studies have shown that the primary reason that parents do not use filters [for online access] is that they think they are unnecessary because they trust their children and do not see a need to block content" (534 F.3d at 203).

67. John Gabriel Woodlee, "Congressional Manipulation of the Sentencing Guideline for Child Pornography Possession: An Argument for or against Deference?" *Duke Law Journal* 60 (2011): 1040–44.

68. Ibid., 1041.

69. Bleistein vs. Donaldson Lithographing Co., 188 U.S. 239, 251 (1903).

70. *Ashcroft*, 542 U.S. at 674–75 (Stevens, J., concurring) (internal quotation marks omitted) (citing Smith vs. United States, 431 U.S. 291, 316 [1977] [Stevens, J., dissenting]).

71. Id. at 675 (Stevens, J., concurring) (internal citations omitted).

72. Sable Communications of California, Inc. vs. F.C.C., 492 U.S. 115, 126 (1989) (citing Butler vs. Michigan, 352 U.S. 380, 383 [1957]).

73. Calvert, "Sex, Cell Phones, Privacy, and the First Amendment," 34 (internal quotation marks omitted) (citing Errol Louis, "Sexting Spawns New Witch Hunt," *Daily News*, April 23, 2009, who to Calvert wrote suggested in the *Daily News* that the solution is "parents, teachers, clergy and counselors—not prosecutors—to steer our kids through the hormone-soaked confusion of adolescence with all the love, understanding and forgiveness we owe them"). See also page 35 (discussing the education campaign of the United Way of Greater Milwaukee as a model alternative to criminalizing our nation's youth for sexting).

74. Ibid. (citing the editorial " 'Sexting' Overreach," *Christian Science Monitor*, April 28, 2009).

75. Laurence Steinberg and Elizabeth S. Scott, "Less Guilty by Reason of Adolescence: Developmental Immaturity, Diminished Responsibility, and the Juvenile Death Penalty," *American Psychologist* 58, no. 12 (2003): 1010.

76. Ibid.

77. Ibid., 1011.

78. Ibid.

79. Ibid., 1012. Cf. "Cognitive capabilities" that "shape the *process* of decision making."

80. Steinberg and Scott, "Less Guilty by Reason of Adolescence," 1012. See also page 1013 (internal citations omitted) ("What is most interesting is that studies of brain development during adolescence, and of differences in patterns of brain activation between adolescents and adults, indicate that the most important

developments during adolescence occur in regions that are implicated in processes of long-term planning, the regulation of emotion, impulse control, and the evaluation of risk and reward. For example, changes in the limbic system around puberty may stimulate adolescents to seek higher levels of novelty and to take more risks and may contribute to increased emotionality. . . . At the same time, patterns of development in the prefrontal cortex, which is active during the performance of complicated tasks involving long-term planning and judgment and decision making, suggest that these higher order cognitive capacities may be immature well into late adolescence").

81. Ibid., 1014.

82. Ibid., 1014.

83. Ibid., 1015.

84. Joanna S. Markman, "Community Notification and the Perils of Mandatory Juvenile Sex Offender Registration: The Dangers Faced by Children and Their Families," *Seton Hall Legislative Journal* 32 (2008): 262. The system was created in 1899 (Ibid., 271).

85. Ibid., 262.

86. Ibid., 271 ("The necessity of a separate juvenile system was based on social scientists' belief that children are less culpable for misconduct and more amenable to rehabilitation").

87. 387 U.S. 1, 15–16 (1967).

88. Id. at 15–16 (internal citations omitted).

89. 543 U.S. 551 (2005). See also id. at 567 (citing Atkins vs. Virginia, 536 U.S. 304, 316 [2002]) ("Today society views juveniles . . . categorically less culpable than the average criminal").

90. *Roper*, 543 U.S. at 561 (citing Thompson vs. Oklahoma, 487 U.S. 815, 835 [1988] [plurality opinion]).

91. See id. at 569 ("Three general differences between juveniles under 18 and adults demonstrate that juvenile offenders cannot with reliability be classified among the worst offenders").

92. Id. (citing Eddings vs. Oklahoma, 455 U.S. 104, 115 [1982]).

93. Id. at 570 (citing Erik Homburger Erikson, *Identity: Youth and Crisis* [1968]).

94. Id. at 574.

95. Id. at 570 (citing Stanford vs. Kentucky, 492 U.S. 361, 395 [1989]).

96. Id. at 570.

97. Id.

98. 130 S.Ct. 2011 (2010). In that case, the court ruled that for nonhomicide crimes, the U.S. Constitution does not allow juveniles to be sentenced to prison for life without parole.

99. Id. at 2023–30. Additionally, in June 2012, in the case Miller vs. Alabama, 2012 WL 2368659 (June 25, 2012), the U.S. Supreme Court reaffirmed the

principles in *Roper* and *Graham* in ruling that juveniles cannot be sentenced to life
without parole for homicides committed while they are juveniles.

100. *Roper*, 543 U.S. at 2026.

101. Id. at 570 (citing Johnson vs. Texas, 509 U.S. 350, 368 [1993]). See also id.
at 367 ("There is no dispute that a defendant's youth is a relevant mitigating
circumstance").

102. Id. at 571.

103. Markman, "Community Notification," 271.

104. Ibid.

105. Ibid., 272 (internal citations and quotation marks omitted).

106. Markman, "Community Notification," 272.

107. B. B. vs. State, 659 So.2d 256 (Fla. 1995) (Kogan, J., concurring). Justice
Kogan made this statement in a case where a 16-year-old boy—B. B.—was criminally charged for sexual relations with a 16-year-old girl (id. at 257–58).

108. A. H., 949 So.2d at 240 (Fla. App. 1 Dist. 2007) (Padovano, J., dissenting).
This was a case involving noncommercial, consensual student-to-student sexting,
though using a computer rather than a cell phone. As Judge Padovano stated,
"Because there is no evidence that the child intended to show the photographs to
third parties, they are as private as the act they depict. . . . The child in this case
did not show the photographs to anyone. Nor has she been charged with doing
so. She stands accused of nothing more than taking photographs of herself and
her boyfriend" (id. at 239–40 [Padovano, J., dissenting]).

109. Id. at 240–41 (Padovano, J., dissenting).

110. *Playboy Entertainment Group, Inc.* 529 U.S. at 817–18. See also Eberle,
"Art as Speech."

111. Jacobson vs. U.S., 503 U.S. 540, 551–52 (1992) (internal quotation marks
omitted) (citing Paris Adult Theatre I vs. Slaton, 413 U.S. 49, 67 [1973; Stanley
vs. Georgia, 394 U.S. 557, 565–566 [1969]).

112. Douglas Kirby, "Understanding What Works and What Doesn't in Reducing Adolescent Sexual Risk-Taking," *Family Planning Perspectives* 33, no. 6 (2001):
280, http://www.guttmacher.org/pubs/journals/3327601.pdf.

113. Ibid. See John W. Maag, "Rewarded By Punishment: Reflections on the Disuse of Positive Reinforcement in Schools," *Exceptional Children* 67, no. 2 (2001)
(contrasting positive reinforcement with punishment and discussing, among other
things, the use of students' peers for positive reinforcement of desired behaviors).

114. Kirby, "Understanding What Works," 280.

115. Ibid.

116. Hinduja and Patchin, "Sexting: A Brief Guide," 4.

117. *Thomas*, 607 F.2d at 1048.

118. Amy F. Kimpel, "Using Laws Designed to Protect as a Weapon: Prosecuting Minors under Child Pornography Laws," *New York University Review of Law
& Social Change* 34 (2010): 315.

119. *Kuhlmeier*, 484 U.S. at 289 (Brennan, J., dissenting) (internal citations and quotation marks omitted).

120. Id. at 290 (Brennan, J., dissenting)

121. *Roper*, 543 U.S. at 571.

122. *Kuhlmeier*, 484 U.S. at 290 (Brennan, J., dissenting) (citing Shanley vs. Northeast Independent School District, Bexar County, Tex., 462 F.2d 960, 972 [5th Cir. 1972]).

Appendix B

1. Ala. Code § 13A-5-6(a)-(d) (2011).
2. Alaska Stat. § 12.55.035(a)-(b) (Michie 2008).
3. Alaska Stat. § 12.55.125(c) (Michie 2008).
4. Alaska Stat. § 12.55.125(d).
5. Alaska Stat. § 12.55.125(e).
6. Alaska Stat. § 12.55.125(g).
7. Alaska Stat. § 12.55.125(h).
8. Alaska Stat. § 12.55.125(i).
9. Alaska Stat. § 12.55.125(l).
10. Alaska Stat. § 12.55.125(o).
11. Ariz. Rev. Stat. Ann. § 13-702 (West 2011). See also Ariz. Rev. Stat. Ann. § 13-703 (West 2009) (covering repeat offenders).
12. Ark. Code Ann. § 5-4-201(a)-(b) (Michie 2009).
13. Ark. Code Ann. § 5-4-401(a)-(b) (Michie 2011).
14. Cal. Penal Code § 311.9 (West 2008).
15. Colo. Rev. Stat. Ann. § 18-1.3-401 (West 2004).
16. Conn. Gen. Stat. Ann. § 53a-35a (West 2010).
17. Conn. Gen. Stat. Ann. § 53a-41 (West 2011).
18. Conn. Gen. Stat. Ann. § 53a-36 (West 2010).
19. Conn. Gen. Stat. Ann. § 53a-42 (West 2011).
20. Del. Code Ann. tit. 11, § 4205 (2003).
21. Fla. Stat. Ann. § 775.082 (West 2011).
22. Fla. Stat. Ann. § 775.083(1) (West 2011).
23. Ga. Code Ann. § 17-10-6.2(a) (2006).
24. Ga. Code Ann. § 17-10-6.2(b).
25. Ga. Code Ann. § 17-10-6.2(c).
26. Ga. Code Ann. § 17-10-6.2(d).
27. Haw. Rev. Stat. § 706-640(1) (2011).
28. Haw. Rev. Stat. § 706-659 (2011).
29. Haw. Rev. Stat. § 706-660 (2011).
30. Idaho Code Ann. § 18-112 (Michie 2011).
31. 730 Ill. Comp. Stat. Ann. 5/5-4.5-50(a)-(b) (West 2011).

32. 730 Ill. Comp. Stat. Ann. 5/5-4.5-30(a) (West 2009).
33. 730 Ill. Comp. Stat. Ann. 5/5-4.5-35(a) (West 2009).
34. 730 Ill. Comp. Stat. Ann. 5/5-4.5-40(a) (West 2009).
35. 730 Ill. Comp. Stat. Ann. 5/5-4.5-25(a) (West 2009).
36. Ind. Code Ann. § 35-50-2-7 (2004).
37. Ind. Code Ann. § 35-50-2-6 (2004).
38. Iowa Code Ann. § 902.9 (West 2003).
39. Kan. Stat. Ann. 21-6611(a) (2011).
40. Kan. Stat. Ann. 21-6611(b).
41. Kan. Stat. Ann. 21-6611(c).
42. Ky. Rev. Stat. Ann. § 532.060 (Michie 2011).
43. La. Code Crim. Proc. Ann. Art. 894.1(A) (West 2011).
44. La. Code Crim. Proc. Ann. Art. 894.1(B).
45. Me. Rev. Stat. Ann. tit. 17-A, § 1252(1)-(2) (West 2007).
46. Md. Code Ann., Crim. Law § 11-207(b) (2010).
47. Md. Code Ann., Crim. Law § 11-208(b) (2009).
48. Mass. Gen. Laws Ann. ch. 272, § 29 (West 2000).
49. Mass. Gen. Laws Ann. ch. 272, § 29A(a) (West 2000).
50. Mass. Gen. Laws Ann. ch. 272, § 29B(a) (West 2000).
51. Mass. Gen. Laws Ann. ch. 272, § 29B(b).
52. Mich. Comp. Laws § 750.145c(2)-(4) (2004).
53. Minn. Stat. Ann. § 617.246 (West 2009).
54. Miss. Code Ann. § 97-5-27(1) (West 2002).
55. Miss. Code Ann. § 97-5-35 (West 2005).
56. Mo. Ann. Stat. § 558.019 (West 2011).
57. Mo. Ann. Stat. § 558.011 (West 2011).
58. Mont. Code Ann. § 46-18-219(1)(a)(iv)(2011). See other statutes on punishments that might apply to sexting teens in the Montana section of the table set forth earlier in Appendix A of this book.
59. Neb. Rev. Stat. § 28-105 (2011).
60. Neb. Rev. Stat. § 28-106(1) (2005).
61. Neb. Rev. Stat. § 28-106(2).
62. Nev. Rev. Stat. 193.130 (2011).
63. N.H. Rev. Stat. Ann. § 625:9 (2009).
64. N.H. Rev. Stat. Ann. § 651:2(I)-(II) (2011).
65. N.J. Stat. Ann. § 2C:43-3(a)-(d) (West 2005).
66. N.J. Stat. Ann. § 2C:43-6(a) (West 2005).
67. N.M. Stat. Ann. § 31-18-15(A) (Michie 2007).
68. N.M. Stat. Ann. § 31-18-15(E).
69. N.Y. Penal Law § 70.00(2) (McKinney 2009).
70. N.Y. Penal Law § 70.05(1)-(2) (McKinney 2003).
71. N.Y. Penal Law § 70.06(3) (McKinney 2011).

72. N.Y. Penal Law § 70.06(3) (McKinney 2013).

73. N.C. Gen. Stat. Ann. § 15A-1340.17 (2009), available at http://www.ncga .state.nc.us/Sessions/2011/Bills/House/PDF/H642v9.pdf.

74. N.C. Gen. Stat. Ann. § 14-3 (2008).

75. N.C. Gen. Stat. Ann. § 15A-1340.14 (2009).

76. N.D. Cent. Code § 12.1-32-01 (2011).

77. Ohio Rev. Code Ann. § 2152.20(A)(1)-(2) (West 2007).

78. Ohio Rev. Code Ann. § 2929.14(B) (West 2011).

79. Ohio Rev. Code Ann. § 2929.18(A)(3) (West 2011).

80. Okla. Stat. Ann. tit. 21, § 1040.13a(D) (West 2007).

81. Okla. Stat. Ann. tit. 21, § 1040.12a(A) (West 2009). See other statutes on punishments that might apply to sexting teens in the Oklahoma section of the table set forth in Appendix A of this book.

82. Or. Rev. Stat. § 137.700(1)-(2) (2011).

83. Or. Rev. Stat. § 161.605 (2003).

84. Or. Rev. Stat. § 161.625(1) (2011).

85. Or. Rev. Stat. § 161.635(1) (2011).

86. 18 Pa. Cons. Stat. Ann. § 106(b) (West 2011).

87. 18 Pa. Cons. Stat. Ann. § 1103 (West 2011).

88. 18 Pa. Cons. Stat. Ann. § 1104 (West 2011).

89. R.I. Gen. Laws § 11-9-1.1 (2011). See other statutes on punishments that might apply to sexting teens in the Rhode Island section of the table set forth in Appendix A of this book.

90. S.C. Code Ann. § 16-1-20(A) (Law. Co-op. 2011).

91. S.C. Code Ann. § 16-1-90(C)-(E) (Law. Co-op. 2010).

92. S.D. Codified Laws § § 22-6-1 (Michie 2005).

93. Tenn. Code Ann. § 40-35-111(a)-(b) (2007).

94. Tenn. Code Ann. § 40-35-111(d)-(e).

95. Tex. Penal Code Ann. §12.21 (Vernon 2011).

96. Tex. Penal Code Ann. §12.22 (Vernon 2011).

97. Tex. Penal Code Ann. §12.23 (Vernon 2011).

98. Tex. Penal Code Ann. §12.42(a)-(c)(1) (Vernon 2011).

99. Tex. Penal Code Ann. §12.32 (Vernon 2011).

100. Tex. Penal Code Ann. §12.33 (Vernon 2011).

101. Tex. Penal Code Ann. §12.34 (Vernon 2011).

102. Tex. Penal Code Ann. §12.43 (Vernon 2011).

103. Utah Code Ann. § 76-3-203 (2003).

104. Utah Code Ann. § 76-3-301(1) (2011).

105. Vt. Stat. Ann. tit. 13, § 2825(c)-(d) (1999). See other statutes on punishments that might apply to sexting teens in the Vermont section of the table set forth in Appendix A of this book.

106. Va. Code Ann. § 18.2-11 (Michie 2000).

107. Va. Code Ann. § 18.2-10 (Michie 2008).

108. Wash. Rev. Code Ann. § 9.94A.035 (West 2010). See also Wash. Rev. Code Ann. § 9.94A.515 (West 2010) and Wash. Rev. Code Ann.§ 9.94A.510 (West 2010).

109. Wash. Rev. Code Ann. § 9A.20.021(1),(3) (West 2011). See also Wash. Rev. Code Ann. § 13.40.0357 (West 2008) (covering juvenile offender sentencing standards).

110. Wash. Rev. Code Ann. § 9.94A.550 (West 2004).

111. W. VA. Code § 61-8C-3 (2011). See other statutes on punishments that might apply to sexting teens in the West Virginia section of the table set forth in Appendix A of this book.

112. Wis. Stat. Ann. § 939.50(3) (West 2005).

113. Wis. Stat. Ann. § 939.51(3) (West 2005).

114. Wyo. Stat. Ann. § 6-4-303(c)-(e) (Michie 2011).

115. Wyo. Stat. Ann. § 6-4-302(b) (Michie 2011). See other statutes on punishments that might apply to sexting teens in the Wyoming section of the table set forth in Appendix A of this book.

Bibliography

"2011 Legislation Related to 'Sexting.'" National Conference of State Legislatures, January 23, 2012. http://www.ncsl.org/default.aspx?tabid=22127.

Adler, Amy. "All Porn All the Time." *New York University Review of Law & Social Change* 31 (2007): 695–700.

Adler, Amy. "Inverting the First Amendment." *University of Pennsylvania Law Review* 149 (2001): 921–1002.

Basbaum, Jesse P. "Inequitable Sentencing for Possession of Child Pornography: A Failure to Distinguish Voyeurs from Pederasts." *Hastings Law Journal* 61 (2010): 1281–1305.

Branch, Alex. "When Is Sexting Just a Huge Mistake, and When Is It a Crime?" Fort-Worth Star Telegram, December 30, 2009, http://sexoffenderresearch. blogspot.com/2009/12/when-is-sexting-just-huge-mistake-and.html.

Calvert, Clay. "Sex, Cell Phones, Privacy, and the First Amendment: When Children Become Child Pornographers and the Lolita Effect Undermines the Law." *CommLaw Conspectus* 18 (2009): 1–65.

Calvert, Clay, Wendy Brunner, Karla Kennedy, and Kara Murrhee. "Judicial Erosion of Protection for Defendants in Obscenity Prosecutions? When Courts Say, Literally, Enough Is Enough and when Internet Availability Does Not Mean Acceptance." *Harvard Journal of Sports & Entertainment Law* 1 (2010): 7–37.

Canlas-LaFlam, Jacqueline. "Has Georgia Gone Too Far—Or Will Sex Offenders Have To?" *Hastings Constitutional Law Quarterly* 35, no. 2 (2008): 309–44.

Collins, W. Andrew. "More than Myth: The Developmental Significance of Romantic Relationships during Adolescence." *Journal of Research on Adolescence* 13, no. 1 (2003): 1–24. http://www.fed.cuhk.edu.hk/~lchang/material/ adol/Reading%20List/Collins.pdf.

Creasy, Shannon. "Defending against a Charge of Obscenity in the Internet Age: How Google Searches Can Illuminate *Miller*'s 'Contemporary Community Standards.'" *Georgia State University Law Review* 16 (2010): 1029–35.

Cumming, Peter E. "Children's Rights, Voices, Technology, Sexuality." Round-table on Youth, Sexuality, Technology, Congress of the Humanities and Social Sciences 2009, Carleton University, Ottawa, May 26, 2009. http://www.yorku.ca/cummingp/documents/TeenSextingbyPeterCummingMay262009.pdf.

Day, Terri. "The New Digital Dating Behavior—Sexting: Teens' Explicit Love Letters: Criminal Justice or Civil Liability." *Hastings Communications and Entertainment Law Journal* 33, no. 1 (2010): 69–73.

Eberle, Edward J. "Art as Speech." *University of Pennsylvania Journal of Law & Social Change* 11 (2007/2008): 1.

"Facts." *Text Ed* (a study conducted by TRU Research on behalf of LG Mobile Comm, 2010). http://www.lg.com/us/mobile-phones/text-education/facts.jsp.

Garfinkle, Elizabeth. "Coming of Age in America: The Misapplication of Sex-Offender Registration and Community-Notification Laws to Juveniles." *California Law Review* 91, no. 1 (2003): 163–208.

Halpern-Felsher, Bonnie L., and Yana Reznik. "Adolescent Sexual Attitudes and Behaviors: A Developmental Perspective." *Prevention Researcher* 16, no. 4 (2009): 3–6.

Handelman, Eric. "Obscenity and the Internet: Does the Current Obscenity Standard Provide Individuals with the Proper Constitutional Safeguards?" *Albany Law Review* 59 (1995): 718.

Hinduja, Sameer, and Justin W. Patchin. "Sexting: A Brief Guide for Educators and Parents." Cyberbullying Research Center, 2010. http://www.scribd.com/doc/58793571/Sexting-A-Brief-Guide-For-Educators-Parents-Hinduja-Patchin.

Hudson, Heather K. "Factors Affecting Sexting Behaviors among Selected Under-graduate Students." PhD diss., Southern Illinois University Carbondale, 2008. http://web.coehs.siu.edu/public/her/sitebefore2012/grad/new/siu/hed/hed_597/hudson/H.%20Hudson%20Prospectus.pdf.

Humbach, John A. " 'Sexting' and the First Amendment." *Hastings Constitutional Law Quarterly* 37 (2010): 433–85.

Kadish, Sanford H. "Legal Norm and Discretion in the Police and Sentencing Pro-cesses." *Harvard Law Review* 75 (1962): 904–31.

Kimpel, Amy F. "Using Laws Designed to Protect as a Weapon: Prosecuting Minors under Child Pornography Laws." *New York University Review of Law & Social Change* 34 (2010): 299–338.

Kirby, Douglas. "Understanding What Works and What Doesn't in Reducing Adolescent Sexual Risk-Taking." *Family Planning Perspectives* 33, no. 6 (2001): 276–81. http://www.guttmacher.org/pubs/journals/3327601.pdf.

Kirby, Douglas, Lynn Short, Janet Collins, Deborah Rugg, Lloyd Kolbe, Marion Howard, Brent Miller, Freya Sonenstein, and Laurie S. Zabin. "School-Based Programs to Reduce Sexual Risk Behaviors: A Review of Effectiveness." *Public Health Reports* 109, no. 3 (1994): 339–60.

Lenhart, Amanda. "Teens and Mobile Phones over the Past Five Years: Pew Internet Looks Back." *Pew Internet and American Life Project.* Washington, DC: Pew Research Center, 2009. http://www.pewinternet.org/~/media/Files/Reports/2009/PIP%20Teens%20and%20Mobile%20Phones%20Data%20Memo.pdf.

Lenhart, Amanda. "Teens and Sexting." *Pew Internet and American Life Project.* Washington, DC: Pew Research Center, 2009. http://pewinternet.org/~/media//Files/Reports/2009/PIP_Teens_and_Sexting.pdf.

Lenhart, Amanda, Rich Ling, Scott Campbell, and Kristen Purcell. "Teens and Mobile Phones." *Pew Internet and American Life Project.* Washington, DC: Pew Research Center, 2010. http://pewinternet.org/Reports/2010/Teens-and-Mobile-Phones/Summary-of-findings.aspx.

Little, Craig B., and Andrea Rankin. "Why Do They Start It? Explaining Reported Early-Teen Sexual Activity." *Sociological Forum* 16, no. 4 (2001): 703–29.

Maag, John W. "Rewarded by Punishment: Reflections on the Disuse of Positive Reinforcement in Schools." *Exceptional Children* 67, no. 2 (2001).

Markman, Joanna S. "Community Notification and the Perils of Mandatory Juvenile Sex Offender Registration: The Dangers Faced by Children and Their Families." *Seton Hall Legislative Journal* 32 (2008): 261–75.

Meola, Olympia. "Legislators Look Into How Va. Laws Cover 'Sexting.'" *Richmond Times-Dispatch*, May 20, 2009.

"MTV-Associated Press Poll Digital Abuse Survey." Menlo Park, CA: Knowledge Networks, September 23, 2009. www.athinline.org/MTV-AP_Digital_Abuse_Study_Full.pdf.

Ott, Mary A., and Elizabeth J. Pfeiffer. "'That's Nasty' to Curiosity: Early Adolescent Cognitions about Sexual Abstinence." *Journal of Adolescent Health* 44, no. 6 (2009): 575–81.

"Policy Statement on Sexting." National Center for Missing & Exploited Children, last modified September 21, 2009. http://www.missingkids.com/missingkids/servlet/NewsEventServlet?LanguageCountry=en_US&PageId=4130.

Richards, David A. J. "Free Speech and Obscenity Law: Toward a Moral Theory of the First Amendment." *University of Pennsylvania Law Review* 123 (1974): 76.

Robbins, H. Franklin Jr., and Steven G. Mason. "The Law of Obscenity—or Absurdity?" *St. Thomas Law Review* 15 (2003): 531.

"Sex and Tech: Results from a Survey of Teens and Young Adults." Washington, DC: National Campaign to Prevent Teen and Unplanned Pregnancy, 2008. http://www.thenationalcampaign.org/sextech/PDF/SexTech_Summary.pdf.

Smith, Stephen F. "Proportionality and Federalization." *Virginia Law Review* 91, no. 4 (2005): 879–903.

Sorenson, Sarah. "Adolescent Romantic Relationships." ACT for Youth Center of Excellence Research Facts and Findings, 2007. http://www.actforyouth.net/resources/rf/rf_romantic_0707.pdf.

Steinberg, Laurence, and Elizabeth S. Scott. "Less Guilty by Reason of Adolescence: Developmental Immaturity, Diminished Responsibility, and the Juvenile Death Penalty." *American Psychologist* 58, no. 12 (2003): 1009–18.

Subrahmanyam, Kaveri, and Patricia Greenfield. "Online Communication and Adolescent Relationships." *Future of Children* 18, no. 1 (2008): 119–46. http://www.futureofchildren.org/futureofchildren/publications/docs/18_01_06 .pdf.

"Teen Online & Wireless Safety Survey." Cox Communications/National Center for Missing and Exploited Children, 2009. http://www.cox.com/takecharge/ safe_teens_2009/research.html.

United States Sentencing Commission. *Final Quarterly Data Report*. Washington, DC: United States Sentencing Commission, 2009. http://www.ussc.gov/Data _and_Statistics/Federal_Sentencing_Statistics/Quarterly_Sentencing_Updates/ USSC_2009_Quarter_Report_Final.pdf).

United States Sentencing Commission. *The History of the Child Pornography Guidelines*. Washington, DC: United States Sentencing Commission, 2009. http://www.ussc.gov/Research/Research_Projects/Sex_Offenses/20091030 _History_Child_Pornography_Guidelines.pdf.

Walters, Lawrence G. "How to Fix the Sexting Problem: An Analysis of the Legal and Policy Considerations for Sexting Legislation." *First Amendment Law Review* 9 (2010): 98–148.

Whitbeck, Les B., Kevin A. Yoder, Dan R. Hoyt, and Rand D. Conger. "Early Adolescent Sexual Activity: A Developmental Study." *Journal of Marriage & the Family* 61 (1999): 934–46.

Wood, Robert H. "The First Amendment Implications of Sexting at Public Schools: A Quandary for Administrators Who Intercept Visual Love Notes." *Journal of Law & Policy* 18 (2010): 701–37.

Woodlee, John Gabriel. "Congressional Manipulation of the Sentencing Guideline for Child Pornography Possession: An Argument for or against Deference?" *Duke Law Journal* 60 (2011): 1015–57.

Index

About the Authors

JOSEPH O. OLUWOLE, PhD, is a professor of education law at Montclair State University. His research interests include constitutional and statutory rights and responsibilities of students, teachers, and public school districts. His expertise also includes educational access and equity. In addition to being a scholar/researcher, he is also an attorney-at-law and has served as an Assistant Attorney General for the State of Ohio. Dr. Oluwole has published several articles analyzing laws and policies affecting education and has given conference and symposium presentations at several venues nationally including the University Council for Educational Administration, the Education Law Association, University of Iowa College of Law, Stanford Law School, and the American Education Research Association. He has been recognized in Marquis' Who's Who in America, Marquis' Who's Who in American Law, and Cambridge's Who's Who Registry among Executives and Professionals. Sage Publications recognized his article in the *Journal of Cases in Educational Leadership* as the Most Downloaded Article in the journal (of all articles published in 2009 and 2010). He was also a recipient of the Emerging Scholar Award from the American Educational Research Association, Law and Education Special Interest Group and a recipient of the Miriam E. Gray Scholarship for Academic Excellence from The Pennsylvania State University. He is the Administrative Affairs Council Chair and an Executive Board Member of the Montclair State University Senate.

PRESTON C. GREEN III, JD, EdD, is Harry Lawrence Batschelet II Chair Professor of Educational Administration and professor of education and law at The Pennsylvania State University. His published works include *Charter Schools and the Law: Establishing New Legal Relationships*; *The Legal and Policy Implications of Value-Added Teacher Assessment Policies*; and *The State Constitutionality of Voucher Programs: Religion Is Not the Sole Component*. Dr. Green holds a juris doctorate from Columbia Law School and a doctorate in educational administration from Columbia University, Teachers College.

MELISSA STACKPOLE is a graduate student at Montclair State University, receiving her Master's in Community Counseling. She has her BA in Psychology from Fairleigh Dickinson University.